Poetry
An Introduction

Bianca Vargas
150-30 71st Ave.
Apt. 6-H
Flushing, NY 11367

Poetry
An Introduction

RUTH MILLER
State University of New York at Stony Brook

ROBERT A. GREENBERG
Queens College of the City University of New York

St. Martin's Press   New York

ACKNOWLEDGMENTS

FLEUR ADCOCK: "The Water Below" from *Tigers* by Fleur Adcock, © Oxford University Press 1967. Reprinted by permission of Oxford University Press, London.

CONRAD AIKEN: "The Road." From *Collected Poems*, Second Edition by Conrad Aiken. Copyright © 1953, 1970 by Conrad Aiken. Reprinted by permission of Oxford University Press, Inc.

SAMUEL ALLEN: "To Satch" from *Ivory Tusks and Other Poems* and "A Moment Please" from *American Negro Poetry* by Samuel Allen. © Samuel Allen and reprinted by permission of the author.

ALURISTA: "Address" from *Floricante en Aztlan*. Copyright © 1971 by the Regents of the University of California, UCLA Chicano Studies Publications. Reprinted by permission.

A. R. AMMONS: "So I Said I Am Ezra" and "Choice." Selections are reprinted from *Collected Poems, 1951–1971*, by A. R. Ammons, with the permission of W. W. Norton & Company, Inc. Copyright © 1972 by A. R. Ammons.

ANONYMOUS: "Hunting Song," originally titled "Comes the Deer to My Singing," from *The Indians Book*, recorded and edited by Natalie Curtis. Published by Dover Publications and reprinted with permission.

ANONYMOUS: "Dinka Song" ("Do You Not Hear, O Divinity"), translated from the Dinka and found in *The Breast of the Earth* by Kofe Awooners and found in *Divinity and Experience: The Religion of the Dinka* by G. Lienhardt, 1961, p. 38. Reprinted by permission of Oxford University Press, London.

ANONYMOUS: "A Spell to Destroy Life" from *Literature of the American Indians* edited by Thomas E. Sanders and Walter W. Peek. © Glencoe Publishing Co., Inc. 1973. Courtesy of Macmillan Publishing Co., Inc.

MARGARET ATWOOD: "We Are Standing Facing Each Other" from *Power Politics* by Margaret Atwood. Copyright © by Margaret Atwood 1971. Reprinted by permission of House of Anansi Press.

W. H. AUDEN: "That Night When Joy Began," Copyright 1945 by W. H. Auden; "If I Could Tell You," Copyright 1945 by W. H. Auden; "In Memory of W. B. Yeats," Copyright © 1940 and renewed 1968 by W. H. Auden; "Luther," Copyright 1940 by W. H. Auden; "The Unknown Citizen," Copyright © 1940 and renewed 1968 by W. H. Auden; and "Musée des Beaux Arts," Copyright 1940 and renewed 1968 by W. H. Auden. All reprinted from *W. H. Auden: Collected Poems*, by W. H. Auden, edited by Edward Mendelson, by permission of Random House, Inc. Reprinted by permission of Faber and Faber Ltd. from *Collected Shorter Poems* by W. H. Auden. "The Cultural Presupposition," Copyright 1945 by W. H. Auden. Reprinted from *The Collected Poetry of W. H. Auden*, by W. H. Auden, by permission of Random House, Inc. Reprinted by permission of Faber and Faber Ltd. from *Collected Shorter Poems* by W. H. Auden.

IMAMU AMIRI BARAKA: "W. W." from *Black Magic: Collected Poetry 1961–1967* by Imamu Amiri Baraka. Copyright © 1969 LeRoi Jones. Reprinted by permission of Sterling Lord Agency.

BASHŌ: "As Firmly Cemented Clam-Shells" and "Only for Morning Glories." From *The Narrow Road to the Deep North and Other Travel Sketches* by Matsuo Bashō, translated by Nobuyuki Yuasa. (Penguin Classics, 1966), pp. 45, 142. Copyright © Nobuyuki Yuasa, 1966. Reprinted by permission of Penguin Books Ltd.

JUANITA BELL: "Indian Children Speak" in *From the Belly of the Shark*, edited by Walter Lowenfels. Copyright © 1973 by Walter Lowenfels. Reprinted by permission of Manna Lowenfels-Perpelitt, Literary Executrix for the Estate of Walter Lowenfels.

JOHN BERRYMAN: from "Eleven Addresses to the Lord (Master of Beauty)" from *Love and Fame* by John Berryman. Copyright © 1970 by John Berryman. "Life, Friends, Is Boring. We Must Not Say So (Dream Song #14)" from *77 Dream Songs* by John Berryman. Copyright © 1959, 1962, 1963, 1964 by John Berryman. Both reprinted by permission of Farrar, Straus and Giroux, Inc.

ELIZABETH BISHOP: "The Fish" from *The Complete Poems* by Elizabeth Bishop. Copyright © 1940, 1969 by Elizabeth Bishop. "North Haven" Copyright © 1978 by Elizabeth Bishop. Reprinted by permission of Farrar, Straus and Giroux, Inc.

ROBERT BLY: "Poem in Three Parts" reprinted from *Silence in the Snowy Fields*, Wesleyan University Press, Middletown, Conn. Copyright © 1962 by Robert Bly, reprinted with his permission. "The Great Society" from *The Light Around the Body* by Robert Bly. Copyright © 1962 by Robert Bly. Reprinted by permission Harper & Row, Publishers, Inc.

LOUISE BOGAN: "To an Artist, To Take Heart" and "Medusa" from *The Blue Estuaries* by Louise Bogan. Copyright © 1923, 1929, 1930, 1931, 1933, 1934, 1935, 1936, 1937, 1938, 1941, 1949, 1951, 1952, 1954, 1957, 1958, 1962, 1963, 1964, 1965, 1966, 1967, 1968 by Louise Bogan. Reprinted by permission of Louise Bogan.

JOSEPH BRODSKY: "Odysseus to Telemachus" from *Selected Poems* by Joseph Brodsky. Translated from the Russian by George L. Kline. English translation and Introduction copyright © 1973 by George L. Kline. Reprinted by permission of Harper & Row, Inc. "Odysseus to Telemachus" by Joseph Brodsky, translated by George L. Kline, as revised by the author for *A Part of Speech*. Copyright © 1980 by Farrar, Straus and Giroux, Inc. Reprinted by permission of Farrar, Straus and Giroux. "Odysseus to Telemachus" by Joseph Brodsky from *Selected Poems* by Joseph Brodsky, translated by George L. Kline (Penguin Modern Europe Poets, 1973), p. 168. Translation and Introduction copyright © George L. Kline, 1973. Reprinted by permission of Penguin Books Ltd.

To T.V.B.

Preface

This book provides an introduction to the elements of poetry, formulates a series of contexts for the interpretation of poems, and offers a substantial anthology. Our purpose throughout is to enable students to read poems with understanding and pleasure and to provide them with a basic vocabulary for analyzing and talking about poems.

Part One comprises a full discussion of the elements of poetry. After a brief opening chapter, we introduce the basic concepts of speaker or persona, setting, subject, and theme and then progress from the particular uses of language and devices of prosody to more general considerations of structure, genre, and tone. The inclusion of a chapter on genre is perhaps unusual in an introductory book on poetry, but we think it is important for the student to see how poems often depend for a part of their meaning on the ways in which they are related to a particular tradition. The larger sense of Part One is of the interplay of all the elements; we repeatedly emphasize the integrative, organic nature of the poem. As much as possible we have avoided the abstract, seeking always to keep particular poems in the forefront of our discussion.

Part Two, "Perspectives," shows how poems may be illuminated when they are considered from various, often complementary, points of view. Its seven chapters take up successively the perspectives of biography, history, society, philosophy, religion, psychology, and myth. Our interest here is in the kinds of new insights and perceptions, the fresh meanings and implications, each perspective makes possible. We are deliberately pluralistic in our treatment, favoring no one approach over another, although we do emphasize that any single approach has its limitations and we point these out as they arise in the course of our discussions. Our aim is to set forth the premises of each approach, to show it in practice, and thus to generate the kind of exciting discussion that results when diverse points of view collide in the give and take of the classroom.

About 350 poems are included in the discussions and exercises in Parts One and Two. Part Three, the anthology, provides some 150 additional poems for further exploration, presented without editorial comment but with occasional glosses and explanatory footnotes. Taken all together, the nearly 500 poems in this book represent every major style, voice, and genre in English and American poetry, beginning with Cædmon and Chaucer and extending to poets whose first significant work has appeared within the past two decades. As a glance through the index of authors and titles will show, many poets are represented by several poems, and quite a few are represented by ten or more. Among the poets who could be studied in some depth are Auden, Blake, Cummings, Dickinson, Donne, Frost, Hardy, Herbert, Hopkins, Housman, Keats, Shakespeare, Whitman, Williams, Wordsworth, and Yeats. Poems in translation appear throughout the volume.

The book incorporates a number of other features that should be mentioned here. A brief chapter, "Writing About Poetry," though not extensive, should be enough to enable students to get started on the kinds of papers they are most likely to be assigned. The listings we have called "Some Groupings of Poems for Comparison" should prove useful not only as a source of writing topics but also generally as a stimulant to exploration and classroom discussion. We especially enjoyed gathering the photographs for "A Gallery of Poets" and believe that students will find it fascinating to see some of the poets who wrote the poems. The "Index of Terms" lists alphabetically all of the important literary terms used in the text, with a reference to the page where each is first introduced and defined.

Except in a few instances—e.g., "Westron Wynde"—where we wanted to give students a sense of the older text, we have modernized spelling and punctuation.

We wish to express our indebtedness to Thomas Broadbent and Nancy Perry of St. Martin's Press, whose skills and guidance have been decisive throughout the planning and evolution of this book.

R. M.
R. A. G.

Topical Table
of Contents

Part Two PERSPECTIVES   **234**

Part Three ANTHOLOGY   **387**

Contents

7. Structure 137

8. Genre   158

Part Two Perspectives   234

11. Poetry and History   262

12. Poetry and Society   279

13. Poetry and Philosophy   299

14. Poetry and Religion   317

15. Poetry and Psychology

Poetry
An Introduction

Part One
Elements

The chapters of Part One focus on what are commonly referred to as the elements of poetry. Our purpose is to enable you to read poems with understanding and pleasure and to provide you with a vocabulary for talking about any poem you may encounter. For instance, in reading most poems you will find it helpful to consider the "speaker," the person in whose voice the words are presented; and you will often discover that a poem suggests—perhaps quite subtly—a particular setting which contributes to its effect and meaning. Certainly you will find it valuable to be able to distinguish subject and theme, and you will always want to be alert and responsive to the use of language and the effects of sound and sound patterns—rhythm, rhyme, and meter. Frequently, too, you may be able to appreciate a poem more fully when you see how it fits into—or perhaps reacts against—a particular poetic tradition, evoking other poems by poets writing in different periods of time. Although in the chapters that follow we must consider such topics as these one by one, always bear in mind that a poem is the result of the interplay of all its elements.

1
Some Impulses to Poetry

People have always found ways to involve poetry in their lives, in their ordinary as well as their more exalted affairs. In this first chapter, as we briefly consider a few of these occasions, we may begin to have a sense of how wide-ranging and how various the impulse to poetic expression is. At the same time, we begin to see, in very different poems, certain features that poems seem to have in common: freshness of perception, economy of language, striking images, pleasing rhythms, and more.

Let us begin with a heightened occasion, the religious ceremony, where poetry will often interweave with music and dance to create a ritual enactment of something that the group or community desires. The hunt was a sacred event in Navaho Indian culture, and the Navahos engaged in several ceremonies before setting out. In the instance below, the singer pretends to be a blackbird, and as he enacts that role he chants the following poem:

Hunting Song

Comes the deer to my singing,
Comes the deer to my song,
Comes the deer to my singing.

He, the blackbird, he am I,
Bird beloved of the wild deer,   5
    Comes the deer to my singing.

From the Mountain Black,
From the summit,
Down the trail, coming, coming now,
    Comes the deer to my singing.   10

Through the blossoms,
Through the flowers, coming, coming now,
    Comes the deer to my singing.

Through the flower dew-drops,
    Coming, coming now,   15
    Comes the deer to my singing.

Through the pollen, flower pollen,
    Coming, coming now,
    Comes the deer to my singing.

Starting with his left fore-foot,   20
Stamping, turns the frightened deer,
    Comes the deer to my singing.

Quarry mine, blessed am I
In the luck of the chase.
    Comes the deer to my singing.   25

    Comes the deer to my singing,
    Comes the deer to my song,
    Comes the deer to my singing.

Anonymous

The poem is a ritual chant to accompany a dance. The lines are short
and repetitious to fit the movements of the dancer. In each stanza the
deer supposedly comes closer and closer, lured by the imitation of the
song of the blackbird. The chant ends in a triumphant repetition of the
opening lines, this time foretelling a favorable hunt.

Before the Cherokee Indians left for battle, they participated in a
ceremonial burial of the enemy. No corpse was present, for the chant
and the dance movement were symbolic; after a symbolic killing, the
victors buried their enemy's spirit, covering it with the clay of the
"Darkening Land" (line 15):

A Spell to Destroy Life

Listen!
Now I have come to step over your soul
    (I know your clan)
    (I know your name)
    (I have stolen your spirit   5
        and buried it
        under earth)
I bury your soul under earth
I cover you over with black rock
I cover you over with black cloth   10
I cover you over with black slabs
You disappear forever
Your path leads to the black coffin
    in the hills
    of the Darkening Land   15
    So let it be for you
The clay of the hills covers you
The black clay of the Darkening Land
    Your soul fades away
    It becomes blue   20
When darkness comes your spirit shrivels
    and dwindles
    to disappear
    forever
Listen!   25

Anonymous

Having symbolically conquered their enemy, the Cherokees were inspired to duplicate that event in reality.

Poetry has long been present in folk medicine, even when no specific religious ceremony is involved. Here is a magic formula, sometimes called a CHARM, that was chanted to protect against the sting of a wasp. The worried person probably muttered it quickly as the wasp flew round and round his or her head:

Wasp, wasp, poison spike.
From Satan you came: you are both alike.
Stick in stone and not in bone.
Stick in pin and not in skin.
Stick in lead and not in head.
If you stick me, you will fall down dead.

Anonymous
(*Trans. from the Swedish by Siv Cedering Fox*)

Ritual poems associated with particular needs and occasions continue to play a role in everyday life. Spoken in private or in public, they may serve to link the persons chanting with some outer force that they hope will hear and respond. For example, some children recite a poem of prayer before climbing into bed:

> Now I lay me down to sleep,
> I pray Thee, Lord, my soul to keep.
> If I should die before I wake
> I pray Thee, Lord, my soul to take;
> And this I ask for Jesus' sake.

Following is a ritual appeal for help sung by the Dinka people in the Sudan:

> Do you not hear, O Divinity?
> The black bull of the rain has been released from the
>   moon's byre°.   *dwelling, stable*
> Do you not hear, O Divinity?
> I have been left in misery indeed.
> Divinity, help me!
> Will you refuse the ants of this country?

Anonymous
(Adapted from the Sudanese by Kofi Awoonor)

To arouse the sympathy of the Divinity, the Dinka poet refers to the people as "ants."

Ritual poems usually express the shared belief of a group. In China during the 1911 uprising against the Manchu Dynasty, a song of protest was chanted on the occasion of cutting off the queue (pigtail) of a revolutionary soldier. Because the Manchus wore queues, the bald head became a symbol of protest. Before the barber began his work, a pair of scissors was placed ritually on the head of the new soldier and the following song was sung:

> Long queues, short queues,
> There will be no more queues.
> No more slaves to the Manchus
> We shall keep our heads bald as members of the Han Tribe.

Anonymous
(Trans. from the Chinese by Betty Wang)

Zilphia Horton wrote the following words originally for union organizers among the coal miners of the Tennessee Valley. She later adapted the song for use in the civil rights movement, and it is now virtually a folk hymn, freely used by many groups pressing for various freedoms. While singing, the participants cross their arms, grasp the hands of the people on either side, and sway in unison from side to side:

We shall overcome,
We shall overcome,
We shall overcome some day.
Oh, deep in my heart
I do believe
We shall overcome some day. ©

Zilphia Horton (1910–1956)

If protest and conflict have moved poets, so has the celebration of peace, a theme transcending the interests of particular groups, tribes, or nations. Walt Whitman wrote "Reconciliation" to mark the end of the American Civil War; but note that for Whitman the occasion has a much larger significance:

Reconciliation

Word over all, beautiful as the sky,
Beautiful that war and all its deeds of carnage must in time be utterly lost,
That the hands of the sisters Death and Night incessantly softly wash
   again, and ever again, this soil'd world;
For my enemy is dead, a man divine as myself is dead,
I look where he lies white-faced and still in the coffin—I draw near,
Bend down and touch lightly with my lips the white face in the coffin.

Walt Whitman (1819–1892)

Whitman embodies his ideas in the images of a funeral service, very much as the Cherokee Indians did, but his poem celebrates the end of conflict rather than its beginning. Moreover, Whitman's poem moves beyond the specific event to express his deep feelings about the divinity and brotherhood of all human beings, including his enemy; reconciliation cleanses our "soil'd world" by the passage of time because there exists a universal harmony of which death itself is an inseparable part.

Poetry has been prompted by other, more mundane, purposes. Here, from seventeenth-century England, is a neatly turned little poem sent with a handkerchief to a lady. It is the handkerchief that speaks the lines:

Pray take me kindly, mistresse,
   Kisse me too:
My master sweares
   Heele do as much for you.

Anonymous

Emily Dickinson often wrote poems to accompany a gift of flowers or fruit or a freshly baked loaf of bread. Among the Dickinson manuscripts is the following poem, still tied to a rosebud which Dickinson sent to a friend:

Baffled for Just a Day or Two

Baffled for just a day or two—
Embarrassed—not afraid—
Encounter in my garden
An unexpected Maid!
She beckons, and the Woods start—
She nods, and all begin—
Surely—such a country
I was never in!

Emily Dickinson (1830–1886)

The "Maid" in the poem is the early rosebud sent to mark the arrival of spring. The flower is seen as a servant girl, baffled and embarrassed on her new job; but taking heart, she asserts herself and begins to transform the scene. She beckons and the woods spring to life; she nods and the rest of nature follows.

RIDDLES have always been a popular literary game, and thousands of riddles have been written in rhymed verse. Here are two (the answers are in the footnote*):

   I am a female of much use,
   I dwell in fields, and wear no shoes;
   I'm a parent to a fam'd Sir Knight
   Whom Britons fed on with delight:
   By some strange process I refine
   Pure water into whitest wine;
   Which certain people much abuse
   And back to water half reduce.

Anonymous

*Cow; Noah's Ark.

A sailor launch'd a ship of force,
A cargo put therein of course;
No goods had he, he wish'd to sell.
Each wind did serve his turn as well;
No pirates dreaded, to no harbour bound,
His strongest wish that he might run aground.

Anonymous

Riddles relate to a long tradition of poems that do not state their subject but challenge the reader to perceive it, describing an object or an action or an idea, using precise details but never stating outright what is meant, leaving the pleasure of discovery to the reader. In the following poem, even though the answer is given away in the closing lines, Ben Jonson is clearly drawing on the riddle tradition to make a satiric point:

On Something, That Walks Somewhere

At court I met it, in clothes brave enough,
To be a courtier; and looks grave enough,
To seem a statesman: as I near it came,
It made me a great face, I ask'd the name.
A lord, it cried, buried in flesh, and blood,
And such from whom let no man hope least good,
For I will do none: and as little ill,
For I will dare none. Good Lord, walk dead still.

Ben Jonson (1573?–1637)

The primary purpose of some poems is to teach, to offer instruction, advice, or moral or spiritual guidance. Such poems are called DIDACTIC poems, and as in the following instance by John Scott, an English Quaker, the message is usually very much in evidence:

I Hate That Drum's Discordant Sound

I hate that drum's discordant sound,
Parading round, and round, and round:
To thoughtless youth it pleasure yields,
And lures from cities and from fields,
To sell their liberty for charms   5
Of tawdry lace, and glittering arms;
And when Ambition's voice commands,
To march, and fight, and fall, in foreign lands.

I hate that drum's discordant sound,
Parading round, and round, and round: 10
To me it talks of ravag'd plains,
And burning town, and ruin'd swains,
And mangl'd limbs, and dying groans,
And widow's tears, and orphan's moans;
And all that Misery's hand bestows, 15
To fill the catalogue of human woes.

John Scott (1730–1783)

An early and intriguing example of didactic poetry is the EMBLEM, written
to explain and point up the moral or spiritual significance of a symbolic
picture, usually a woodcut or an engraving. From the Renaissance into
the nineteenth century, books of emblems were popular sources of
instruction. A typical emblem comprises a motto illustrated by a picture
and a poem. The subject might be, for instance, a stage in the journey
toward salvation, the temptations of earthly love, or some principle of
good conduct. The emblem that follows illustrates a biblical text:

Psalm 142.7

*Bring my soul out of prison, that I may praise
thy name.*

My soul is like a bird, my flesh the cage,
Wherein she wears her weary pilgrimage
Of hours, as few as evil, daily fed
With sacred wine and sacramental bread;
The keys that lock her in and let her out,
Are birth and death, 'twixt both she hops about
From perch to perch. . . .

Francis Quarles (1592–1644)

The poem goes on for many lines with the soul reflecting bitterly on its fate, imprisoned in its body like a bird in a cage, and concludes with St. Paul's advising the soul as he liberates it from the cage:

> Paul's midnight voice prevail'd; his music's thunder
> Unhing'd the prison-doors, split bolts in sunder:
> And sitt'st thou here, and hang'st the feeble wing?
> And, whin'st to be enlarg'd? soul, learn to sing.

Poems explicitly intended to teach are written less often in the twentieth century than they were in earlier periods. But the impulse to offer a moral corrective remains very much present. Consider, for example, the following poem by Robinson Jeffers, which comes as close to the didactic mode as a twentieth-century poet is likely to come:

Shine, Perishing Republic

While this America settles in the mold of its vulgarity, heavily thickening to
    empire,
And protest, only a bubble in the molten mass, pops and sighs out, and the
    mass hardens,

I sadly smiling remember that the flower fades to make fruit, the fruit rots
    to make earth.
Out of the mother; and through the spring exultances, ripeness and deca-
    dence; and home to the mother.

You making haste haste on decay: not blameworthy; life is good, be it
    stubbornly long or suddenly   5
A mortal splendor: meteors are not needed less than mountains: shine,
    perishing republic.

But for my children, I would have them keep their distance from the thick-
    ening center; corruption
Never has been compulsory, when the cities lie at the monster's feet there
    are left the mountains.

And boys, be in nothing so moderate as in love of man, a clever servant,
    insufferable master.
There is the trap that catches noblest spirits, that caught—they say—God,
    when he walked the earth.   10

Robinson Jeffers (1887–1962)

Moral and religious impulses are evident in another long poetic tra-
dition—that of the EPITAPH, a poem used as an inscription on a tomb

or gravestone. For obvious reasons of space, epitaphs had to be brief, and they commonly taught a moral lesson. Certain epitaphs achieved considerable popularity and were used over and over by tombstone carvers. Almanacs and newspapers of the eighteenth and nineteenth centuries printed them as space fillers and gave them wide circulation.

> Friends and Physicians could not save
> This mortal body from the grave.
> Nor can the grave confine it here.
> When Jesus calls it must appear.

> This shall our mouldering members teach,
> What now our senses learn.
> For dust and ashes loudest preach
> Man's infinite concern.

Eventually poets came to see in the epitaph form a chance for some purely literary games, as in this witty play on the prospects of the deceased for life after death:

On an Old Woman Who Sold Pots

Beneath this stone lies Cath'rine Gray
Changed to a lifeless lump of clay:
By earth and clay she got her pelf,
Yet now she's turned to earth herself.
Ye weeping friends; let me advise.   5
Abate your grief, and dry your eyes:
For what avails a flood of tears?
Who knows but in a run of years,
In some tall pitcher, or broad pan,
She in her shop may be again?   10

Anonymous

The eighteenth-century poet John Gay, in a fit of despair at the government's banning of one of his plays, wrote to his friend and fellow poet Alexander Pope that he wanted these words inscribed on his tomb:

> Life's a jest, and all things show it,
> I thought so once, but now I know it.

Gay invited his friend to add "what more you may think proper," and Pope, in good humor, accommodated him:

Well, then, poor Gay lies underground!
   So there's an end of Honest Jack.
So little justice here he found,
   'Tis ten to one he'll ne'er come back.

The seventeenth-century poet Robert Herrick wrote a number of epitaphs, both serious and comic. In the one that follows he deftly compresses into just four lines both an affectionate memorial for the dead and a celebration of life:

Upon Prue, His Maid

In this little urn is laid
Prudence Baldwin, once my maid,
From whose happy spark here let
Spring the purple violet.

Robert Herrick (1591–1674)

Herrick's lines are clearly in the epitaph form. William Wordsworth's poem that follows also draws upon the tradition of the epitaph but moves beyond it for purposes of a private lament:

A Slumber Did My Spirit Seal

A slumber did my spirit seal;
  I had no human fears:
She seemed a thing that could not feel
  The touch of earthly years.

No motion has she now, no force;
  She neither hears nor sees;
Rolled round in earth's diurnal course,
  With rocks, and stones, and trees.

William Wordsworth (1770–1850)

The second stanza, taken separately, might serve as an epitaph, but the poem as a whole is more: it both embodies and reflects on a powerful experience, that of a confrontation with human mortality.

A final instance of a poet's enlarging upon the traditional epitaph is provided by one of Emily Dickinson's best-known poems. Notice that here the words are those of the persons interred within the tomb. In the last two lines the poem becomes a comment on the vanity and futility of the epitaph itself:

I Died for Beauty—But Was Scarce

I died for Beauty—but was scarce
Adjusted in the Tomb
When One who died for Truth, was lain
In an adjoining Room—

He questioned softly "Why I failed"?   5
"For Beauty", I replied—
"And I—for Truth—Themself are One—
We Brethren, are", He said—

And so, as Kinsmen, met a Night—
We talked between the Rooms—   10
Until the Moss had reached our lips—
And covered up—our names—

Emily Dickinson (1830–1886)

So far we have looked at a few occasions for poetry and a few of the countless forms poems may take. But when we enjoy poems, what is it that we enjoy? When a poem moves us, what is it that we find affecting? Much of this book will be devoted to answering such questions. But we may say this much briefly now: whatever the occasion for a poem may have been, it is the freshness and clarity of the poet's vision and the originality—or simply the extraordinary precision and "rightness"—of the poet's expression that make poems the kind of valuable experience they become for us and give them a validity that cuts easily across boundaries of time and space. Five hundred years separate the two poems that follow, but despite the differences in spelling and reference, see how vividly each conveys the experience of loneliness.

Westron Wynde

Westron wynde when wyll thow blow
the smalle rayne downe can rayne
Chryst yf my love wer in my armys
and I yn my bed agayne

Anonymous (Fifteenth Century)

You Know It's Really Cold

You know it's really cold
  when you wake up hurtin
    in the middle of the night
      and the only one you know to
        call is the operator and she
          puts you through to the police.

Shirley Williams (b. 1944)

William Blake's poem that follows forces us, at least temporarily, to revise our ordinary conceptions about the common experience of being born. He dramatizes what happens to a child at birth by presenting birth from the child's point of view:

Infant Sorrow

My mother groan'd! my father wept.
Into the dangerous world I leapt:
Helpless, naked, piping loud;
Like a fiend hid in a cloud.

Struggling in my father's hands,
Striving against my swaddling bands,
Bound and weary I thought best
To sulk upon my mother's breast.

William Blake (1757–1827)

The child arrives full of undirected energies; its first moments are a battle, a struggle in its father's hands, which are then replaced by swaddling bands. The child is bound, imprisoned, worn down; defeated, it sulks upon its mother's breast—not a conventional image of a newborn child.

T. S. Eliot, in the following poem, uses an astonishing comparison to mount a criticism of the institutional church. The idea of a hippopotamus taking wing and ascending to heavenly redemption is fresh and original, to say the least:

The Hippopotamus

The broad-backed hippopotamus
Rests on his belly in the mud;
Although he seems so firm to us
He is merely flesh and blood.

Flesh and blood is weak and frail,　　　　　　　　　　5
Susceptible to nervous shock;
While the True Church can never fail
For it is based upon a rock.

The hippo's feeble steps may err
In compassing material ends,　　　　　　　　　　　10
While the True Church need never stir
To gather in its dividends.

The 'potamus can never reach
The mango on the mango-tree;
But fruits of pomegranate and peach　　　　　　　　15
Refresh the Church from over sea.

At mating time the hippo's voice
Betrays inflexions hoarse and odd,
But every week we hear rejoice
The Church, at being one with God.　　　　　　　　20

The hippopotamus's day
Is passed in sleep; at night he hunts;
God works in a mysterious way—
The Church can sleep and feed at once.

I saw the 'potamus take wing　　　　　　　　　　　25
Ascending from the damp savannas,
And quiring angels round him sing
The praise of God, in loud hosannas.

Blood of the Lamb shall wash him clean
And him shall heavenly arms enfold,　　　　　　　　30
Among the saints he shall be seen
Performing on a harp of gold.

He shall be washed as white as snow,
By all the martyr'd virgins kist,
While the True Church remains below　　　　　　　35
Wrapt in the old miasmal mist.

T. S. Eliot (1888–1965)

Eliot chooses a clumsy and slothful animal and attributes to it human qualities of frailty, nervousness, proneness to error and frustration, sensual need, weakness. The "True Church," on the other hand, is described as solid, successful, rich, powerful, and joined to God. Yet it is the hippo that flies to heaven and is welcomed by angels; the church remains below, "Wrapt in the old miasmal mist." The conception is extraordinary, but it is not only the image of the hippo and the church that we enjoy. It is also Eliot's use of language, his choice of details, the interweaving of rhyme and meter, the structure—in short, it is a combination of many elements that gives us pleasure. In the eight chapters that follow we shall look at these elements more closely.

2
Speaker, Setting, Subject, and Theme

Speaker

It is always important in reading a poem to consider *who* is talking. Even though the word "I" is used in the poem, the poet may not be the speaker. The voice, whatever its origin—whether real or imagined, personal or impersonal—has an important function in a poem, for it is the owner of that voice to whom things happen, who feels an emotion or has a reflection to share; it is that speaker through whose eyes or from whose point of view a sequence of events or a series of details is presented.

In the following poem the speaker is clearly the poet, Peter Meinke, who addresses his son, advising him how to act as well as what to expect:

Advice to My Son

The trick is, to live your days
as if each one may be your last
(for they go fast, and young men lose their lives
in strange and unimaginable ways)

but at the same time, plan long range 5
(for they go slow: if you survive
the shattered windshield and the bursting shell
you will arrive
at our approximation here below
of heaven or hell). 10

To be specific, between the peony and the rose
plant squash and spinach, turnips and tomatoes;
beauty is nectar
and nectar, in a desert, saves—
but the stomach craves stronger sustenance 15
than the honied vine.
Therefore, marry a pretty girl
after seeing her mother;
show your soul to one man,
work with another; 20
and always serve bread with your wine.

But, son,
always serve wine.

J. Peter Meinke (b. 1932)

The poet's is the only voice heard, though it is controlled to some extent by the occasion: he is speaking as a father, not in anger or jest, but thoughtfully, with some wit, offering his best wisdom. Were Meinke speaking still in his own voice but in another role as, say, a lover or a war casualty, a different view of things might have emerged and another dimension of the poet been uncovered.

Poems by the same poet, expressing different moods or perceptions, can show considerable variety. Here are two by Walt Whitman that differ in mood and outlook but that contain nothing to indicate that the "I" in each is not Whitman:

As Adam Early in the Morning

As Adam early in the morning,
Walking forth from the bower refresh'd with sleep,
Behold me where I pass, hear my voice, approach,
Touch me, touch the palm of your hand to my body as I pass,
Be not afraid of my body.

Walt Whitman (1819–1892)

Animals

I think I could turn and live with animals, they are so placid and self-
    contained;
I stand and look at them long and long.
They do not sweat and whine about their condition;
They do not lie awake in the dark and weep for their sins;
They do not make me sick discussing their duty to God;
Not one is dissatisfied—not one is demented with the mania of owning
    things;
Not one kneels to another, nor to his kind that lived thousands of years
    ago;
Not one is respectable or industrious over the whole earth.

Walt Whitman (1819–1892)

QUESTIONS

1. How would you describe Whitman's mood in each of the poems?
2. To what extent is the language he uses in each poem affected by his mood?
3. To whom is he speaking in "As Adam early in the morning"?
4. Do you see any basic consistency (for example, with regard to the poet's
   view of nature) that might relate the two poems to each other?

We may prefer one Whitman poem to the other, judging one more
moving or more skillfully executed, but they both represent aspects of
the same poet. In the following poem, however, though we encounter
two speakers, neither may safely be identified with the poet:

Two Voices in a Meadow

A Milkweed

Anonymous as cherubs
Over the crib of God,
White seeds are floating
Out of my burst pod.
What power had I   5
Before I learned to yield?
Shatter me, great wind:
I shall possess the field.

A Stone

As casual as cow-dung
Under the crib of God,   10
I lie where chance would have me,
Up to the ears in sod.
Why should I move? To move
Befits a light desire.
The sill of Heaven would founder,   15
Did such as I aspire.

Richard Wilbur (b. 1921)

Wilbur could, of course, have begun with something like, "One day I
heard/Two voices in a field," and then have proceeded to relate, in his
own words, what he heard. But by eliminating his own presence, he
shifts interest from the poet and his view to the points of view of the
"two voices" and to how they reflect back on each other. The reader,
not the poet, must make the interpretation.

Wilbur seems, in fact, to have modeled his poem on an earlier one
by William Blake, but with a major change:

The Clod & the Pebble

"Love seeketh not Itself to please,
Nor for itself hath any care;
But for another gives its ease,
And builds a Heaven in Hell's despair."

So sang a little Clod of Clay,   5
Trodden with the cattle's feet;
But a Pebble of the brook,
Warbled out these metres meet°:   *appropriate*

"Love seeketh only Self to please,
To bind another to its delight;   10
Joys in another's loss of ease,
And builds a Hell in Heaven's despite."

William Blake (1757–1827)

Blake's middle stanza intervenes between the speakers to provide certain
crucial information: the clod is accustomed to being trodden upon, while

the pebble is soothed by the flowing brook waters. Put another way, the clod is malleable, the pebble hard and integral. The poem seems, then, to be implying certain things about the way we see, most of all that our perceptions—in this case, as they corrupt or limit our vision of love—are determined by our prior experience. Are there similar implications, perhaps less evident, in Wilbur's poem?

The information Blake provides (trodden with the cattle's feet, pebble in a brook) helps clarify the speakers' points of view. Were they not a clod and a pebble but human speakers, other kinds of information— age, sex, vocation, social status—might be offered to help establish points of view. T. S. Eliot's "Gerontion" (the title means "little old man") opens with a firm sense of the speaker's status and condition:

> Here I am, an old man in a dry month,
> Being read to by a boy, waiting for rain. . . .
> My house is a decayed house . . .
> The woman keeps the kitchen, makes tea,
> Sneezes at evening, poking the peevish gutter.

All that follows in the poem (see p. 418) grows out of the characterization conveyed by these first lines.

More often than not, information about a speaker is implied rather than stated and must therefore be inferred from the poem. See what can be inferred from the following poem:

"next to of course god america i

"next to of course god america i
love you land of the pilgrims' and so forth oh
say can you see by the dawn's early my
country 'tis of centuries come and go
and are no more what of it we should worry   5
in every language even deafanddumb
thy sons acclaim your glorious name by gorry
by jingo by gee by gosh by gum
why talk of beauty what could be more beau-
tiful than these heroic happy dead   10
who rushed like lions to the roaring slaughter
they did not stop to think they died instead
then shall the voice of liberty be mute?"

He spoke. And drank rapidly a glass of water

e. e. cummings (1894–1962)

1. What is the evidence that the speaker is not the poet?
2. What seem to be the occasion and the setting of the poem? How does your answer clarify the speaker's social position?
3. How would you describe the speaker's language (for example, in lines 1–4 and line 8)? Is Cummings transcribing everyday speech, or is he doing something else?
4. What attitudes does the speaker reveal on such issues as history, war, country?
5. Can you infer what Cummings himself thinks of the speaker? If so, how?

Although the speaker in Cummings's poem refers to soldiers killed in battle as "these heroic happy dead," this view is obviously not endorsed by the poet. Randall Jarrell also creates a speaker who is clearly not the poet, but the poem suggests that Jarrell's own attitude toward war is not substantially different from the speaker's:

Gunner

Did they send me away from my cat and my wife
To a doctor who poked me and counted my teeth,
To a line on a plain, to a stove in a tent?
Did I nod in the flies of the schools?

And the fighters rolled into the tracer like rabbits,   5
The blood froze over my splints like a scab—
Did I snore, all still and grey in the turret,
Till the palms rose out of the sea with my death?

And the world ends here, in the sand of a grave,
All my wars over? . . . It was easy as that!   10
Has my wife a pension of so many mice?
Did the medals go home to my cat?

Randall Jarrell (1914–1965)

QUESTIONS

1. The poem contrasts the speaker's experience before and after he was drafted into military service. What details in the poem establish this contrast?
2. What can you conclude about the speaker's attitude toward his death? toward war?

Whereas poet and speaker seem to converge in Jarrell's poem, no such identification is likely in the poem that follows by Robert Browning, who detaches himself from the character speaking and from the event described:

Porphyria's Lover

The rain set early in tonight,
    The sullen wind was soon awake,
It tore the elm-tops down for spite,
    And did its worst to vex the lake:
    I listened with heart fit to break.   5
When glided in Porphyria; straight
    She shut the cold out and the storm,
And kneeled and made the cheerless grate
    Blaze up, and all the cottage warm;
    Which done, she rose, and from her form   10
Withdrew the dripping cloak and shawl,
    And laid her soiled gloves by, untied
Her hat and let the damp hair fall,
    And, last, she sat down by my side
    And called me. When no voice replied,   15
She put my arm about her waist,
    And made her smooth white shoulder bare,
And all her yellow hair displaced,
    And, stooping, made my cheek lie there,
    And spread, o'er all, her yellow hair,   20
Murmuring how she loved me—she
    Too weak, for all her heart's endeavor,
To set its struggling passion free
    From pride, and vainer ties dissever,
    And give herself to me forever.   25
But passion sometimes would prevail,
    Nor could tonight's gay feast restrain
A sudden thought of one so pale
    For love of her, and all in vain:
    So, she was come through wind and rain.   30
Be sure I looked up at her eyes
    Happy and proud; at last I knew
Porphyria worshiped me: surprise
    Made my heart swell, and still it grew
    While I debated what to do.   35
That moment she was mine, mine, fair,
    Perfectly pure and good: I found

A thing to do, and all her hair
　　In one long yellow string I wound
　　Three times her little throat around,　　　　　　40
And strangled her. No pain felt she;
　　I am quite sure she felt no pain.
As a shut bud that holds a bee,
　　I warily oped her lids: again
　　Laughed the blue eyes without a stain.　　　　45
And I untightened next the tress
　　About her neck; her cheek once more
Blushed bright beneath my burning kiss:
　　I propped her head up as before,
　　Only, this time my shoulder bore　　　　　　　50
Her head, which droops upon it still:
　　The smiling rosy little head,
So glad it has its utmost will,
　　That all it scorned at once is fled,
　　And I, its love, am gained instead!　　　　　　55
Porphyria's love: she guessed not how
　　Her darling one wish would be heard.
And thus we sit together now,
　　And all night long we have not stirred,
　　And yet God has not said a word!　　　　　　　60

Robert Browning (1812–1889)

The opening lines, with their violent and highly subjective view of
nature, suggest a speaker who is locked into his own vision of things.
His obsessiveness is suggested in other ways as well, for example, in
his repeated attention to Porphyria's hair. Because everything is expe-
rienced through the speaker's eyes, the reader is compelled to see things
his way until there is a recoil at the realization of what the speaker has
done.

QUESTIONS

1. What is the setting of Browning's poem?
2. What do lines 6–15 suggest about the speaker's need for Porphyria? Which
   lines suggest his fears with regard to her?
3. Explain in your own words the speaker's justification for killing Porphyria.
4. What are the implications of the final lines?
5. It is not clear to whom the speaker is telling his story. Explain the effect of
   such ambiguity.
6. Try rewriting this poem as an objective news story. What differences in effect
   do you find?

Poems like "Porphyria's Lover" and Jarrell's "Gunner," in which there is only one speaker, are called MONOLOGUES and are to be distinguished from DIALOGUES, in which two or more speakers interact. Wilbur's "Two Voices in a Meadow" tends to the monologue form since there is no direct interaction between the speakers; there is even less interaction in Blake's "The Clod & the Pebble." One could argue, however, that the speakers in these poems are engaged in a cosmic dialogue in which they answer each other by endlessly reiterating what they are.

A purer version of the dialogue form can be seen in the following poem by Thomas Hardy:

"Ah, Are You Digging on My Grave?

"Ah, are you digging on my grave
    My loved one?—planting rue?"
—"No: yesterday he went to wed
One of the brightest wealth has bred.
'It cannot hurt her now,' he said,   5
    'That I should not be true.' "

"Then who is digging on my grave?
    My nearest dearest kin?"
—"Ah, no: they sit and think, 'What use!
What good will planting flowers produce?   10
No tendance of her mound can loose
    Her spirit from Death's gin.' "

"But some one digs upon my grave?
    My enemy?—prodding sly?"
—"Nay: when she heard you had passed the Gate   15
That shuts on all flesh soon or late,
She thought you no more worth her hate,
    And cares not where you lie."

"Then, who is digging on my grave?
    Say—since I have not guessed!"   20
—"O it is I, my mistress dear,
Your little dog, who still lives near,
And much I hope my movements here
    Have not disturbed your rest?"

"Ah, yes! *You* dig upon my grave . . .   25
    Why flashed it not on me
That one true heart was left behind!

What feeling do we ever find
To equal among human kind
   A dog's fidelity!"

        30

"Mistress, I dug upon your grave
   To bury a bone, in case
I should be hungry near this spot
When passing on my daily trot.
I am sorry, but I quite forgot
   It was your resting-place."

        35

Thomas Hardy (1840–1928)

The dialogue is between a woman and her dog: a woman who has carried with her into the grave certain expectations and misperceptions about life, a dog that continues to pursue its own interests. Each has distinctive character traits that affect their different outlooks on life.

Setting

Thomas Hardy's poem takes place in a cemetery, Robert Browning's in the privacy of a room; and in each instance the SETTING of the event is crucial to our understanding of the poem. To imagine the scenes reversed is to begin to imagine very different kinds of works. Though not all poems are so dependent on setting, determining *where* the events of a poem occur will often help clarify the theme as well as the mood and the action. The setting may be subtly implied or clearly stated; it may remain fixed or undergo change; it may be urban or rural, indoors or out, dreary or comfortable, rich or poor. The more pronounced or unusual the setting, the more significant its contribution to the poem is likely to be, as in the following poem:

In the Desert

In the desert
I saw a creature, naked, bestial,
Who, squatting upon the ground,
Held his heart in his hands,
And ate of it.

        5

I said, "Is it good, friend?"
"It is bitter—bitter," he answered;
"But I like it
Because it is bitter,
And because it is my heart."

        10

Stephen Crane (1871–1900)

1. Why is the desert setting especially appropriate to the poem as a whole?
2. Explain the strange phenomenon described in lines 4–5.
3. What can you infer about the condition of the creature encountered? What can you infer about the "I" of the poem?

Nature also serves as a strong presence in the two poems that follow by Theodore Roethke and Robert Bly, but unlike Crane they treat it as a vital, life-supporting force. However, as the settings of the Bly and Roethke poems differ, so do the poems' moods and implications.

Root Cellar

Nothing would sleep in that cellar, dark as a ditch,
Bulbs broke out of boxes hunting for chinks in the dark,
Shoots dangled and drooped,
Lolling obscenely from mildewed crates,
Hung down long yellow evil necks, like tropical snakes.   5
And what a congress of stinks!
Roots ripe as old bait,
Pulpy stems, rank, silo-rich,
Leaf-mold, manure, lime, piled against slippery planks.
Nothing would give up life: 10
Even the dirt kept breathing a small breath.

Theodore Roethke (1908–1963)

Poem in Three Parts

1

Oh, on an early morning I think I shall live forever!
I am wrapped in my joyful flesh,
As the grass is wrapped in its clouds of green.

2

Rising from a bed, where I dreamt
Of long rides past castles and hot coals,   5
The sun lies happily on my knees;
I have suffered and survived the night
Bathed in dark water, like any blade of grass.

3

The strong leaves of the box-elder tree,
Plunging in the wind, call us to disappear   10
Into the wilds of the universe,
Where we shall sit at the foot of a plant,
And live forever, like the dust.

Robert Bly (b. 1926)

QUESTIONS

1. Compare the settings of the two poems, noting their differences in particular.
2. What qualities in nature seem most to arouse Roethke? Bly?
3. How do the speakers differ in their reactions? Which details justify your answer?
4. How comfortable would the poet of "Poem in Three Parts" be in the root cellar described by Roethke? Explain.

The following poem has an indoor setting and describes a late-night encounter of two poets, one considerably older than the other. Note how Robert Lowell uses the setting to create a mood and context for the dialogue:

Robert Frost

Robert Frost at midnight, the audience gone
to vapor, the great act laid on the shelf in mothballs,
his voice is musical and raw—he writes in the flyleaf:
For Robert from Robert, his friend in the art.
"Sometimes I feel too full of myself," I say.   5
And he, misunderstanding, "When I am low,
I stray away. My son wasn't your kind. The night
we told him Merrill Moore would come to treat him,
he said, 'I'll kill him first.' One of my daughters thought things,
thought every male she met was out to make her;   10
the way she dressed, she couldn't make a whorehouse."
And I, "Sometimes I'm so happy I can't stand myself."
And he, "When I am too full of joy, I think
how little good my health did anyone near me."

Robert Lowell (1917–1977)

Some useful information: Merrill Moore was both a psychiatrist and a poet; Frost's son had taken his own life.

QUESTIONS

1. What details establish the setting for the encounter?
2. In what way is Lowell's comment (line 5) misunderstood by Frost?
3. How would you describe Frost's attitude to his children?
4. What sense of Frost do you get from the poem? How is it likely to differ from the audience's perception of Frost?
5. Lowell is both the speaker of the poem and a character who speaks in the poem. Distinguish between the two Lowells.

The settings considered so far have ranged from cemetery to auditorium, desert to root cellar, but each has also remained constant within its particular poem. The one exception is Bly's "Poem in Three Parts," which provides two scenes from nature as well as a brief indoor flashback to the night before. In Emily Dickinson's poem that follows, the action consists of a ride in a carriage through the countryside, and because the carriage is in constant movement, so—from the occupant's perspective—is the landscape:

Because I Could Not Stop for Death

Because I could not stop for Death—
He kindly stopped for me—
The Carriage held but just Ourselves—
And Immortality.

We slowly drove—He knew no haste   5
And I had put away
My labor and my leisure too,
For His Civility—

We passed the School, where Children strove
At Recess—in the Ring—   10
We passed the Fields of Gazing Grain—
We passed the Setting Sun—

Or rather—He passed Us—
The Dews drew quivering and chill—
For only Gossamer, my Gown—   15
My Tippet°—only Tulle°—   *overscarf/stiffened gauze*

We paused before a House that seemed
A Swelling of the Ground—
The Roof was scarcely visible—
The Cornice—in the Ground—   20

Since then—'tis Centuries—and yet
Feels shorter than the Day
I first surmised the Horses' Heads
Were toward Eternity—

Emily Dickinson (1830–1886)

QUESTIONS

1. The landscape changes continuously through the poem. Identify each place passed and the activities associated with it.
2. How many are in the carriage? Explain your answer.
3. What is the significance of the garments worn by the speaker? Why are they mentioned in stanza 4 rather than earlier?
4. What is the effect of characterizing death as a gallant gentleman caller?

Subject and Theme

In Emily Dickinson's poem above, the carriage conveys the speaker beyond the constraints of space and time into eternity, where centuries seem moments. Attention to the setting suggests, moreover, that though the poem describes a carriage ride, it is really about the nature of death and immortality. We can distinguish, then, between a poem's SUBJECT, which is its action or events, and its THEME, which is its central idea or conception.

The difference between subject and theme can be seen in the painting *Hunger*, by Ben Shahn, on the following page. It is a painting *of* a young boy in a particular posture; it is a painting *about* hunger. Theme and subject are obviously interconnected: were the subject a boy who was chubby and symmetrically proportioned, the theme would perhaps be "satisfaction," but it surely would not be "hunger."

In the poem that follows, the subject is an encounter between an elderly suitor and a genteel young woman whom he intends to possess. The theme is mortality and human refusal to acknowledge it.

Piazza Piece

—I am a gentleman in a dustcoat trying
To make you hear. Your ears are soft and small
And listen to an old man not at all,
They want the young men's whispering and sighing.

But see the roses on your trellis dying 5
And hear the spectral singing of the moon;
For I must have my lovely lady soon,
I am a gentleman in a dustcoat trying.

—I am a lady young in beauty waiting
Until my truelove comes, and then we kiss. 10
But what grey man among the vines is this
Whose words are dry and faint as in a dream?
Back from my trellis, Sir, before I scream!
I am a lady young in beauty waiting.

John Crowe Ransom (1888–1974)

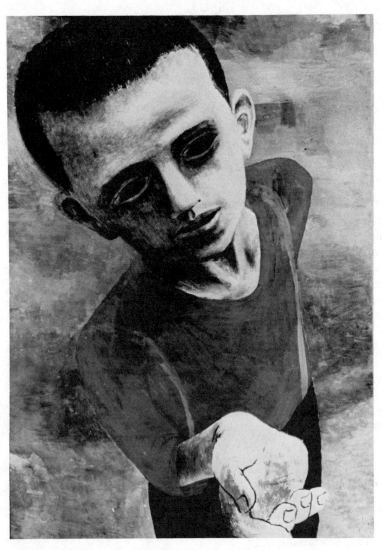

Hunger by Ben Shahn (1898–1969)

One useful way of determining the theme, especially in a long or complex poem, is to try first to paraphrase the poem. A PARAPHRASE is a restatement of the poem in your own words, offering a summary of what is happening segment by segment. Consider, for example, Abraham Cowley's extended argument in favor of drinking wine:

Drinking

The thirsty earth soaks up the rain,
And drinks, and gapes for drink again.
The plants suck in the earth, and are
With constant drinking fresh and fair.
The sea itself, which one would think   5
Should have but little need of drink,
Drinks ten thousand rivers up,
So filled that they o'erflow the cup.
The busy sun—and one would guess
By's drunken, fiery face no less—   10
Drinks up the sea, and when he's done,
The moon and stars drink up the sun.
They drink and dance by their own light;
They drink and revel all the night.
Nothing in nature's sober found,   15
But an eternal health goes round.
Fill up the bowl, then, fill it high,
Fill all the glasses there, for why
Should every creature drink but I?
Why, man of morals, tell me why?   20

Abraham Cowley (1618–1667)

The poem is obviously about drinking, and though there is a kind of comic excess to the argument, each segment does add further evidence for taking a merry cup. The proposition in line 15 is proved by the preceding 14 lines: rain falls on earth and soaks in; plants drink that; the sea drinks the rivers to the point of overflowing; the sun drinks up the waters of the sea, and the moon and stars drink in the sunlight. Water, now in the heavens, falls back to earth as rain. Thus the water goes round and round in a natural cycle. And since all nature is drunk and reveling—the fiery face of the sun, the dancing moon and stars— why should not a man fill up his bowl and from that fill all the glasses and drink? The speaker presents an empirical argument from the world of nature, his theme being that theories of virtue cannot stand up against contrary evidence from nature.

As useful as paraphrase is, its effectiveness may often require the prior clarification of other aspects of the poem. The argument in Ralph Waldo Emerson's poem is spoken by Brahma, a god in the Hindu religion:

Brahma

If the red slayer think he slays,
  Or if the slain think he is slain,
They know not well the subtle ways
  I keep, and pass, and turn again.

Far or forgot to me is near;   5
  Shadow and sunlight are the same;
The vanished gods to me appear;
  And one to me are shame and fame.

They reckon ill who leave me out;
  When me they fly, I am the wings;   10
I am the doubter and the doubt,
  And I the hymn the Brahmin sings.

The strong gods pine for my abode,
  And pine in vain the sacred Seven°,   *those who rank below Brahma*
But thou, meek lover of the good!   15
  Find me, and turn thy back on heaven.

Ralph Waldo Emerson (1803–1882)

Before attempting a paraphrase, you will want to know that Brahma is conceived of as the supreme soul or essence of the universe, a pure intelligence, uncreated, immaterial, timeless and spaceless. The world he creates lasts over two billion years, at which point he allows it to disintegrate until, after a fallow time of the same duration, he renews it once more. Brahma's cycle is eternal, and the world and all that is in it partake of the god's singular regenerative power. With this information in hand, a paraphrase is the next step:

> If a slayer thinks he is the means of slaying, or if a victim thinks he has been killed, they do not understand my cyclical essence; the slayer will die, the dead will be born again.
> Nothing is lost; what is far becomes near, what is forgotten will in due course be remembered (or return again), dark will become light, and light fade to shadow. Vanished gods will return and reputations reverse.
> Nonbelievers must take my way of cyclical return into account. There is no distinction—in the very long run—between belief and nonbelief, doubt and praise. The singer of hymns will become a doubter; the doubter will eventually sing hymns.

There are no other gods as powerful, and one need not be a member of any hierarchy to participate in Brahma's way. The merest creature, any "meek lover of the good," can find Brahma and turn his back on established religions such as Christianity.

The god's reflection on his own nature is the subject of the poem. The theme is the oneness of all things and the ultimate reconciliation of apparent contraries.

Paraphrase is a helpful device, but it is obviously only a beginning, a way into a poem. To compare the paraphrase of any poem with the poem itself is to see how many essential elements have been stripped away. Poems are more than merely statements with subjects and themes. Some of the other elements that give them their unique quality as poems—the richness, complexity, and evocativeness of their language and the rhythms and patterns of sound—will be dealt with in the next several chapters.

EXERCISES

I. Explain the attitude of the speaker toward the various social issues engaged in the following poems.

Stanzas

When a Man Hath No Freedom to Fight For at Home

When a man hath no freedom to fight for at home,
    Let him combat for that of his neighbors;
Let him think of the glories of Greece and of Rome,
    And get knocked on his head for his labors.

To do good to mankind is the chivalrous plan,
    And is always as nobly requited;
Then battle for freedom wherever you can,
    And, if not shot or hanged, you'll get knighted.

George Gordon, Lord Byron (1788–1824)

American Primitive

Look at him there in his stovepipe hat,
His high-top shoes, and his handsome collar;
Only my Daddy could look like that,
And I love my Daddy like he loves his Dollar.

The screen door bangs, and it sounds so funny,   5
There he is in a shower of gold;
His pockets are stuffed with folding money,
His lips are blue, and his hands feel cold.

He hangs in the hall by his black cravat,
The ladies faint, and the children holler: 10
Only my Daddy could look like that,
And I love my Daddy like he loves his Dollar.

William Jay Smith (b. 1918)

II.   The speaker in "The Gallows" has little character and appears to be objective in his tone and choice of details. As you read, consider the effect of this apparently neutral stance.

The Gallows

There was a weasel lived in the sun
With all his family,
Till a keeper shot him with his gun
And hung him up on a tree,
Where he swings in the wind and rain,   5
In the sun and in the snow,
Without pleasure, without pain,
On the dead oak tree bough.

There was a crow who was no sleeper,
But a thief and a murderer   10
Till a very late hour; and this keeper
Made him one of the things that were,
To hang and flap in rain and wind,
In the sun and in the snow.
There are no more sins to be sinned   15
On the dead oak tree bough.

There was a magpie, too,
Had a long tongue and a long tail;
He could both talk and do—
But what did that avail?   20
He, too, flaps in the wind and rain
Alongside weasel and crow,
Without pleasure, without pain,
On the dead oak tree bough.

And many other beasts   25
And birds, skin, bone, and feather,
Have been taken from their feasts
And hung up there together,
To swing and have endless leisure
In the sun and in the snow,   30
Without pain, without pleasure,
On the dead oak tree bough.

Edward Thomas (1878–1917)

1. Explain the meaning of the title.
2. What is the effect of starting the first three stanzas in the same way and then varying the last stanza?
3. What relationship exists between the weasel, the crow, and the magpie?
4. What does the limit placed on the number and kind of examples suggest about the "many other beasts" (line 25) that are hung up?
5. Describe the mood of the poem and explain why the objective voice is an effective device.

III. How do the settings in the following poems contribute to the effect and meaning?

The Encounter

All the while they were talking the new morality
Her eyes explored me.
And when I arose to go
Her fingers were like the tissue
Of a Japanese paper napkin.

Ezra Pound (1885–1972)

The Solitary Reaper

Behold her, single in the field,
Yon solitary Highland° Lass!   *Scottish*
Reaping and singing by herself;
Stop here, or gently pass!
Alone she cuts and binds the grain,   5
And sings a melancholy strain;
O listen! for the Vale profound
Is overflowing with the sound.

No Nightingale did ever chaunt
More welcome notes to weary bands   10
Of travelers in some shady haunt,
Among Arabian sands;
A voice so thrilling ne'er was heard
In springtime from the Cuckoo bird,
Breaking the silence of the seas   15
Among the farthest Hebrides°.   *islands near Scotland*

Will no one tell me what she sings?—
Perhaps the plaintive numbers flow
For old, unhappy, far-off things,
And battles long ago;   20
Or is it some more humble lay,
Familiar matter of today?
Some natural sorrow, loss, or pain,
That has been, and may be again?

Whate'er the theme, the Maiden sang   25
As if her song could have no ending;
I saw her singing at her work,
And o'er the sickle bending—
I listened, motionless and still;
And, as I mounted up the hill,   30
The music in my heart I bore,
Long after it was heard no more.

William Wordsworth (1770–1850)

In a Surrealist Year

In a surrealist year
                of sandwichmen and sunbathers
                        dead sunflowers and live telephones
        house-broken politicos with party whips
        performed as usual   5
        in the rings of their sawdust circuses
        where tumblers and human cannonballs
                        filled the air like cries
            when some cool clown
                        pressed an inedible mushroom button   10
        and an inaudible Sunday bomb
                        fell down
        catching the president at his prayers
                        on the 19th green

O it was a spring
        of fur leaves and cobalt flowers
when cadillacs fell thru the trees like rain
    drowning the meadows with madness
while out of every imitation cloud
        dropped myriad wingless crowds   20
        of nutless nagasaki° survivors   *Japanese city*
                                             destroyed by
And lost teacups   *atom bomb*
full of our ashes
floated by

               Lawrence Ferlinghetti (b. 1919)

IV.   Identify the subject and the theme in each of the following. Comment on the appropriateness of the subject to the theme.

The Tide Rises, The Tide Falls

The tide rises, the tide falls,
The twilight darkens, the curlew calls;
Along the sea-sands damp and brown
The traveller hastens toward the town,
    And the tide rises, the tide falls.   5

Darkness settles on roofs and walls,
But the sea, the sea in the darkness calls;
The little waves, with their soft, white hands,
Efface the footprints in the sands,
    And the tide rises, the tide falls.   10

The morning breaks; the steeds in their stalls
Stamp and neigh, as the hostler calls;
The day returns, but nevermore
Returns the traveller to the shore,
    And the tide rises, the tide falls.   15

       Henry Wadsworth Longfellow (1807–1882)

The Eagle

He clasps the crag with crooked hands;
Close to the sun in lonely lands,
Ringed with the azure world, he stands.

The wrinkled sea beneath him crawls;
He watches from his mountain walls,
And like a thunderbolt he falls.

Alfred, Lord Tennyson (1809–1892)

The Year's at the Spring*

The year's at the spring
And day's at the morn;
Morning's at seven;
The hill-side's dew-pearled;

The lark's on the wing,
The snail's on the thorn:
God's in his heaven—
All's right with the world!

Robert Browning (1812–1889)

V. Paraphrase the poems below, segment by segment, and on the basis of your summary, state the theme of each.

In Drear-Nighted December

1

In drear-nighted December,
   Too happy, happy tree,
Thy branches ne'er remember
   Their green felicity:
  The north cannot undo them   5
  With a sleety whistle through them;
  Nor frozen thawings glue them
   From budding at the prime.

2

In drear-nighted December,
   Too happy, happy brook,   10
Thy bubblings ne'er remember
   Apollo's° summer look;   *god of the sun*

---

* These lines are sung by Pippa, the heroine of Browning's longer work *Pippa Passes*.

But with a sweet forgetting,
They stay their crystal fretting,
Never, never petting   15
    About the frozen time.

        3
Ah! would 'twere so with many
    A gentle girl and boy!
But were there ever any
    Writhed not of passéd joy?   20
The feel of *not* to feel it,
When there is none to heal it
Nor numbéd sense to steel it,
    Was never said in rhyme.

        John Keats (1795–1821)

The Pardon

My dog lay dead five days without a grave
In the thick of summer, hid in a clump of pine
And a jungle of grass and honeysuckle-vine.
I who had loved him while he kept alive

Went only close enough to where he was   5
To sniff the heavy honeysuckle-smell
Twined with another odor heavier still
And hear the flies' intolerable buzz.

Well, I was ten and very much afraid.
In my kind world the dead were out of range   10
And I could not forgive the sad or strange
In beast or man. My father took the spade

And buried him. Last night I saw the grass
Slowly divide (it was the same scene
But now it glowed a fierce and mortal green)   15
And saw the dog emerging. I confess

I felt afraid again, but still he came
In the carnal sun, clothed in a hymn of flies,
And death was breeding in his lively eyes.
I started in to cry and call his name,   20

Asking forgiveness of his tongueless head.
. . . I dreamt the past was never past redeeming:
But whether this was false or honest dreaming
I beg death's pardon now. And mourn the dead.

        Richard Wilbur (b. 1921)

3
Words and
Word Order

Robert Penn Warren has whimsically defined a poem as a group of lines that are printed evenly along the left-hand margin of a page. After that, he says, you're on your own. Robert Frost said, "Poetry is the kind of things poets write." Both are telling us that poetry is so varied in its potential that no definition, not even by a poet, is likely to be adequate.

But poems are discussable, and one way to talk about them is to focus on the literary devices and modes of expression that poets use and that have become more or less intrinsic to the idea of poetry. Poets experiment with these, as well as with new modes and devices, hoping to create particular effects that will enable them to express, and to give order to, their thoughts and feelings. You can learn to identify these elements of poetry and in the process acquire a vocabulary to explain their use in any poem. Though you will find that not everything in a poem can be named or explained, enough can be to sharpen your perception as a reader and to permit a fuller understanding of what it is in a poem that gives pleasure and creates form and meaning.

Diction: Denotation and Connotation

Through the next several chapters we shall be discussing the various elements of poetry. We begin here with DICTION, which refers to the selection and use of words to convey meaning. It is generally agreed that there are two ways to understand the meaning of particular words: through their DENOTATION, which refers to an exact, or dictionary, meaning, and through their CONNOTATION, which refers to an implied meaning, all the associations the word brings into play.

Every word has a dictionary meaning, but seldom a single one, and the larger the dictionary, the greater the number of definitions. Having a good dictionary at hand is indispensable, though you can trust your common sense in reading many poems. The two that follow should present no problems of definition:

Poem

As the cat
climbed over
the top of

the jamcloset
first the right   5
forefoot

carefully
then the hind
stepped down

into the pit of   10
the empty
flowerpot

William Carlos Williams (1883–1963)

Fog

The fog comes
on little cat feet.
It sits looking
over harbor and city
on silent haunches
and then moves on.

Carl Sandburg (1878–1967)

"Pit," in line 10 of "Poem," means a hollow space in the flowerpot, not the pit of a fruit. Jamclosets may be out of fashion, but the context of the poem makes clear that "jamcloset" is some kind of cupboard, containing a stock of jams. "Fog" has no difficult words, though something unexpected seems to occur as you move from "little cat feet" to "silent haunches." The latter phrase implies a larger, more forceful creature: the haunches have a potency, "silent" until the fog/cat "moves on." As the fog/cat "sits" it seems to spread out over the city and harbor. Thus the arrival and departure of the fog appear to differ in quality.

In "Fog" the implications emerge from a willingness to read the poem closely; we require no external help. In the following stanza by Emily Dickinson, however, we are likely to require a dictionary to determine the exact meaning of "brake" in line 4:

> A Wounded Deer—leaps highest—
> I've heard the Hunter tell—
> 'Tis but the Ecstasy of *death*—
> And then the Brake is still!

Webster's Third New International Dictionary defines "brake" as a secluded area in the woods where large ferns may grow. Knowing this, we can visualize the scene. When the ferns become "still," motionless and soundless, the deer's "ecstasy" is complete, the deer dead.

The dictionary offers several other definitions of "brake"—an instrument for separating flax fiber, a pump handle, a device applied to a wheel to slow down its motion, the man who applies the brake, marshy land, an ancient instrument of torture—but it is easy to pick the right one. The context of the word in the line and of the line in the poem guides the reader to the likely choice.

Fully to enjoy the exuberance of the following poem, you need to activate several meanings of the word "star":

To Satch

Sometimes I feel like I will *never* stop
Just go on forever
Till one fine mornin'
I'm gonna reach up and grab me a handfulla stars
Throw out my long lean leg
And whip three hot strikes burnin' down the heavens
And look over at God and say
How about that!

Samuel Allen (b. 1917)

The monologue is spoken by Satchelfoot Paige, a legendary black baseball pitcher excluded from major league baseball for most of his best years. Satch is both a performer and a "star" of baseball; the ball he usually pitches becomes successively a fixed star (line 4) and, as he throws it, a comet "burnin' down the heavens" (line 6). In controlling the stars he seems, indeed, to be competing with God, or at least to be showing off his powers (*"How about that!"*). His sense that he "will *never* stop/Just go on forever" (lines 1–2) is rooted in the actual fact that Paige continued pitching until into his early fifties. The poem suggests that Paige may well be an immortal "star": that he will continue to perform in heaven as he has on earth, startling God, pitching comets through the sky.

Allen's poem is a lively, extravagant celebration. But notice how the nuances and associations attached to "star" are controlled by the context of the poem: the game of baseball, the speed of Paige's fastball, his actual fame, his long public life.

Awareness of CONTEXT can often be decisive since the power of words to foster associations seems at moments almost limitless. When the word "white," for example, appears in a line, some readers think of snow, winter, cold, and death; others might think of snow and winter, but veer off to an association with polar bears, hibernation, spring, and new green worlds; to some readers "white" may connote bridal dress, which in turn they may associate with the idea of purity and perhaps of virgin birth, Christ, and salvation; others, hearing "white," think of race and perhaps of racism.

Consider the curious and macabre effects of Robert Frost's use of "white" in the following poem:

Design

I found a dimpled spider, fat and white,
On a white heal-all, holding up a moth
Like a white piece of rigid satin cloth—
Assorted characters of death and blight
Mixed ready to begin the morning right,   5
Like the ingredients of a witches' broth—
A snow-drop spider, a flower like froth,
And dead wings carried like a paper kite.

What had that flower to do with being white,
The wayside blue and innocent heal-all?   10
What brought the kindred spider to that height,
Then steered the white moth thither in the night?
What but design of darkness to appall?—
If design govern in a thing so small.

Robert Frost (1874–1963)

The poem begins casually enough, "I found," but then turns suddenly by associating a positively connotated term, "dimpled" (cute, charming), with a distinctly negative creature (to most humans), the spider. The spider, moreover, is described as white and fat, a description that reverses our usual expectations. The combination of dimpled, white, and fat suggests not a spider but perhaps a prospering, well-fed, harmless baby. The spider rests on a flower called a "heal-all" (an ironical name for this deadly occasion), which is usually blue, though in this instance it is white, as is the moth being held up by the spider in what seems to be a gesture of triumph, the moth a kind of trophy of conquest. The moth is rigid, dead, but is associated with "satin," a rich and expensive cloth that is typically worn on formal occasions or used to line coffins. Spider, moth, and heal-all are (lightly) described as "assorted characters" of (more heavily) "death and blight." Line 5 seems to be describing a breakfast concoction, "Mixed ready to begin the morning right," which turns out to be a witches' "broth." The same play of negative and positive occurs in "snow-drop spider" (line 7) and in the flower's association with "froth." The next line reminds us that the moth is, after all, only "dead wings," lifeless like a paper kite (a happy plaything of children).

There are other possible implications in these lines—for example, the presence of witches may activate a heard connection between "satin" and "Satan." Satan is traditionally seen as the prime cause of "death and blight," and the poet will later speculate that the convergence of moth, spider, and flower may have been calculated, have been a "design of darkness" (Satan is the Prince of Darkness).

QUESTIONS

1. What opposing connotations do you sense in "snow-drop spider"? in "flower like froth" (line 7)?
2. Check the dictionary meanings of "appall." Which relate to the context Frost has been developing?
3. Lines 9–13 are structured as three questions. Which of the three is less a question than an assertion? Explain.
4. In what sense is line 14 both a question and an assertion?

"Design" seems consciously to pursue contradictory effects, but Frost is also the master of less violent connotative tones. Note how delicately he brings the black crow, white snow, and hemlock tree into union in the following poem:

Dust of Snow

The way a crow
Shook down on me
The dust of snow
From a hemlock tree

Has given my heart
A change of mood
And saved some part
Of a day I had rued.

Robert Frost (1874–1963)

The poem is virtually a replay of "Design," but with entirely different results. Here, too, the poet experiences an event in nature and this event also leads to a change of awareness. But the impact is reassuring rather than threatening, and to make it so Frost must defeat certain negative connotations normally associated with the images in the opening stanza.

QUESTIONS

1. What connotations usually attach to "crow" (as distinct, say, from "peacock" or "lark")? to "dust"? to "snow"?
2. Check the dictionary for possible meanings of "hemlock" that are appropriate to the poem.
3. What had been the speaker's mood prior to the experience? What has caused the change?

Syntax

"Dust of Snow" is remarkable not only for its connotative effects but for its SYNTAX, that is, its ordering of words into a verbal pattern. Note the movement of the poem, how the whole of it is structured as one sentence, as if to correspond to the oneness or totality of the experience being rendered. The sentence subject opens the first stanza and then carries through, finding its related verbs in the second stanza:

The way . . . (line 1)
Has given . . . (line 5)
And saved . . . (line 7)

Much the opposite effect is achieved in the last six lines of "Design," where Frost is shaken by the study in white he has witnessed. His uncertainty is reflected not only in the questions he asks but in their frequency: three or perhaps four compressed into a total of six lines.

The syntax of the poem below, by Lord Byron, creates a logical progression that gives the poem its basic structure:

So We'll Go No More A-Roving

So we'll go no more a-roving
  So late into the night,
Though the heart be still as loving,
  And the moon be still as bright.

For the sword outwears its sheath,   5
  And the soul wears out the breast,
And the heart must pause to breathe,
  And Love itself have rest.

Though the night was made for loving,
  And the day returns too soon,   10
Yet we'll go no more a-roving
  By the light of the moon.

George Gordon, Lord Byron (1788–1824)

Note first the grammatical relationship between "So," with which the poem opens, and "Yet," which appears near the close (line 11). Though they are two colorless words, the poem is going to take us from "So" to "Yet" in an interesting manner, picking up two companion words in lines 3 and 4, "Though" and "still." *So, though, still, yet*—the words seem to set up a kind of condition, or imply a question. Indeed, the first stanza does raise a question at the same time that it portrays an activity of lovers. To "rove" means to wander freely, at random, as one wishes; but though love is still possible, though the moon is still bright, the speaker won't rove any more. Why not?

The answer is given in the second stanza in a series of four strong parallel examples (sword, soul, heart, Love) that point to the wearing out, not of love, but of the lover. The third stanza repeats key phrases from the opening to remind us of what once was true, grammatically and literally, and what still remains true—nights are made for loving, day returns too soon. But now there is just the wistful awareness of a weary lover no longer capable of roaming.

PARALLEL STRUCTURE can be an effective persuasive device since it allows for both repetition and enlargement of the theme or idea. We have seen this technique elsewhere, for example in Abraham Cowley's "Drinking" (p. 35), which makes a witty case for imbibing. It is central to *"Sic Vita,"* in which Henry King argues his point—"such is life"— through a series of comparisons that reach from sky to earth to ocean:

Sic Vita

Like to the falling of a star;
Or as the flights of eagles are;
Or like the fresh Spring's gaudy hue;
Or silver drops of morning dew;
Or like a wind that chafes the flood°;   *disturbs the waters* 5
Or bubbles which on water stood;
Even such is man, whose borrow'd light
Is straight call'd in, and paid to night.

   The wind blows out; the bubble dies;
   The Spring entomb'd in Autumn lies;   10
   The dew dries up; the star is shot;
   The flight is past; and man forgot.

Henry King (1592–1669)

To lessen the danger of monotony, King varies his syntax twice in the opening stanza (lines 4 and 6), and when he drives his point home in the second stanza, he replaces one type of parallel structure with another. The assertions are briefer, a series of simple subject-verb statements: wind blows, bubble dies, and so forth. But even here the parallelism is varied by the insertion of a modifying phrase, "entomb'd in Autumn," between subject and verb (line 10). Tedium is avoided without blunting the force of the argument.

   William Wordsworth's use of parallel structure in combination with other forms of syntax proves especially dramatic in the following poem:

My Heart Leaps Up When I Behold

My heart leaps up when I behold
   A rainbow in the sky:
So was it when my life began;
So is it now I am a man;
So be it when I shall grow old,
   Or let me die!
The Child is father of the Man;
And I could wish my days to be
Bound each to each by natural piety.

William Wordsworth (1770–1850)

QUESTIONS

1. How are lines 3, 4, and 5 similar? How do they differ?
2. What is the effect of breaking the parallelism in line 6?
3. The statements in lines 1–2 and 8–9 are the only ones that require more than one line. Can you explain this in terms of the poem's structure?

When parallel structures serve to set up opposing terms or phrases, the effect is called ANTITHESIS.

> Oh, thoughtless mortals, ever blind to fate,
> Too soon dejected, and too soon elate.
>
> *Alexander Pope (1688–1744)*

> Plots, true or false, are necessary things,
> To raise up commonwealths and ruin kings.
>
> *John Dryden (1631–1700)*

In the first instance, the parallelism suggested by the repeated "Too soon" is turned antithetical in the contrast of "dejected" and "elate." In the second instance, the nouns "commonwealths" and "kings" are balanced against each other, as are the verbs "raise up" and "ruin." Antithesis need not be confined, as above, to one line but can run into the next:

> Be not the first by whom the new are tried,
> Nor yet the last to lay the old aside.
>
> *Alexander Pope (1688–1744)*

> Heard melodies are sweet, but those unheard
>   Are sweeter; . . .
>
> *John Keats (1795–1821)*

Pope's lines urge a middle position between "first" and "last," "new" and "old." The contrast in Keats between the "heard" and "unheard" melodies is developed in a further antithesis between the sensual ear and the spirit as the passage continues:

> . . . therefore, ye soft pipes, play on;
> Not to the sensual ear, but, more endeared,
>   Pipe to the spirit . . .

INVERSION, the reversal of the normally expected word order, is another device commonly used to create emphasis or a particular effect. Shakespeare's line

>   That time of year thou mayst in me behold

runs counter to the anticipated order: "Thou mayst behold in me that time of year." But to rewrite it in this way shifts emphasis away from "time of year," which is the central theme the sonnet develops (see p. 154). John Milton's description in *Paradise Lost* of Satan's being thrown headfirst from Heaven gains much of its effectiveness from the use of inversion in the first lines:

>   Him the Almighty Power
>   Hurled headlong flaming from the ethereal sky
>   With hideous ruin and combustion down
>   To bottomless perdition . . .

The upside-down effect is then made explicit in "ethereal sky . . . down/ To bottomless perdition." Note, too, Milton's use of another poetic device, QUALIFICATION, the introduction or unusual placement of a modifying phrase to achieve a special effect. It is partly by inserting the very long phrase beginning with "flaming" in the second line and continuing through "combustion" in the third line that Milton brilliantly conveys to the reader an almost physical sense of Satan's plummeting for a great distance and length of time through space. To see how this works, try reading aloud—several times if necessary—first the same lines with the qualifying phrase omitted, as they are printed below, and then the lines above just as Milton wrote them.

>   Him the Almighty Power
>   Hurled headlong down to bottomless perdition.

In the poem below, the poet utilizes both inversion and qualification, recasting the bare statement "The moon hangs above the water."

Niagara

Seen on a Night in November

How frail
Above the bulk
Of crashing water hangs
Autumnal, evanescent, wan,
The moon.

Adelaide Crapsey (1878–1914)

Poets will occasionally violate accepted grammatical forms to the
extent of creating a syntax of their own for a particular poem. E. E.
Cummings does this often; see, for example, "next to of course god
america i" (p. 24) and "All in green went my love riding" (p. 166).
Consider the following poem by Gary Snyder, which consists of a series
of sentence fragments:

Some Good Things to Be Said for the Iron Age

A ringing tire iron
      dropped on the pavement

Whang of a saw
brusht on limbs

          the taste
          of rust.

Gary Snyder (b. 1930)

QUESTIONS

1. What is being argued in this poem? Would the point be as clear as if the title
   were "Sound and Flavor"?
2. How can you tell that "dropped" (line 2) is being used to modify "iron"
   rather than as a verb?
3. What connotations of "limbs" and "brusht" make the statement in lines 3–4
   especially unpleasant?
4. Rewrite each of the three pairs of lines as complete sentences. What qualities
   that contribute to the effectiveness of the poem are lost?

Snyder's meaning is enforced by the syntax he has chosen. The same
is true of Williams's "Poem," discussed at the beginning of this chapter
(p. 45). By presenting the entire action in a single continuous sentence,
but divided into four units suggesting pauses at unexpected—that is,
syntactically illogical—points, the poem simultaneously suggests both
the fluidity and grace and also the stop-and-start wariness that cats
uniquely combine in their movement. It is the complexity of the per-
ceived event that the syntax helps to re-create in the poem. In the
following poem, Williams does employ sentence divisions, each sen-
tence serving a precisely defined function. Each sentence is then broken
into qualifying phrases that are spatially separated:

The Artist

Mr. T.
>   bareheaded
>>   in a soiled undershirt
his hair standing out
>   on all sides   5
>>   stood on his toes
heels together
>   arms gracefully
>>   for the moment
curled above his head.   10
>   Then he whirled about
>>   bounded
into the air
>   and with an *entrechat*°   *a ballet movement*
>>   perfectly achieved   15
completed the figure.
>   My mother
>>   taken by surprise
where she sat
>   in her invalid's chair   20
>>   was left speechless.
Bravo! she cried at last
>   and clapped her hands.
>>   The man's wife
came from the kitchen: 25
>   What goes on here? she said.
>>   But the show was over.

William Carlos Williams (1883–1963)

QUESTIONS

1. Show that each sentence provides its own distinct kind of information.
2. What is the effect of the varying sentence lengths? How are the differences justified by the sentence content?
3. Analyze the effects of qualification as it is used in the first and third sentences.

A poem's syntax may, of course, be grammatically correct and yet profoundly strained and involuted. Inversions of word order, interruptions of logical flow with qualifiers, odd constructions—each or all may be necessary to reflect the complexities of a perception or an argument or the emotional stress of the speaker. Gerard Manley Hopkins commonly employs such fracturings of expected patterns:

> Wert thou my enemy, O thou my friend,
> How wouldst thou worse, I wonder, than thou dost
> Defeat, thwart me? . . .

> Not, I'll not, carrion comfort, Despair, not feast on thee;
> Not untwist—slack they may be—these last strands of man
> In me or, most weary, cry *I can no more*. I can;
> Can something, hope, wish day come, not choose not to be.

The lines do, in fact, hold up grammatically. They also suggest the tension, indeed anguish, of the imagination that created them.

Allusion

In addition to drawing upon the connotative richness of words and the many possibilities of syntactical arrangement, poets often enlarge the implications of their poems by reference to specific events, characters, or scenes of a religious, historical, scientific, or literary nature. Such references are called ALLUSIONS, and their use assumes a certain shared knowledge between poet and reader. So Ezra Pound opens his "Portrait d'une Femme" (printed in full on p. 476) in this manner:

> Your mind and you are our Sargasso Sea,
> London has swept about you this score years
> And bright ships left you this or that in fee:
> Ideas, old gossip, oddments of all things,
> Strange spars of knowledge and dimmed wares of price.

The Sargasso Sea is an extensive area of the North Atlantic notable for its massive accumulation of seaweed. According to legend, ships caught in its weed rarely survive or, if they do, lose their cargo and equipment.

QUESTIONS

1. Show how this information about the Sargasso Sea is built into Pound's lines.
2. Read the entire poem (p. 476) and decide whether Pound's allusion is meant to compliment the woman being addressed.

The possibilities for poetic allusion are virtually limitless: Greece and Rome; the Old and New Testaments; classical myths and medieval and folk legends; poets, painters, and scientists. Or, as William Wordsworth put it, describing the multitude of door signs he encountered in London:

> Land warriors, kings, or admirals of the sea,
> Boyle, Shakespeare, Newton, or the attractive head
> Of some quack doctor, famous in his day.

Shakespeare we know; Robert Boyle and Isaac Newton were among the most notable scientists of the seventeenth century. But allusions may be more obscure and still be as richly suggestive for the reader who is willing to take the trouble to track them down.

Occasionally a poem may depend entirely on the reader's understanding of an allusion. Ralph Waldo Emerson's "Brahma," considered earlier (p. 36), can hardly be comprehended without an awareness of the deity's role in Hindu religion. In the following poem, the poet expects us to know, or find out, certain things about another poet named Ovid:

Penal Law

Burn Ovid with the rest. Lovers will find
A hedge-school for themselves and learn by heart
All that the clergy banish from the mind,
When hands are joined and head bows in the dark.

Austin Clarke (b. 1896)

A reader unfamiliar with Ovid could find out from an encyclopedia or a reference work such as the *New Century Classical Handbook* that Ovid was a Roman poet of the first century, that he wrote *The Art of Love,* and that this work was banned by the Roman Catholic Church as immoral. Assuming that the reader has such knowledge, Clarke's poem argues that the suppression of Ovid and other supposedly immoral writers ("the rest") accomplishes nothing since lovers will discover on their own, by natural instinct, what the clergy would hope to banish.

In the following poem, Wilfred Owen finds his subject in the Old Testament but goes beyond allusion to retell a biblical story as a means of commenting on modern war. The form he uses is the PARABLE, a brief anecdote devised to illustrate a moral—in this instance, the story of Abraham and Isaac. In the Old Testament account, Abraham is commanded by God to sacrifice his son, Isaac. Abraham lays the boy on the sacrificial altar, but as he is about to kill Isaac, God intervenes and a ram miraculously appears to take the boy's place. Owen revises the happy ending to make a powerful new statement of his own:

The Parable of the Old Man and the Young

So Abram rose, and clave the wood, and went,
And took the fire with him, and a knife.
And as they sojourned both of them together,
Isaac the first-born spake and said, My Father,
Behold the preparations, fire and iron,   5
But where the lamb for this burnt offering?
Then Abram bound the youth with belts and straps,
And builded parapets and trenches there,
And strechèd forth the knife to slay his son.
When lo! an angel called him out of heaven,   10
Saying, Lay not thy hand upon the lad,
Neither do anything to him. Behold,
A ram, caught in a thicket by its horns;
Offer the Ram of Pride instead of him.
But the old man would not so, but slew his son,   15
And half the seed of Europe, one by one.

Wilfred Owen (1893–1918)

QUESTIONS

1. At what precise point does the poet leave the Bible story and proceed to tell
   his own?
2. What are the differences between the biblical world and the world Owen
   describes?
3. What are the indications that Owen is talking about war?
4. Explain the connotation of "half the seed of Europe" (line 16).

Note, finally, how Owen's diction evokes the biblical origins of his
story. Words like "clave" and "spake"; phrasings like "they sojourned
both of them together" and "builded parapets and trenches" establish
a formal verbal context far removed from the normal usage of the poet's
own time. Though archaic words and syntax seem appropriate to this
poem, in another they might well seem simply false and pompous.
Poets of the last three hundred years, like the rest of us, are more likely
to have said "split" than "clave" the wood, and if they surprise us with
an archaic or unusual usage, there is likely to be a good reason.

Ultimately, it is the context provided by the whole poem that validates
the diction, syntax, and allusions, or indeed that fails to do so if the
poem is unsuccessful. Within this one constraint of appropriateness to
the whole poem, however, the possible varieties of diction, of syntax,
of allusion are virtually unlimited, as the brief poems that follow only
begin to suggest.

On Our Crucified Lord, Naked and Bloody

Th' have left Thee naked, Lord, O that they had;
This garment too I would they had denied.
Thee with Thyself they have too richly clad,
Opening the purple wardrobe of Thy side.
  O never could be found garments too good
  For Thee to wear, but these, of Thine own blood.

Richard Crashaw (1613?–1649)

Merry-Go-Round

Colored Child at Carnival

Where is the Jim Crow section
On this merry-go-round,
Mister, cause I want to ride?
Down South where I come from
White and colored   5
Can't sit side by side.
Down South on the train
There's a Jim Crow car.
On the bus we're put in the back—
But there ain't no back   10
To a merry-go-round!
Where's the horse
For a kid that's black?

Langston Hughes (1902–1967)

Dirce

Stand close around, ye Stygian set,
  With Dirce in one boat conveyed!
Or Charon, seeing may forget
  That he is old and she a shade.

Walter Savage Landor (1775–1864)

Dirce. In classical myth, Charon ferried the shades of the dead over the river Styx to Hades.

Long-Legged Fly

That civilization may not sink,
Its great battle lost,
Quiet the dog, tether the pony
To a distant post;
Our master Caesar is in the tent   5
Where the maps are spread,
His eyes fixed upon nothing,
A hand under his head.
Like a long-legged fly upon the stream
His mind moves upon silence.   10

That the topless towers° be burnt   *of Troy*
And men recall that face°,   *of Helen*
Move most gently if move you must
In this lonely place.
She thinks, part woman, three parts a child,   15
That nobody looks; her feet
Practice a tinker shuffle
Picked up on a street.
Like a long-legged fly upon the stream
Her mind moves upon silence.   20

That girls at puberty may find
The first Adam in their thought,
Shut the door of the Pope's chapel°,   *Sistine Chapel, in Rome*
Keep those children out.
There on that scaffolding reclines   25
Michael Angelo.
With no more sound than the mice make
His hand moves to and fro.
Like a long-legged fly upon the stream
His mind moves upon silence.   30

William Butler Yeats (1865–1939)

The Destruction of Sennacherib

The Assyrian came down like the wolf on the fold,
And his cohorts were gleaming in purple and gold;
And the sheen of their spears was like stars on the sea,
When the blue wave rolls nightly on deep Galilee.

Like the leaves of the forest when summer is green,   5
That host with their banners at sunset were seen:
Like the leaves of the forest when autumn hath blown,
That host on the morrow lay withered and strown.

For the Angel of Death spread his wings on the blast,
And breathed in the face of the foe as he passed;   10
And the eyes of the sleepers waxed deadly and chill,
And their hearts but once heaved, and forever grew still!

And there lay the steed with his nostril all wide,
But through it there rolled not the breath of his pride;
And the foam of his gasping lay white on the turf,   15
And cold as the spray of the rock-beating surf.

And there lay the rider distorted and pale,
With the dew on his brow, and the rust on his mail:
And the tents were all silent, the banners alone,
The lances unlifted, the trumpet unblown.   20

And the widows of Ashur° are loud in their wail,   *Assyria*
And the idols are broke in the temple of Baal°;   *Assyrian god*
And the might of the Gentile, unsmote by the sword,
Hath melted like snow in the glance of the Lord!

George Gordon, Lord Byron (1788–1824)

The Destruction of Sennacherib. Sennacherib was an Assyrian king whose forces were
destroyed by plague while attacking Jerusalem (see II Kings 19:32–37).

Song

Why so pale and wan, fond lover?
    Prithee why so pale?
Will, when looking well can't move her,
    Looking ill prevail?
    Prithee why so pale?   5

Why so dull and mute, young sinner?
    Prithee why so mute?
Will, when speaking well can't win her,
    Saying nothing do' t?
    Prithee why so mute?   10

Quit, quit, for shame; this will not move,
    This cannot take her;
If of herself she will not love,
    Nothing can make her:
    The devil take her!   15

Sir John Suckling (1609–1642)

EXERCISES

I. John Masefield's poem depends almost entirely on the use of connotation for its effect.

Cargoes

Quinquireme of Nineveh from distant Ophir,
Rowing home to haven in sunny Palestine,
With a cargo of ivory,
And apes and peacocks,
Sandalwood, cedarwood, and sweet white wine.   5

Stately Spanish galleon coming from the Isthmus,
Dipping through the Tropics by the palm-green shores,
With a cargo of diamonds,
Emeralds, amethysts,
Topazes, and cinnamon, and gold moidores.   10

Dirty British coaster with a salt-cake smoke stack,
Butting through the Channel in the mad March days,
With a cargo of Tyne coal,
Road-rails, pig-lead,
Firewood, iron-ware, and cheap tin trays.   15

John Masefield (1878–1967)

1. Where are Nineveh, Ophir, and Tyne (lines 1, 13) located?
2. What is the denotative meaning of "galleon" (line 6)? of "coaster" (line 11)? Compare the connotative effects of "Spanish galleon" and "British coaster."
3. What are the connotations of such items as emeralds, amethysts, and topazes (lines 9–10)? ivory and cedarwood (lines 3, 5)? How do these connotations compare with those associated with the cargo in stanza 3?
4. Show how the poem develops its argument through parallel syntax.

II. William Cartwright's lively and witty poem about love plays with the possibilities of connotation and denotation.

No Platonique Love

Tell me no more of minds embracing minds,
    And hearts exchanged for hearts;
That spirits spirits meet, as winds do winds,
    And mix their subtlest parts;
That two unbodied essences may kiss,   5
And then like angels, twist and feel one bliss.

I was that silly thing that once was wrought
    To practise this thin love;
I climbed from sex to soul, from soul to thought;
    But thinking there to move,   10
Headlong I rolled from thought to soul, and then
From soul I lighted at the sex again.

As some strict down-looked men pretend to fast
    Who yet in closets eat,
So lovers who profess they spirits taste,   15
    Feed yet on grosser meat;
I know they boast they souls to souls convey;
Howe'er they meet, the body is the way.

Come, I will undeceive thee: they that tread
    Those vain aerial ways   20
Are like young heirs and alchemists, misled
    To waste their wealth and days;
For searching thus to be forever rich,
They only find a med'cine for the itch.

William Cartwright (1611–1643)

1. Explain the meanings of Platonic ("Platonique") love and of "alchemist" (line 21).
2. Which ideas in the poem exemplify Platonic love?
3. What are the connotations of "silly thing" and "thin love" (lines 7–8)? of "the itch" (line 24)?
4. What connotations usually associated with eating suggest the speaker's attitude in the third stanza?
5. Heirs, alchemists, and Platonic love are not normally associated with one another. Explain the linkage here.

III. Poets often achieve striking syntactical effects in their initial lines. Analyze the effects of syntax in the following examples.

Smudged eyeballs,
mouth stale as air,
I'm newly dead, a corpse

so fresh the grave unnerves me . . .

Adrienne Rich (b. 1929)

Captain Carpenter rose up in his prime
Put on his pistols and went riding out
But had got wellnigh nowhere at that time
Till he fell in with ladies in a rout.

John Crowe Ransom (1888–1974)

My own heart let me more have pity on; let
Me live to my sad life hereafter kind,
Charitable; not live this tormented mind
With this tormenting mind tormenting yet.

Gerard Manley Hopkins (1844–1889)

Although the aepyornis
   or roc that lived in Madagascar, and
the moa are extinct,
the camel-sparrow, linked
   with them in size—the large sparrow
Xenophen saw walking by a stream—was and is
a symbol of justice.

Marianne Moore (1887–1972)

IV.   Consider the effects of syntax in the following poem.

A Noiseless Patient Spider

A noiseless patient spider,
I mark'd where on a little promontory it stood isolated,
Mark'd how to explore the vacant vast surrounding,
It launch'd forth filament, filament, filament, out of itself,
Ever unreeling them, ever tirelessly speeding them.

And you O my soul where you stand,
Surrounded, detached, in measureless oceans of space,
Ceaselessly musing, venturing, throwing, seeking the spheres to connect
   them,
Till the bridge you will need be form'd, till the ductile anchor hold,
Till the gossamer thread you fling catch somewhere, O my soul.   10

Walt Whitman (1819–1892)

1. What is unusual about the sentence structure of the first three lines? How is the effect resolved in the next two lines?
2. Identify the parallel structures throughout the poem.
3. What distinctions are being made in the repetitions that occur in lines 9–10?
4. The filament is coming out of the spider and the spider is being compared to the soul: what, then, may be said to come out of the soul?
5. Describe the nature of the soul as presented by the analogy with the spider.

V.   Work out the allusions in the following stanzas.

    It was a kind and northern face
    That mingled in such exile guise
    The everlasting eyes of Pierrot
    And of Gargantua, the laughter.

Hart Crane (1899–1932)

1. Who are Pierrot and Gargantua? How do they differ in character and temperament?
2. What qualities of the face are conveyed by the allusions?

    Roman Virgil, thou that singest
      Ilion's lofty temples robed in fire,
    Ilion falling, Rome arising,
      wars, and filial faith, and Dido's pyre.

Alfred, Lord Tennyson (1809–1892)

1. Who was Virgil?
2. Explain the three allusions in lines 2–4 and how Virgil is connected with them.

4
Figurative Language and Imagery

When you hear such things as "He's all thumbs," "I'm at the end of my rope," "She doesn't know enough to come in out of the rain," you know that the speaker isn't talking about thumbs, rope, or rain. Something else is intended: he's graceless; I'm desperate; she's dull. The speaker is using FIGURATIVE LANGUAGE, that is, a means of indirect statement that says one thing in terms of another. The effectiveness of such usage can, of course, vary widely. It can seem tedious and uninteresting if the particular expression has too often been used; or it can seem foolish if it is simply showy or not especially appropriate. But as often as not the effect can be a liveliness of expression that manages to press very closely to the essence of an object or idea while also conveying a strong sense of the speaker's attitudes and feelings. For the poet, whose tendency is to see and think figuratively, the use of figurative language is virtually inescapable.

Old English poets, for example, used a device of figurative language called the KENNING, a compound word or phrase that identifies an object without naming it directly: *ring-giver* for king, *whale-road* for the sea, *hate-bite* for a wound. They had a large storehouse of kennings for their most frequently used nouns; instead of "ocean" they could say "sea-street" or "foaming fields" or "realm of monsters" or "sea-fowl's bath."

There were approximately twenty-five kennings for a spear and many more than that for a warrior.

Here is a contemporary writer playing at the kenning, mustering a series to convey the sense of ocean in winter:

Winter Ocean

Many-maned scud-thumper, tub
of male whales, maker of worn wood, shrub-
ruster, sky-mocker, rave!
portly pusher of waves, wind-slave.

John Updike (b. 1932)

QUESTIONS

1. How many kennings can you find in "Winter Ocean"?
2. Which seem especially comic? Which might pass as serious efforts in a less playful context?
3. Add two or three kennings of your own devising to Updike's list.

Though later poets tended to abandon formal use of the kenning, they devised other, more varied means of figurative statement. When Lord Byron responds admiringly to woman's beauty, he writes in terms of night and day and gradations of light:

> She walks in beauty, like the night
>   Of cloudless climes and starry skies;
> And all that's best of dark and bright
>   Meet in her aspect and her eyes:
> Thus mellowed to that tender light
>   Which heaven to gaudy day denies.

When Dylan Thomas writes of youth and mortality, he says:

>   Time held me green and dying
> Though I sang in my chains like the sea.

What is it in "green" that is opposed to dying, or in the sea that resists chains? As the answers become clear, so does the poet's meaning.

We have seen earlier (p. 45) that when Carl Sandburg wishes to describe the fog he chooses what seems to him its essential aspect, its soundless movement, and writes six small lines about a cat. The same combination of fog and cat appears in T. S. Eliot's "The Love Song of J. Alfred Prufrock" (printed in full on pp. 420–423), but with totally different effect:

> The yellow fog that rubs its back upon the window-panes,
> The yellow smoke that rubs its muzzle on the window-panes,
> Licked its tongue into the corners of the evening,
> Lingered upon the pools that stand in drains,
> Let fall upon its back the soot that falls from chimneys,
> Slipped by the terrace, made a sudden leap,
> And seeing that it was a soft October night,
> Curled once about the house, and fell asleep.

QUESTIONS

1. What does the use of "yellow" suggest about the fog?
2. How do the cat's actions in Eliot's lines differ from the cat's actions in Sandburg's "Fog"? What do the differences indicate about the nature of the fog in the two poems?
3. How does the length of the lines in each poem help create different effects?

Of course, not all cats in poetry are associated with fog. Eliot's use of the cat here contrasts not only with Sandburg's but with Marianne Moore's below; here the cat conveys a sense of the supposedly superior person impervious to all but its own needs:

> Self-reliant like the cat—
> that takes its prey to privacy,
> the mouse's limp tail hanging like a shoelace from its mouth—

The cat's action is precisely visualized, and if you think a moment about that limp tail hanging from its mouth, you will grasp the assessment being made of the effect of a superior person on someone more timid (see the complete poem on p. 360).

Understanding the implications of figurative language brings us close to the center of poetic statement. Here is Shakespeare using the language of seasonal change to convey the sense of aging.

> That time of year thou mayst in me behold
> When yellow leaves, or none, or few, do hang
> Upon those boughs which shake against the cold,
> Bare ruined choirs, where late the sweet birds sang.

The season is late autumn, early winter, suggested by the yellow leaves (few or none) that remain upon the boughs shaking in the cold. They shake (suggesting frailty, old age, perhaps palsy) because they are subject to the wind's blowing, a phenomenon we are made to hear in the last line as the boughs become choirs: bare and ruined now but once full (as the boughs were of leaves) of sweet birds singing. The song of the choristers has been replaced by the wind's song—a moan, perhaps, or a wail, but certainly not the song of sweet birds as in his youth and young manhood.

Our initial reaction on reading these lines, that their effect is single, unified, is reinforced when we analyze the figurative languge. D. H. Lawrence's stanza from "Gloire de Dijon," below, is less complex, but notice again the essential rightness of the expression: how the "sunbeams" mellow into a "golden shadow" and then reassert themselves as the "yellow" of the roses; how the detailed perception of the woman finds its perfect resolution at the close:

> When she rises in the morning
> I linger to watch her;
> She spreads the bath-cloth underneath the window
> And the sunbeams catch her
> Glistening white on the shoulders,   5
> While down her sides the mellow
> Golden shadow glows as
> She stoops to the sponge, and her swung breasts
> Sway like full-blown yellow
> Gloire de Dijon roses.   10

Though critics and scholars have identified well over two hundred FIGURES OF SPEECH (the term used to refer to the various details of figurative language), we need to learn only a few at this point to enlarge our understanding and enjoyment of poetry. Among the most common is the SIMILE, which is a figure that makes an explicit comparison between two entities using words such as "like" or "as." The elements being compared are essentially different in nature but come together in the poet's perception.

> Her goodly eyes like Sapphires shining bright . . .
> Her cheeks like apples which the sun hath redded,
> Her lips like cherries charming men to bite.

> *Edmund Spenser (1552–1599)*

> I wandered lonely as a cloud
> That floats on high o'er vales and hills.

> *William Wordsworth (1770–1850)*

For hope grew round me, like the twining vine,
And fruits, and foliage, not my own, seemed mine.

Samuel Taylor Coleridge (1772–1834)

Ben Jonson gives a negative twist to his statement, but it is a simile nonetheless:

> It is not growing like a tree
> In bulk, doth make man better be.

Each of these passages clarifies one thing by taking for its simile an aspect of nature—sapphires, apples, cherries, clouds, vines, trees. But the poet may draw as readily on any realm of awareness or experience. Adelaide Crapsey reverses the above pattern, clarifying a natural event by comparison with a supernatural one:

November Night

Listen . . .
With faint dry sound,
Like steps of passing ghosts,
The leaves, frost-crisped, break from the trees
And fall.

Adelaide Crapsey (1878–1914)

What in the condition of the leaves makes the simile appropriate?
   Crapsey envisions ghosts, but Henry Vaughan sets himself the more difficult task of describing eternity as he apprehended it one night:

> I saw eternity the other night
> Like a great ring of pure and endless light,
> All calm as it was bright.

The light is calm, unflickering, yet bright; it is endless and yet circumscribed within a ring. If the size of the ring ("great") is left open, it is presumably because it was not to be encompassed by the poet's merely human measurement.

METAPHOR, like simile, involves a comparison of two unlike elements, but it omits the linking word ("like," "as"), thus creating a more thorough identification between the two and giving rise to further implications.

And the hands of the clock still knock without entering

A clock might also be identified with the brain or a procession or the universe in order to say something about rationality, inevitability, or entropy. When scientists speak of our "genetic clock," they are using a striking metaphor that suggests a greater certitude than would the simile "Our genes are like a clock."

Here are some other clear and expressive metaphors:

But at my back I always hear
Time's wingèd chariot hurrying near;

Andrew Marvell (1621–1678)

When the young man was flaming out his thoughts
Upon a palace-wall for Rome to see,

Robert Browning (1812–1889)

Come, fill the Cup, and in the fire of Spring
Your Winter-garment of Repentence fling:

Edward Fitzgerald (1809–1883)

Consider the following lines, in which one metaphor is expanded by another:

Once did my thoughts both ebb and flow,
    As passion did them move.

Anonymous

The metaphor in the first line identifies the speaker's thoughts with the tidal flow of a sea or ocean, and then the second line expands and fulfills the first metaphor with another, identifying his passion with the moon: his passion moves his thoughts as the moon controls the tides. The implication is especially interesting in this context because mental disorders were long associated with lunar effects (as can be seen in the common word "lunacy"). The poet seems to be implying, then, that the effect of his passion on his thoughts included at least a touch of madness.

EPIC SIMILES are extended comparisons that go well beyond the obvious point of similarity. Typically, they have three stages: A is compared to B; B is then given considerable development in terms that will clarify A; A is returned to. In the passage from the *Iliad*, below, Homer describes the departure of Paris, son of the Trojan king, but does so through an extended comparison with the flight of a horse.

But Paris in turn did not linger long in his high house,
but when he had put on his glorious armour with bronze elaborate
he ran in the confidence of his quick feet through the city.
As when some stalled horse who has been corn-fed at the manger
breaking free of his rope gallops over the plain in thunder   5
to his accustomed bathing place in a sweet-running river
and in the pride of his strength holds high his head, and the mane
 floats
over his shoulders; sure of his glorious strength, the quick knees
carry him to the loved places and the pasture of horses;
so from uttermost Pergamos came Paris, the son of   10
Priam.

     (Trans. from the Greek by Richmond Lattimore)

Much that may be associated with stallions running free across the plain
may also be said of Paris, the passionate, sensual man who abducted
Helen from Greece and brought her home to Troy, thus initiating a ten-
year war.

 Like epic similes, EXTENDED METAPHORS carry the figure of speech
beyond the simple phrase or line of poetry:

Word

The word bites like a fish.
Shall I throw it back free
Arrowing to that sea
Where thoughts lash tail and fin?
Or shall I pull it in
To rhyme upon a dish?

       Stephen Spender (b. 1909)

QUESTIONS

1. Is it "word" in general or a specific word that interests Spender?
2. What are the connotations of "sea"? of "dish"?
3. Explain how the "word," the "fish," and "thoughts" each inhabit the same
   "sea."

 As we noted earlier, every metaphor or simile involves a comparison.
In analyzing such figures, particularly extended metaphors and similes,
it is helpful to distinguish between what are called the primary and
secondary, or major and minor, terms. *Primary term* refers to the abstract
idea or the elusive or intangible notion the poet aims to clarify. *Secondary*

term refers to the more concrete and familiar element with which the primary term is being identified. In Spender's poem, "word" is the primary or major term; "fish" is the secondary or minor term. It is the minor term that the poet expands into a complex metaphor. In the following poem, Ted Hughes allows the minor term to determine the flow of the entire poem:

The Dove-Breeder

Love struck into his life
Like a hawk into a dovecote.
What a cry went up!
Every gentle pedigree dove
Blindly chattered and beat,   5
And the mild-mannered dove-breeder
Shrieked at that raider.

He might well wring his hands
And let his tears drop:
He will win no more prizes   10
With fantails or pouters°,   *types of doves*
(After all these years
Through third, up through second places
Till they were all world beaters. . . .)

Yet he soon dried his tears.   15

Now he rides the morning mist
With a big-eyed hawk on his fist.

Ted Hughes (b. 1930)

QUESTIONS

1. What is the primary term? the secondary term?
2. What are the usual connotations of "dove" and "hawk"? To what extent do these connotations apply in the poem?
3. Paraphrase the last two lines.
4. Describe in your own words the dove-breeder's transformation.

Closely related to metaphor are two figures of speech that are similar in function, SYNECDOCHE and METONYMY. In *synecdoche*, the part is named for the whole: the line, "The hand that sways the King beguiles the state," refers to the power behind the throne by naming only one aspect, the hand. Shakespeare uses the same figure:

> Nay, if you read this line, remember not
> The hand that writ it.

In the following lines by Thomas Gray, "heart" (line 2) and "hands" (line 3) are synecdoches for the unknown person buried in the country churchyard who, the poet speculates, might have been inspired to great statesmanship or poetic achievement:

> Perhaps in this neglected spot is laid
>   Some heart once pregnant with celestial fire;
> Hands that the rod of empire might have swayed,
>   Or waked to ecstasy the living lyre.

In *metonymy*, an object, idea, or event is referred to by naming some attribute or quality associated with it. For instance, when we say, "The pen is mightier than the sword," "pen" and "sword" are metonymies for written ideas and military force. The following lines by William Collins isolate an admirable soldierly quality, bravery, to refer to those slain in battle:

> How sleep the brave who sink to rest
> By all their country's wishes blest!

PERSONIFICATION is a figure of speech in which an abstract idea, inanimate object, or aspect of nature is described as if it were human. To say that "Time intrudes and steals my days" is to see time as a thief, that is, to see it as human. James Stephens personifies the wind, explaining its nature in terms suggestive of a violent man:

The Wind

The wind stood up, and gave a shout;
He whistled on his fingers, and

Kicked the withered leaves about,
And thumped the branches with his hand,

And said he'd kill, and kill, and kill;
And so he will! And so he will!

James Stephens (1882–1950)

T. L. Beddoes manages to concentrate three personifications in these lines:

> . . . Despair has married wildest mirth
> And to their wedding-banquet all the earth
> Is bade to bring its enmities and loves.

Another figure of speech, often found in connection with personification, is APOSTROPHE, in which the speaker of the poem makes a direct address to a person, thing, or idea:

> With how sad steps, O moon, thou climb'st the skies.

Sir Philip Sidney (1554–1586)

> Busy old fool, unruly sun,
>   Why dost thou thus,
> Through windows and through curtains call on us?
> Must to thy motions lovers' seasons run?

John Donne (1572–1631)

> O Lady! we receive but what we give,
> And in our life alone does Nature live.

Samuel Taylor Coleridge (1772–1834)

In the following poem, Donne both personifies and apostrophizes death in the first step of a strategy that will lead to the humbling and finally the death of death. Put another way, Donne must first give life to death in order to eliminate him.

Death, Be Not Proud, Though Some Have Calléd Thee

Death, be not proud, though some have calléd thee
Mighty and dreadful, for thou art not so;
For those whom thou think'st thou dost overthrow,
Die not, poor Death, nor yet canst thou kill me.
From rest and sleep, which but thy pictures° be,   *copies*   5
Much pleasure; then from thee, much more must flow,
And·soonest our best men with thee do go,

Rest of their bones, and soul's delivery.
Thou art slave to fate, chance, kings, and desperate men,
And dost with poison, war, and sickness dwell,   10
And poppy or charms can make us sleep as well
And better than thy stroke; why swell'st thou then?
One short sleep past, we wake eternally
And death shall be no more; Death, thou shalt die.

John Donne (1572–1631)

We come, finally, to three figures of speech in which the element of play is important: the oxymoron, the pun, and the conceit. OXYMORON is the joining of words with apparently opposing meanings to make a new union. John Keats, describing a lover's response, terms it "making sweet moan" in an effort to fuse the elements of pleasure and pain. When the speaker in William Blake's "The Tiger" (p. 338), addressing the animal, asks

> What immortal hand or eye
> Could frame thy fearful symmetry?

he is using an oxymoron (terror linked to beauty) to reflect his awe and bewilderment. William Butler Yeats more than a century later employs a similar oxymoron in the phrase "A terrible beauty is born," referring to the "new" Ireland born in rebellion against England during Easter of 1916.

George Herbert builds an entire poem upon oxymoron:

Bitter-Sweet

Ah my dear angry Lord,
Since thou dost love, yet strike;
Cast down, yet help afford;
Sure I will do the like.

I will complain, yet praise;
I will bewail, approve:
And all my sour-sweet days
I will lament, and love.

George Herbert (1593–1633)

A PUN is a play on a single word that has two different meanings or sometimes on two words that have the same sound but different meanings. Lawrence Ferlinghetti's lines contain a pun on the name of St. Peter:

> Him just hang there
>> on His Tree
>>> looking real Petered out

Thomas Hardy puns when describing an architect as an "arch-designer," the context making clear that he means both a designer of arches and a cunning man.

Puns offer the pleasure of recognition, but they can also intensify the seriousness of a poem. John Donne, ill and perhaps fearful of imminent death, puns repeatedly on his own name in a poem seeking forgiveness of God:

A Hymn to God the Father

1

Wilt thou forgive that sin where I begun,
  Which is my sin, though it were done before?
Wilt thou forgive those sins, through which I run,
  And do run still: though still I do deplore?
    When thou hast done, thou hast not done,   5
      For, I have more.

2

Wilt thou forgive that sin by which I have won
  Others to sin, and, made my sin their door?
Wilt thou forgive that sin which I did shun
  A year, or two, but wallowed in, a score?   10
    When thou hast done, thou hast not done,
      For, I have more.

3

I have a sin of fear, that when I have spun
  My last thread, I shall perish on the shore;
Swear by thyself, that at my death thy son   15
  Shall shine as he shines now, and heretofore;
    And, having done that, Thou hast done,
      I fear no more.

John Donne (1572–1631)

QUESTIONS

1. How does the punning in lines 5–6 and 11–12 relate to the stanzas in which they occur? What does "more" refer to?

2. How do the verbal changes in lines 17–18 (compared with lines 5–6 and 11–12) help to resolve the poem?
3. Explain the puns in lines 2 and 15–16.
4. Hymns are usually sung in unison. How, then, has Donne adapted the form? Is there possibly a pun on the word "Hymn"?

A CONCEIT is a figure of speech that presents an elaborate, often ingenious, parallel between two things or ideas. Like metaphors and similes, conceits find resemblances between unlike objects or situations, but the conceit carries the comparison to unexpected extremes.

Cherry-Ripe

Cherry-ripe, ripe, ripe, I cry,
Full and fair ones; come and buy:
If so be, you ask me where
They do grow? I answer, there,
Where my Julia's lips do smile;
There's the land, or cherry-isle:
Whose plantations fully show
All the year, where cherries grow.

Robert Herrick (1591–1674)

Rather than use a simple metaphor, "Her lips are ripe cherries," Herrick extends the possibilities by fabricating a "cherry-isle" on which "plantations" flourish; and because the cherries grow "all the year," we assume the season there is always summer. Herrick's conceit takes no more than a few lines; Richard Crashaw's is sustained through a longer poem and is put to a more serious purpose:

An Epitaph upon a Young Married Couple Dead and Buried Together

To these, whom Death again did wed,
This grave's their second marriage-bed;
For though the hand of Fate could force
'Twixt soul and body a divorce,
It could not sunder man and wife,   5
Because they both lived but one life.
Peace, good Reader, do not weep.
Peace, the lovers are asleep.

They, sweet turtles°, folded lie   *turtledoves*
In the last knot Love could tie.   10
And though they lie as they were dead,
Their pillow stone, their sheets of lead,
(Pillow hard, and sheets not warm)
Love made the bed; they'll take no harm.
Let them sleep: let them sleep on,   15
Till this stormy night be gone,
Till the eternal morrow dawn;
Then the curtains will be drawn
And they wake into a light,
Whose day shall never die in night.   20

Richard Crashaw (1613?–1694)

QUESTIONS

1. How do "again" and "second" (lines 1, 2) function in relation to the whole poem?
2. Trace the analogy, detail by detail, between bed and grave.
3. In what sense did the couple live "but one life" (line 6)?
4. Explain the implications of the day-night contrast (lines 16–20). How does this contrast function in the poem as a whole?

The term IMAGERY requires separate discussion. It is often used in a general sense to refer to the various figures of speech, as when we say: Crashaw develops the image of a couple in bed; Herrick uses the image of a plantation. Strictly speaking, however, imagery refers not to a figurative device so much as to the stuff of which most similes and metaphors are made. More exactly, the materials of imagery are drawn by the poet from the world of the five senses and then are re-created as word pictures—specific representations—that register on the reader's imagination. We can thus speak of images as being primarily visual, aural (appealing to the ear), or tactile (appealing to the sense of touch); we can say that an image appeals to our sense of smell or of taste, though in fact we neither taste nor smell it except as our imagination is able to activate those responses. To the extent that images are verbal pictures, most will have a strong visual component, but they will often also combine the visual with one or more of the other senses.

Notice how in the brief simile that follows, from T. S. Eliot's *The Waste Land*, we are likely to respond first to the visual image of a woman sitting at a marble table, and then secondly, as the other sensual details ("burnished," "Glowed") are absorbed, to become aware of the connotations of "throne" with its implied comparison of the woman to a queen:

The chair she sat in, like a burnished throne,
Glowed on the table . . .

In the same poem, Eliot offers a series of nightmare images that depend
for their effect on the reader's vulnerability to imagined sense impressions:

A woman drew her long black hair out tight
And fiddled whisper music on those strings
And bats with baby faces in the violet light
Whistled, and beat their wings
And crawled head downward down a blackened wall
And upside down in air were towers
Tolling reminiscent bells, that kept the hours,
And voices singing out of empty cisterns and exhausted wells.

QUESTIONS

1. Which of the senses are appealed to in lines 1–2? lines 3–4?
2. What time of day is implied by "violet light"? Is the image aural, visual, or
   tactile?
3. What is the visual relationship between the bats and the towers?

In the following lines from Alfred, Lord Tennyson's "Ulysses" (p.
373), the imagery moves from what is seen to what is heard:

The lights begin to twinkle from the rocks;
The long day wanes; the slow moon climbs; the deep
Moans round with many voices;

while in these lines from Tennyson's "Mariana" the imagery shifts from
the predominantly aural to the visual to the aural again:

All day within the dreamy house
  The doors upon their hinges creaked;
The blue fly sung in the pane; the mouse
  Behind the moldering wainscot shrieked,
Or from the crevice peered about.
  Old faces glimmered through the doors,
  Old footsteps trod the upper floors,
Old voices called her from without.

Show the points of transition in the excerpt from "Mariana" where the
imagery turns from aural to visual; from visual back to aural.

Images strike us differently, with varying degrees of intensity, even when they relate to the same sense. Eliot's baby-faced bats and Tennyson's "slow moon climbs" are both visual images, but the effects the poets seek are radically different and so is our response. Compare the quality of sound in Tennyson's "The blue fly sung in the pane" with that created by John Milton in *Paradise Lost* as he describes the battle in heaven between the angels loyal to God and those loyal to Satan:

> . . . now storming fury rose,
> And clamor such as heard in heaven till now
> Was never, arms on armor clashing brayed
> Horrible discord, and the madding° wheels   *frenzied*
> Of brazen chariots raged; dire was the noise
> Of conflict; overhead the dismal hiss
> Of fiery darts in flaming volleys flew
> And flying vaulted either host° with fire.   *both groups*

QUESTIONS

1. How does "brayed" (line 3) affect the kind of sound heard in the clash of arms on armor?
2. How would you relate "brayed" to "hiss" (line 6)?
3. What sort of weaponry are you invited to visualize?
4. Show how the imagery in the last three lines, beginning with "overhead," relates to both sight and sound and perhaps also to touch.

Sometimes clusters of images are joined to create a special effect similar to the extended metaphor or the epic simile. In the following stanza from "Ode to a Nightingale" (p. 448), John Keats embeds in his description of wine a thumbnail history: grapes, grown in the country, are pressed and stored and decanted; the glass, taken by the speaker, is held to his lips; the wine is swallowed and goes to his head—all in the course of the ten lines. In the process, Keats manages to draw upon all five senses:

> O, for a draught of vintage! that hath been
>   Cooled a long age in the deep-delved earth,
> Tasting of Flora and the country green,
>   Dance, and Provençal song, and sunburnt mirth!
> O for a beaker full of the warm South,   5
>   Full of the true, the blushful Hippocrene,
>   With beaded bubbles winking at the brim,
>   And purple-stained mouth;
> That I might drink, and leave the world unseen,
>   And with thee fade away into the forest dim: 10

When an image mingles two or more senses, using one sense to describe another, we call the device SYNESTHESIA. "Silken tones" and "sweet song" are examples. The following lines from Emily Dickinson's poem "I Heard a Fly Buzz—When I Died" (p. 412) provide another:

> There interposed a Fly—
>
> With Blue—uncertain stumbling Buzz—
> Between the light—and me—

Dickinson may well have recalled Tennyson's "The blue fly sung in the pane," but whereas in Tennyson's lines the visual and aural are kept in sequential relation, the speaker in Dickinson's poem, describing the approach of death, mixes up the senses of sight and sound, producing the effect of a more deranged sense perception.

The possibilities of figurative language and imagery are virtually limitless. The reader who wishes to experience a poem fully will approach it as D. H. Lawrence does the apple, "with all [the] senses awake":

Mystic

They call all experience of the senses *mystic*, when the experience is
   considered.
So an apple becomes *mystic* when I taste in it
the summer and the snows, the wild welter of earth
and the insistence of the sun.
All of which things I can surely taste in a good apple.   5
Though some apples taste preponderantly of water, wet and sour
and some of too much sun, brackish sweet
like lagoon-water, that has been too much sunned.

If I say I taste these things in an apple, I am called *mystic*, which means a
   liar.
The only way to eat an apple is to hog it down like a pig   10
and taste nothing
that is *real*.

But if I eat an apple, I like to eat it with all my senses awake.
Hogging it down like a pig I call the feeding of corpses.

D. H. Lawrence (1885–1930)

EXERCISES

I. The following poem depends almost entirely on simile for its effect.

"It Was Wrong to Do This," Said the Angel

"It was wrong to do this," said the angel.
"You should live like a flower,
Holding malice like a puppy,
Waging war like a lambkin."

"Not so," quoth the man   5
Who had no fear of spirits;
"It is only wrong for angels
Who can live like the flowers,
Holding malice like the puppies,
Waging war like the lambkins."   10

Stephen Crane (1871–1900)

1. Point out three similes in stanza 1 and indicate how they are related to each other.
2. Describe the effect of repeating the same similes in stanza 2.
3. From the nature of the similes, infer what it was the man did.

II. The following passages contain many of the figures of speech discussed in this chapter. Analyze each passage, identifying the figures of speech and explaining each in the context of the passage.

> Fear no more the frown o' the great,
>   Thou art past the tyrant's stroke;
> Care no more to clothe and eat,
>   To thee the reed is as the oak.
> The scepter, learning, physic, must
> All follow this, and come to dust.

William Shakespeare (1564–1616)

> Now as I was young and easy under the apple boughs
> About the lilting house and happy as the grass was green,
>   The night above the dingle° starry,   *narrow valley*
>   Time let me hail and climb
>   Golden in the heydays of his eyes,
> And honoured among wagons I was prince of the apple towns
> And once below a time I lordly had the trees and leaves
>   Trail with daisies and barley
>   Down the rivers of the windfall light.

Dylan Thomas (1914–1953)

Old age is
a flight of small
cheeping birds
skimming
bare trees
above a snow glaze.

William Carlos Williams (1883–1963)

III. Concentrate on the use of personification in the following poem, which was written to commemorate those who had died the previous year in defense of England.

Ode Written in the Beginning of the Year 1746

How sleep the brave who sink to rest
By all their country's wishes blest!
When Spring, with dewy fingers cold,
Returns to deck° their hallowed mold,   *dress*
She there shall dress a sweeter sod   5
Than Fancy's feet have ever trod.

By fairy hands their knell is rung,
By forms unseen their dirge is sung;
There Honor comes, a pilgrim gray,
To bless the turf that wraps their clay,   10
And Freedom shall awhile repair,
To dwell a weeping hermit there!

William Collins (1721–1759)

1. Find four instances of personification. Which of the four is most developed? which least developed?
2. Explain the function each personification serves in the development of the poem.
3. Explain the distinction between a pilgrim and a hermit as it applies in this poem.
4. Do you agree that lines 7–8 fall short of true personification? Justify your answer.

IV. Read the following poem by John Keats with attention to its imagery.

To Autumn

1

Season of mists and mellow fruitfulness,
  Close bosom-friend of the maturing sun;
Conspiring with him how to load and bless
  With fruit the vines that round the thatch-eves run;
To bend with apples the moss'd cottage-trees,   5
  And fill all fruit with ripeness to the core;
    To swell the gourd, and plump the hazel shells
With a sweet kernel; to set budding more,
  And still more, later flowers for the bees,
  Until they think warm days will never cease,   10
    For Summer has o'er-brimm'd their clammy cells.

2

Who hath not seen thee oft amid thy store?
  Sometimes whoever seeks abroad may find
Thee sitting careless on a granary floor,
  Thy hair soft-lifted by the winnowing wind;   15
Or on a half-reap'd furrow sound asleep,
  Drows'd with the fume of poppies, while thy hook
    Spares the next swath and all its twined flowers:
And sometimes like a gleaner thou dost keep
  Steady thy laden head across a brook;   20
  Or by a cyder-press, with patient look,
    Thou watchest the last oozings hours by hours.

3

Where are the songs of Spring? Ay, where are they?
  Think not of them, thou hast thy music too,—
While barred clouds bloom the soft-dying day,   25
  And touch the stubble-plains with rosy hue;
Then in a wailful choir the small gnats mourn
  Among the river sallows°, borne aloft   *willows*
    Or sinking as the light wind lives or dies;
And full-grown lambs loud bleat from hilly bourn°;   *realm* 30
  Hedge-crickets sing; and now with treble soft
    The red-breast whistles from a garden-croft°;   *enclosure*
    And gathering swallows twitter in the skies.

John Keats (1795–1821)

1. Which of the senses (sight, hearing, smell, taste, touch) pervades stanza 1?
   stanza 2? stanza 3? What progression can you find in the shift from one sense
   to another?

2. Which season of the year is not directly alluded to? Explain why.
3. Describe the comparison between spring and autumn. What subjects would be appropriate to the songs of spring (line 23)?
4. Analyze the poem for figures of speech such as personification, synecdoche, metonymy, simile, metaphor.

V.   Find the epic simile in the lines that follow from *The Aeneid* and show how it functions to characterize Aeneas.

> Such were her prayers, and such the tearful entreaties her agonized
> Sister conveyed to Aeneas again and again. But unmoved by
> Tearful entreaties he was, adamant against all pleadings:
> Fate blocked them, heaven stopped his ears lest he turn complaisant.
> As when some stalwart oak-tree, some veteran of the Alps,   5
> Is assailed by a wintry wind whose veering gusts tear at it,
> Trying to root it up; wildly whistle the branches,
> The leaves come flocking down from aloft as the bole is battered;
> But the tree stands firm on its crag, for high as its head is carried
> Into the sky, so deep do its roots go down towards Hades: 10
> Even thus was the hero belaboured for long with every kind of
> Pleading, and his great heart thrilled through and through with the
>   pain of it;
> Resolute, though, was his mind; unavailingly rolled her tears.

Virgil (70–19 B.C.*)*
(Trans. from the Latin by C. D. Lewis)

VI.   Try your hand at writing a few of the figures of speech described in this chapter.

1. Write three kennings—for a sports car, a boat, a professor you know.
2. Write a simile for the ring of a telephone; for the way someone you know drives a car.
3. Write a metaphor conveying an idea you have about sunset, or Washington, D.C., or dreams, or outer space.
4. Write three or four lines personifying any inanimate object in the room you are now in.

5
Symbols and Allegory

Symbols

Each week thousands of people visit an ancient wall in Jerusalem and are moved by the experience; the wall may or may not be the remnant of Solomon's temple but it has acquired that meaning, and to stand there and perhaps scribble a wish on a piece of paper and hide it between the cracks is a symbolic act of community with the God of Israel. Not far away, thousands of people climb a dozen stairs and gaze at a shapeless mound of ancient rock which has been designated as the place of the Crucifixion. To stand thus is a symbolic act of Christian community. A farmer from Wisconsin visiting the marketplace in Jaipur, India, is astonished to see how the cow is treated there; but he soon learns that it is a sacred symbol in the Hindu religion and may not be hindered in its wandering or harmed in any way.

Through custom and wide usage, specific objects or acts have come to have fixed meanings that may be recognized immediately, serving as a kind of shorthand to arouse familiar associations leading to a whole complex of ideas and emotions. A multicolored piece of cloth arouses feelings of patriotism. A comet is interpreted as a sign of impending doom. A dove suggests peace. Like synecdoche and metonymy, symbols imply the whole, as when a plain golden ring symbolizes marriage or a burnished cross symbolizes Christianity. A concrete object, a gesture, a mark on the forehead may signify a general truth or an abstract idea. We eat symbolic meals on Thanksgiving and deafen our ears with fireworks on the Fourth of July. Just glance at the following phrases and consider your associations and you will sense at once how symbols work: "roll out the red carpet"; "he drives a Rolls Royce"; "ivory tower"; "eternal flame."

Symbols may undergo changes in meaning over the centuries. In Greek and Roman times the rose was often a symbol of sensual love; by the Middle Ages it had become part of a new context, serving primarily as a symbol of spiritual love. In the Renaissance the associations shifted once again, and "rose" tended to signify youth and physical beauty, but with the further sense of vulnerability to age and decay. Both aspects are brought into play in the opening stanzas of Robert Herrick's "To the Virgins, to Make Much of Time":

> Gather ye rosebuds while ye may,
>   Old time is still a-flying;
> And this same flower that smiles today
>   Tomorrow will be dying.

The short-lived flower suggests all that is fresh and lovely but also ephemeral and transient; by implication, love that is smiling now will be dead on the morrow. The virgins addressed in the title would do well to "make much" of the time allowed them (for the complete poem, see p. 440).

In Edmund Spenser's stanza, taken from *The Faerie Queene*, the rose is similarly a symbol of love and transience, and as Spenser develops the symbol, it becomes associated with time and a proud lady and her impatient lover.

> So passeth, in the passing of a day,
>   Of mortal life the leaf, the bud, the flower;
> No more doth flourish after first decay,
> That erst° was sought to deck both bed and bower,   *first*
> Of many a lady, and many a paramour:
> Gather therefore the rose, whilst yet is prime,
> For soon comes age that will her pride deflower:
> Gather the rose of love, whilst yet is time,
> Whilst loving thou mayst lovéd be with equal crime.

The poet begins by speaking of the rose as a flower, subject to natural decay; and if we take that to relate to all things mortal, we understand the important corollary, that it cannot rejuvenate itself, cannot return again. The same is true of a lady and her lover. Lovers cannot rely on the permanence of love, and if the proud lady delays, age will violate her virtue ("her pride deflower"). She should therefore "Gather the rose of love, whilst yet is time."

Spenser and Herrick assume that their readers will share similar associations with regard to the rose. But common symbols can be made to change their meanings when placed in new contexts, and to respond adequately to the poet's new perception it is necessary for the reader to be alert to the new implications. In William Blake's poem "The Sick Rose," the rose is no longer merely the conventional symbol of youth and beauty; it seems also to suggest a type of innocence that would resist passion. And in opposition to the rose, Blake introduces a further symbol, the worm, which in this context seems to signify dark and brooding passion, a force capable under certain circumstances of destroying the rose.

The Sick Rose

O rose, thou art sick!
The invisible worm
That flies in the night,
In the howling storm,

Has found out thy bed
Of crimson joy,
And his dark secret love
Does thy life destroy.

William Blake (1757–1827)

QUESTIONS

1. Define as best you can what has made Blake's rose "sick."
2. What do the details in lines 3–4 suggest about the worm?
3. What is suggested by the phrases "crimson joy" and "dark secret love" (lines 6–7)?
4. What is implied of the rose's innocence by the phrase "has found out" (line 5)?
5. Compare Blake's use of the rose as symbol with that of Spenser and Herrick.

Your reading of "The Sick Rose" should make clear that symbols do not merely "stand for" something: they *are* the thing, embodying in themselves the meanings they evoke. As Samuel Taylor Coleridge wrote, defining the symbol: "It partakes of the reality which it renders intelligible." In the stanzas that follow, part of the poet's lament for a dead friend, the tree functions symbolically:

Old Yew, Which Graspest at the Stones*

Old yew, which graspest at the stones
  That name the underlying dead,
  Thy fibres net the dreamless head,
Thy roots are wrapt about the bones.

The seasons bring the flower again,   5
  And bring the firstling to the flock;
  And in the dusk of thee the clock
Beats out the little lives of men.

O, not for thee the glow, the bloom,
  Who changest not in any gale,   10
  Nor branding summer suns avail
To touch thy thousand years of gloom;

And gazing on thee, sullen tree,
  Sick for thy stubborn hardihood,
  I seem to fail from out my blood   15
And grow incorporate into thee.

Alfred, Lord Tennyson (1809–1892)

The yew is visualized in a graveyard setting and is rich in attributes: it is enduring, changeless, seemingly eternal; it is sullen, gloomy, not very hopeful; its roots go deep, reach to and envelop the "underlying dead." As the poet seems to "fail from out [his] blood" and "grow incorporate" into the tree, he finds a symbolic way of uniting with the dead friend he is lamenting and of freeing himself from the anguish of loss and separation.

    Herrick and Spenser write of the rose, Blake of the rose and the worm; Tennyson writes of the yew tree but makes a passing reference to flowers, flocks, and gales, which suggest other aspects of nature and especially the recurrence of the seasons:

> The seasons bring the flower again,
>   And bring the firstling to the flock . . .
>
> O, not for thee the glow, the bloom . . .

As in this instance, seasonal patterns provide poets with a rich source of symbolic reference, since each of the seasons seems capable of arousing certain associations that readers share. When Percy Bysshe Shelley

* From Tennyson's *In Memoriam.*

asks, "If Winter comes, can Spring be far behind?" we sense that he is setting up opposing symbols that enable him to look forward to the promise of rebirth after a period of dormancy. Shakespeare, as we have seen (p. 68), expresses the sense of aging in the lines:

> That time of year thou mayst in me behold
> When yellow leaves, or none, or few, do hang . . .

The poet assumes that his reader will have no trouble identifying the signs of coming winter with the speaker's own advanced "time of year." His summer, a time of vitality and flourishing, is clearly behind him.

But even summer may take on negative implications, as in these lines sung on the supposed death of a character in Shakespeare's play *Cymbeline:*

> Fear no more the heat o' the sun,
>   Nor the furious winter's rages;
> Thou thy worldly task hast done,
>   Home are gone, and ta'en thy wages.

The lines make death seem a consolation by excluding the usual pleasant associations of summer, stressing instead its destructive aspect, and then linking summer to winter personified as a furious creature inflicting its rage on the world. In her death, the subject of the song escapes all that is symbolized here by the seasonal cycle and returns "Home," a symbol of eternity, which is seasonless.

Autumn proves perhaps the most complex of the seasonal symbols since it bears the ambiguity of a fully fulfilled time that suggests, nonetheless, in its very ripeness, the threat of winter decline and death. Autumn is virtually spent in Shakespeare's image of "yellow leaves, or none, or few." But in John Keats's "To Autumn," read earlier for its imagery (p. 85), the season shows "ripeness to the core" through the first two stanzas, and only then seems to edge to its inevitable decline in the final stanza, which, like the others, is addressed to autumn:

> Where are the songs of Spring? Ay, where are they?
>   Think not of them, thou hast thy music too,—
> While barred clouds bloom the soft-dying day,
>   And touch the stubble-plains with rosy hue;
> Then in a wailful choir the small gnats mourn   5
>   Among the river sallows°, borne aloft   *willows*
>   Or sinking as the light wind lives or dies;
> And full-grown lambs loud bleat from hilly bourn°;   *realm*
>   Hedge-crickets sing; and now with treble soft
>   The red-breast whistles from a garden-croft°;   *enclosure* 10
>   And gathering swallows twitter in the skies.

The "soft-dying day," the "wailful choir," the wind that "lives or dies," the lambs "full-grown" and ready for the market—all suggest the inevitability of autumn's end. In the "gathering swallows" of the final line, we find a kind of summary symbol suggesting both the completion of a pattern (the gathering) and the imminence of departure.

"To Autumn" activates associations that we, as readers, are prepared to bring to the poem. The opening lines of T. S. Eliot's *The Waste Land* activate and simultaneously repudiate our usual expectations about springtime as a period of freshness, growth, and renewal:

> April is the cruellest month, breeding
> Lilacs out of the dead land, mixing
> Memory and desire, stirring
> Dull roots with spring rain.
> Winter kept us warm, covering
> Earth in forgetful snow, feeding
> A little life with dried tubers.

Spring is cruel because it invites rebirth in one who feels incapable of it, who is more at ease in the winter death world, where hope does not beckon.

James Wright, in "Saint Judas," makes similar demands—that his readers revise their associations—in choosing to write of Judas, a symbol identified for some two thousand years with villainy and betrayal. In casting the poem as a monologue, with Judas as speaker, Wright humanizes the conventional symbol and invites us to a more complex appreciation of it:

Saint Judas

When I went out to kill myself, I caught
A pack of hoodlums beating up a man.
Running to spare his suffering, I forgot
My name, my number, how my day began,
How soldiers milled around the garden stone   5
And sang amusing songs; how all that day
Their javelins measured crowds; how I alone
Bargained the proper coins, and slipped away.

Banished from heaven, I found this victim beaten,
Stripped, kneed, and left to cry. Dropping my rope   10
Aside, I ran, ignored the uniforms:
Then I remembered bread my flesh had eaten.
The kiss that ate my flesh. Flayed without hope,
I held the man for nothing in my arms.

James Wright (1927–1980)

1. What events or actions in the poem alter the conventional symbol of Judas as the arch-betrayer?
2. Explain the relevance of the last line to the entire poem.
3. Does the provocative title seem justified or frivolous?

Not all symbols used in a poem have symbolic status apart from their use in that particular poem. Wallace Stevens takes the most common-place and least promising of things, a jar, and manages by the poem's close to imbue it with symbolic meaning:

Anecdote of the Jar

I placed a jar in Tennessee,
And round it was, upon a hill.
It made the slovenly wilderness
Surround that hill.

The wilderness rose up to it,   5
And sprawled around, no longer wild.
The jar was round upon the ground
And tall and of a port° in air.   *portliness*

It took dominion everywhere.
The jar was gray and bare.   10
It did not give of bird or bush,
Like nothing else in Tennessee.

Wallace Stevens (1879–1955)

QUESTIONS

1. Gather all the details descriptive of the jar and redescribe it in your own words.
2. Trace the jar's effect on the wilderness and explain the change. In what sense does the jar make things happen?
3. What are the connotations of "dominion" (line 9)? Do they seem appropriate to a jar? Are they appropriate here?
4. Explain the symbolism of the jar.

Clearly, the meaning of Stevens's symbol derives from the context of the poem rather than from traditional associations. The same dependence on context is evident in the following poem, in which Stevens registers "disillusionment" with drab reality by creating a lively symbolism based on the interplay of color and outlandish things:

Disillusionment of Ten O'Clock

The houses are haunted
By white night-gowns.
None are green,
Or purple with green rings,
Or green with yellow rings,   5
Or yellow with blue rings.
None of them are strange,
With socks of lace
And beaded ceintures°.   *waistbands*
People are not going   10
To dream of baboons and periwinkles.
Only, here and there, an old sailor,
Drunk and asleep in his boots,
Catches tigers
In red weather.   15

Wallace Stevens (1879–1955)

QUESTIONS

1. Who are wearing the white nightgowns?
2. How do the color patterns in lines 3–6 relate to the white nightgowns? to the socks of lace and the beaded ceintures?
3. Why is it a bad thing that people won't dream of baboons and periwinkles? a good thing that the sailor dreams of "red weather"?

To ask exactly what "red weather" is, or what a drunken old sailor in boots is doing catching tigers in his sleep, is to realize that Stevens's poem creates a symbolic system of its own.

How poets arrive at the private symbols that enter their work can only remain a mystery to the reader, and may indeed be one to the poets. But the poems that follow by William Wordsworth and William Butler Yeats suggest something about the process.

I Wandered Lonely As a Cloud

I wandered lonely as a cloud
That floats on high o'er vales and hills,
When all at once I saw a crowd,
A host, of golden daffodils;
Beside the lake, beneath the trees,   5
Fluttering and dancing in the breeze.

Continuous as the stars that shine
And twinkle on the Milky Way,
They stretched in never-ending line
Along the margin of a bay: 10
Ten thousand saw I at a glance,
Tossing their heads in sprightly dance.

The waves beside them danced; but they
Outdid the sparkling waves in glee:
A poet could not but be gay,   15
In such a jocund company:
I gazed—and gazed—but little thought
What wealth the show to me had brought:

For oft, when on my couch I lie
In vacant or in pensive mood,   20
They flash upon that inward eye
Which is the bliss of solitude;
And then my heart with pleasure fills,
And dances with the daffodils.

William Wordsworth (1770–1850)

QUESTIONS

1. What do the opening lines suggest about the poet's state prior to his encounter with the daffodils?
2. What evidence in the poem suggests the nature of the poet's reaction to his encounter with the daffodils?
3. What is meant by "inward eye" (line 21)? What sort of vision is implied?

The symbol that evolves in Yeats's poem, and the source of the symbol, are quite different from Wordsworth's, but notice as you read that he goes through the same three stages: a state of need or irresolution, a vision, and a sense of comprehension that is imaged forth in a new symbol:

The Second Coming

Turning and turning in the widening gyre°   *cone-like spirals*
The falcon cannot hear the falconer;
Things fall apart: the center cannot hold;
Mere anarchy is loosed upon the world,
The blood-dimmed tide is loosed, and everywhere   5
The ceremony of innocence is drowned;
The best lack all conviction, while the worst
Are full of passionate intensity.

Surely some revelation is at hand;
Surely the Second Coming is at hand.   10
The Second Coming! Hardly are those words out
When a vast image out of *Spiritus Mundi*°   *world spirit*
Troubles my sight: somewhere in sands of the desert
A shape with lion body and the head of a man,
A gaze blank and pitiless as the sun,   15
Is moving its slow thighs, while all about it
Reel shadows of the indignant desert birds.
The darkness drops again; but now I know
That twenty centuries of stony sleep
Were vexed to nightmare by a rocking cradle,   20
And what rough beast, its hour come round at last,
Slouches towards Bethlehem to be born?

William Butler Yeats (1865–1939)

QUESTIONS

1. In what sense is the relationship of falcon to falconer an unnatural one (lines 1–2)? How is the relationship restated in line 3?
2. Paraphrase lines 5–6 and lines 7–8.
3. In what sense is the speaker prepared for the vision that follows?
4. Explain the symbol in lines 11–17. How does it answer to the condition of the poet and of the world as established in the preceding lines?
5. What, in your own words, does the poet now "know" (lines 18–22)?

Whether poets are reinterpreting familiar public symbols, as Blake does the rose, Eliot the spring, and Wright the Apostle Judas, or are creating their own symbols, as Stevens, Wordsworth, and Yeats do in the poems we have examined, the context of the poem will usually guide us to the meaning. As you read the following group of poems, consider the relation between the symbols and their contexts.

Crossing the Bar

Sunset and evening star,
   And one clear call for me!
And may there be no moaning of the bar°,   *sandbar*
   When I put out to sea,

But such a tide as moving seems asleep,   5
   Too full for sound and foam,
When that which drew from out the boundless deep
   Turns again home.

Twilight and evening bell,
   And after that the dark!   10
And may there be no sadness of farewell,
   When I embark;

For tho' from out our bourne° of Time and Place   *boundary, realm*
   The flood may bear me far,
I hope to see my Pilot face to face   15
   When I have crost the bar.

Alfred, Lord Tennyson (1809–1892)

Fire and Ice

Some say the world will end in fire,
Some say in ice.
From what I've tasted of desire
I hold with those who favor fire.
But if it had to perish twice,
I think I know enough of hate
To say that for destruction ice
Is also great
And would suffice.

Robert Frost (1874–1963)

The Coming of Wisdom with Time

Though leaves are many, the root is one;
Through all the lying days of my youth
I swayed my leaves and flowers in the sun;
Now I may wither into the truth.

William Butler Yeats (1865–1939)

Allegory

ALLEGORY may be defined as a structured narrative in which a system of abstract concepts is represented by persons, objects, and events. As we read an allegory, we recognize that the tale is not merely about, say, the pursuit of a beautiful maiden. The maiden, we perceive, personifies virtue, and her pursuer is not simply a lover on a dangerous journey through the woods at night but the soul in search of salvation. A deceptive lady who distracts him from his pursuit represents temptation, and though he may linger with her for a time, he unites finally with the beautiful maiden. Soul embraces Virtue, having repudiated Temptation, and achieves True Love, or Salvation.

Though many poems may have allegorical overtones, in strict allegory there ought to be no possibility of differing interpretations. The interplay between characters, incidents, objects, and the external framework is fixed by a one-to-one correspondence between the surface action of the narrative and the external system of ideas. The poem below, for example, appears to be a striking instance of allegory, but because of the ambiguity of the outside system of ideas and the inconclusive nature of the ending, we can say only that it is loosely allegorical, teasing us to solve its meaning.

Once There Came a Man

Once there came a man
Who said,
"Range me all men of the world in rows."
And instantly
There was terrific clamour among the people   5
Against being ranged in rows.
There was a loud quarrel, world-wide.
It endured for ages;
And blood was shed
By those who pined to stand in rows.   10
Eventually, the man went to death, weeping.
And those who stayed in bloody scuffle
Knew not the great simplicity.

Stephen Crane (1871–1900)

The poem has an action: a man speaks to a mass of people, generates a quarrel, and dies. The story reminds us of what may happen when a new religion is proposed, perhaps Christianity, for it does seem possible to identify the "man" as Jesus, although he may simply be called a prophet of religion. Those who agree with the new religion fight with those who do not. The prophet is himself destroyed, but the people fight on for ages, unaware that—well, unaware of what? Now we confront in the final line the ambiguity of the "great simplicity." Is the line suggesting that it makes no difference whether people are ranged in rows and that the prophet should have been ignored? Is the poem arguing that religion arouses men to violent quarrels? There are no clear answers, and because so much is left unresolved, the poem falls short of allegory despite its allegorical overtones.

Now read a poem that is indeed an allegory, embodying a pattern of unequivocal one-to-one correspondences. As the title suggests, the poem is a narrative of a spiritual quest. The action is presented in terms of a lover—a woman—seeking her beloved.

Songs of the Soul in Rapture at Having Arrived at the Height of Perfection, Which Is Union with God by the Road of Spiritual Negation

Upon a gloomy night,
With all my cares to loving ardours flushed,
(O venture of delight!)
With nobody in sight
I went abroad when all my house was hushed.   5

In safety, in disguise,
In darkness up the secret stair I crept,
(O happy enterprise!)
Concealed from other eyes
When all my house at length in silence slept.   10

Upon that lucky night
In secrecy, inscrutable to sight,
I went without discerning
And with no other light
Except for that which in my heart was burning.   15

It lit and led me through
More certain than the light of noonday clear
To where One waited near
Whose presence well I knew,
There where no other presence might appear.   20

Oh night that was my guide!
Oh darkness dearer than the morning's pride,
Oh night that joined the lover°   *Christ*
To the beloved bride°   *bride-to-be*
Transfiguring them each into the other.   25

Within my flowering breast
Which only for himself entire I save
He sank into his rest
And all my gifts I gave
Lulled by the airs with which the cedars wave.   30

Over the ramparts fanned
While the fresh wind was fluttering his tresses,
With his serenest hand
My neck he wounded, and
Suspended every sense with its caresses.   35

Lost to myself I stayed
My face upon my lover having laid
From all endeavor ceasing:
And all my cares releasing
Threw them amongst the lilies there to fade.   40

St. John of the Cross (1542–1591)
(Trans. from the Spanish by Roy Campbell)

The speaker leaves her house in disguise; she climbs a secret stairway
and reaches her lover, who caresses and soothes her; they lie in loving
embrace with all passion allayed and all cares forgotten. This is the
action from which we infer the correspondences. The woman represents
the soul seeking Christ; the beloved is the "One"—Christ—who rep-
resents God; the gloomy night she passes through is the state of spiritual
darkness; the house she leaves behind is the body; the stairway she
climbs represents stages in the process of meditation that bring her
closer to Christ; the light burning in her heart is the light of intuition;
the gifts given are all that the soul relinquishes to achieve union; the
wounding is the moment of grace; and the consequent suspension of
all senses is the annihilation of the physical self. The last stanza shows
the soul in rapture at having arrived at the height of perfection; and the
lilies amongst which all cares are thrown to fade represent pure virtue.

Not all allegories are religious, though through the centuries allegories
have most often dealt with religious themes and especially with the
experience of the spiritual quest. The allegory presented by the speaker
in Edgar Lee Masters's "Carl Hamblin" is concerned not with religion
but with social protest. It refers to an historical event, the Haymarket

Riot of 1886, a gathering to protest police brutality, during which a bomb was thrown, causing fatalities. The person who threw the bomb was never identified, but eight Anarchists were convicted and four of them hanged on the basis of evidence that a dispassionate jury would probably have found inadequate.

Carl Hamblin

The press of the Spoon River *Clarion* was wrecked,
And I was tarred and feathered,
For publishing this on the day the Anarchists were hanged in Chicago:
"I saw a beautiful woman with bandaged eyes
Standing on the steps of a marble temple.   5
Great multitudes passed in front of her,
Lifting their faces to her imploringly.
In her left hand she held a sword.
She was brandishing the sword,
Sometimes striking a child, again a laborer,   10
Again a slinking woman, again a lunatic.
In her right hand she held a scale;
Into the scale pieces of gold were tossed
By those who dodged the strokes of the sword.
A man in a black gown read from a manuscript: 15
'She is no respecter of persons.'
Then a youth wearing a red cap
Leaped to her side and snatched away the bandage.
And lo, the lashes had been eaten away
From the oozy eye-lids;   20
The eye-balls were seared with a milky mucus;
The madness of a dying soul
Was written on her face—
But the multitude saw why she wore the bandage."

Edgar Lee Masters (1868–1950)

QUESTIONS

1. Establish correspondences for each of the following: the marble temple; the beautiful woman; her sword and scale; the multitudes; the man in the black gown; the youth in the red cap.
2. Paraphrase the poem using the correspondences you have found.

The effectiveness of an allegory, as we have seen, depends on the reader's willingness to accept the chain of correspondences forged by the poet. The writing of allegories, therefore, has tended to flourish in periods when poets and readers have shared a single, generally accepted system of beliefs—especially, in the predominantly Christian tradition of poetry in English, beliefs about the nature of this world and of another beyond it. In the absence of such a presumed faith, as in the twentieth century, we are likely to have, at most, poems in which there seem to be orderly correspondences but the symbols cannot confidently be said to "stand for" specific concepts or abstractions.

To compare Masters's modern allegory, "Carl Hamblin," with one written centuries ago by George Herbert is to sense both the strain placed upon a modern poet choosing to work in an essentially alien form and the ease of movement for a seventeenth-century poet for whom allegory was a tenable, indeed a favorite, mode.

Redemption

Having been tenant long to a rich lord,
    Not thriving, I resolvéd to be bold,
    And make a suit unto him, to afford
A new small-rented lease, and cancel the old.

In heaven at his manor I him sought;   5
    They told me there that he was lately gone
    About some land, which he had dearly bought
Long since on earth, to take possessiön.

I straight returned, and knowing his great birth,
    Sought him accordingly in great resorts;   10
    In cities, theaters, gardens, parks, and courts;
At length I heard a ragged noise and mirth
    Of thieves and murderers; there I him espied,
    Who straight, *Your suit is granted*, said, and died.

George Herbert (1593–1633)

EXERCISES

I. Determine the symbols in the following poems and show how they function to create meaning.

The Golf Links

The golf links lie so near the mill
  That almost every day
The laboring children can look out
  And see the men at play.

Sarah N. Cleghorn (1876–1959)

A Lyke-Wake° Song

Corpse-Watch

Fair of face, full of pride,
Sit ye down by a dead man's side.

Ye sang songs a' the day;
Sit down at night in the red worm's way.

Proud ye were a' day long;   5
Ye'll be but lean at evensong.

Ye had gowd kells° on your hair;   *gold nets*
Nae man kens° what ye were.   *knows*

Ye set scorn by the silken stuff;
Now the grave is clean enough.   10

Ye set scorn by the rubis° ring;   *ruby*
Now the worm is a saft sweet thing.

Fine gold and blithe fair face,
Ye are come to a grimly place.

Gold hair and glad grey een°,   *eyes* 15
Nae man kens if ye have been.

Algernon Charles Swinburne (1837–1909)

The Water Below

This house is floored with water,
Wall to wall, a deep green pit,
Still and gleaming, edged with stone.
Over it are built stairways
And railed living-areas   5
In wrought iron. All rather
Impractical; it will be
Damp in winter, and we shall
Surely drop small objects—keys,
Teaspoons, or coins—through the chinks   10
In the ironwork, to splash
Lost into the glimmering
Depths (and do we know how deep?)
It will have to be rebuilt:
A solid floor of concrete   15

Over this dark well (perhaps
Already full of coins, like
The flooded crypt of that church
In Ravenna°). You might say   *city in Italy*
It could be drained, made into   20
A useful cellar for coal.
But I am sure the water
Would return; would never go.
Under my grandmother's house
In Drury, when I was three,   25
I always believed there was
Water: lift up the floorboards
And you would see it—a lake,
A subterranean sea.
True, I played under the house   30
And saw only hard-packed earth,
Wooden piles, gardening tools,
A place to hunt for lizards.
That was different: below
I saw no water. Above,   35
I knew it must still be there,
Waiting. (For why did we say
'Forgive us our trespasses,
Deliver us from evil?')
Always beneath the safe house   40
Lies the pool, the hidden sea
Created before we were.
It is not easy to drain
The waters under the earth.

Fleur Adcock (b. 1934)

On the Subject of Poetry

I do not understand the world, father.
By the millpond at the end of the garden
There is a man who slouches listening
To the wheel revolving in the stream, only
There is no wheel there to revolve.   5

He sits in the end of March, but he sits also
In the end of the garden; his hands are in
His pockets. It is not expectation
On which he is intent, nor yesterday
To which he listens. It is a wheel turning.   10

When I speak, father, it is the world
That I must mention. He does not move
His feet nor so much as raise his head
For fear he should disturb the sound he hears
Like a pain without a cry, where he listens.   15

I do not think I am fond, father,
Of the way in which always before he listens
He prepares himself by listening. It is
Unequal, father, like the reason
For which the wheel turns, though there is no wheel.   20

I speak of him, father, because he is
There with his hands in his pockets, in the end
Of the garden listening to the turning
Wheel that is not there, but it is the world,
Father, that I do not understand.   25

W. S. Merwin (b. 1927)

II. The following poems evoke aspects of the seasonal cycle. Show how each symbol in each poem incorporates the attributes of the season for symbolic effect.

Shall I Compare Thee to a Summer's Day?

Shall I compare thee to a summer's day?
Thou art more lovely and more temperate.
Rough winds do shake the darling buds of May,
And summer's lease hath all too short a date.
Sometime too hot the eye of heaven shines,   5
And often is his gold complexion dimmed;
And every fair° from fair sometime declines,   *beauty*
By chance, or nature's changing course, untrimmed°:   *stripped*
But thy eternal summer shall not fade
Nor lose possession of that fair thou ow'st°,   *ownest* 10
Nor shall Death brag thou wand'rest in his shade
When in eternal lines to time thou grow'st.
  So long as men can breathe or eyes can see,
  So long lives this, and this gives life to thee.

William Shakespeare (1564–1616)

After Apple-Picking

My long two-pointed ladder's sticking through a tree
Toward heaven still,
And there's a barrel that I didn't fill
Beside it, and there may be two or three
Apples I didn't pick upon some bough.   5
But I am done with apple-picking now.
Essence of winter sleep is on the night,
The scent of apples: I am drowsing off.
I cannot rub the strangeness from my sight
I got from looking through a pane of glass   10
I skimmed this morning from the drinking trough
And held against the world of hoary grass.
It melted, and I let it fall and break.
But I was well
Upon my way to sleep before it fell,   15
and I could tell
What form my dreaming was about to take.
Magnified apples appear and disappear,
Stem end and blossom end,
And every fleck of russet showing clear.   20
My instep arch not only keeps the ache,
It keeps the pressure of a ladder-round.
I feel the ladder sway as the boughs bend.
And I keep hearing from the cellar bin
The rumbling sound   25
Of load on load of apples coming in.
For I have had too much
Of apple-picking: I am overtired
Of the great harvest I myself desired.
There were ten thousand thousand fruit to touch,   30
Cherish in hand, lift down, and not let fall.
For all
That struck the earth,
No matter if not bruised or spiked with stubble,
Went surely to the cider-apple heap   35
As of no worth.
One can see what will trouble
This sleep of mine, whatever sleep it is.
Were he not gone,
The woodchuck could say whether it's like his   40
Long sleep, as I describe its coming on,
Or just some human sleep.

Robert Frost (1874–1963)

Brief Autumnal

Green grape, and you refused me.
        Red grape, and you sent me packing.
            Must you deny me a bite of your raisin?

Anonymous
(Trans. from the Greek by Dudley Fitts)

III. Read the following allegorical poem by George Herbert. Explain the action, identify the symbols, and describe the one-to-one correspondence between the symbols or incidents and the external system of ideas they represent.

The Pilgrimage

I traveled on, seeing the hill, where lay
        My expectation.
    A long it was and weary way.
    The gloomy cave of Desperation
I left on the one, and on the other side   5
        The rock of Pride.

And so I came to Fancy's meadow strowed
        With many a flower:
    Fain would I here have made abode,
    But I was quickened by my hour.   10
So to Care's copse° I came, and there got through   *woods*
        With much ado.

That led me to the wild of Passion, which
        Some call the wold°;   *moors*
    A wasted place, but sometimes° rich.   *once* 15
    Here I was robbed of all my gold,
Save one good Angel°, which a friend had tied   *gold coin; heavenly angel*
        Close to my side.

At length I got unto the gladsome hill,
        Where lay my hope,   20
    Where lay my heart; and climbing still,
    When I had gained the brow and top,
A lake of brackish° waters on the ground   *muddy*
        Was all I found.

With that abashed and struck with many a sting   25
        Of swarming fears,
    I fell, and cried, Alas my King!
    Can both the way and end be tears?
Yet taking heart I rose, and then perceived
        I was deceived: 30

My hill was further; so I flung away,
    Yet heard a cry
Just as I went, *None goes that way*
And lives. If that be all, said I,
After so foul a journey death is fair,   35
    And but a chair.

                    George Herbert (1593–1633)

IV.   Explain the symbols in the following poems. What allegorical implications do you find, and how do you interpret them?

I Was a Stricken Deer, That Left the Herd*

I was a stricken deer, that left the herd
Long since; with many an arrow deep infixt
My panting side was charged, when I withdrew
To seek a tranquil death in distant shades.
There was I found by one who had himself   5
Been hurt by th' archers. In his side he bore,
And in his hands and feet, the cruel scars.
With gentle force soliciting the darts,
He drew them forth, and heal'd and bade me live.
Since then, with few associates, in remote   10
And silent woods I wander, far from those my
Former partners of the peopled scene;
With few associates, and not wishing more.

                    William Cowper (1731–1800)

In an Empty Field at Night

for Peter

A man carries a skull of red yarn
that unravels as he walks.
With his steps he traces
the labyrinth scratched on his palm.
At its center he discovers the tree
whose leaves open underground
and whose white roots toss in the wind.

                    Gregory Orr (b. 1947)

* From Cowper's lengthy discursive poem *The Task.*

6
Rhyme, Rhythm, and Stanza

The very best way to read a poem is to read it aloud, for although poems usually come to us as a visual experience, as words locked into the printed page, they are intended to be heard as well as seen. An attentiveness to the sounds and patterns of sound is essential to the full appreciation of most poems. For example, the rhythm and other sound patterns may contribute to a sense of dignity and stateliness, as in the opening lines of John Milton's "On the Morning of Christ's Nativity":

> This is the month, and this the happy morn,
> Wherein the Son of Heaven's Eternal King,
> Of wedded maid and virgin mother born,
> Our great redemption from above did bring;
> For so the holy sages once did sing,
>   That he our deadly forfeit should release,
> And with his Father work us a perpetual peace.

The sounds of another poem may approach those of ordinary conversation, as in the opening lines of W. H. Auden's "The Unknown Citizen":

> He was found by the Bureau of Statistics to be
> One against whom there was no official complaint,
> And all the reports on his conduct agree
> That, in the modern sense of an old-fashioned word, he was a saint.

Milton is writing of the exceptional, Auden of the commonplace, and they choose their language and rhythms accordingly. In each instance, however, the sound and the sense of the lines work inseparably to create the total meaning of the poem.

We saw earlier, in chapters 3, 4, and 5, how the poet's choice and arrangement of words, figures of speech, images, and symbols contribute to the highly concentrated meaning that is characteristic of poetry. In this chapter we shall see how patterns of sound—the poet's use of rhyme, rhythm, stress, and variations of sound and silence—help to determine and intensify the experience and meaning of a poem.

Rhyme

The poems most of us grew up with as children were rhymed poems—in fact, we call some of them nursery rhymes—so it is quite natural that when we think of poetry we tend to think first of RHYME. Rhyme, in its broadest sense, refers to the repetition of sounds from word to word or line to line.

> Hey diddle diddle,
> The cat and the fiddle,
> The cow jumped over the moon.
> The little dog laughed,
> To see such sport,
> And the dish ran away with the spoon.

Poems need not rhyme to be good poems: in previous chapters we have seen many that do not. But rhyme certainly is one of the most effective ways of binding a poem into a single unit, and it also gives pleasure in itself. Compare the following version with the original printed above and account for what has been lost.

> Hey diddle diddle,
> The cat and the cello,
> The cow jumped over the moon.
> The little dog laughed,
> To see such sport,
> And the dish ran away with the knife.

Generally speaking, a rhyme occurs when two or more words (or in some instances, phrases) have matching sounds. It is *sound*, not spelling, that determines rhyme.

Who comes here?
    A Grenadier.
What do you want?
    A Pot of Beer.

When rhyme occurs at the close of lines, it is called END RHYME:

Upon a Child That Died

Here she lies, a pretty bud,
Lately made of flesh and blood,
Who as soon fell fast asleep
As her little eyes did peep.
Give her strewings°, but not stir   *strew flowers*
The earth that lightly covers her.

Robert Herrick (1591–1674)

When the rhyme occurs elsewhere than at ends of lines, it is called INTERNAL RHYME. In the following example from Samuel Taylor Coleridge, note the internal rhymes in the first and third lines:

The fair breeze blew, the white foam flew,
The furrow followed free:
We were the first that ever burst
Into that silent sea.

EXACT RHYME, the kind we have seen above, occurs when the accented vowel sounds, as well as any following consonants and vowels, are identical:

When Lovely Woman Stoops to Folly

When lovely woman stoops to folly,
    And finds too late that men betray,
What charm can soothe her melancholy,
    What art can wash her guilt away?

The only art her guilt to cover,
    To hide her shame from every eye,
To give repentance to her lover,
    And wring his bosom—is to die.

Oliver Goldsmith (1730–1774)

Poets, especially modern poets, often favor an approximate rhyme, called SLANT RHYME, in which the sounds are similar but not identical. W. H. Auden's poem uses six end rhymes, each of which is a slant rhyme:

That Night When Joy Began

That night when joy began
Our narrowest veins to flush,
We waited for the flash
Of morning's levelled gun.

But morning let us pass,   5
And day by day relief
Outgrows his nervous laugh,
Grown credulous of peace.

As mile by mile is seen
No trespasser's reproach,   10
And love's best glasses reach
No fields but are his own.

W. H. Auden (1907–1973)

Often exact and approximate rhyme are combined in the same poem. In the following lines from Theodore Roethke's "My Papa's Waltz" (for the entire poem, see p. 480), the rhyme in the first and third lines is exact, in the second and fourth lines, approximate:

The whiskey on your breath
Could make a small boy dizzy;
But I hung on like death:
Such waltzing was not easy.

Roethke's lines serve also to illustrate another distinction that is often useful in talking about the effects of rhyme—the distinction between MASCULINE RHYME and FEMININE RHYME. In a masculine rhyme, the accent or stress is always on the final syllable (*support/distort*; or, in the lines above, *breath/death*). In a feminine rhyme, however, the accented syllable is followed by one or more unaccented ones: *burning/turning; attitude/ latitude*. In Roethke's lines, *dizzy* and *easy* are a feminine slant rhyme, while in the following lines from Robert Browning we find feminine exact rhyme:

To carry pure death in an earring, a casket,
A signet, a fan-mount, a filigree basket.

Lord Byron was a master of rhyme, and in his comic epic, *Don Juan* (pronounced Jóo-an in this poem), he carries feminine rhyme to deliberately absurd lengths:

> Sagest of women, even of widows, she
> > Resolved that Juan should be quite a paragon,
> And worthy of the noblest pedigree,
> > (His Sire was of Castile, his Dam from Aragon):
> Then, for accomplishments of chivalry,
> > In case our Lord the King should go to war again,
> He learned the arts of riding, fencing, gunnery,
> And how to scale a fortress—or a nunnery.

Paragon and *Aragon* are an exact feminine rhyme, and are then slant rhymed with *war again*. The rhyming of *she, pedigree*, and *chivalry* is picked up in the final rhyme, *gunnery* and *nunnery*, which is exact feminine. The unexpected rhyming of two such seemingly incompatible words as *gunnery* and *nunnery* brings a comic stanza to a comic conclusion.

In order to talk about the pattern of end rhyme, called the RHYME SCHEME, of stanzas or poems, we use a simple shorthand system based on the letters of the alphabet. Lines with the same end rhyme are given the same letters, the first rhyme the letter *a*, the second rhyme the letter *b*, and so on. The first passage below, by Alexander Pope, has an *aa* rhyme scheme; the second, by William Wordsworth, has an *abab* rhyme scheme:

| But when to mischief mortals bend their will, | a |
| How soon they find fit instruments of ill. | a |

To her fair works did Nature link	a
The human soul that through me ran;	b
And much it grieved my heart to think	a
What man has made of man.	b

More complicated rhyme schemes require us to go beyond *a* and *b*:

Sigh No More, Ladies, Sigh No More

Sigh no more, ladies, sigh no more,	a
Men were deceivers ever;	b
One foot in sea, and one on shore,	a
To one thing constant never.	b

Then sigh not so,	c
But let them go,	c
And be you blithe and bonny,	d
Converting all your sighs of woe	c
Into Hey nonny, nonny.	d

William Shakespeare (1564–1616)

Before we move on to other sound patterns, read aloud the stanza below from Edgar Allan Poe's "The Raven" and find instances of end rhyme, internal rhyme, masculine rhyme, and feminine rhyme.

> Once upon a midnight dreary, while I pondered, weak and weary,
> Over many a quaint and curious volume of forgotten lore—
> While I nodded, nearly napping, suddenly there came a tapping,
> As of some one gently rapping, rapping at my chamber door.
> " 'Tis some visitor," I muttered, "tapping at my chamber door—
> Only this and nothing more."

In reading poems, much of the pleasure we get derives not only from the kinds of rhymes we have been discussing, but from other repetitions of sound that produce echoes within and between lines. Such repetitions help unify the poem much as a formal rhyme scheme may do and also contribute in complex ways, as we shall see, to the particular effect the poem has on the reader. These repetitions of sound are called *alliteration, consonance,* and *assonance.* You can much better explain why a particular poem has a particular effect if you understand these three terms and make them a part of your vocabulary for discussing poetry.

Perhaps the easiest to understand is ALLITERATION, which is the repetition of consonant sounds at the beginnings of words (*b*ully *b*oys; *w*indow on the *w*orld). In the following lines from Gerard Manley Hopkins's "Pied Beauty," note in the first line the repetition of the hard *g* sound (that is, *g* as in *g*low), and in the second line the hard *c* sound (as in *c*ore).

> *G*lory be to *G*od for dappled things—
> For skies of *c*ouple-*c*olor, as a brinded *c*ow;

As you read the following lines aloud from Samuel Taylor Coleridge's "Kubla Khan," note the repetition of the *m* and *r* and the effect such repetition produces:

> Five miles meandering with a mazy motion
> Through wood and dale the sacred river ran,
> Then reached the caverns measureless to man,
> And sank in tumult to a lifeless ocean.

To get a sense of the quite different effects that alliteration may produce, read again, aloud, first the two lines from Hopkins, with their hard *g* and *c* sounds, and then the lines from Coleridge with their softer and more flowing *m* and *r* sounds.

Below are some additional brief instances for study and comparison:

Westron wynde when wyll thow blow

Winds, whisper gently whilst she sleeps

And death shall have no dominion

A sweet disorder in the dress
Kindles in clothes a wantonness.

The sound must seem an echo of the sense.

When to the sessions of sweet silent thought
I summon up remembrance of things past

CONSONANCE refers to the repetition of consonant sounds that are not confined to alliteration, though they may support a particular alliterative pattern. In the last of the passages above, by Shakespeare, the alliterative use of *s* is reinforced by similar internal sounds: se*ss*ions, remembrance, thing*s*, pa*st*. The preponderance of the *s* sound seems to create a hushed or whispering effect appropriate to the notion of "silent thought." On the other hand, John Milton opens *Paradise Lost* with emphasis on firmer, more precise consonants than the drawn-out *s*:

Of man's first disobedience, and the fruit
Of that forbidden tree . . .

Alliteration brings together *first, fruit,* and *forbidden,* all key words in Milton's argument. Notice, too, how *first* and *fruit* end in the same consonants; how the *t* in *first* edges into the *d* of *disobedience* and is resumed in *that* and *tree;* and how diso*bed*ience is reaffirmed in for*bid*den.

Observe the interplay of alliteration and consonance in the following lines by Algernon Charles Swinburne:

For winter's rains and ruins are over,
And all the season of snows and sins;
The days dividing lover and lover,
The light that loses, the night that wins;

Consonance and alliteration, as we have seen, involve the repetition of consonant sounds. ASSONANCE refers to the repetition of vowel sounds, as in the following line by John Milton:

Methought I saw my late espoused saint

The two halves of William Butler Yeats's line

That dolphin-torn, that gong-tormented sea—

show verbal repetition (*That*), alliteration (*t*), consonance (*t*, *n*), and strong assonance (dol/gong; orn/orm). *Sea* is the one word free of aural echo, an isolation that gives it emphasis. Below, in Thomas Gray's lines, the assonance moves from line to line, helping to bind the stanza into a whole. Listen especially to the variations on the *o* sound:

> The curfew tolls the knell of parting day,
>   The lowing herd wind slowly o'er the lea,
> The plowman homeward plods his weary way,
>   And leaves the world to darkness and to me.

QUESTIONS

1. Show the use of assonance in lines 2 and 4. Find the same sound in other lines.
2. What alliterative effects seem especially prominent? Are any of these reinforced by consonance?

The sounds of certain words seem to imitate the sounds of what they describe. A few obvious examples are *buzz, drip, click.* The use of such words in poetry to reflect a particular sound—for instance, a horse galloping over cobblestones—is called ONOMATOPOEIA. Very often onomatopoeia is heightened by alliteration, consonance, or assonance:

> Over the cobbles he clattered and clashed

> The moan of doves in immemorial elms,
> And murmur of innumerable bees

> I should have been a pair of ragged claws
> Scuttling across the floors of silent seas.

Rhythm

You now have a vocabulary for talking about rhyme and a sense of the ways in which alliteration, consonance, and assonance contribute to the meaning and pleasure of a poem. Let us turn to another pattern in poetry, RHYTHM, which may be defined as a pattern of recurring stresses and pauses.

Rhythms are all around us, in the ticking of a clock or the dripping of a faucet, the wheels of a train, rain on the roof, the pounding of a sledge hammer, the ocean surf. Why we respond to rhythm is not entirely clear, but there is no question that we do. The reason may be physiological, stemming from some inner rhythm of our nature, such as our heartbeat or breathing; or it may be psychological, stemming from some need we have for evidence of order in things outside ourselves. Although in art we seem to resist too persistent a pattern, calling it tedious or monotonous, some pattern is essential to our enjoyment of music or dance, painting or poetry. Indeed, rhythm is more fundamental to poetry than the repetitions of particular sounds we have been discussing, for although there are many poems with no rhyme at all and scarcely any effect of consonance, assonance, or alliteration, rhythm is everywhere in poetry, as it is everywhere in life.

Read each of the following lines aloud and notice how they fall into strong but quite different rhythms:

Down the Mississippi where the boats go push!

Oh brave Miss Pritchett!

Sometimes I feel like a motherless child.

Star light, star bright, first star I see tonight.

Here comes the Judge!

I hit the man with a frying pan!

here is little Effie's head
whose brains are made of gingerbread

We can analyze poetic rhythm and, to some extent at least, account for the effects of rhythm in any particular poem. As in music, we look for the beat—a regular pattern of stressed and unstressed sounds. In most poetry written in English, the beat comes out of a pattern of stressed and unstressed syllables. This basic pattern is called the METER.

Hannah Bantry, in the pantry,
Gnawing at a mutton bone,
How she gnawed it,
How she clawed it,
When she found herself alone.

The regular rhythmic pattern in the lines above is created by an alternation of strong and weak syllables. To describe meter, we use a set of signs that suggest how the line is to be read. Below is a list of the most common signs:

- ′ is used to indicate a strong or stressed syllable.
- ‿ is used for a weak or unstressed syllable.
- | is called a *bar*, and is used to mark metrical divisions in a line. Each unit thus marked is called a FOOT, consisting (usually) of one stressed and one or two unstressed syllables.
- ‖ indicates a CAESURA—a pause—in the line of verse.

The process of marking the meter is called SCANSION. To scan a line of poetry, first mark the accented, or strong, syllables:

Agaínst an elm a shéep was tíed,

The bútcher's knífe in blóod was dýed;

Next, place a mark over the unaccented or weak syllables:

Ăgaínst ăn elm ă shéep wăs tíed,

Thĕ bútchĕr's knífe ĭn blóod wăs dýed;

Mark off the feet with vertical bars, and where a pause (caesura) occurs within the line, use the double bar to indicate it:

Ăgaínst | ăn elm ‖ ă shéep | wăs tíed,

Thĕ bútch|ĕr's knífe | ĭn blóod | wăs dýed;

Following this step-by-step process, try a simple exercise of scansion on the passages below, by Alexander Pope and Lord Byron.

Be not the first by whom the new are tried,
Nor yet the last to lay the old aside.

She walks in beauty, like the night
    Of cloudless climes and starry skies;
And all that's best of dark and bright
    Meet in her aspect and her eyes:

When you scan the brief poem by W. H. Auden that follows, you will discover that the feet are irregular, perhaps to match the discomfort of the speaker;

Óvĕr thĕ | héathĕr | thĕ wét | wĭnd blóws,

I'vĕ líce | ĭn mў | túnĭc | ănd ă cóld | ĭn mў nóse.

These lines by Lord Byron seem to gallop along, simulating the motion
of the Assyrians on horseback:

> The Assýr|iăn cáme dówn | líke thĕ wólf | ŏn thĕ fóld,
>
> Ănd hĭs có|hŏrts wĕre gléam|ĭng ĭn púr|plĕ ănd góld;
>
> Ănd thĕ shéen | ŏf thĕir spéars | wăs lĭke stárs | ŏn thĕ séa,
>
> Whĕn thĕ blúe | wăve rólls níght|lў ŏn déep | Gălĭlée.

In Sterling A. Brown's lines below, the metrical pattern appears to wind
down, the meter and the dog seemingly both asleep at the end:

> Sŏ yŏu cain't | nĕvĕr téll
>
> Hŏw fás' | ă dóg | căn rún
>
> Whĕn yŏu sée | hĭm ă-sleep|ĭng,
>
> Ĭn thĕ sún.

Notice that at the close of the first and second lines above, you move
with virtually no pause to the next line. Such lines are called RUN-ON,
and the effect of continuity they give is termed ENJAMBMENT. When the
lines close on a strong pause, as in this passage by John Lyly, we call
them END-STOPPED:

> My Daphne's hair is twisted gold,
> Bright stars apiece her eyes do hold;
> My Daphne's brow enthrones the graces,
> My Daphne's beauty stains all faces.

Following are a few examples to experiment with. In each, mark the
stressed and unstressed syllables, use the single bar to mark off the feet,
and use the double bar to indicate caesuras where appropriate.

> Sweetest love, I do not go
>   For weariness of thee,
> Nor in hope the world can show
>   A fitter love for me;
>   But since that I
> Must die at last, 'tis best
> To use myself in jest,
>   Thus by feigned° deaths to die.   *pretended*

John Donne (1572–1631)

I went to the Garden of Love,
And saw what I never had seen:
A Chapel was built in the midst,
Where I used to play on the green.

William Blake (1757–1827)

Go, lovely rose,
Tell her that wastes her time and me
   That now she knows,
When I resemble her to thee,
How sweet and fair she seems to be.

Edmund Waller (1606–1687)

His Being Was in Her Alone

His being was in her alone:
And he not being, she was none.

They joyed one joy, one grief they grieved;
One love they loved, one life they lived.
The hand was one, one was the sword,
That did his death, her death afford.

As all the rest, so now the stone
That tombs the two is justly one.

Sir Philip Sidney (1554–1586)

QUESTIONS

1. Which of the four passages has the most regular metrical pattern? In which is the meter most varied?
2. Which of the four is most dependent on caesura? Explain the effect in that poem of the use of caesura.
3. In which of the four passages are the lines predominantly end-stopped? In which predominantly run-on?

In the process of scanning, you have been dividing each line into a unit of measurement called the *foot*, consisting of two or three syllables, one of which is stressed. The four most common feet in English poetry are:

name	sign	example
IAMB	⌣ ′	invĕnt
TROCHEE	′ ⌣	mótiŏn
ANAPEST	⌣ ⌣ ′	iñtĕrrúpt
DACTYL	′ ⌣ ⌣	téndĕrlў

The following feet occur less frequently:

AMPHIBRACH	⌣ ′ ⌣	Ăláskă
SPONDEE	′ ′	heártbréak
PYRRHIC	⌣ ⌣	sŏ-sŏ

Remember that two or more one-syllable words may be thought of as joined ("Hĕ lovĕs | tŏ lóve") when we wish to identify a metrical foot. The partial line, "Tŏ die | iñ mў arḿs," consists of two feet, one an iamb, the other an anapest; but no pattern is clear until we know the whole line: "Tŏ die | ĭn mў arḿs | wăs lóve | sĕréne." The dominant meter is thus iambic.

You may have noticed that the iamb and the trochee are reversals of each other, and the same may be said of the anapest and the dactyl. Many believe that the IAMBIC is the basic English metrical pattern and all other meters are variations of it. In any case, when words are joined into lines of verse, we assign distinct names to specify the meter that prevails. Below are examples of the four principal meters used in English poetry:

IAMBIC:

Hăd wĕ | bŭt worĺd | ĕnoúgh, | ănd time,

TROCHAIC:

Láy yoŭr | sléepiñg | heád, mў | love,*

ANAPESTIC:

Fŏr thĕ móon | ñevĕr beáms, | withŏut bríng|iñg mĕ dréams

DACTYLIC:

Jŭst fŏr ă | handfŭl ŏf | silvĕr hĕ | léft ŭs,

* The last foot in this line, as in the dactylic line, is incomplete. Such omission of one or more syllables is called catalexis and is one of many devices by which poets achieve metrical variety.

Notice that in the examples we have just considered, each line has four feet. Such lines are said to be written in tetrameter (*tetra,* meaning "four," plus *meter*), and as the instances above show, we may have iambic tetrameter, trochaic tetrameter, and so forth. When we wish to indicate the number of feet in a line, we use the following terms:

MONOMETER: 1 foot in a line

Helen
Led 'em!

DIMETER: 2 feet in a line

The sea of faith

TRIMETER: 3 feet in a line

Down to a sunless sea

TETRAMETER: 4 feet in a line

My heart is like a singing bird

PENTAMETER: 5 feet in a line

Are falling like a ton of bricks and bones

HEXAMETER: 6 feet in a line

Eye of the earth, and what it watches is not our wars.

Though poems tend to have a prevalent meter, few are written entirely in iambs or trochees, in anapests or dactyls. For one thing, such poems probably would very quickly lead us into an annoying or distracting singsong monotony. But there is a more important general point to be made about meter. Although, like four beats or three beats to a measure in a piece of music, a poem's metrical pattern may give us pleasure in itself (so long as it is *not* allowed to become merely monotonous), both that metrical pattern and any variations from it are finally inseparable from the meaning of the poem if the poem is successful. Indeed, our main purpose in having learned the fundamentals of meter (since this is not a book about how to write poetry) is to enable us as readers to examine the various ways in which a poem might be read so that we may arrive at the very best way, the one that comes nearest the meaning of the poem.

Consider, for instance, the four lines that follow from a poem by William Wordsworth, in which the speaker mourns for a loved one now dead and buried. The basic meter is unquestionably iambic. But try reading the lines aloud, first in a *perfectly regular* iambic meter (strictly alternating unstressed and stressed syllables) and with *no pauses* (cae-

suras) within any of the lines. This is the way we have first marked
(scanned) them. Then read the lines as they are scanned the second
time, with a spondee (rather than an iamb) as the first and last foot of
the first line and as the first foot of the second and third lines, and with
the caesuras marked in the first and fourth lines. If necessary, try this
comparison two or three times, until you feel you have a sense of the
real difference between the two readings. You may even wish to have
someone else read the lines aloud while you listen.

No mó|tĭon hás | sĭe ňow, | ňo for̆ce;
   Sĭe néi|tĭer héars | nŏr sées;
Rol̆led róund | ĭn eárth's | dĭúr|năl coúrse,
   Wĭth rocks, | aňd stónes, | aňd trées.

Nó mŏ|tĭon hás | sĭe nów, ‖ ňo for̆ce;
   Sĭe néi|tĭer héars | nŏr sées;
Rol̆led róund | ĭn eárth's | dĭúr|năl coúrse.
   Wĭth rócks, ‖ aňd stónes, ‖ aňd trées.

A detailed analysis of these lines could yield many insights into the
craft of poetry, but we need not make any such exhaustive study to
appreciate some of the ways in which metrical considerations have an
important bearing on meaning. Consider, for instance, just the first foot
of the first line in each of the two versions. Surely it is not *motion* (as
in the first version) but the absence of motion, *no motion* (as in the
second), that the poet wishes to stress. This impression of motionless-
ness is then reinforced when we come to rest at the caesura after *now*—
a pause it is in fact hard not to make in reading the line aloud. (You
might consider, as well, the effects of both assonance and alliteration
in this line.)

Turning briefly to the second line: it seems unlikely that as readers
we are meant to skip without any stress over *she* (the subject, after all,
of the speaker's reflections) and simply emphasize *neither*, as in the first
version. Read the line as scanned in the second version and consider
the difference. And note one other thing in the second line: how perfectly
the last two (iambic) feet emphasize the key words, *hears* and *sees*.

Finally, consider just two more metrical features in Wordsworth's
lines. One is in the first foot of the third line: read both versions of the
line aloud and consider how much more effectively the first foot of the
second version, a spondee, by slowing the reading of *rolled round*,
suggests the slow, massive turning of the earth (here, too, notice how
alliteration and assonance work together with meter to help create the
sense). The other notable feature is the effect of the two caesuras in the

last line of the second version. The difference in the line when read with and without these pauses is almost astonishing; without them, the rhythm tends to be singsong, almost "jingly," certainly inappropriate to the gravity of the poem. With the pauses (which, in fact, the poet here indicates for us with commas that need not otherwise have been inserted), the line has a stateliness that accords with the serious theme. (For the entire poem, see p. 15.)

Stanza

So far in this chapter, our concern has been primarily with lines and the effects within lines. Now we turn to the larger units within poems. The one with which you are probably most familiar is the STANZA, a unit which is repeated in the poem. Each stanza has the same number of lines, the same metrical pattern, and usually the same rhyme scheme. Notice the regular line division and rhyme scheme in the following poem:

Richard Cory

Whenever Richard Cory went down town,
We people on the pavement looked at him:
He was a gentleman from sole to crown,
Clean favored, and imperially slim.

And he was always quietly arrayed,   5
And he was always human when he talked;
But still he fluttered pulses when he said,
"Good-morning," and he glittered when he walked.

And he was rich—yes, richer than a king—
And admirably schooled in every grace: 10
In fine, we thought that he was everything
To make us wish that we were in his place.

So on we worked, and waited for the light,
And went without the meat, and cursed the bread;
And Richard Cory, one calm summer night,   15
Went home and put a bullet through his head.

Edwin Arlington Robinson (1869–1935)

Certain line lengths, meters, and rhyme schemes have come to be associated with particular stanza forms. COUPLETS are two lines that rhyme and usually are iambic tetrameter or iambic pentameter:

> What poet would not grieve to see,
> His brethren write as well as he?

> *Jonathan Swift (1667–1745)*

> Two principles in human nature reign;
> Self-love to urge, and reason to restrain.

> *Alexander Pope (1688–1744)*

Pope composed many thousands of pentameter couplets, and when he translated Homer, he put all of the *Iliad* and parts of the *Odyssey* into rhymed couplets, exercising incredible skill to vary a potentially predictable form.

The following poem by Theodore Roethke proceeds through pentameter couplets, each comprising a stanza that presents a further aspect of its subject:

The Bat

By day the bat is cousin to the mouse.
He likes the attic of an aging house.

His fingers make a hat about his head.
His pulse beat is so slow we think him dead.

He loops in crazy figures half the night   5
Among the trees that face the corner light.

But when he brushes up against a screen,
We are afraid of what our eyes have seen:

For something is amiss or out of place
When mice with wings can wear a human face.   10

> *Theodore Roethke (1908–1963)*

Each of Roethke's couplet stanzas is end-stopped, producing a sharp and incisive effect. Compare the effect of W. H. Auden's poem below, which consists of a series of TERCETS, or three-line units, each locked into the other as well by the repeated lines and rhymes.

If I Could Tell You

Time will say nothing but I told you so,
Time only knows the price we have to pay;
If I could tell you I would let you know.

If we should weep when clowns put on their show,
If we should stumble when musicians play,   5
Time will say nothing but I told you so.

There are no fortunes to be told, although,
Because I love you more than I can say,
If I could tell you I would let you know.

The winds must come from somewhere when they blow,   10
There must be reasons why the leaves decay;
Time will say nothing but I told you so.

Perhaps the roses really want to grow,
The vision seriously intends to stay;
If I could tell you I would let you know.   15

Suppose the lions all get up and go,
And all the brooks and soldiers run away;
Will Time say nothing but I told you so?
If I could tell you I would let you know.

W. H. Auden (1907–1973)

Auden's skillful use of the double refrain of repeated lines helps weave together the fabric of the poem: line 1 recurs in lines 6, 12, and 18; line 3 recurs in lines 9, 15, and 19; and both come together in the final stanza, which is structured as a quatrain. (The design is known technically as a VILLANELLE; see p. 219n for further discussion.)

Four-line stanzas are called QUATRAINS. The quatrain is among the most commonly used of stanza forms:

Grown-up

Was it for this I uttered prayers,
And sobbed and cursed and kicked the stairs,
That now, domestic as a plate,
I should retire at half-past eight?

Edna St. Vincent Millay (1892–1950)

The example just read consists of four lines of four feet each, but quatrains may take many forms. Here is an example from William Butler Yeats in which four-foot lines alternate with three-foot lines. Note that the rhyme schemes in the two examples also are different.

> The old priest Peter Gilligan
> Was weary night and day;
> For half his flock were in their beds,
> Or under green sods lay.

The five-line stanza, called a QUINTAIN or QUINTET, is evident in Edmund Waller's "Go, Lovely Rose." The rose has three missions to perform: to go to the lady; to bring her a message; and to die:

Go, Lovely Rose

> Go, lovely rose,
> Tell her that wastes her time and me
>   That now she knows,
> When I resemble her to thee,
> How sweet and fair she seems to be.   5
>
>   Tell her that's young
> And shuns to have her graces spied
>   That hadst thou sprung
> In deserts where no men abide,
> Thou must have uncommended died.   10
>
>   Small is the worth
> Of beauty from the light retired;
>   Bid her come forth,
> Suffer herself to be desired,
> And not blush so to be admired.   15
>
>   Then die, that she
> The common fate of all things rare
>   May read in thee:
> How small a part of time they share
> That are so wondrous sweet and fair!   20

Edmund Waller (1606–1687)

The LIMERICK is a special use of the five-line stanza form; it is a single unit, with a fixed metrical pattern and rhyme scheme, and a final line that has a witty turn of thought:

There was an Old Man with a beard,
Who said, "It is just as I feared—
   Two Owls and a Hen,
   Four Larks and a Wren,
Have all built their nests in my beard!"

Edward Lear (1812–1888)

Notice the balancing of trimeter and dimeter lines and the shifts from iambs to anapests.

As stanzas build up to constitute the total poem, so smaller units are often used to build larger stanzas. In Percy Bysshe Shelley's "Ode to the West Wind," the unit is a form of interlocking tercets (also called, from the Italian, TERZA RIMA), in which the first and third lines rhyme, with the middle line providing the rhyme for the first and third lines of the succeeding unit. The pattern in this instance is completed by use of a couplet.

If I were a dead leaf thou mightest bear;
If I were a swift cloud to fly with thee;
A wave to pant beneath thy power, and share

The impulse of thy strength, only less free
Than thou, O uncontrollable! If even   5
I were as in my boyhood, and could be

The comrade of thy wanderings over Heaven,
As then, when to outstrip thy skiey speed
Scarce seemed a vision; I would ne'er have striven

As thus with thee in prayer in my sore need.   10
Oh! lift me as a wave, a leaf, a cloud!
I fall upon the thorns of life! I bleed!

A heavy weight of hours has chained and bowed
One too like thee: tameless, and swift, and proud.

The entire poem (pp. 185–187) consists of five parts, each containing, as above, four tercets and a couplet.

Ben Jonson's poem below uses interlocking quatrains to build an eight-line stanza, an OCTAVE.

Song: To Celia

Drink to me only with thine eyes,
   And I will pledge with mine;
Or leave a kiss but in the cup,
   And I'll not ask for wine.

The thirst that from the soul doth rise   5
  Doth ask a drink divine;
But might I of Jove's nectar sup,
  I would not change for thine.

I sent thee late° a rosy wreath,   *recently*
  Not so much honoring thee   10
As giving it a hope that there
  It could not withered be.
But thou thereon didst only breathe,
  And sent'st it back to me;
Since when it grows, and smells, I swear,   15
  Not of itself, but thee.

Ben Jonson (1573?–1637)

The SONNET (considered in greater detail later, p. 175) offers an ideal instance of an established form that is built out of smaller units. The Italian (or Petrarchan) version combines an octave of eight lines (*abbaabba*) and a sestet of six lines (*cdecde* or *cdcdcd* or a variant), thus providing two basic units; the English (or Shakespearean) sonnet combines three quatrains and a couplet, potentially providing four units (*abab*, *cdcd*, *efef*, *gg*). The following sonnet by Shakespeare indicates how the basic structure, cemented by rhyme and meter, can help organize a poet's thoughts:

My Mistress' Eyes Are Nothing Like the Sun

My mistress' eyes are nothing like the sun;   a
Coral is far more red than her lips' red;   b
If snow be white, why then her breasts are dun;   a
If hairs be wires, black wires grow on her head.   b
I have seen roses damask'd, red and white,   c   5
But no such roses see I in her cheeks,   d
And in some perfumes there is more delight   c
Than in the breath that from my mistress reeks.   d
I love to hear her speak, yet well I know   e
That music hath a far more pleasing sound.   f   10
I grant I never saw a goddess go;   e
My mistress, when she walks, treads on the ground: f
    And yet, by heaven, I think my love as rare   g
    As any she belied with false compare.   g

William Shakespeare (1564–1616)

In the first quatrain, the poet tells us about the appearance of the mistress, mentioning her eyes, her lips, her breasts, and her hair. In the second quatrain, he tells us that her skin does not resemble rose petals; neither does her breath smell like perfume. And in the third quatrain he describes how she sounds; her voice is unmusical, and when she walks she makes a heavy noise. We move, then, from images of sight to images of smell and sound, all focused on her physical attributes. The couplet then makes a summary, and surprising, point: for all her apparent failings, the poet's mistress is a rare person, and he need not reach for the false comparisons so often employed by other poets when they write of their mistresses.

Along with its many stanzaic forms, English poetry developed a well-defined but remarkably flexible form called BLANK VERSE, consisting of a sequence of unrhymed iambic pentameter lines. The sequence may be of any length, ranging from a few lines to hundreds or even thousands. The iambic meter is perhaps the closest to the rhythms of ordinary speech, and the five-footed line is more open and flexible than tetrameter or trimeter, less ponderous and unwieldy than hexameter. The regular but unobtrusive rhythm of successive pentameter lines creates a patterned effect, while the absence of rhyme and stanzaic breaks permits a naturalness and fluidity of movement especially appropriate to the telling of a story or the working out of an argument. Shakespeare, some of whose sonnets and songs we have discussed, was also the first great poet to commit his imagination consistently to the possibilities of blank verse. Here is Hamlet, alone on stage, expressing his inner conflict, arguing out the question of suicide, in a blank verse that moves in rhythm with his thoughts:

from *Hamlet**

HAMLET To be, or not to be: that is the question:
  Whether 'tis nobler in the mind to suffer
  The slings and arrows of outrageous fortune,
  Or to take arms against a sea of troubles,
  And by opposing end them. To die: to sleep: 5
  No more; and by a sleep to say we end
  The heart-ache, and the thousand natural shocks
  That flesh is heir to, 'tis a consummation°   *goal*
  Devoutly to be wish'd. To die, to sleep;
  To sleep: perchance to dream: ay, there's the rub°;   *obstacle* 10
  For in that sleep of death what dreams may come,
  When we have shuffled off this mortal coil,
  Must give us pause: there's the respect
  That makes calamity of so long life:

* Act III, Scene 1, lines 56–88.

For who would bear the whips and scorns of time,   15
The oppressor's wrong, the proud man's contumely°,   *contempt*
The pang of despised love, the law's delay,
The insolence of office, and the spurns
That patient merit of the unworthy takes,
When he himself might his quietus° make   *release (from life)* 20
With a bare bodkin°? who would fardels° bear,   *dagger/burdens*
To grunt and sweat under a weary life,
But that the dread of something after death,
The undiscover'd country from whose bourn°   *boundary*
No traveller returns, puzzles the will,   25
And makes us rather bear those ills we have
Than fly to others that we know not of?
Thus conscience does make cowards of us all,
And thus the native hue° of resolution   *natural color*
Is sicklied o'er with the pale cast of thought,   30
And enterprises of great pith and moment°   *importance*
With this regard their currents turn awry
And lose the name of action.

William Shakespeare (1564–1616)

QUESTIONS

1. Analyze Hamlet's soliloquy, indicating where the shifts in his argument for and against suicide occur. Explain the relationship of lines 28–33 to that argument.
2. Note where the lines are heavily caesured, where lightly caesured, and where the run-on lines become end-stopped. Explain how these variations relate to stages in the argument.
3. Imagine Hamlet's words cast in couplets or quatrains. What differences in effect seem to you likely?

Blank verse and the various stanzaic forms persisted as the dominant modes in English and American poetry until well into the nineteenth century, when poets, straining against both modes and seeking new structures for poetic statement, began experimenting with a type of poetry that has loosely been called FREE VERSE (or, from the French, *vers libre*). In place of rhyme patterns and a consistent meter, we find reliance on a series of other devices: repetition of grammatical elements; a strong stress pattern with no concern for the number of syllables in a line; occasional rhymes, slant rhymes, or more often no rhymes at all; sound recurrence by means of alliteration, consonance, and assonance; lists (called *catalogues*) or words organized as a series; and significant use of the caesura to distinguish shifts in thought or emotion. Several of these qualities are in evidence in the following poem by Walt Whitman, who was among the earliest of the major poets to experiment with the possibilities of free verse:

When I Heard the Learn'd Astronomer

When I heard the learn'd astronomer,
When the proofs, the figures, were ranged in columns before me,
When I was shown the charts and diagrams, to add, divide, and measure
    them,
When I sitting heard the astronomer where he lectured with much
    applause in the lecture-room,
How soon unaccountable I became tired and sick,
Till rising and gliding out I wander'd off by myself,
In the mystical moist night-air, and from time to time,
Look'd up in perfect silence at the stars.

Walt Whitman (1819–1892)

QUESTIONS

1. Find examples of alliteration and assonance.
2. Find instances of grammatical elements that are repeated and explain their effect.
3. Lines 3 and 8 can in fact be scanned in a fairly conventional way. What is the basic foot in each? How many feet in each?

Whitman's poem falls visually into one unit, but many—perhaps most—poems in free verse separate into a series of units called STROPHE, a convenient term to use when there are no patterned stanzas. Much of a poem's dramatic effect, as in Charles Olson's "La Chute," can result from open spaces forcing a pause between or within strophes.

La Chute

my drum, hollowed out thru the thin slit,
carved from the cedar wood, the base I took
when the tree was felled

o my lute, wrought from the tree's crown

my drum, whose lustiness   5
was not to be resisted
                              my lute,
from whose pulsations
not one could turn away

                                    They   10
are where the dead are, my drum fell
where the dead are, who
will bring it up, my lute
who will bring it up where it fell in the face of them
where they are, where my lute and drum have fallen?   15

Charles Olson (1910–1970)

QUESTIONS

1. What is the effect of open space surrounding line 4? within lines 5–9?
2. How do the varying lengths of the strophes contribute to the poem's meaning?

  Before we turn from this chapter on rhyme, rhythm, and stanza to
other aspects of poetry, we should point out once again that not all
poems rhyme and not all have consistent metrical or stanzaic patterns.
But all do have a structure, an inner coherence, which we will take up
in the next chapter.

EXERCISES

I. Study the following poem by Gerard Manley Hopkins:

Heaven-Haven

A Nun Takes the Veil

      I have desired to go
            Where springs not fail,
To fields where flies no sharp and sided hail
      And a few lilies blow.

      And I have asked to be
            Where no storms come,
Where the green swell is in the havens dumb,
      And out of the swing of the sea.

Gerard Manley Hopkins (1844–1889)

1. Underline each example of assonance; circle the instances of alliteration.
2. Mark the poem with signs for scansion and name the prevailing meter.
3. Mark the rhyme scheme. How does it seem to organize or give structure to each of the stanzas?

II. Consider the unexpected variations in meter and rhyme in William Blake's poem:

The Garden of Love

I went to the Garden of Love,
And saw what I never had seen:
A Chapel was built in the midst,
Where I used to play on the green.

And the gates of this Chapel were shut,   5
And "Thou shalt not" writ over the door;
So I turn'd to the Garden of Love,
That so many sweet flowers bore,

And I saw it was filled with graves,
And tomb-stones where flowers should be: 10
And Priests in black gowns were walking their rounds,
And binding with briars my joys & desires.

William Blake (1757–1827)

1. Determine the poem's basic meter and rhyme scheme.
2. Explain the effects of the internal rhymes and the use of caesura in lines 11–12.
3. Explain the emphasis achieved by the stress pattern in line 6. Explain how the consonance in lines 5–6 contributes to that emphasis.
4. Notice that each line is end-stopped. What is the effect on the poem as a whole?

III. Elinor Wylie's poem below conveys an impression of quiet, tranquility, peace, an effect achieved largely by the use of assonance, consonance, alliteration, and end-stopped lines. Identify as many specific instances as you can.

Velvet Shoes

Let us walk in the white snow
    In a soundless space;
With footsteps quiet and slow,
    At a tranquil pace,
    Under veils of white lace.   5

I shall go shod in silk,
   And you in wool,
White as a white cow's milk,
   More beautiful
   Than the breast of a gull.   10

We shall walk through the still town
   In a windless peace;
We shall step upon white down,
   Upon silver fleece,
   Upon softer than these.   15

We shall walk in velvet shoes:
   Wherever we go
Silence will fall like dews
   On white silence below.
   We shall walk in the snow.   20

Elinor Wylie (1885–1928)

IV.   Below are three sonnets, each with a different rhyme scheme. Analyze
the relationship between the smaller units in each sonnet and then show how
they contribute to the larger design.

When I Have Fears That I May Cease to Be

When I have fears that I may cease to be
Before my pen has gleaned my teeming brain,
Before high piléd books, in charactry°,   *letters, writing*
Hold like rich garners the full-ripened grain;
When I behold, upon the night's starred face,   5
Huge cloudy symbols of a high romance,
And think that I may never live to trace
Their shadows, with the magic hand of chance;
And when I feel, fair creature of an hour!
That I shall never look upon thee more,   10
Never have relish in the faery power
Of unreflecting love!—then on the shore
Of the wide world I stand alone, and think
Till Love and Fame to nothingness do sink.

John Keats (1795–1821)

Composed upon Westminster Bridge
Sept. 3, 1802

Earth has not anything to show more fair:
Dull would he be of soul who could pass by
A sight so touching in its majesty:
This city now doth, like a garment, wear
The beauty of the morning; silent, bare,   5
Ships, towers, domes, theatres, and temples lie
Open unto the fields, and to the sky;
All bright and glittering in the smokeless air.
Never did sun more beautifully steep
In his first splendour, valley, rock, or hill;   10
Ne'er saw I, never felt, a calm so deep!
The river glideth at his own sweet will:
Dear God! The very houses seem asleep;
And all that mighty heart is lying still!

William Wordsworth (1770–1850)

What Guile Is This, That Those Her Golden Tresses

What guile is this, that those her golden tresses,
She doth attire under a net of gold;
And with sly skill so cunningly them dresses,
That which is gold or hair, may scarce be told?
Is it that men's frail eyes, which gaze too bold,   5
She may entangle in that golden snare;
And being caught may craftily enfold,
Their weaker hearts, which are not well aware?
Take heed therefore, mine eyes, how ye do stare
Henceforth too rashly on that guileful net,   10
In which if ever ye entrappèd are,
Out of her bands ye by no means shall get.
Fondness° it were for any being free,   *foolishness*
To covet fetters, though they golden be.

Edmund Spenser (1552?–1599)

V. (a) Select a metrical pattern from those listed on page 121; using this basic pattern, write two lines of verse with end rhyme, taking as your subject a season of the year, a time of day, or an aberration in the weather.

(b) Write a four-line poem in any meter, using the rhyme scheme *abab*. Then try another poem on the same theme, changing the rhyme scheme to *abba*. See whether your own poems include instances of alliteration, consonance, and assonance.

7
Structure

STRUCTURE is best understood as the organization of the parts or units of a poem into an order that is coherent and meaningful in terms of the content of the poem as a whole. Perhaps the simplest structure is that of a story, in which events are recounted in a sequence, as in the following poem by Robert Frost:

"Out, Out—"

The buzz saw snarled and rattled in the yard
And made dust and dropped stove-length sticks of wood,
Sweet-scented stuff when the breeze drew across it.
And from there those that lifted eyes could count
Five mountain ranges one behind the other   5
Under the sunset far into Vermont.
And the saw snarled and rattled, snarled and rattled,
As it ran light, or had to bear a load.
And nothing happened: day was all but done.
Call it a day, I wish they might have said   10
To please the boy by giving him the half hour
That a boy counts so much when saved from work.
His sister stood beside them in her apron
To tell them "Supper." At the word, the saw,
As if to prove saws knew what supper meant,   15

Leaped out at the boy's hand, or seemed to leap—
He must have given the hand. However it was,
Neither refused the meeting. But the hand!
The boy's first outcry was a rueful laugh,
As he swung toward them holding up the hand   20
Half in appeal, but half as if to keep
The life from spilling. Then the boy saw all—
Since he was old enough to know, big boy
Doing a man's work, though a child at heart—
He saw all spoiled. "Don't let him cut my hand off—   25
The doctor, when he comes. Don't let him, sister!"
So. But the hand was gone already.
The doctor put him in the dark of ether.
He lay and puffed his lips out with his breath.
And then—the watcher at his pulse took fright.   30
No one believed. They listened at his heart.
Little—less—nothing!—and that ended it.
No more to build on there. And they, since they
Were not the one dead, turned to their affairs.

Robert Frost (1874–1963)

Although Frost's lines are not divided into stanzas or strophes, it is easy to see how the unfolding of the action—the calling of the boy to dinner, the accident, the doctor's visit, the death of the boy—gives order to the poem. The opening lines prepare the scene and build into the action; the closing lines are the speaker's caustic observation, rounding off the action. In between is the sequence of events, given in chronological order.

The structure in the poem that follows is also readily apparent—that of a simple question and answer. In this case, however, the stanza division coincides with the structural design:

A Question

I asked if I got sick and died, would you
With my black funeral go walking too,
If you'd stand close to hear them talk or pray
While I'm let down in that steep bank of clay.

And, No, you said, for if you saw a crew
Of living idiots pressing round that new
Oak coffin—they alive, I dead beneath
That board—you'd rave and rend them with your teeth.

John Millington Synge (1871–1909)

The two stanzas serve to balance the question and the reply, the speaker's quiet description of the solemn funeral procession and the extreme reaction of the person addressed.

As you read the next poem, you will sense that it, too, is developing coherently: each event is presented in a couplet-stanza possessing its own focus; at the same time, each stanza contributes to the poem's unifying theme—what it means to be human:

The Four Ages of Man

He with body waged a fight,
But body won; it walks upright.

Then he struggled with the heart;
Innocence and peace depart.

Then he struggled with the mind;
His proud heart he left behind.

Now his wars on God begin;
At stroke of midnight God shall win.

William Butler Yeats (1865–1939)

The first couplet speaks of the body, the second of the heart, the third of the mind, the fourth of the approaching annihilation of all three—the death of the man. Reconsidering the poem, we see a further structural principle: each couplet is rooted in conflict and loss. In the first, the subject resists in vain the physical processes of becoming a man and must give up the crawling posture of childhood. In the second, he is drawn into an emotional conflict and loses his innocence and peace. In the third, whatever passion or emotion may be associated with his proud heart is lost in an intellectual conflict. His final struggle is with God, as he faces the ultimate loss that awaits all humanity. Notice that the structure also involves a succession in time: the first three stanzas describe progressive stages in the past; the last stanza places the action in the present ("Now") and also foretells the future ("shall win").

Each of the three poems we have considered has a distinctive structure, which may be described as an arrangement of parts that conforms in Frost to stages in a narrative, in Synge to a pattern of question and reply, and in Yeats to the development of a conception ordered as a narrative sequence. The speaker in A. E. Housman's poem below is only twenty years old and does not appear, on first reading, to be lamenting the inevitability of death. He speaks rather of the exquisite beauty to be found in nature and tells us that life is not long enough to enable him to perceive that beauty adequately:

Loveliest of Trees, the Cherry Now

Loveliest of trees, the cherry now
Is hung with bloom along the bough,
And stands about the woodland ride
Wearing white for Eastertide.

Now, of my threescore years and ten,   5
Twenty will not come again,
And take from seventy springs a score,
It only leaves me fifty more.

And since to look at things in bloom
Fifty springs are little room,   10
About the woodlands I will go
To see the cherry hung with snow.

A. E. Housman (1859–1936)

Each stanza has a different focus: in the first stanza the cherry trees are remembered in their setting; in the second stanza the speaker makes a reckoning of his age—what time has gone by (twenty years) and what is left to him (fifty years); in the third stanza the speaker resolves, on the basis of what the first two stanzas revealed to him, to go forth to view the trees. On rereading, you discover that the blossoming trees wear white, for Eastertide, a time associated with rebirth; that the calculation of the speaker's age ends with the awareness of a life span that is limited; and that nature continues, but he will not, and therefore he had better go to the woodlands to see "the cherry hung with snow." In the first stanza the trees have blossoms; by the third stanza the blossoms have changed to a metaphoric snow, with implications of winter and death, in contrast to the initial celebration of springtime and youth.

In the poems by Housman and Yeats we have seen that the progress or movement from part to part has been steady, almost relentless, as if there were an unwavering forward movement—from youth to maturity to death in Yeats, from scene to calculation to decision in Housman. In the following poem by Thomas Hardy, the movement seems less orderly, in keeping with the thought processes of a speaker who is working out the implications of an encounter that troubles him from the past:

The Man He Killed

"Had he and I but met
  By some old ancient inn,
We should have sat us down to wet
  Right many a nipperkin°!   *glass of beer*

"But ranged as infantry, 5
  And staring face to face,
I shot at him as he at me,
  And killed him in his place.

"I shot him dead because—
  Because he was my foe, 10
Just so—my foe of course he was;
  That's clear enough; although

"He thought he'd 'list°, perhaps, *enlist*
  Off-hand like—just as I—
Was out of work—had sold his traps— 15
  No other reason why.

"Yes; quaint and curious war is!
  You shoot a fellow down
You'd treat if met where any bar is,
  Or help to half-a-crown." 20

Thomas Hardy (1840–1928)

Here again the stanza divisions and the structure coincide. Thinking of the man he killed, the speaker in the first stanza conjectures how he and his adversary might have met (in an inn) and what they might have done (taken a glass of beer together); in the second and third stanzas he recalls how, in fact, they did meet (as infantrymen on opposite sides) and what, in fact, they did do (shoot at each other). In the fourth stanza he speculates on why his so-called enemy joined the war, and supposes it was for no compelling cause, "off-hand like," or because he was unemployed—"just as I." The fifth stanza concludes with a rueful comment and brings us back to the opening stanza. In his meditation the speaker has realized that he and his foe were quite alike, both in a sense victims, killing and being killed for no really adequate reason. The uncertainty expressed in the middle stanza, as the speaker tries to understand, persists to the end.

As we have seen, a poem may use any one of a number of structural patterns. Certain patterns, however, seem to recur more consistently than others, and we turn now to several of the more common ones. Poems with a strong narrative thrust, like Frost's "Out, Out—," are likely to adhere to a *chronological* ordering of the units. John Clare's narrative below on the fate of a badger begins at midnight and carries through the next day. Within that time span we find event piled upon event in a dizzying pursuit and combat that falls essentially into three major parts: the badger is caught, the badger is harassed, the badger dies:

Badger

When midnight comes a host of dogs and men
Go out and track the badger to his den,
And put a sack within the hole, and lie
Till the old grunting badger passes by.
He comes and hears—they let the strongest loose.   5
The old fox hears the noise and drops the goose.
The poacher shoots and hurries from the cry,
And the old hare half wounded buzzes by.
They get a forked stick to bear him down
And clap the dogs and take him to the town,   10
And bait him all the day with many dogs,
And laugh and shout and fright the scampering hogs.
He runs along and bites at all he meets:
They shout and hollo down the noisy streets.

He turns about to face the loud uproar   15
And drives the rebels to their very door.
The frequent stone is hurled where'er they go;
When badgers fight, then everyone's a foe.
The dogs are clapped and urged to join the fray;
The badger turns and drives them all away.   20
Though scarcely half as big, demure and small,
He fights with dogs for hours and beats them all.
The heavy mastiff, savage in the fray,
Lies down and licks his feet and turns away.
The bulldog knows his match and waxes cold,   25
The badger grins and never leaves his hold.
He drives the crowd and follows at their heels
And bites them through—the drunkard swears and reels.

The frighted women take the boys away,
The blackguard laughs and hurries on the fray.   30
He tries to reach the woods, an awkward race,
But sticks and cudgels quickly stop the chase.
He turns again and drives the noisy crowd
And beats the many dogs in noises loud.
He drives away and beats them every one,   35
And then they loose them all and set them on.
He falls as dead and kicked by dogs and men,
Then starts and grins and drives the crowd again;
Till kicked and torn and beaten out he lies
And leaves his hold and cackles, groans, and dies.   40

John Clare (1793–1864)

The events are fewer and time seems to move more slowly in William Stafford's poem, allowing for a meditative effect not possible in the helter-skelter of Clare's "Badger":

Traveling Through the Dark

Traveling through the dark I found a deer
dead on the edge of the Wilson River road.
It is usually best to roll them into the canyon:
that road is narrow; to swerve might make more dead.

By glow of the tail-light I stumbled back of the car   5
and stood by the heap, a doe, a recent killing;
she had stiffened already, almost cold.
I dragged her off; she was large in the belly.

My fingers touching her side brought me the reason—
her side was warm; her fawn lay there waiting,   10
alive, still, never to be born.
Beside that mountain road I hesitated.

The car aimed ahead its lowered parking lights;
under the hood purred the steady engine.
I stood in the glare of the warm exhaust turning red;   15
around our group I could hear the wilderness listen.

I thought hard for us all—my only swerving—
then pushed her over the edge into the river.

William Stafford (b. 1914)

QUESTIONS

1. Show how the action develops stanza by stanza.
2. At what point does the physical action cease, to be replaced by another kind? Analyze the effect.
3. How do the last two lines complete both types of action?

Chronology is obviously a factor in Ted Hughes's "Owl's Song": the owl sings of this and this and this and then stops. But the poem's prime interest is not as a narrative; its impact depends rather on a *cause-effect* relationship that gives meaning to the events. Note that though the poem consists of five strophes, it divides structurally into two major units:

Owl's Song

He sang
How the swan blanched forever
How the wolf threw away its telltale heart
And the stars dropped their pretence
The air gave up appearances   5
Water went deliberately numb
The rock surrendered its last hope
And cold died beyond knowledge

He sang
How everything had nothing more to lose   10

Then sat still with fear

Seeing the clawtrack of star
Hearing the wingbeat of rock

And his own singing

Ted Hughes (b. 1930)

Strophes one and two convey the content of the owl's song, first in detail (lines 1–8) and then in summary (lines 9–10). The extravagant song, culminating in the owl's recognition of its meaning in line 10, leads to terror and silence, conveyed by the spareness of the last three strophes.

Walt Whitman's "When I Heard the Learn'd Astronomer" (discussed in another context on p. 132) also falls into two units, in a relationship that is in a sense cause and effect: what the poet hears causes the reaction he has. But the reaction itself is contrary to what the astronomer intended, and we find, in fact, by the poem's close, that the poem's structure has set up two opposed ways of seeing the same thing, the astronomer's and the poet's. The impact of the poem depends primarily on the *contrast* between the parts rather than on a causal relationship.

When I Heard the Learn'd Astronomer

When I heard the learn'd astronomer,
When the proofs, the figures, were ranged in columns before me,
When I was shown the charts and diagrams, to add, divide, and measure
    them,
When I sitting heard the astronomer where he lectured with much
    applause in the lecture-room,

How soon unaccountable I became tired and sick,
Till rising and gliding out I wander'd off by myself,
In the mystical moist night-air, and from time to time,
Look'd up in perfect silence at the stars.

Walt Whitman (1819–1892)

A similar use of contrast underlies the structure of E. E. Cummings's poem, which is more tightly organized than it might seem were one to judge simply by the openness of its appearance or its apparent defiance of printing conventions:

O sweet spontaneous

O sweet spontaneous
earth how often have
the
doting

     fingers of   5
prurient philosophers pinched
and
poked

thee
, has the naughty thumb   10
of science prodded
thy

  beauty   . how
often have religions taken
thee upon their scraggy knees   15
squeezing and

buffeting thee that thou mightest conceive
gods
    (but
true   20

to the incomparable
couch of death thy
rhythmic
lover

    thou answerest   25

them only with

      spring)

e. e. cummings (1894–1962)

QUESTIONS

1. What do philosophy, science, and religion have in common in the first three strophes?
2. How does the material in parentheses relate structurally to what has gone before?
3. Comment on the way in which structure may be said to contribute to the meaning of Cummings's poem.

Where Whitman and Cummings proceed by contrast, Jonathan Swift structures his poem "A Description of the Morning" through *parallelism*, a series of parallel elements each of which attests to the approach of morning. The poem conveys a sense of simultaneous action: Betty, the apprentice, Moll, and the kennel boy act in apparent unison, though they are physically separated; as the "flock" returns, the schoolboys go forth. By the last lines, as the scene has gradually filled out, a noisy and somewhat sordid morning seems well under way.

A Description of the Morning

Now hardly here and there an hackney coach
Appearing, showed the ruddy morn's approach.
Now Betty from her master's bed had flown,
And softly stole to discompose her own;
The slipshod 'prentice from his master's door   5
Had pared the dirt, and sprinkled round the floor.
Now Moll had whirled her mop with dextrous airs,
Prepared to scrub the entry and the stairs.
The youth with broomy stumps began to trace
The kennel's edge, where wheels had worn the place.   10
The small-coal man was heard with cadence deep,
Till drowned in shriller notes of chimney sweep:
Duns at his lordship's gate began to meet;
And brickdust Moll had screamed through half the street.
The turnkey now his flock returning sees,   15
Duly let out a-nights to steal for fees:
The watchful bailiffs take their silent stands,
And schoolboys lag with satchels in their hands.

Jonathan Swift (1667–1745)

QUESTIONS

1. What action ties together the kennel boy, Moll, and the apprentice? What image ties together the coal man, the chimney sweep, and the bill collectors (duns)?

2. Comment on the relationship between turnkey, flock, and bailiffs (lines 15–17). What is the effect of turning from them to end on the image of the schoolboys?

For Dorothy Parker the use of parallel structure permits the formulation of a series of alternatives, none of which proves viable:

Résumé

Razors pain you;
Rivers are damp;
Acids stain you;
And drugs cause cramp.
Guns aren't lawful;
Nooses give;
Gas smells awful;
You might as well live.

Dorothy Parker (1893–1967)

Yet another structural pattern depends on the detailed elaboration of an *analogy*, that is, an extended comparison that explains one thing in terms of another. Poems so structured are often ingenious (we have seen something of this earlier when discussing conceit and extended metaphors in chapter 4), and they conclude when the potential implications of the analogy have been more or less exhausted.

What Is Our Life? A Play of Passion

What is our life? A play of passion,
Our mirth the music of division.
Our mothers' wombs the tiring-houses° be,   *dressing rooms*
Where we are dressed for this short comedy.
Heaven the judicious sharp spectator is,   5
That sits and marks still who doth act amiss.
Our graves that hide us from the searching sun
Are like drawn curtains when the play is done.
Thus march we, playing, to our latest rest,
Only we die in earnest, that's no jest.   10

Sir Walter Raleigh (1552–1618)

1. What is the basic analogy? Explain how the poem is structured stage by stage in terms of that analogy.
2. Explain the effect of the sudden shift away from analogy at the end of the poem.

We have examined a few of the more common structural patterns, but the variations and combinations are, finally, infinite. Poets devise new structures, and familiar structures may be combined in all sorts of fresh ways. In the following poem, we find two strands of action that proceed simultaneously, each interrupting the other but fulfilling its own line of development. One strand renders a direct encounter retrieved from memory; the other, a series of reflections on time and space:

A Moment Please

When I gaze at the sun
  I walked to the subway booth
  for change for a dime.
and know that this great earth
  Two adolescent girls stood there   5
  alive with eagerness to know
is but a fragment from it thrown
  all in their new found world
  there was for them to know
in heat and flame a billion years ago,   10
  they looked at me and brightly asked
  "Are you Arabian?"
that when this world was lifeless
  I smiled and cautiously
  —for one grows cautious—   15
  shook my head.
as, a billion hence,
  "Egyptian?"
it shall again be,
  Again I smiled and shook my head   20
  and walked away.
what moment is it that I am betrayed,
  I've gone but seven paces now
oppressed, cast down,
  and from behind comes swift the sneer   25
or warm with love or triumph?
  "Or Nigger?"
  A moment, please

What is it that to fury I am roused?
  for still it takes a moment   30
What meaning for me
  and now
in this homeless clan
  I'll turn
the dupe of space   35
  and smile
the toy of time?
  and nod my head.

Samuel Allen (b. 1917)

QUESTIONS

1. Describe the structural pattern dominant in each of the two strands of action.
2. How do the two strands relate to each other? Are there any points at which they intersect in an especially telling way?
3. How would you describe the structure of the poem as a whole?

  The three poems that follow provide further instances of how poets may mix their structural designs. The important thing as you read is not simply to identify the patterns employed but to see how they contribute to the total effect of the poem.

  John Webster's poem is technically a DIRGE, a song commemorating the dead. In its original context, Webster's play *The White Devil*, the dirge is sung by a mother over the body of her son, murdered by his brother. Something of the mother's distress is reflected in the movement of the three parts: the first two, parallel in structure, seem intended to console, but in the third part the structural pattern shifts, creating a striking dramatic effect:

Call for the Robin Redbreast and the Wren

Call for the robin redbreast and the wren
Since o'er shady groves they hover,
And with leaves and flowers do cover
The friendless bodies of unburied men.
Call to his funeral dole°   *lament*   5
The ant, the field mouse, and the mole,
To rear him hillocks that shall keep him warm,
And (when gay tombs are robbed) sustain no harm;
But keep the wolf far thence that's foe to men,
For with his nails he'll dig them up again.   10

John Webster (1580?–1634?)

1. Explain the parallel relationship of lines 1–4 and lines 5–8.
2. How is the structure altered in lines 9–10? What is the new effect?

Denise Levertov's "Sunday Afternoon," like Swift's "A Description of the Morning," focuses on a time of day; but unlike Swift, she organizes the events of her poem in a chronological sequence. Chronology, however, proves to be but one aspect of its structural complexity:

Sunday Afternoon

After the First Communion
and the banquet of mangoes and
bridal cake, the young daughters
of the coffee merchant lay down
for a long siesta, and their white dresses   5
lay beside them in quietness
and the white veils floated
in their dreams as the flies buzzed.
But as the afternoon
burned to a close they rose   10
and ran about the neighborhood
among the halfbuilt villas
alive, alive, kicking a basketball, wearing
other new dresses, of bloodred velvet.

Denise Levertov (b. 1923)

Lines 1–3 fill in the morning and noontime activities, which are followed by the midday sleeping (lines 4–8) and then, later in the afternoon, by the awakening and very different kind of activities. But as we read, we sense that the effect lies not simply in the time sequence but in the use of contrast as enforced by the images. The girls change their clothes; white becomes "bloodred velvet"; they kick and run instead of sleep. The speaker intrudes—"alive, alive" (line 13)—implying a value judgment about the late afternoon activities as against the earlier ones. And there is still a further use of contrast in the structure of the fourteen lines, which, though lacking in rhyme and consistent meter, are patterned according to the structure of the Italian sonnet: the octave establishes a situation which is played against in the sestet, itself introduced by "But" (line 9). Levertov seems, then, to have depended on chronology to provide a framework and on contrast to establish the theme. How would you define that theme?

As a concluding instance of mixed patterning, consider Richard Wilbur's "A Late Aubade." An AUBADE is a morning song, usually relating to the awakening of lovers, and much of the pleasure of Wilbur's version derives from a recognition of the various conventions he manages to employ (for example, the allusion to "The rosebuds-theme of centuries of verse," a symbol we have already considered in chapter 5). Notice how this poem is structured as an argument and how the argument draws upon parallelism, contrast, and chronology:

A Late Aubade

You could be sitting now in a carrel°   *library cubicle*
Turning some liver-spotted page,
Or rising in an elevator-cage
Toward Ladies' Apparel.

You could be planting a raucous bed   5
Of salvia, in rubber gloves,
Or lunching through a screed° of someone's loves   *a long discourse*
With pitying head,

Or making some unhappy setter
Heel, or listening to a bleak   10
Lecture on Schoenberg's° serial technique.   *Arnold Schoenberg, 1874–1951,*
Isn't this better?   *invented the 12-tone*
    system of composition

Think of all the time you are not
Wasting, and would not care to waste,
Such things, thank God, not being to your taste.   15
Think what a lot

Of time, by woman's reckoning,
You've saved, and so may spend on this,
You who had rather lie in bed and kiss
Than anything.   20

It's almost noon, you say? If so,
Time flies, and I need not rehearse
The rosebuds-theme of centuries of verse.
If you *must* go,

Wait for a while, then slip downstairs   25
And bring us up some chilled white wine,
And some blue cheese, and crackers, and some fine
Ruddy-skinned pears.

        Richard Wilbur (b. 1921)

I. Each of the poems below is structured primarily by chronology, contrast, or parallelism. Identify the structural pattern in each poem and explain how it contributes to the meaning.

On the Vanity of Earthly Greatness

The tusks that clashed in mighty brawls
Of mastodons, are billiard balls.

The sword of Charlemagne the Just
Is ferric oxide, known as rust.

The grizzly bear whose potent hug
Was feared by all, is now a rug.

Great Caeser's bust is on the shelf,
And I don't feel so well myself.

Arthur Guiterman (1871–1943)

On Hurricane Jackson

Now his nose's bridge is broken, one eye
will not focus and the other is a stray;
trainers whisper in his mouth while one ear
listens to itself, clenched like a fist;
generally shadow-boxing in a smoky room,   5
his mind hides like the aching boys
who lost a contest in the Pan-Hellenic° games   *ancient Greek contests*
and had to take the back roads home,
but someone else, his perfect youth,
laureled in newsprint and dollar bills,   10
triumphs forever on the great white way
to the statistical Sparta° of the champs.   *city in ancient Greece*
                                                       known for its militarism

Alan Dugan (b. 1923)

John Anderson My Jo, John

John Anderson my jo°, John,	*dear*
When we were first acquent°,	*acquainted*
Your locks were like the raven,	
Your bonny brow was brent°;	*clear*
But now your brow is beld, John,	5
Your locks are like the snaw;	
But blessings on your frosty pow°,	*head*
John Anderson my jo.	
John Anderson my jo, John,	
We clamb the hill thegither;	10
And mony a canty° day, John,	*happy*
We've had wi' ane anither:	
Now we maun° totter down, John,	*must*
And hand in hand we'll go,	
And sleep thegither at the foot,	15
John Anderson my jo.	

Robert Burns (1759–1796)

Music, When Soft Voices Die

Music, when soft voices die,
Vibrates in the memory—
Odors, when sweet violets sicken,
Live within the sense they quicken.
Rose leaves, when the rose is dead,
Are heaped for the belovèd's bed;
And so thy thoughts, when thou art gone,
Love itself shall slumber on.

Percy Bysshe Shelly (1792–1822)

The Dream

Someone approaches to say his life is ruined
and to fall down at your feet
and pound his head upon the sidewalk.
Blood spreads in a puddle.

And you, in a weak voice, plead   5
with those nearby for help;
your life takes on his desperation.
He keeps pounding his head.
It is you who are fated;
and you fall down beside him.   10
It is then you are awakened,
the body gone, the blood washed from the ground,
the stores lit up with their goods.

David Ignatow (b. 1914)

II. Below are three sonnets, each with a different rhyme scheme. In each
sonnet, analyze the relationships between the smaller units and then show how
the units contribute to the larger structure.

That Time of Year Thou Mayst in Me Behold

That time of year thou mayst in me behold
When yellow leaves, or none, or few, do hang
Upon those boughs which shake against the cold,
Bare ruined choirs° where late the sweet birds sang.   *church choirs, stalls*
In me thou see'st the twilight of such day   5
As after sunset fadeth in the west,
Which by-and-by black night doth take away,
Death's second self that seals up all in rest.
In me thou see'st the glowing of such fire
That on the ashes of his youth doth lie,   10
As the deathbed whereon it must expire,
Consumed with that which it was nourished by.
   This thou perceiv'st, which makes thy love more strong,
   To love that well which thou must leave ere long.

William Shakespeare (1564–1616)

At the Round Earth's Imagined Corners Blow

At the round earth's imagined corners blow
Your trumpets, angels, and arise, arise
From death, you numberless infinities
Of souls, and to your scattered bodies go,
All whom the flood did, and fire shall o'erthrow,   5

All whom war, dearth, age, agues°, tyrannies,   *fevers*
Despair, law, chance, hath slain, and you whose eyes
Shall behold God, and never taste death's woe.
But let them sleep, Lord, and me mourn a space;
For, if above all these my sins abound,   10
'Tis late to ask abundance of Thy grace,
When we are there. Here on this lowly ground,
Teach me how to repent, for that's as good
As if Thou hadst sealed my pardon with Thy blood.

John Donne (1572–1631)

Ozymandias

I met a traveler from an antique land
Who said: Two vast and trunkless legs of stone
Stand in the desert. Near them, on the sand,
Half sunk, a shattered visage lies, whose frown,
And wrinkled lip, and sneer of cold command,   5
Tell that its sculptor well those passions read
Which yet survive, stamped on these lifeless things,
The hand that mocked them and the heart that fed;
And on the pedestal these words appear:
"My name is Ozymandias, king of kings: 10
Look on my works, ye Mighty, and despair!"
Nothing beside remains. Round the decay
Of that colossal wreck, boundless and bare
The lone and level sands stretch far away.

Percy Bysshe Shelley (1792–1822)

III. Explain the structural pattern of each of the following poems:

Lebensraum

Life should be a humane
undertaking. I know. I
undertook it.
            Yet have found
that in my every move   5
I prevent someone
from stepping where I step.

So I must run into the open,
alone, to wait on the
untrodden acres of snow   10
among black trunks, till
the bacillus of despair is
rendered harmless:
isolated and frozen over.

Thom Gunn (b. 1929)

Lebensraum. *Lebensraum* (German) means "living space."

Good Times

My Daddy has paid the rent
and the insurance man is gone
and the lights is back on
and my uncle Brud has hit
for one dollar straight   5
and they is good times
good times
good times

My Mama has made bread
and Grampaw has come   10
and everybody is drunk
and dancing in the kitchen
and singing in the kitchen
oh these is good times
good times   15
good times

oh children think about the
good times

Lucille Clifton (b. 1936)

The Uses of Light

It warms my bones
          say the stones

I take it into me and grow
Say the trees
Leaves above   5
Roots below

A vast vague white
Draws me out of the night
Says the moth in his flight—

Some things I smell   10
Some things I hear
And I see things move
Says the deer—

A high tower
on a wide plain.   15
If you climb up
One floor
You'll see a thousand miles more.

Gary Snyder (b. 1930)

8
Genre

The term GENRE refers to a mode of writing that follows certain literary rules or conventions that have come down to the poet through custom and use. When we say that a poem belongs to a particular genre, we are relating the poem to others of its kind, regardless of who the author is or when the poem was written; we are cutting across boundaries of time, personality, and even nationality. Attempting to place a poem in a particular genre may bring us closer to the meaning or effect intended by the poet, for poets are readers themselves and often draw very deliberately upon inherited conventions. Hence our awareness of these conventions becomes a part of our understanding of the poem. To put this differently, just as a word has connotations, a particular genre has a wealth of associations the poet may use. Further, the consideration of genre—that is, of certain features poems have in common—makes us more sensitive to the ways in which each poet's achievement is special or unique.

The term *genre* is used both broadly and specifically. Using the term quite broadly, we can say that there are three genres of poetic discourse—narrative, dramatic, and lyric—and that each of these broad categories includes certain specific types of poems that also are often referred to as genres. In narrative poetry we include such types as the epic, romance, and ballad because all primarily tell a story; within the category of dramatic poetry we classify plays, such as *Hamlet* and *Oedipus Rex*, as well as soliloquies, monologues, and dialogues, to the extent that they represent characters (other than the poet) in conflict. In the most inclusive of the three genres, lyric poetry, we place poems such as hymns, meditations, songs, elegies, odes, and most sonnets, because they tend to have a strongly subjective core and are devoted primarily to the expression of an emotion or thought or of a reflection on experience.

We should bear in mind that although distinctions of genre are important for readers and often for poets, poems do not always fit neatly into one category or another. For example, a narrative poem may have dramatic or lyric elements; dramatic poems usually do have some narrative thrust; and lyric poems, too, may have narrative or dramatic aspects. Generally, however, we are able to say that a poem is primarily narrative, dramatic, or lyric. Although it is possible here to discuss only a few of the more familiar genres—ballads, soliloquies, dramatic monologues, dialogues, elegies, sonnets, and odes—these will suffice to show how certain characteristics define each type and enable us to say that a particular poem is, for instance, a sonnet, an ode, or a ballad.

Narrative Poetry

NARRATIVE POEMS tell a story, recount a series of events. They may be very long, running to many thousands of lines in epics such as Homer's *Odyssey* or John Milton's *Paradise Lost*. But a narrative may be compressed to the brevity of a single quatrain:

> Jack and Jill went up the hill
> To fetch a pail of water.
> Jack fell down and broke his crown
> And Jill came tumbling after.

More commonly, a narrative extends over several stanzas, as in Edwin Arlington Robinson's "The Mill," a domestic tale of two suicides.

The Mill

The miller's wife had waited long,
  The tea was cold, the fire was dead;
And there might yet be nothing wrong
  In how he went and what he said:
"There are no millers any more,"   5
  Was all that she had heard him say;
And he had lingered at the door
  So long that it seemed yesterday.

Sick with a fear that had no form
  She knew that she was there at last;   10
And in the mill there was a warm
  And mealy fragrance of the past.
What else there was would only seem
  To say again what he had meant;
And what was hanging from a beam   15
  Would not have heeded where she went.

And if she thought it followed her,
  She may have reasoned in the dark
That one way of the few there were
  Would hide her and would leave no mark: 20
Black water, smooth above the weir
  Like starry velvet in the night,
Though ruffled once, would soon appear
  The same as ever to the sight.

Edwin Arlington Robinson (1869–1935)

Ballads

Originally, FOLK or POPULAR BALLADS were part of an oral tradition, sung by poets whose names are lost to us. Dating from at least as far back as the thirteenth century, ballads were handed down from generation to generation, in the process undergoing changes in many of their details—an inevitable consequence for stories orally transmitted over a long period. Not until the eighteenth century did they begin to find their way into print in any significant numbers and achieve anything like a permanent form. Between 1882 and 1898 a Harvard professor, F. J. Child, gathered all the British ballads he could find into five huge volumes. Many of these are recognizable as American and Canadian folk songs because immigrants to the New World brought their songs with them, adapting them to local settings. The old chieftains and warriors became frontiersmen, miners, railroaders, outlaws, and soldiers; they drank whiskey instead of mead, used guns instead of swords.

The heart of the ballad is the story, with incidents taken from the supernatural, from folklore, from political and family histories. We hear of battles and private quarrels, famous contests and romantic encounters, but little of their causes or motives, which are less important than the story itself. The story is usually presented from a neutral, impersonal point of view and with a minimum of descriptive detail.

The ballad below is among the best known in English and utilizes many of the typical ballad devices:

Lord Randal

"O where ha' you been, Lord Randal, my son?
And where ha' you been, my handsome young man?"
"I ha' been at the greenwood; mother, mak my bed soon,
For I'm wearied wi' huntin', and fain wad° lie down."   *gladly would*

"And wha° met ye there, Lord Randal, my son?   *who* 5
And wha met you there, my handsome young man?"
"O I met wi' my true-love; mother, mak my bed soon,
For I'm wearied wi' huntin', and fain wad lie down."

"And what did she give you, Lord Randal, my son?
And what did she give you, my handsome young man?"   10
"Eels fried in a pan; mother, mak my bed soon,
For I'm wearied wi' huntin', and fain wad lie down."

"And wha gat your leavin's°, Lord Randal, my son?   *leftovers*
And wha gat your leavin's, my handsome young man?"
"My hawks and my hounds; mother, mak my bed soon,   15
For I'm wearied wi' huntin', and fain wad lie down."

"And what becam of them, Lord Randal, my son?
And what becam of them, my handsome young man?"
"They stretched their legs out and died; mother, mak my bed soon,
For I'm wearied wi' huntin', and fain wad lie down."   20

"O I fear you are poisoned, Lord Randal, my son!
I fear you are poisoned, my handsome young man!"
"O yes, I am poisoned; mother, mak my bed soon,
For I'm sick at the heart, and I fain wad lie down."

"What d' ye leave to your mother, Lord Randal, my son?   25
What d' ye leave to your mother, my handsome young man?"
"Four and twenty milk kye°; mother, mak my bed soon,   *cows*
For I'm sick at the heart, and I fain wad lie down."

"What d' ye leave to your sister, Lord Randal, my son?
What d' ye leave to your sister, my handsome young man?"   30
"My gold and my silver; mother, mak my bed soon,
For I'm sick at the heart, and I fain wad lie down."

"What d' ye leave to your brother, Lord Randal, my son?
What d' ye leave to your brother, my handsome young man?"
"My houses and my lands; mother, mak my bed soon,   35
For I'm sick at the heart, and I fain wad lie down."

"What d' ye leave to your true-love, Lord Randal, my son?
What d' ye leave to your true-love, my handsome young man?"
"I leave her hell and fire; mother, mak my bed soon,
For I'm sick at the heart, and I fain wad lie down."   40

Anonymous

The most obvious characteristic here is the use of dialogue, with each
question and answer providing hints about what happened: where have
you been? whom did you meet? what did she give you? and so forth.
The recognition that the hero·has been poisoned leads to yet other
questions and answers: what do you leave to your mother? your sister?
your brother? your true love?

Another characteristic of the ballad is the REFRAIN, a phrase or line
repeated at intervals. Such repetition may either by exact, as "Lord
Randal, my son?" and "my handsome young man?" or take the form
of INCREMENTAL REPETITION, in which a few words in the refrain are
changed to provide additional information and carry the story forward.
Lines 3, 7, 11, 15, 19, 27, 31, 35, and 39 offer a series of incremental
repetitions.

Because ballads were intended to be heard, the rhythm is strong and
the words are simple, usually of one or two syllables. Stanzas are brief
and follow identical rhyme schemes, usually *abcb* or *abab* or *aabb*, with
the lines occasionally all tetrameter but more often, as in the following
excerpt from "Bonny Barbara Allen" (see p. 391), a mixture of tetrameter
(lines 1 and 3) and trimeter (lines 2 and 4).

"O mother, mother, make my bed
    O make it soft and narrow
My love has died for me today
    I'll die for him tomorrow."

Ballads were carried from place to place by minstrel poets, who
traveled about singing the news and entertaining their audiences. In
the process these poets created new versions of old stories or made up
their own tales, and though they continued to use the typical ballad
devices, they introduced additional refinements, dwelling more on de-
scriptive detail and on the feelings of the characters.

Sir Patrick Spens

The king sits in Dumferling town,
    Drinking the blude-reid° wine: blood-red
"O whar will I get guid sailor,
    To sail this ship of mine?"

Up and spak an eldern knicht   5
   Sat at the king's richt knee:
"Sir Patrick Spens is the best sailor
   That sails upon the sea."

The king has written a braid° letter   *open, broad*
   And signed it wi' his hand,   10
And sent it to Sir Patrick Spens,
   Was walking on the sand.

The first line that Sir Patrick read,
   A loud lauch° lauched he;   *laugh*
The next line that Sir Patrick read,   15
   The tear blinded his ee°.   *eye*

"O wha is this has done this deed,
   This ill deed done to me,
To send me out this time o' the year,
   To sail upon the sea?   20

"Mak haste, mak haste, my mirry men all,
   Our guid ship sails the morn."
"O say na sae°, my master dear,   *so*
   For I fear a deadly storm.

"Late, late yestre'en° I saw the new moon   *last evening*   25
   Wi' the auld moon in hir arm,
And I fear, I fear, my dear master,
   That we will come to harm."

O our Scots nobles were richt laith°   *loath*
   To weet° their cork-heeled shoon°,   *wet/shoes*   30
But lang or° a' the play were played   *before*
   Their hats they swam aboon°.   *above (on the surface)*

O lang, lang may their ladies sit,
   Wi' their fans into their hand,
Or ere they see Sir Patrick Spens   35
   Come sailing to the land.

O lang, lang may the ladies stand
   Wi' their gold kems° in their hair,   *combs*
Waiting for their ain dear lords,
   For they'll see them na mair.   40

Half o'er, half o'er to Aberdour
   It's fifty fadom deep,
And there lies guid Sir Patrick Spens
   Wi' the Scots lords at his feet.

Anonymous

QUESTIONS

1. Explain the action, indicating how each stanza contributes to the narrative.
2. Comment on how the changes of place (beginning with the great hall in stanza 1) contribute to the parallel structure.
3. Explain the effect of such added details as the references to the ladies' fans (stanza 9) and gold combs (stanza 10).

LITERARY BALLADS employ most of the devices characteristic of the folk ballad but, more recent in date, are conceived in terms of a printed medium rather than an oral one by poets for whom this very old form suggests new possibilities. John Keats, for example, writing in the early nineteenth century, tried his hand at a variety of genres, including the ballad, to which he brought a complexity of language and implication rarely found in the original tradition. As you read his ballad below, note how Keats adheres to the ballad conventions while varying them for his own purposes, and decide whether the action is meant to be understood literally or symbolically.

La Belle Dame sans Merci

O what can ail thee, knight-at-arms,
    Alone and palely loitering?
The sedge has withered from the lake,
    And no birds sing.

O what can ail thee, knight-at-arms,   5
    So haggard and so woe-begone?
The squirrel's granary is full,
    And the harvest's done.

I see a lily on thy brow
    With anguish moist and fever dew,   10
And on thy cheek a fading rose
    Fast withereth too.

I met a lady in the meads,
    Full beautiful—a faery's child;
Her hair was long, her foot was light,   15
    And her eyes were wild.

I made a garland for her head,
    And bracelets too, and fragrant zone°;   *belt, girdle*
She looked at me as she did love,
    And made sweet moan.   20

I set her on my pacing steed,
    And nothing else saw all day long,
For sidelong would she bend, and sing
    A faery's song.

She found me roots of relish sweet,   25
    And honey wild, and manna dew,
And sure in language strange she said—
    "I love thee true."

She took me to her elfin grot,
    And there she wept and sighed full sore,   30
And there I shut her wild eyes
    With kisses four.

And there she lullèd me asleep,
    And there I dreamed—ah! woe betide!
The latest dream I ever dreamed   35
    On the cold hill's side.

I saw pale kings and princes too,
    Pale warriors, death-pale were they all;
They cried—"La Belle Dame sans Merci
    Hath thee in thrall!"   40

I saw their starved lips in the gloam,
    With horrid warning gapèd wide,
And I awoke and found me here,
    On the cold hill's side.

And this is why I sojourn here,   45
    Alone and palely loitering,
Though the sedge is withered from the lake
    And no birds sing.

John Keats (1795–1821)

QUESTIONS

1. Isolate the elements that make this poem a ballad.
2. What is the meter of the last line of each stanza? How does it differ from the typical ballad meter?
3. What is the effect of the extended use of the first-person point of view?
4. How do you interpret the dream (lines 37–42) in terms of the poem as a whole? Explain why the knight wakes up on "the cold hill's side."

Below is a more recent ballad that departs in significant ways from the tradition but manages nonetheless to evoke it in various ways, especially in the use of refrain and incremental repetition.

All in green went my love riding

All in green went my love riding
on a great horse of gold
into the silver dawn.

four lean hounds crouched low and smiling
the merry deer ran before.   5

Fleeter be they than dappled dreams
the swift sweet deer
the red rare deer.

Four red roebuck at a white water
the cruel bugle sang before.   10

Horn at hip went my love riding
riding the echo down
into the silver dawn.

four lean hounds crouched low and smiling
the level meadows ran before.   15

Softer be they than slippered sleep
the lean lithe deer
the fleet flown deer.

Four fleet does at a gold valley
the famished arrow sang before.   20

Bow at belt went my love riding
riding the mountain down
into the silver dawn.

four lean hounds crouched low and smiling
the sheer peaks ran before.   25

Paler be they than daunting death
the sleek slim deer
the tall tense deer.

Four tall stags at a green mountain
the lucky hunter sang before.   30

All in green went my love riding
on a great horse of gold
into the silver dawn.

four lean hounds crouched low and smiling
my heart fell dead before.   35

e. e. cummings (1894–1962)

Dramatic Poetry

Though DRAMATIC POETRY may, like narrative, have a strong story
component, its primary emphasis is on character. The essential feature
in all dramatic poems is the PERSONA, a character created by the poet
and placed in a situation that involves some conflict or action (even
though the action may consist of no more than an internal debate). A
dramatic poem may involve a single character or more than one, but the
characters speak always in their own voices, which are not to be confused
with the voice of the poet. However, the poet's attitude toward the
speaker—which may range from sympathy to repugnance—will prob-
ably be more or less evident from the poem.

Soliloquies

In the SOLILOQUY one person speaks aloud and does so with no one
else present to hear the words. When this occurs in a play, it is usually
a means of providing information so that the plot can move forward or
the hidden self can be revealed, enabling the audience to recognize
motives and eventually understand the conflict played out before them.
Hamlet's soliloquy beginning "To be or not to be" (p. 130) offers a good
instance of self-revelation, as does the following passage from the last
act of Shakespeare's *Othello*. Othello here soliloquizes over the sleeping
form of his wife, Desdemona, whom he has come to kill, thinking her
unfaithful to him. Notice how the soliloquy slips into dialogue as the
innocent Desdemona awakens and how Othello must shift from a direct
to a veiled expression of his thoughts.

from *Othello**

[*State Bedroom in the Citadel. Enter Othello with a light, and Desdemona
in her bed.*]

OTHELLO   It is the cause, it is the cause, my soul.
   Let me not name it to you, you chaste stars!
   It is the cause. Yet I'll not shed her blood,
   Nor scar that whiter skin of hers than snow,
   And smooth as monumental alabaster.   5

*Act V, Scene 2, lines 1–34.

Yet she must die, else she'll betray more men.
Put out the light, and then put out the light.
If I quench thee, thou flaming minister,
I can again thy former light restore,
Should I repent me; but once put out thy light,   10
Thou cunning'st pattern of excelling nature,
I know not where is that Promethean heat°   *god-given fire*
That can thy light relume. When I have plucked the rose,
I cannot give it vital growth again;
It needs must wither. I'll smell thee on the tree.   15

                                        He kisses her.

O balmy breath, that dost almost persuade
Justice to break her sword! One more, one more!
Be thus when thou art dead, and I will kill thee,
And love thee after. One more, and this the last!
So sweet was ne'er so fatal. I must weep,   20
But they are cruel tears. This sorrow's heavenly;
It strikes where it doth love. She wakes.
DESDEMONA   Who's there? Othello?
OTHELLO   Ay, Desdemona.
DESDEMONA   Will you come to bed, my lord?
OTHELLO   Have you prayed to-night, Desdemona?   25
DESDEMONA   Ay, my lord.
OTHELLO   If you bethink yourself of any crime
    Unreconciled as yet to heaven and grace,
    Solicit for it straight.
DESDEMONA   Alack, my lord, what may you mean by that?
OTHELLO   Well, do it, and be brief; I will walk by.   30
    I would not kill thy unpreparèd spirit.
    No, heaven forfend! I would not kill thy soul.
DESDEMONA   Talk you of killing?
OTHELLO   Ay, I do.
DESDEMONA   Then heaven
    Have mercy on me!
OTHELLO   Amen, with all my heart!

William Shakespeare (1564–1616)

   We have the whole of *Othello* to bring to bear on this scene, but when
soliloquies are written as independent pieces, they must be complete
in themselves. In the following poem, A. R. Ammons uses the persona
of Ezra, the Old Testament prophet who reestablished law as the guiding
spirit of the Hebrew community. Ammons shows Ezra wrestling with
his awareness of weakness and failure, searching for confirmation of
his identity.

So I Said I Am Ezra

So I said I am Ezra
and the wind whipped my throat
gaming for the sounds of my voice
   I listened to the wind
go over my head and up into the night   5
Turning to the sea I said
       I am Ezra
but there were no echoes from the waves
The words were swallowed up
   in the voice of the surf   10
or leaping over the swells
lost themselves oceanward
   Over the bleached and broken fields
I moved my feet and turning from the wind
   that ripped sheets of sand   15
   from the beach and threw them
   like seamists across the dunes

swayed as if the wind were taking me away
and said
       I am Ezra   20
As a word too much repeated
falls out of being
so I Ezra went out into the night
like a drift of sand
and splashed among the windy oats   25
that clutch the dunes
of unremembered seas

A. R. Ammons (b. 1926)

There is no sign that anyone else is present; Ezra reminds himself how he thrice declared "I am Ezra." The first time the wind reacted, the second time the sea; his voice was lost in the wind and swallowed up by the sea. Then he turned to the fields, declaring his name a third time, but the words had lost all meaning.

Edgar Lee Masters exploited the possibilities of the soliloquy in a remarkable way, creating an imaginary town, Spoon River, and its history, through some two hundred soliloquies. His characters, the townspeople, are all dead and speak from the grave about their lives. The two instances below can stand alone and are interesting individually, but a greater impact comes from their being read in relation to each other.

Elsa Wertman

I was a peasant girl from Germany,
Blue-eyed, rosy, happy and strong.
And the first place I worked was at Thomas Greene's.
On a summer's day when she was away
He stole into the kitchen and took me   5
Right in his arms and kissed me on my throat,
I turning my head.   Then neither of us
Seemed to know what happened.
And I cried for what would become of me.
And cried and cried as my secret began to show.   10
One day Mrs. Greene said she understood,
And would make no trouble for me,
And, being childless, would adopt it.
(He had given her a farm to be still.)
So she hid in the house and sent out rumors,   15
As if it were going to happen to her.
And all went well and the child was born—They were so kind to me.
Later I married Gus Wertman, and years passed.
But—at political rallies when sitters-by thought I was crying
At the eloquence of Hamilton Greene—   20
That was not it.
No!   I wanted to say:
That's my son!   That's my son!

Edgar Lee Masters (1868–1950)

Hamilton Greene

I was the only child of Frances Harris of Virginia
And Thomas Greene of Kentucky,
Of valiant and honorable blood both.
To them I owe all that I became,
Judge, member of Congress, leader in the State.   5
From my mother I inherited
Vivacity, fancy, language;
From my father will, judgment, logic.
All honor to them
For what service I was to the people!   10

Edgar Lee Masters (1868–1950)

Note that it is Elsa Wertman and Hamilton Greene, not Masters, who
reflect on their experience, just as it is Ezra, not Ammons. Each speaker

is placed in a situation which makes possible the revelation of character—Ezra searching, bewildered, rejected, and lonely; Elsa proud, long-suffering, a little stupid; Hamilton pompous and ignorant of the truth.

Dramatic Monologues

Poets developed the dramatic potential of the soliloquy into DRAMATIC MONOLOGUE by building an audience into the poem. In both there is a single speaker, a setting in time and place, an event or incident usually marked by conflict; but the dramatic monologue provides the added dimension of an interaction between the speaker and one or more listeners. The reaction, or indeed lack of one, on the listener's part may affect the speaker, causing, for example, an outburst of excessive speech or bringing some other change in the tone or direction of the argument.

In the poem that follows by William Carlos Williams, a man addresses members of a funeral party. As his easy manner in the opening lines changes to an outburst of anger and grief, we sense the underlying tensions in his speech—an almost desperate resistance to the ease with which death is managed by conventional ritual practice.

Tract

I will teach you my townspeople
how to perform a funeral
for you have it over a troop
of artists—
unless one should scour the world— 5
you have the ground sense necessary.

See! the hearse leads.
I begin with a design for a hearse.
For Christ's sake not black—
nor white either—and not polished! 10
Let it be weathered—like a farm wagon—
with gilt wheels (this could be
applied fresh at small expense)
or no wheels at all:
a rough dray to drag over the ground. 15

Knock the glass out!
My God—glass, my townspeople!
For what purpose? Is it for the dead
to look out or for us to see
how well he is housed or to see 20
the flowers or the lack of them—
or what?

To keep the rain and snow from him?
He will have a heavier rain soon:
pebbles and dirt and what not.   25
Let there be no glass—
and no upholstery, phew!
and no little brass rollers
and small easy wheels on the bottom—
my townspeople what are you thinking of?   30

A rough plain hearse then
with gilt wheels and no top at all.
On this the coffin lies
by its own weight.

                    No wreaths please—   35
especially no hot house flowers.
Some common memento is better,
something he prized and is known by:
his old clothes—a few books perhaps—
God knows what! You realize   40
how we are about these things
my townspeople—
something will be found—anything
even flowers if he had come to that.
So much for the hearse.   45

For heaven's sake though see to the driver!
Take off the silk hat! In fact
that's no place at all for him—
up there unceremoniously
dragging our friend out to his own dignity!   50
Bring him down—bring him down!
Low and inconspicuous! I'd not have him ride
on the wagon at all—damn him—
the undertaker's understrapper!
Let him hold the reins   55
and walk at the side
and inconspicuously too!

Then briefly as to yourselves:
Walk behind—as they do in France,
seventh class, or if you ride   60
Hell take curtains! Go with some show
of inconvenience; sit openly—
to the weather as to grief.
Or do you think you can shut grief in?
What—from us? We who have perhaps   65

nothing to lose? Share with us
share with us—it will be money
in your pockets.

         Go now
I think you are ready.   70

William Carlos Williams (1883–1963)

QUESTIONS

1. Which lines convey shifts in the speaker's tone?
2. On the basis of everything he says, describe how the speaker's values differ
   from the values of those he addresses.

    Robert Browning, writing in the mid-nineteenth century, was a master
of the dramatic monologue and did much to develop its possibilities.
His speakers range from rabbis to bishops, poets to painters, noblemen
to charlatans. And he not only reveals their quirks, flaws, and occasionally admirable qualities but often, at the same time, illuminates a
period of history, the nature of an institution°, or a way of life. In the
following poem, the speaker bears the name of a powerful principality
and cultural center in Renaissance Italy, and he and his former wife are
probably based in part on actual people. However, the painter Frà
Pandolf (line 3) and the sculptor Claus of Innsbruck (line 56) are both
fictional characters, created by Browning for the occasion.

My Last Duchess

Ferrara

That's my last Duchess painted on the wall,
Looking as if she were alive. I call
That piece a wonder, now; Frà Pandolf's hands
Worked busily a day, and there she stands.
Will 't please you sit and look at her? I said   5
"Frà Pandolf" by design, for never read
Strangers like you that pictured countenance,
The depth and passion of its earnest glance,
But to myself they turned (since none puts by
The curtain I have drawn for you, but I)   10
And seemed as they would ask me, if they durst°,   *dared*
How such a glance came there; so, not the first

Are you to turn and ask thus. Sir, 'twas not
Her husband's presence only, called that spot
Of joy into the Duchess' cheek: perhaps   15
Frà Pandolf chanced to say, "Her mantle laps
Over my lady's wrist too much," or "Paint
Must never hope to reproduce the faint
Half-flush that dies along her throat": such stuff
Was courtesy, she thought, and cause enough   20
For calling up that spot of joy. She had
A heart—how shall I say?—too soon made glad,
Too easily impressed: she liked whate'er
She looked on, and her looks went everywhere.
Sir, 'twas all one! My favor at her breast,   25
The dropping of the daylight in the West,
The bough of cherries some officious fool
Broke in the orchard for her, the white mule
She rode with round the terrace—all and each
Would draw from her alike the approving speech,   30
Or blush, at least. She thanked men,—good! but thanked
Somehow—I know not how—as if she ranked
My gift of a nine-hundred-years-old name
With anybody's gift. Who'd stoop to blame
This sort of trifling? Even had you skill   35
In speech—(which I have not)—to make your will
Quite clear to such an one, and say, "Just this
Or that in you disgusts me; here you miss,
Or there exceed the mark"—and if she let
Herself be lessoned so, nor plainly set   40
Her wits to yours, forsooth, and made excuse,
—E'en then would be some stooping; and I choose
Never to stoop. Oh sir, she smiled, no doubt.
Whene'er I passed her; but who passed without
Much the same smile? This grew; I gave commands;   45
Then all smiles stopped together. There she stands
As if alive. Will't please you rise? We'll meet
The company below, then. I repeat,
The Count your master's known munificence
Is ample warrant that no just pretence   50
Of mine for dowry will be disallowed;
Though his fair daughter's self, as I avowed
At starting, is my object. Nay, we'll go
Together down, sir. Notice Neptune°, though,   *Roman god of the seas*
Taming a sea-horse, thought a rarity,   55
Which Claus of Innsbruck cast in bronze for me!

Robert Browning (1812–1889)

QUESTIONS

1. To whom is the Duke speaking? What is the occasion?
2. What attributes of his "last Duchess" does the Duke find offensive? What does this tell you about the Duke?
3. It has been said that the Duke talks too much for the occasion. Comment.
4. What is the effect of ending the poem by reference to the bronze statue? How, in fact, has art functioned in the poem?

Lyric Poetry

As we have seen, narrative poetry focuses on telling a story and dramatic poetry on revealing character in a dramatic situation. LYRIC POETRY is the most inclusive of our three broad categories and the least easy to define. The derivation of the term *lyric* from "lyre," a musical instrument, relates the genre to song, suggesting brevity, a strongly musical component, a significant presence of emotion, and a direct involvement of the singer or poet, who seems to be speaking in his or her own person rather than through the developed persona characteristic of dramatic poetry. Almost any subject or mood, public or private, can be accommodated by the lyric mode. The discussion here of three types of lyric poems—the sonnet, elegy, and ode—suggests a few of the many possibilities of lyric expression.

Sonnets

A lyric form remarkable for the range of emotions and ideas it can encompass is the SONNET, which means, literally, "little song." The variety of the sonnet is all the more astonishing given both its brevity and its quite rigid metrical and structural pattern. The design originated in Italy, where Dante used it for his passionate lyrics to Beatrice; his countryman Petrarch, writing to eulogize Laura, made it so popular that by the time of Shakespeare in the late sixteenth century the sonnet was established as a favorite poetic structure. The anthology contains examples by Edmund Spenser, John Donne, John Milton, William Wordsworth, Gerard Manley Hopkins, and others, all of them exhibiting a harmony of technical design, complex thought, and deep feeling.

Our previous discussion of the sonnet (p. 129) focused briefly on its structural pattern—fourteen lines of iambic pentameter rhymed according to one or the other of the two major sonnet traditions: the *Italian* (or *Petrarchan*) and the *English* (or *Shakespearean*). We may now consider each type in fuller detail.

The Italian sonnet divides into two unequal parts: an opening octave, invariably rhyming *abbaabba*, followed by a sestet whose lines may rhyme *cdecde* or *cdcdcd* or indeed, more erratically, *cedce*. The poet's relative freedom in the sestet is reflected in the content as well as the rhyme. So the octave will tend to propose an issue: a question perhaps, or a premise, a doubt, an experience, a principle. The sestet in turn disposes of the issue, presenting (as the case may be) an answer, a conclusion, a reassurance, an application, a reversal. The structure depends on the relation of the two parts.

Here are two sonnets, one a translation from Petrarch, the other an instance from Keats showing his use, nearly five hundred years later, of the same form. Petrarch writes to commemorate the death of Laura, Keats to express his reaction to the discovery of a seventeenth-century translation of Homer by George Chapman.

The Eyes That Drew from Me Such Fervent Praise

The eyes that drew from me such fervent praise,
The arms and hands and feet and countenance
Which made me a stranger in my own romance
And set me apart from the well-trodden ways;

The gleaming golden curly hair, the rays   5
Flashing from a smiling angel's glance
Which moved the world in paradisal dance,
Are grains of dust, insensibilities.

And I live on, but in grief and self-contempt,
Left here without the light I loved so much,   10
In a great tempest and with shrouds unkempt.

No more love songs, then, I have done with such;
My old skill now runs thin at each attempt.
And ears are heard within the harp I touch.

Francesco Petrarch (1304–1374)
(Trans. from the Italian by Edwin Morgan)

On First Looking into Chapman's Homer

Much have I travell'd in the realms of gold,
  And many goodly states and kingdoms seen;
  Round many western islands have I been
Which bards in fealty to Apollo hold.
Oft of one wide expanse had I been told   5
  That deep-brow'd Homer ruled as his demesne;

Yet did I never breathe its pure serene
Till I heard Chapman speak out loud and bold:
Then felt I like some watcher of the skies
    When a new planet swims into his ken;   10
Or like stout Cortez when with eagle eyes
    He star'd at the Pacific—and all his men
Look'd at each other with a wild surmise—
    Silent, upon a peak in Darien°.   *in Panama*

John Keats (1795–1821)

On First Looking into Chapman's Homer. ll. 11–12: In fact, the first European to view the Pacific was Balboa, not Cortez.

QUESTIONS

1. Show how the octave in each sonnet makes a roughly complete unit.
2. Explain the relationship between the octave and the sestet in each sonnet.

In the English sonnet, brought to perfection by Shakespeare, the fourteen lines divide into three quatrains and a couplet, the whole typically rhyming *ababcdcdefefgg*. The segments are smaller than in the Italian sonnet and open to more varied use: the quatrains may, for instance, provide examples of a general idea or give three instances of some theory or develop a thought from three points of view. The terse couplet may draw a conclusion, offer a summary, or carry the argument of the quatrain a step further; sometimes it surprises with an ironical twist or a reversal of all that has been declared in the preceding twelve lines. In a sense, the couplet functions much as the sestet does in the Italian form. Note how the couplet is used in the following sonnet by Michael Drayton, a contemporary of Shakespeare:

Since There's No Help, Come Let Us Kiss and Part

Since there's no help, come let us kiss and part;
Nay, I have done, you get no more of me;
And I am glad, yea, glad with all my heart,
That thus so cleanly I myself can free.
Shake hands for ever, cancel all our vows,   5
And when we meet at any time again,
Be it not seen in either of our brows
That we one jot of former love retain.
Now at the last gasp of love's latest breath,
When, his pulse failing, passion speechless lies,   10

When faith is kneeling by his bed of death,
And innocence is closing up his eyes,
Now if thou wouldst, when all have given him over,
From death to life thou might'st him yet recover.

Michael Drayton (1563–1631)

QUESTIONS

1. Explain how the couplet reverses the three quatrains.
2. Explain the structural principle that ties lines 1–12 together. What is the shift that occurs between lines 1–8 and lines 9–12?

Like folk ballads, sonnets are highly compressed, but instead of presenting a story, the sonnet is likely to develop a thought, emotion, or argument through the use of an extended metaphor or three related metaphors or figures of speech. Shakespeare's sonnet below makes an intricate weave of argument and metaphor, all building to the final couplet:

Not Marble, nor the Gilded Monuments

Not marble, nor the gilded monuments
Of princes, shall outlive this powerful rhyme;
But you shall shine more bright in these contents
Than unswept stone, besmeared with sluttish° time.   *dirty, dusty*
When wasteful war shall statues overturn,   5
And broils° root out the work of masonry,   *battles*
Nor Mars his sword nor war's quick fire shall burn
The living record of your memory.
'Gainst death and all-oblivious enmity
Shall you pace forth; your praise shall still find room   10
Even in the eyes of all posterity
That wear this world out to the ending doom°.   *Judgment Day*
   So, till the judgment that yourself arise,
   You live in this, and dwell in lovers' eyes.

William Shakespeare (1564–1616)

Shakespeare's sonnet compares poetry with two other arts and declares poetry to be the most lasting. Each quatrain is related to some aspect of art and the idea of longevity. The first four lines name marble and monuments; together they become "unswept stone." The second quatrain names statues and masonry, less abstract than marble and monuments, while the third turns to poetry, which will outlast sculpture and architecture. The final couplet concludes the argument ("So, . . .") with a particular reference to "this" poem.

Coupled with this movement in the sonnet is another that progresses from princes who are forgotten, to Mars who would destroy, to lovers who endure, ending again with "this" poem. The collaboration of "sluttish time" and "wasteful war" causes stones to disintegrate, statues to fall, and masonry to crumble, but the poem (poetry) remains intact, invulnerable to time and war. Though princes will be forgotten, the subject of the poem shall "pace forth" (in the metrical lines of verse) and the praise endure through "all posterity" until the day of judgment, when the loved one shall "arise."

The gilt on the monuments is less than the brightness of the poem; fire is unable to destroy the living record of the beloved; and death and oblivion will wear the world out but have no power against a fourteen-line sonnet.

The couplet serves as a distillation of what has preceded: the loved one lives in the sonnet, and the sonnet lives to the end of human time. It is deathless because the eyes of lovers will read it and there will always be lovers.

Though the Italian and English sonnets make up the dominant tradition, poets have experimented with other rhyme patterns and structures. Even as the English sonnet was taking hold, Edmund Spenser devised a fourteen-line unit with a more interlocking rhyme: *ababbcbccdcdee*. John Donne, in the seventeenth century, favored a scheme that draws on both the Italian and English forms: *abbaabbacdcdee*. In the mid-nineteenth century, some two hundred and fifty years after Shakespeare's death, George Meredith composed a SONNET CYCLE (a series of sonnets organized to tell a story or to work through a conception) consisting of fifty sonnets of sixteen lines each, rhyming *abbacddceffeghhg*. Contemporary poets have even experimented with an unrhymed sonnet, one of which you have already read: Robert Lowell's "Robert Frost" (p. 31). Reread it to determine how Lowell has managed to sustain most of the sonnet conventions despite the abandonment of rhyme.

Elegies

The ELEGY, a lyric poem which commemorates the dead, may convey profound personal emotion but tends to do so according to a set of long-established literary conventions. The most notable of these conventions are found in the PASTORAL ELEGY, which had its beginnings in ancient Greece. In the classical elegy, the setting is rural, and the characters are shepherds; gods and goddesses rule over an idyllic natural world, which is thrown into mourning by a death. John Milton, writing in the seventeenth century, makes use of many of the traditional elements, adapting them to his own Christian vision in perhaps the greatest English pastoral elegy, "Lycidas" (p. 465). The grief is stated, the cause of death told; earlier, happier days are recalled; nature sympathizes and joins in the lament; the body is attended, and mourners arrive to pay last respects; finally, there is a reflection on death and immortality, ending with consolation. The language is elevated in tone, and the entire conception highly ritualistic.

Although modern elegies have given up the pastoral elements, and some aspects are curtailed or eliminated entirely, the formal tone and general design usually remain in evidence. In the elegy by W. H. Auden that follows, you can find hints of the pastoral tradition, but the innovations and departures are perhaps more fascinating. Their effect depends, of course, on a knowledge of the conventions of the fixed form.

In Memory of W. B. Yeats

(D. Jan. 1939)

1

He disappeared in the dead of winter:
The brooks were frozen, the airports almost deserted,
And snow disfigured the public statues;
The mercury sank in the mouth of the dying day.
O all the instruments agree   5
The day of his death was a dark cold day.

Far from his illness
The wolves ran on through the evergreen forests,
The peasant river was untempted by the fashionable quays;
By mourning tongues   10
The death of the poet was kept from his poems.

But for him it was his last afternoon as himself,
An afternoon of nurses and rumors;
The provinces of his body revolted,
The squares of his mind were empty,   15
Silence invaded the suburbs,
The current of his feeling failed: he became his admirers.

Now he is scattered among a hundred cities
And wholly given over to unfamiliar affections;
To find his happiness in another kind of wood   20
And be punished under a foreign code of conscience.
The words of a dead man
Are modified in the guts of the living.

But in the importance and noise of tomorrow
When the brokers are roaring like beasts on the floor of the French 25
  Bourse°, stock exchange
And the poor have the sufferings to which they are fairly
  accustomed,
And each in the cell of himself is almost convinced of his
  freedom;
A few thousand will think of this day
As one thinks of a day when one did something slightly unusual.

O all the instruments agree 30
The day of his death was a dark cold day.

2

You were silly like us: your gift survived it all;
The parish of rich women, physical decay,
Yourself; mad Ireland hurt you into poetry.
Now Ireland has her madness and her weather still, 35
For poetry makes nothing happen: it survives
In the valley of its saying where executives
Would never want to tamper; it flows south
From ranches of isolation and the busy griefs,
Raw towns that we believe and die in; it survives, 40
A way of happening, a mouth.

3

Earth, receive an honored guest;
William Yeats is laid to rest:
Let the Irish vessel lie
Emptied of its poetry. 45

In the nightmare of the dark
All the dogs of Europe bark,
And the living nations wait,
Each sequestered° in its hate; isolated, cut off

Intellectual disgrace 50
Stares from every human face,
And the seas of pity lie
Locked and frozen in each eye.

Follow, poet, follow right
To the bottom of the night, 55
With your unconstraining voice
Still persuade us to rejoice;

With the farming of a verse
Make a vineyard of the curse,
Sing of human unsuccess   60
In a rapture of distress;

In the deserts of the heart
Let the healing fountain start,
In the prison of his days
Teach the free man how to praise.   65

W. H. Auden (1907–1973)

Auden's elegy begins with a description of a wintry setting appropriate to the condition of the dying poet Yeats (lines 1–17); the passage is comparable to that describing the bereavement in the traditional pastoral elegy, and although the scene is modern, traditional pastoral images (wolves, the evergreen forests, the "peasant river") are used for symbolic effect. In the same way, the traditional response of nature to the death is changed to society's response—but with a bitter, modern, twist: the response is indifference (lines 24–31), which is cause enough for lamentation. In place of the conventional funeral procession, Auden gives us a glimpse of Yeats's passage through life, and instead of noting a separation of the physical body from the spirit, he focuses on the separation of the man and his poetry (lines 42–45):

> Earth, receive an honored guest;
> William Yeats is laid to rest:
> Let the Irish vessel lie
> Emptied of its poetry.

Rather than reflect on the immortality of the soul, the speaker informs us that the poems will be immortal; instead of meditating on an afterlife, the speaker reflects on the bleak world the poet has left behind—prewar Europe in the year 1939 (lines 46–53). And, finally, instead of consolation, there is appeal (lines 54–65).

Elegies usually offer comfort with arguments taken from religion or philosophy. Among the poems in the anthology you will find an elegy written by Walt Whitman (p. 507) on the death of Abraham Lincoln, which turns from lamentation to consolation because of Whitman's belief in immortality. When the speaker in Auden's poem turns back to face a brutal world, he can find no religious or philosophical consolation; if there is consolation, it is in the endurance of art.

Theodore Roethke's elegy, both briefer and more directly personal than Auden's, seems almost entirely free of the usual elegiac conventions. In fact, however, it draws upon a number of the traditional elements:

Elegy for Jane

My Student, Thrown by a Horse

I remember the neckcurls, limp and damp as tendrils;
And her quick look, a sidelong pickerel smile;
And how, once startled into talk, the light syllables leaped for her,
And she balanced in the delight of her thought,

A wren, happy, tail into the wind,   5
Her song trembling the twigs and small branches.
The shade sang with her;
The leaves, their whispers turned to kissing;
And the mold sang in the bleached valleys under the rose.

Oh, when she was sad, she cast herself down into such a pure depth,   10
Even a father could not find her:
Scraping her cheek against straw;
Stirring the clearest water.

My sparrow, you are not here,
Waiting like a fern, making a spiny shadow.   15
The sides of wet stones cannot console me,
Nor the moss, wound with the last light.

If only I could nudge you from this sleep,
My maimed darling, my skittery pigeon.
Over this damp grave I speak the words of my love: 20
I, with no rights in this matter,
Neither father nor lover.

Theodore Roethke (1908–1963)

QUESTIONS

1. How do the references to nature function in the poem?
2. Show how Roethke has used the convention of remembering happier times.
3. In what ways do lines 14–22 evoke the conventional funeral/burial procession?
4. How does the poem deal with the issues of immortality and consolation?
5. Having answered the previous questions, can you determine why the poem seems free of the conventions it evokes?

Odes

ODES, like sonnets and elegies, belong to the genre of the lyric but tend to be less private, addressing themes such as liberty, justice, immortality, the nature of art and truth. Like the elegy, the ode originated in ancient Greece, deriving from the choral chant in Greek drama. The diction is elevated, the rhythms stately, the progression of ideas orderly.

When the strophes are different in length or design, we speak of the IRREGULAR ODE; for an example, see in the anthology (p. 516) William Wordsworth's "Ode: Intimations of Immortality from Recollections of Early Childhood." When the strophes take the form of identical stanzas, the ode is called a HOMOSTROPHIC ODE:

Ode on Solitude

Happy the man whose wish and care
  A few paternal acres bound,
Content to breathe his native air,
      In his own ground.

Whose herds with milk, whose fields with bread,   5
  Whose flocks supply him with attire,
Whose trees in summer yield him shade,
      In winter fire.

Blest, who can unconcernedly find
  Hours, days, and years slide soft away,   10
In health of body, peace of mind,
      Quiet by day,

Sound sleep by night; study and ease,
  Together mixed; sweet recreation;
And innocence, which most does please   15
      With meditation.

Thus let me live, unseen, unknown;
  Thus unlamented let me die;
Steal from the world, and not a stone
      Tell where I lie.   20

Alexander Pope (1688–1744)

Addressing the abstract theme of solitude, Pope seems to speak for all who long for a life of peace and tranquility. The steady iambic meter, the regular rhyme scheme, and the carefully balanced stanzas all join to reinforce the sense of stately argument.

By contrast, Percy Bysshe Shelley's ode, while also stately in form, is far more personal. It consists of two interrelated parts, with sections

I, II, and III pertaining to the wind and preparing for sections IV and V, which pertain to the poet, his condition, and the desires he has for his poems:

Ode to the West Wind

I

O wild West Wind, thou breath of Autumn's being,
Thou, from whose unseen presence the leaves dead
Are driven, like ghosts from an enchanter fleeing,

Yellow, and black, and pale, and hectic red,
Pestilence-stricken multitudes: O thou,   5
Who chariotest to their dark wintry bed

The wingèd seeds, where they lie cold and low,
Each like a corpse within its grave, until
Thine azure sister of the Spring shall blow

Her clarion° o'er the dreaming earth, and fill   *trumpet* 10
(Driving sweet buds like flocks to feed in air)
With living hues and odours plain and hill:

Wild Spirit, which art moving everywhere;
Destroyer and preserver; hear, oh, hear!

II

Thou on whose stream, mid the steep sky's commotion,   15
Loose clouds like earth's decaying leaves are shed,
Shook from the tangled boughs of Heaven and Ocean,

Angels° of rain and lightning: there are spread   *heralds, messengers*
On the blue surface of thine aëry surge,
Like the bright hair uplifted from the head   20

Of some fierce Maenad°, even from the dim verge   *frenzied woman follower*
Of the horizon to the zenith's height,   *of Dionysus*
The locks of the approaching storm. Thou dirge

Of the dying year, to which this closing night
Will be the dome of a vast sepulchre,   25
Vaulted with all thy congregated might

Of vapours, from whose solid atmosphere
Black rain, and fire, and hail will burst: oh, hear!

III

Thou who didst waken from his summer dreams
The blue Mediterranean, where he lay,   30
Lulled by the coil of his crystàlline streams,

Beside a pumice° isle in Baiae's bay°,   *volcanic stone/near Naples*
And saw in sleep old palaces and towers
Quivering within the wave's intenser day,

All overgrown with azure moss and flowers   35
So sweet, the sense faints picturing them! Thou
For whose path the Atlantic's level powers

Cleave themselves into chasms, while far below
The sea-blooms and the oozy woods which wear
The sapless foliage of the ocean, know   40

Thy voice, and suddenly grow gray with fear,
And tremble and despoil themselves: oh, hear!

IV

If I were a dead leaf thou mightest bear;
If I were a swift cloud to fly with thee;
A wave to pant beneath thy power, and share   45

The impulse of thy strength, only less free
Than thou, O uncontrollable! If even
I were as in my boyhood, and could be

The comrade of thy wanderings over Heaven,
As then, when to outstrip thy skiey speed   50
Scarce seemed a vision; I would ne'er have striven

As thus with thee in prayer in my sore need.
Oh! lift me as a wave, a leaf, a cloud!
I fall upon the thorns of life! I bleed!

A heavy weight of hours has chained and bowed   55
One too like thee: tameless, and swift, and proud.

V

Make me thy lyre°, even as the forest is: *aeolian lyre or harp*
What if my leaves are falling like its own!
The tumult of thy mighty harmonies

Will take from both a deep, autumnal tone,   60
Sweet though in sadness. Be thou, spirit fierce,
My spirit! Be thou me, impetuous one!

Drive my dead thoughts over the universe
Like withered leaves to quicken a new birth;
And, by the incantation of this verse,   65

Scatter, as from an unextinguished hearth
Ashes and sparks, my words among mankind!
Be through my lips to unawakened earth

The trumpet of a prophecy! O Wind,
If Winter comes, can Spring be far behind?   70

Percy Bysshe Shelley (1792–1822)

QUESTIONS

1. Describe the action of the wind in sections I, II, and III. Explain how, in each
   section, the wind acts as both "Destroyer and preserver."
2. Explain how lines 43–45 serve as transition from the first part of the poem
   to the second part. What bearing do these lines have on section V?
3. Explain the appeal the poet makes in the concluding lines.

Pope and Shelley represent very different kinds of poetic tempera-
ment, and the poems they write are separated by roughly a hundred
years. It is in their choice of genre—in this case, the ode—that they can
be said to come together and to warrant our reading them in terms of
each other.

Awareness of genre helps us, then, to relate one poem to another,
to see how poems can participate in lengthy traditions and yet remain
unique in themselves. Poets who choose to write sonnets or ballads,
elegies or dramatic monologues, accept certain formal restraints and
find in such fixed modes challenges and possibilities not available in
freer forms. Poems such as Roethke's "Elegy for Jane" and Keats's "La
Belle Dame sans Merci" are committed to the genres they reinterpret,
and for the reader not to know that is to lose part of their meaning.

EXERCISES

I. Read the group of short poems that follow as examples of narrative, dramatic,
or lyric poetry and classify each poem. Explain how you arrived at your decision
and, where appropriate, describe how the poem departs from the mode.

The Twa Corbies

As I was walking all alane,
I herd twa corbies° making a mane°;   *two crows/moan*
The tane unto the t' other say,
"Where sall we gang and dine to-day?"

"In behint yon auld fail dyke°,   *behind the old wall* 5
I wot° there lies a new slain knight;   *know*
And naebody kens° that he lies there,   *knows*
But his hawk, his hound, and lady fair.

"His hound is to the hunting gane,
His hawk to fetch the wild-fowl hame,   10
His lady's ta'en another mate,
So we may mak our dinner sweet.

"Ye'll sit on his white hause-bane°,   *neck bone*
And I'll pike out his bonny blue een°;   *eyes*
Wi ae lock o his gowden hair   15
We'll theek° our nest when it grows bare.   *thatch*

"Mony a one for him makes mane,
But nane sall ken where he is gane;
O'er his white banes when they are bare,
The wind sall blaw for evermair."   20

Anonymous

Meeting at Night

The gray sea and the long black land;
And the yellow half-moon large and low;
And the startled little waves that leap
In fiery ringlets from their sleep,
As I gain the cove with pushing prow,   5
And quench its speed i' the slushy sand.

Then a mile of warm sea-scented beach;
Three fields to cross till a farm appears;
A tap at the pane, the quick sharp scratch
And blue spurt of a lighted match,   10
And a voice less loud, through its joys and fears,
Than the two hearts beating each to each!

Robert Browning (1812–1889)

Parting at Morning

Round the cape of a sudden came the sea,
And the sun looked over the mountain's rim:
And straight was a path of gold for him°,   *the sun*
And the need of a world of men for me.

Robert Browning (1812–1889)

from *Romeo and Juliet**

ROMEO   He jests at scars that never felt a wound.
   But soft, what light through yonder window breaks?
   It is the East and Juliet is the sun.
   Arise fair Sun and kill the envious Moon,
   Who is already sick and pale with grief   5
   That thou her maid art far more fair than she.
   Be not her maid, since she is envious,
   Her vestal liv'ry° is but sick and green,   *virginal attire*
   And none but fools do wear it, cast it off.
                 [Enter Juliet at the window.]
   It is my lady! O it is my love!   10
   O that she knew she were!
   She speaks yet she says nothing, what of that?
   Her eye discourses, I will answer it.
   I am too bold, 'tis not to me she speaks.
   Two of the fairest stars in all the heaven,   15
   Having some business, do entreat her eyes
   To twinkle in their spheres till they return.
   What if her eyes were there, they in her head?
   The brightness of her cheek would shame those stars
   As daylight doth a lamp; her eye in heaven   20
   Would through the airy region stream so bright
   That birds would sing and think it were not night.
   See how she leans her cheek upon her hand!
   O that I were a glove upon that hand
   That I might touch that cheek.   25

William Shakespeare (1564–1616)

the Cambridge ladies who live in furnished souls

the Cambridge ladies who live in furnished souls
are unbeautiful and have comfortable minds
(also, with the church's protestant blessings
daughters, unscented shapeless spirited)
they believe in Christ and Longfellow, both dead,   5
are invariably interested in so many things—
at the present writing one still finds
delighted fingers knitting for the is it Poles?
perhaps. While permanent faces coyly bandy

*Act II, Scene I, lines 43–67.

scandal of Mrs. N and Professor D   10
. . . . the Cambridge ladies do not care, above
Cambridge if sometimes in its box of
sky lavender and cornerless, the
moon rattles like a fragment of angry candy

                    e. e. cummings (1894–1962)

Bells for John Whiteside's Daughter

There was such speed in her little body,
And such lightness in her footfall,
It is no wonder her brown study
Astonishes us all.

Her wars were bruited in our high window.   5
We looked among orchard trees and beyond
Where she took arms against her shadow,
Or harried unto the pond

The lazy geese, like a snow cloud
Dripping their snow on the green grass,   10
Tricking and stopping, sleepy and proud,
Who cried in goose, Alas,

For the tireless heart within the little
Lady with rod that made them rise
From their noon apple-dreams and scuttle   15
Goose-fashion under the skies!

But now go the bells, and we are ready,
In one house we are sternly stopped
To say we are vexed at her brown study,
Lying so primly propped.   20

                    John Crowe Ransom (1888–1974)

Bonie Doon

Ye flowery banks o' bonie Doon,
  How can ye blume sae fair?
How can ye chant, ye little birds,
  And I sae fu'° o' care?   *so full*

Thou'll break my heart, thou bonie bird,   5
  That sings upon the bough;
Thou minds me o' the happy days,
  When my fause luve was true.

Thou'll break my heart, thou bonie bird,
  That sings beside thy mate;   10
For sae I sat, and sae I sang,
  And wist na° o' my fate.   *knew not*

Aft hae° I roved by bonie Doon   *often have*
  To see the wood-bine twine,
And ilka° bird sang o' its luve,   *that same*   15
  And sae did I o' mine.

Wi' lightsome heart I pu'd a rose
  Frae aff its thorny tree;
And my fause luver staw° my rose   *stole*
  But left the thorn wi' me.   20

Robert Burns (1759–1796)

II. The small collection that follows has examples of both folk and literary ballads. Read them for their stories first, paying particular attention to the manner in which the narrative is compressed. Then:

1. Explain how each poem treats a subject typical of the ballad.
2. Show how the sequence of the story provides structure to the poem.
3. Find instances of incremental repetition, refrain, and dialogue in the folk ballads. Show how the literary ballads also use these devices.

The Three Ravens

1

There were three ravens sat on a tree,
  Down a down, hay down, hay down
There were three ravens sat on a tree,
  With a down
There were three ravens sat on a tree,   5
They were as black as they might be.
  With a down derry, derry, derry, down, down.

2

The one of them said to his make°,   *mate*
"Where shall we our breakfast take?"

3

"Down in yonder greene field,   10
There lies a knight slain under his shield.

4

"His hounds they lie down at his feet,
So well they can their master keep.

5

"His hawks they fly so eagerly°,   *fiercely*
There's no fowl dare him come nigh."   15

6

Down there comes a fallow° doe,   *yellow-brown*
As great with young as she might go.

7

She lift up his bloody head
And kissed his wounds that were so red.

8

She got him up upon her back   20
And carried him to earthen lake°.   *a grave*

9

She buried him before the prime°,   *early morning*
She was dead herself ere even-song° time.   *vespers*

10

God send every gentleman
Such hawks, such hounds, and such a leman°.   *lover*   25

Anonymous

The Sisters

We were two daughters of one race:
She was the fairest in the face:
   The wind is blowing in turret and tree.
They were together, and she fell;
Therefore revenge became me well.   5
   O the Earl was fair to see!

She died: she went to burning flame°:   *hell*
She mix'd her ancient blood with shame.
    The wind is howling in turret and tree.
Whole weeks and months, and early and late,   10
To win his love I lay in wait:
    O the Earl was fair to see!

I made a feast; I bade him come:
I won his love, I brought him home.
    The wind is roaring in turret and tree.   15
And after supper, on a bed,
Upon my lap he laid his head:
    O the Earl was fair to see!

I kiss'd his eyelids into rest:
His ruddy cheek upon my breast.   20
    The wind is raging in turret and tree.
I hated him with the hate of hell,
But I loved his beauty passing well.
    O the Earl was fair to see!

I rose up in the silent night: 25
I made my dagger sharp and bright.
    The wind is raving in turret and tree.
As half-asleep his breath he drew,
Three times I stabb'd him thro' and thro'.
    O the Earl was fair to see!   30

I curl'd and comb'd his comely head,
He look'd so grand when he was dead.
    The wind is blowing in turret and tree.
I wrapt his body in the sheet,
And laid him at his mother's feet.   35
    O the Earl was fair to see!

Alfred, Lord Tennyson (1809–1892)

Edward

"Why dois your brand° sae drap° wi bluid,   *sword/drip*
    Edward, Edward,
Why dois your brand sae drap wi bluid,
    And why sae sad gang° yee O?"   *go*

"O I hae killed my hauke sae guid,   5
   Mither, mither,
O I hae killed my hauke sae guid,
   And I had nae mair bot° hee O."   *no more but*

"Your haukis bluid was nevir sae reid,
   Edward, Edward,   10
Your haukis bluid was nevir sae reid,
   My deir son I tell thee O."
"O I hae killed my reid-roan steid°,   *chestnut steed*
   Mither, mither,
O I hae killed my reid-roan steid,   15
   That erst° was sae fair and frie O."   *once*

"Your steid was auld, and ye hae got mair,
   Edward, Edward,
Your steid was auld, and ye hae got mair,
   Sum other dule° ye drie° O."   *sorrow/suffer* 20
"O I hae killed my fadir deir,
   Mither, mither,
O I hae killed my fadir deir,
   Alas, and wae° is mee O!"   *woe*

"And whatten penance wul ye drie° for that,   *do* 25
   Edward, Edward,
And whatten penance will ye drie for that?
   My deir son, now tell me O."
"Ile set my feit in yonder boat,
   Mither, mither,   30
Ile set my feit in yonder boat,
   And Ile fare ovir the sea O."

"And what wul ye doe wi your towirs and your ha°,   *hall*
   Edward, Edward?
And what wul ye doe wi your towirs and your ha,   35
   That were sae fair to see O?"
"Ile let thame stand tul they doun fa,
   Mither, mither,
Ile let thame stand tul they doun fa,
   For here nevir mair maun° I bee O."   *must* 40

"And what wul ye leive to your bairns° and your wife,   *children*
   Edward, Edward?
And what wul ye leive to your bairns and your wife,
   Whan ye gang ovir the sea O?"
"The warldis room°, late them beg thrae° life,   *world's space/through* 45
   Mither, mither,
The warldis room, late them beg thrae life,
   For thame nevir mair wul I see O."

"And what wul ye leive to your ain° mither deir,   *own*
    Edward, Edward?   50
And what wul ye leive to your ain mither deir?
  My deir son, now tell me O."
"The curse of hell frae me sall° ye beir,   *shall*
    Mither, mither,
The curse of hell frae me sall ye beir,   55
  Sic° counseils ye gave to me O."   *such*

Anonymous

Eldorado

    Gaily bedight°,   *arrayed*
    A gallant knight,
In sunshine and in shadow,
    Had journeyed long,
    Singing a song   5
In search of Eldorado.

    But he grew old—
    This knight so bold—
And o'er his heart a shadow
    Fell, as he found   10
    No spot of ground
That looked like Eldorado.

    And, as his strength
    Failed him at length,
He met a pilgrim shadow—   15
    "Shadow," said he,
    "Where can it be—
This land of Eldorado?"

    "Over the Mountains
    Of the Moon,   20
Down the Valley of the Shadow,
    Ride, boldly ride,"
    The shade replied,—
"If you seek for Eldorado!"

Edgar Allan Poe (1809–1849)

III. After you read the following folk ballad, "Thomas Rhymer," reread John Keats's "La Belle Dame sans Merci" (p. 164).

1. How do the two ballads compare in terms of storytelling, use of dialogue, characterization, and imagery?
2. What events present in "Thomas Rhymer" are either missing from or condensed in Keats's ballad? What new events does Keats's ballad contain?
3. In what sense do the two ballads have a similar theme? How do they seem to differ thematically?
4. Which of the two do you prefer? Why?

Thomas Rhymer

True Thomas lay on Huntlie bank,
   A ferlie° he spied wi' his ee,   *wondrous sight*
And there he saw a lady bright,
   Come riding down by the Eildon Tree.

Her shirt° was o' the grass-green silk,   *skirt* 5
   Her mantle o' the velvet fine,
At ilka tett° of her horse's mane   *every lock*
   Hang fifty siller° bells and nine.   *silver*

True Thomas, he pulled aff his cap,
   And louted° low down to his knee: *bowed* 10
"All hail, thou mighty Queen of Heaven!
   For thy peer on earth I never did see."

"O no, O no, Thomas," she said,
   "That name does not belang to me;
I am but the queen of fair Elfland,   15
   That am hither come to visit thee.

"Harp and carp°, Thomas," she said,   *play and sing*
   "Harp and carp along wi' me,
And if ye dare to kiss my lips,
   Sure of your body I will be."   20

"Betide me weal, betide me woe,
   That weird° shall never daunton me";   *fate*
Syne° he has kissed her rosy lips,   *then*
   All underneath the Eildon Tree.

"Now, ye maun° go wi' me," she said,   *must* 25
   "True Thomas, ye maun go wi' me,
And ye maun serve me seven years,
   Thro weal or woe, as may chance to be."

She mounted on her milk-white steed,
    She's taen True Thomas up behind,   30
And aye° whene'er her bridle rung,   *always*
    The steed flew swifter than the wind.

O they rade on, and farther on—
    The steed gaed° swifter than the wind—   *went*
Until they reached a desart wide,   35
    And living land was left behind.

"Light down, light down, now, True Thomas,
    And lean your head upon my knee;
Abide and rest a little space,
    And I will shew you ferlies° three.   *wonders* 40

"O see ye not yon narrow road,
    So thick beset with thorns and briars?
That is the path of righteousness,
    Though after it but few enquires.

"And see not ye that braid° braid road,   *broad* 45
    That lies across that lily leven°?   *lovely plain*
That is the path of wickedness,
    Though some call it the road to heaven.

"And see not ye that bonny road,
    That winds about the ferny brae°?   *hillside* 50
That is the road to fair Elfland,
    Where thou and I this night maun gae°.   *must go*

"But, Thomas, ye maun hold your tongue,
    Whatever ye may hear or see,
For, if you speak word in Elfyn land,   55
    Ye'll ne'er get back to your ain countrie."

O they rade on, and farther on,
    And they waded thro rivers aboon the knee,
And they saw neither sun nor moon,
    But they heard the roaring of the sea.   60

It was mirk° mirk night, and there was nae stern° light,   *murky/star*
    And they waded thro red blude to the knee;
For a' the blude that's shed on earth
    Rins thro the springs o' that countrie.

Syne° they came on to a garden green,   *then* 65
    And she pu'd an apple frae a tree:
"Take this for thy wages, True Thomas,
    It will give the tongue that can never lie."

"My tongue is mine ain," True Thomas said;
  "A gudely gift ye wad gie to me!
I neither dought° to buy or sell,   70   *dare*
  At fair or tryst° where I may be.   *market*

"I dought neither speak to prince or peer,
  Nor ask of grace from fair ladye":
"Now hold thy peace," the lady said,   75
  "For as I say, so must it be."

He has gotten a coat of the even° cloth,   *smooth*
  And a pair of shoes of velvet green,
And till seven years were gane and past
  True Thomas on earth was never seen.   80

Anonymous

Thomas Rhymer. Thomas of Erceldoune, a Scottish minstrel of the thirteenth century, was the subject of several poems focusing on his powers of prophecy.

IV. Read the two poems below, one a dramatic monologue, the other a soliloquy. Focus first on the kinds of situations portrayed, and second on the characters.

The Flea

Mark but this flea, and mark in this
How little that which thou deny'st me is;
It sucked me first, and now sucks thee,
And in this flea our two bloods mingled be;
Thou know'st that this cannot be said   5
A sin, nor shame, nor loss of maidenhead,
  Yet this enjoys before it woo,
  And pampered swells with one blood made of two,
  And this, alas, is more than we would do.

Oh stay, three lives in one flea spare,   10
Where we almost, yea more than married are.
This flea is you and I, and this
Our marriage bed, and marriage temple is;
Though parents grudge, and you, we're met
And cloistered in these living walls of jet.   15
  Though use° make you apt to kill me,   *custom*
  Let not to that, self-murder added be,
  And sacrilege, three sins in killing three.

Cruel and sudden, hast thou since
Purpled thy nail in blood of innocence?   20
Wherein could this flea guilty be,
Except in that drop it sucked from thee?
Yet thou triumph'st, and say'st that thou
Find'st not thyself, nor me, the weaker now;
   'Tis true; then learn how false, fears be;   25
   Just so much honor, when thou yield'st to me,
   Will waste, as this flea's death took life from thee.

John Donne (1572–1631)

1. Whom does the speaker address? Explain the circumstances.
2. Paraphrase the speaker's argument in the first and second stanzas.
3. What event, or near event, determines the particulars of the argument in the second and third stanzas?
4. What attitude toward the listener seems to pervade each of the stanzas?
5. From the nature of the argument, how would you describe the speaker's character? Can you infer anything about the listener's character?

The Moss of His Skin

Young girls in old Arabia were often buried alive next to their dead fathers, apparently as sacrifice to the goddesses of the tribes . . .

HAROLD FELDMAN, "Children of the Desert"
Psychoanalysis and Psychoanalytic Review, Fall 1958

It was only important
to smile and hold still,
to lie down beside him
and to rest awhile,
to be folded up together   5
as if we were silk,
to sink from the eyes of mother
and not to talk.
The black room took us
like a cave or a mouth   10
or an indoor belly.
I held my breath
and daddy was there,
his thumbs, his fat skull,
his teeth, his hair growing   15
like a field or a shawl.

I lay by the moss
of his skin until
it grew strange. My sisters
will never know that I fall

20

out of myself and pretend
that Allah will not see
how I hold my daddy
like an old stone tree.

Anne Sexton (1928–1975)

1. Explain the scene of the poem.
2. What is the relationship of the headnote to the poem?
3. To what extent does the speaker assume the character of an Arabian girl? to
   what extent does she not?

V. T. S. Eliot's "The Love Song of J. Alfred Prufrock" (in the anthology, p.
420) combines qualities of the soliloquy and the dramatic monologue. Prufrock
seems at one moment to be addressing an audience ("Let us go then, you and
I,") and at other times to be speaking of his inner conflict to no one in particular.
With this in mind, read the poem and respond to the questions below:

1. Where is Prufrock going? Though he never does arrive, in what sense is he
   there from the start?
2. Isolate Prufrock's various references to women (such as in lines 13–14 and
   63–69) and determine the quality of his emotions toward them.
3. What assessment of himself does Prufrock seem to be making in lines 111–119?
   How do you interpret his judgment that he is "ridiculous," almost the
   "Fool"?
4. Prufrock's reference to disturbing the "universe" (lines 45–46) can be read
   as disturbing his world. What details help to clarify the nature of that world?
   In what ways would it be possible for Prufrock to "disturb" his world? What
   prevents him from doing so?
5. The scene shifts from indoors to out in the last lines (lines 122–130). What
   do the mermaids seem to represent? Why is Prufrock drawn to them?
6. Prufrock ends with a vision of himself drowning (lines 129–131). Explain the
   lines.

VI. In the anthology you will find the pastoral elegy "Lycidas," by John Milton
(p. 465), and the elegy "When Lilacs Last in the Dooryard Bloom'd," by Walt
Whitman (p. 507). As you read each poem, keep the following structure for
elegies before you:

   (a) the cause of grief
   (b) the reference to earlier days
   (c) lamentation

    (d) funeral preparations

    (e) procession of mourners

    (f) reflections on immortality

    (g) consolation

1. Make an outline of "Lycidas," indicating which lines belong to each of the segments listed above. Do the same for "When Lilacs Last in the Dooryard Bloom'd," taking into account Whitman's adaptations (for example, instead of the procession of mourners, the funeral train passes the standing crowds).
2. Edward King, the "learned friend" whose death was the occasion for "Lycidas," had hopes of being a poet but was essentially an untested and unfulfilled young man; Abraham Lincoln, the subject of Whitman's elegy, was of course a great, if controversial, statesman. How do the elegies make use of the status of their subjects?
3. Milton's headnote alluding to the corrupt clergy suggests a public dimension to the poem. Which lines fulfill that expectation? Find lines in Whitman's poem that suggest a public, indeed a political, concern.
4. Whitman's poem uses three major symbols—the bird, the star, and the lilac. Show how they function to support the structure of the elegy.

VII.   John Keats is looking at an ancient Greek vase. As he studies its several scenes, he wonders not only about what he sees but about his own life:

Ode on a Grecian Urn

Thou still unravished bride of quietness,	
Thou foster-child of silence and slow time,	
Sylvan° historian, who canst thus express	*of the forest*
A flowery tale more sweetly than our rhyme:	
What leaf-fringed legend haunts about thy shape	5
Of deities or mortals, or of both,	
In Tempe° or the dales of Arcady?°	*ideal pastoral landscapes in Greek tradition*
What men or gods are these? What maidens loth?	
What mad pursuit? What struggle to escape?	
What pipes and timbrels? What wild ecstasy?	10

Heard melodies are sweet, but those unheard
   Are sweeter; therefore, ye soft pipes, play on;
Not to the sensual ear, but, more endeared,
   Pipe to the spirit ditties of no tone:
Fair youth, beneath the trees, thou canst not leave   15
   Thy song, nor ever can those trees be bare;
     Bold Lover, never, never canst thou kiss,
Though winning near the goal—yet, do not grieve;
   She cannot fade, though thou hast not thy bliss,
     For ever wilt thou love, and she be fair!   20

Ah, happy, happy boughs! that cannot shed
 Your leaves, nor ever bid the spring adieu;
And, happy melodist, unwearièd,
 For ever piping songs for ever new;
More happy love! more happy, happy love!   25
 For ever warm and still to be enjoyed,
  For ever panting, and for ever young;
All breathing human passion far above,
 That leaves a heart high-sorrowful and cloyed,
  A burning forehead, and a parching tongue.   30

Who are these coming to the sacrifice?
 To what green altar, O mysterious priest,
Lead'st thou that heifer lowing at the skies,
 And all her silken flanks with garlands dressed?
What little town by river or sea shore,   35
 Or mountain-built with peaceful citadel,
  Is emptied of this folk, this pious morn?
And, little town, thy streets for evermore
 Will silent be; and not a soul to tell
  Why thou art desolate, can e'er return.   40

O Attic° shape! Fair attitude! with brede°   *Greek/with pattern*
 Of marble men and maidens overwrought,
With forest branches and the trodden weed;
 Thou, silent form, dost tease us out of thought
As doth eternity: Cold Pastoral!   45
 When old age shall this generation waste,
  Thou shalt remain, in midst of other woe
Than ours, a friend to man, to whom thou say'st,
 "Beauty is truth, truth beauty,"—that is all
  Ye know on earth, and all ye need to know.   50

John Keats (1795–1821)

1. Describe each "leaf-fringed legend" that "haunts about" the shape of the vase. Which of the scenes described is not in fact on the urn? What is its source and how does it relate to the others?
2. In what sense does line 14 have meaning for the lines that follow through line 40? How do you interpret lines 49–50?
3. Compare the use of apostrophe in the opening and closing stanzas. How is each appropriate to its place in the poem?
4. Analyze the stanza structure and show how it relates to the development of the thought.
5. Although the ode seems to be a personal reflection, with profound personal meaning, how would you argue for its having a wider application?

9

Tone and

Attitude

We have occasionally used the words "tone" and "attitude" in commenting on the effect of particular poems, and though we have not formally defined these terms, their meanings in general were probably easy enough to grasp from the context of the discussion. But tone and attitude are sufficiently important to the understanding of poetry to merit more detailed consideration.

In its most basic sense, TONE is an aspect of the speaking voice, especially the inflections of the voice from which we infer the attitude of the speaker. We may sense that a speaker's tone is gay, nasty, melancholy, soothing, bitter, somber, angry, or meditative, as the case may be, and the more attentive we are to the precise intonation, the closer we seem to come to an exact notion of a speaker's attitude toward the subject. When we hear someone say "Good try" or "I don't believe it!" it is the tone of voice that reveals, for instance, mockery, reverence, or contempt. We usually associate a snarl with "Get off my back," admiration with "Nice guy!" or contentment with "a sheer delight," but the same phrases, with a shift in context as well as tone, can take on different meanings. "Nice guy!" applied to a despised politician, may well suggest disgust, disillusionment, or bitterness. "Get off my back," directed to a lively eight-year-old who has made a pert remark, can imply disguised affection, while "a sheer delight," uttered after a taste of murky coffee, is not likely to be misheard as praise.

Read the brief poems that follow and try to hear the tone of voice in each. The variations, you will discover, are considerable:

We Real Cool

The Pool Players.
Seven at the Golden Shovel.

We real cool. We
Left school. We

Lurk late. We
Strike straight. We

Sing sin. We
Thin gin. We

Jazz June. We
Die soon.

Gwendolyn Brooks (b. 1917)

Buffalo Bill's

Buffalo Bill's
defunct
     who used to
     ride a watersmooth-silver
           stallion   5
and break onetwothreefourfive pigeonsjustlikethat
                  Jesus

he was a handsome man
          and what i want to know is

how do you like your blueeyed boy   10
Mister Death

e. e. cummings (1894–1962)

For the Children

The rising hills, the slopes,
of statistics
lie before us.
the steep climb
of everything, going up,   5
up, as we all
go down.

In the next century
or the one beyond that,
they say,   10
are valleys, pastures,
we can meet there in peace
if we make it.

To climb these coming crests
one word to you, to   15
you and your children:

stay together
learn the flowers
go light

                    Gary Snyder (b. 1930)

The three poems have obviously contrasting tones. The voice we hear
in Brooks is offhand, laconic, conversational; in Cummings, assertive,
brassy, boastful; in Snyder, thoughtful, somewhat resigned, and yet
reassuring.

Tone in a poem is a product of many factors—choice of words and
details; associations of imagery, rhythms and sound effects, speaker
and situation—in other words, most of the elements we have been
describing in the preceding chapters. The seven voices of the seven pool
players at the Golden Shovel are indistinguishable and culminate in a
kind of choral assertion, "We/Die soon," which suggests their acceptance
of a brutal reality that the poet herself is by no means indifferent to.
Cummings's typographical devices, which speed up the rhythm, and
the fragmentary look of the poem, which slows it down, the use of
cliché ("Jesus/he was a handsome man," "and what i want to know
is"), and the presence of striking verbal usage *(watersmooth-silver stallion,*
defunct) suggest a voice that is rough-hewn, matter-of-fact rather than
meditative, and yet capable of challenging Mister Death. Snyder's med-
itative tone comes from the composure of a speaker who will not be
defeated by his century's steep climb of statistics, who takes a detached
view of any promise that in the century to come there will be peace,
and who, with just a trace of acid in his parenthetical "if we make it,"
counsels that, despite all, we must keep going:

    stay together
    learn the flowers
    go light

Tone, then, as we have been describing it, is more than an inflection
of the speaking voice; it is the mood or quality of feeling that informs
the poem as a whole. The sadness and sense of isolation that pervade

the following poem about loneliness are created by the situation—that of an office worker whose only home is a hotel room—and the poet's use of parallel syntax to convey the day's commonplace events: "he" wakens to an alarm clock, dresses, locks his door, waits for his bus, dozes over his newspaper, passes the day in the office without communicating with any of his fellow workers, takes his evening meal alone in a cafeteria, goes for a walk, and returns to the hotel room:

And the Hotel Room Held Only Him

And the hotel room held only
him

    and the alarm would ring
    and he would dress
    and lock the door   5

and the hotel room held only
him

    and the bus would come
    and he would open his paper
    and then he would nod   10

and the hotel room held only
him

    and the hot dank coffee smelled of people
    and fans whirred, drawers slammed, typewriters clattered
    and emptied eyes excluded him   15

and the hotel room held only
him

    and he just missed the last seat on the bus
    and he sat a long time in the cafeteria over his paper
    and he walked slowly down the neoned streets   20

and the hotel room held only
him

    and he threw up his hand and smiled at the desk clerk
    and he took the half-silent self-service to seven
    and he walked slowly down the worn corridor   25

    and he unlocked his door and closed it . . . slowly

and the hotel room held only
him

Mari Evans

We do not enter the mind of the man, but there are many details to reveal how he feels: the coffee is *dank,* drawers *slam,* typewriters *clatter,* eyes *exclude* him; he walks *slowly* down the *worn* corridor, and he closes his door *slowly.* The tone never shifts; all through the leaden day he seems haunted by his empty hotel room, and that is the effect of the refrain:

> and the hotel room held only
> him

QUESTION

How would you characterize the poet's attitude toward her subject?

The mood is altogether different in Randall Jarrell's "Bats," which describes a flying mammal, usually an object that generates horror. Jarrell's scientific detachment never wavers as it conveys a precise sense of bat behavior. At the same time, the bat is characterized as a devoted mother to whom her baby clings: she takes it with her wherever she goes, nurses it, and puts it gently to sleep. Decide for yourself whether this surprising description heightens the sense of the grotesque or diminishes it.

Bats

A bat is born
Naked and blind and pale.
His mother makes a pocket of her tail
And catches him. He clings to her long fur
By his thumbs and toes and teeth.   5
And then the mother dances through the night
Doubling and looping, soaring, somersaulting—
Her baby hangs on underneath.
All night, in happiness, she hunts and flies.
Her high sharp cries   10
Like shining needlepoints of sound
Go out into the night and, echoing back,
Tell her what they have touched.
She hears how far it is, how big it is,
Which way it's going: 15
She lives by hearing.
The mother eats the moths and gnats she catches
In full flight; in full flight

The mother drinks the water of the pond
She skims across. Her baby hangs on tight.   20
Her baby drinks the milk she makes him
In moonlight or starlight, in mid-air.
Their single shadow, printed on the moon
Or fluttering across the stars,
Whirls on all night; at daybreak   25
The tired mother flaps home to her rafter.
The others all are there.
They hang themselves up by their toes,
They wrap themselves in their brown wings.
Bunched upside-down, they sleep in air.   30
Their sharp ears, their sharp teeth, their quick sharp faces
Are dull and slow and mild.
All the bright day, as the mother sleeps,
She folds her wings about her sleeping child.

Randall Jarrell (1914–1965)

QUESTIONS

1. Enumerate the details that are unique to bats.
2. Describe the mood of the poem. Show how the details build up to create that mood.
3. Read Theodore Roethke's "The Bat" (p. 125), and compare the two poems, focusing on mood and use of details.

The somberness of Thomas Nashe's LITANY (a poem solemn in character, based on church prayer) builds its effect stanza by stanza, with each stanza punctuated by the same refrain. So pronounced is the mood Nashe creates that it is likely to remain in memory long after the impact of the individual images fades:

A Litany in Time of Plague

Adieu, farewell, earth's bliss;
This world uncertain is;
Fond° are life's lustful joys;   *foolish*
Death proves them all but toys°;   *trifles*
None from his darts can fly;   5
I am sick, I must die.
    Lord, have mercy on us!

Rich men, trust not in wealth,
Gold cannot buy you health;
Physic° himself must fade.   *medical skill*   10
All things to end are made,
The plague full swift goes by;
I am sick, I must die.
   Lord, have mercy on us!

Beauty is but a flower   15
Which wrinkles will devour;
Brightness falls from the air;
Queens have died young and fair;
Dust hath closed Helen's° eye.   *Helen of Troy*
I am sick, I must die.   20
   Lord, have mercy on us!

Strength stoops unto the grave,
Worms feed on Hector° brave;   *warrior hero of Troy*
Swords may not fight with fate,
Earth still holds ope her gate.   25
"Come, come!" the bells do cry.
I am sick, I must die.
   Lord, have mercy on us.

Wit with his wantonness
Tasteth death's bitterness;   30
Hell's executioner
Hath no ears for to hear
What vain art can reply.
I am sick, I must die.
   Lord, have mercy on us.   35

Haste, therefore, each degree°,   *class, type*
To welcome destiny;
Heaven is our heritage,
Earth but a player's stage;
Mount we unto the sky.   40
I am sick, I must die.
   Lord, have mercy on us.

Thomas Nashe (1567–1601)

QUESTIONS

1. Show that the poem develops topically and that in each instance the speaker's
   attitude is the same.
2. The argument turns in the last stanza. To what extent does the shift affect
   the poem's mood?

For Nashe's speaker, hearing everywhere the death knell, the sense of life's transience undermines all other values—beauty, bravery, reputation, even the inventiveness of the human mind. Robert Frost approaches much the same theme, though in briefer compass and more modest terms:

Nothing Gold Can Stay

Nature's first green is gold,
Her hardest hue to hold.
Her early leaf's a flower;
But only so an hour.
Then leaf subsides to leaf.
So Eden sank to grief,
So dawn goes down to day.
Nothing gold can stay.

Robert Frost (1874–1963)

As in Nashe's poem the lines are short, the meter predominantly iambic trimeter, the rhyme pattern couplets. But where Nashe is expansive, reaching for another and yet another instance, Frost is compact.

QUESTIONS

1. Explain how such elements as syntax, rhyme, and imagery contribute to the mood of Frost's poem.
2. Describe Frost's attitude toward the theme of transience.

The two poems that follow both deal with the same subject—war—but note the differences in tone and attitude. The speaker in Richard Lovelace's poem is going off to battle; the speaker in the segment from *Hugh Selwyn Mauberley* by Ezra Pound thinks of the war retrospectively.

To Lucasta, Going to the Wars

Tell me not, sweet, I am unkind
That from the nunnery
Of thy chaste breast and quiet mind,
To war and arms I fly.

True, a new mistress now I chase,   5
The first foe in the field;
And with a stronger faith embrace
A sword, a horse, a shield.

Yet this inconstancy is such
As you too shall adore;   10
I could not love thee, dear, so much,
Loved I not honor more.

Richard Lovelace (1618–1658)

The choice the speaker faces is difficult, but he resolutely pursues his
new "mistress," confident that Lucasta, too, shall "adore" (in the re-
ligious sense of worship) once she understands the reasons for his
decision: that his love for her is meaningless if he is without honor, and
that his honor dictates his "inconstancy." To betray his honor is to
betray as well his love.

   Lovelace's ardor and idealism have little place in Ezra Pound's estimate
of World War I, written soon after its close:

from *Hugh Selwyn Mauberley*

There died a myriad,
And of the best, among them,
For an old bitch gone in the teeth,
For a botched civilization.

Charm, smiling at the good mouth,
Quick eyes gone under earth's lid,

For two gross of broken statues,
For a few thousand battered books.

Ezra Pound (1885–1972)

QUESTIONS

1. To what does the "old bitch" of line 3 refer? What does the image suggest
   about the poet's attitude?
2. The tone shifts in lines 5–6 and then shifts again in the last two lines. What
   attitude is implied in each instance?
3. How would you describe the overall tone of the eight lines?

The tone of a poem may prove elusive and escape simple formulation. Is it the wit and ingenuity, the teasing and cajoling, the tenderness, or somehow a mixture of the three, that we finally respond to in the following poem? "Song" is addressed to a weeping wife from whom the poet must soon part:

Song

Sweetest love, I do not go
   For weariness of thee,
Nor in hope the world can show
   A fitter love for me;
     But since that I   5
Must die at last, 'tis best
To use myself in jest,
   Thus by feigned° deaths to die.   *pretended*

Yesternight the sun went hence,
   And yet is here today;   10
He hath no desire nor sense,
   Nor half so short a way:
     Then fear not me,
But believe that I shall make
Speedier journeys, since I take   15
   More wings and spurs than he.

O how feeble is man's power,
   That if good fortune fall,
Cannot add another hour,
   Nor a lost hour recall!   20
     But come bad chance,
And we join to'it our strength,
And we teach it art and length,
   Itself o'er us to'advance.

When thou sigh'st, thou sigh'st not wind,   25
   But sigh'st my soul away;
When thou weep'st, unkindly kind,
   My life's blood doth decay.
     It cannot be
That thou lov'st me, as thou say'st,   30
If in thine my life thou waste;
   Thou art the best of me.

Let not thy divining heart
  Forethink me any ill;
Destiny may take thy part   35
  And may thy fears fulfill;
    But think that we
Are but turned aside to sleep;
They who one another keep
  Alive, ne'er parted be.   40

John Donne (1572–1631)

QUESTIONS

1. Rephrase the argument of the first two stanzas. Given the fact that the poet is departing on a brief journey, how credible is the argument?
2. What change of tone is evident in the third stanza? In the fourth and fifth?
3. What attitude does the poet take toward his wife?

Donne must win his wife from her sorrow; to that end he uses a number of rhetorical strategies, the most common being VERBAL IRONY, that is, saying one thing but intending another. Because he must ultimately die, he is journeying now, in jest, testing his inevitable state by "feigned deaths" (lines 5–8). The irony, of course, is that he expects not to be believed and that his witty treatment of the situation will transform his wife's sorrow.

The irony is more direct and as central to the tone in the following poem, composed, like Pound's above, at the close of World War I:

Does It Matter?

Does it matter—losing your legs? . . .
For people will always be kind,
And you need not show that you mind
When the others come in after hunting
To gobble their muffins and eggs.   5

Does it matter—losing your sight? . . .
There's such splendid work for the blind;
And people will always be kind,
As you sit on the terrace remembering
And turning your face to the light.   10

Do they matter—those dreams from the pit? . . .
You can drink and forget and be glad,
And people won't say that you're mad;
For they'll know that you've fought for your country,
And no one will worry a bit.   15

Siegfried Sassoon (1886–1967)

Sassoon's irony is felt not only in the replies given to the questions
with which each stanza begins but in the laconic tone of the questions
themselves. A phrase like "Does it matter" is monstrously inappropriate
when joined to consequences like "losing your legs," "losing your
sight," or suffering harsh dreams.

In verbal irony there is a disparity between what is said and what is
intended; in SITUATIONAL IRONY the disparity lies between what seems
to be taking place and what does in fact occur, a contrast between
expectation and fulfillment. A. E. Housman was a master at recording
life's ironies:

"Is My Team Ploughing

"Is my team ploughing,
    That I was used to drive
And hear the harness jingle
    When I was man alive?"

Aye, the horses trample,   5
    The harness jingles now;
No change though you lie under
    The land you used to plough.

"Is football playing
    Along the river shore,   10
With lads to chase the leather,
    Now I stand up no more?"

Aye, the ball is flying,
    The lads play heart and soul;
The goal stands up, the keeper   15
    Stands up to keep the goal.

"Is my girl happy,
    That I thought hard to leave,
And has she tired of weeping
    As she lies down at eve?"   20

Aye, she lies down lightly,
    She lies not down to weep:
Your girl is well contented.
    Be still, my lad, and sleep.

"Is my friend hearty,   25
    Now I am thin and pine;
And has he found to sleep in
    A better bed than mine?"

Yes, lad, I lie easy,
    I lie as lads would choose;   30
I cheer a dead man's sweetheart,
    Never ask me whose.

                    A. E. Housman (1859–1936)

QUESTIONS

1. Explain the disparity between what is expected and what indeed has occurred.
2. Describe the different tones of the two speakers and show how their interplay
   establishes the tone of the poem as a whole.
3. On the basis of this poem, how would you describe Housman's attitude
   toward human events?

    In the brief dramatic episode that follows, Thomas Hardy takes an
ironical look at human behavior, playing with the disparity between
what is expected and what is taking place. The sleep of the dead in a
churchyard is disturbed by the sound of gunfire from battleships on
war exercises off the English coast. The dead believe it is "Judgment-
day"; God says no, it is nations practicing for war, and adds an ironical
comment in parentheses.

Channel Firing

That night your great guns, unawares,
Shook all our coffins as we lay,
And broke the chancel window-squares,
We thought it was the Judgment-day

And sat upright. While drearisome   5
Arose the howl of wakened hounds:
The mouse let fall the altar-crumb,
The worms drew back into the mounds,

The glebe° cow drooled. Till God called, "No;   *field*
It's gunnery practice out at sea   10
Just as before you went below;
The world is as it used to be:

"All nations striving strong to make
Red war yet redder. Mad as hatters
They do no more for Christés sake   15
Than you who are helpless in such matters.

"That this is not the judgment-hour
For some of them's a blessed thing,
For if it were they'd have to scour
Hell's floor for so much threatening . . .   20

"Ha, ha. It will be warmer when
I blow the trumpet (if indeed
I ever do; for you are men,
And rest eternal sorely need)."

So down we lay again. "I wonder,   25
Will the world ever saner be,"
Said one, "than when He sent us under
In our indifferent century!"

And many a skeleton shook his head.
"Instead of preaching forty year,"   30
My neighbor Parson Thirdly said,
"I wish I had stuck to pipes and beer."

Again the guns disturbed the hour,
Roaring their readiness to avenge,
As far inland as Stourton Tower,   35
And Camelot, and starlit Stonehenge.

Thomas Hardy (1840–1928)

Channel Firing. ll. 35–36: Hardy alludes to ancient English sites: Stourton Tower commemorates the accomplishments of Alfred the Great; Camelot served as the center of King Arthur's realm; Stonehenge survives as a mysterious prehistoric stone structure.

QUESTIONS

1. Describe the series of events and show how, as the events change, the tone shifts.
2. Show how the details of horror are mingled with the commonplace. How does this contribute to the ironical effect?

3. What attitude does God take toward his creation?
4. What does the last stanza suggest about Hardy's attitude toward human behavior?

Akin to irony is PARADOX, which refers to a statement or situation that seems absurd or contradictory on the face of it and yet may well be true in essence. John Donne's sonnet "Death, Be Not Proud, Though Some Have Calléd Thee," discussed earlier (p. 75), plays with the idea of conquering death and ends on a seeming absurdity, the death of death, although for the believing Christian the concept is obviously not outlandish:

> One short sleep past, we wake eternally,
> And death shall be no more; death, thou shalt die.

So, too, Wordsworth's formulation, "The Child is father of the Man" (in "My Heart Leaps Up When I Behold," p. 51), is seemingly absurd since everyone knows it is the father who sires the child. What the poet intends to say, and we quickly sense this after the initial surprise, is that childhood experiences create the man, obviously a tenable conception. The poem that follows, by Chidiock Tichborne, is developed through a series of related paradoxes:

Elegy
Written with his Own Hand in the Tower
Before his Execution

My prime of youth is but a frost of cares,
My feast of joy is but a dish of pain,
My crop of corn is but a field of tares,
And all my good is but vain hope of gain;
The day is past, and yet I saw no sun,   5
And now I live, and now my life is done.

My tale was heard and yet it was not told,
My fruit is fallen and yet my leaves are green,
My youth is spent and yet I am not old,
I saw the world and yet I was not seen;   10
My thread is cut and yet it is not spun,
And now I live, and now my life is done.

I sought my death and found it in my womb,
I looked for life and saw it was a shade,
I trod the earth and knew it was my tomb,   15
And now I die, and now I was but made;
My glass is full, and now my glass is run,
And now I live, and now my life is done.

Chidiock Tichborne (1558?–1586)

Two other devices are worth noting for the contribution they make to tone: MEIOSIS, which is understatement, and HYPERBOLE, which is overstatement or exaggeration. Consider, for instance, Robert Burns's extravagance in expressing his constancy and affection:

A Red, Red Rose

O, my luve is like a red red rose
   That's newly sprung in June:
O, my luve is like the melodie
   That's sweetly played in tune.

As fair art thou, my bonie lass,   5
   So deep in luve am I;
And I will luve thee still, my dear,
   Till a' the seas gang dry.

Till a' the seas gang dry, my dear,
   And the rocks melt wi' the sun;   10
And I will luve thee still, my dear,
   While the sands o' life shall run.

And fare thee weel, my only luve!
   And fare thee weel a while!
And I will come again, my luve,   15
   Tho' it were ten thousand mile.

Robert Burns (1759–1796)

Dylan Thomas, confronting the idea of his father's death, reacts with a passion conveyed largely by the use of hyperbole:

Do Not Go Gentle into That Good Night

Do not go gentle into that good night,
Old age should burn and rave at close of day;
Rage, rage against the dying of the light.

Though wise men at their end know dark is right,
Because their words had forked no lightning they   5
Do not go gentle into that good night.

Good men, the last wave by, crying how bright
Their frail deeds might have danced in a green bay,
Rage, rage against the dying of the light.

Wild men who caught and sang the sun in flight,   10
And learn, too late, they grieved it on its way,
Do not go gentle into that good night.

Grave men, near death, who see with blinding sight
Blind eyes could blaze like meteors and be gay,
Rage, rage against the dying of the light.   15

And you, my father, there on the sad height,
Curse, bless, me now with your fierce tears, I pray.
Do not go gentle into that good night.
Rage, rage against the dying of the light.

Dylan Thomas (1914–1953)

Words such as *burn, rave, rage, fierce* and phrases such as *forked no lightning, caught and sang the sun in flight, blinding sight, blaze like meteors*— all highly colored and implicitly violent—give the poem a ferocity that defines Thomas's attitude to the prospect of his father's death. At the same time, however, he manages to control the potential excesses of his language through a tightly woven structure modeled on the VIL- LANELLE, the intricate rhyme and line repetitions of which suggest a highly conscious formal concern.*

Opposed to hyperbole is *meiosis,* or understatement. Note how much is left unsaid in Raymond Patterson's skeletal dialogue. What makes the poem effective is that the minimal conversation is so much at odds with the imagined event outside the bedroom:

When I Awoke

When I awoke, she said:
Lie still, do not move.
They are all dead,
She said.

Who?   5
I said.

* The *villanelle* is divided into five tercets (each *aba*) and a final four-line stanza (*abaa*) and uses only two rhymes: line 1 is repeated in lines 6, 12, and 18; line 3 is repeated in lines 9, 15, and 19.

The world,
She said.

I had better go,
I said.   10

Why?
She said,
What good
Will it do?

I have to see,   15
I said.

Raymond Patterson (b. 1929)

In the following poem, a few vivid and concrete details imply the complex emotions of a mother at the marriage of her son.

Mother of the Groom

What she remembers
Is his glistening back
In the bath, his small boots
In the ring of boots at her feet.

Hands in her voided lap,   5
She hears a daughter welcomed.
It's as if he kicked when lifted
And slipped her soapy hold.

Once soap would ease off
The wedding ring   10
That's bedded forever now
In her clapping hand.

Seamus Heaney (b. 1939)

QUESTIONS

1. What emotions are implied by the details in the first stanza? in the third stanza?
2. How do you characterize the mood of the poem as a whole?

Let us consider a final example of tone which seems deceptively simple but becomes more complex the closer we look. Unquestionably the tone of Donald Justice's "Counting the Mad" is deeply ironical. The tone depends partly on understatement, in this case the use of flat, matter-of-fact language to describe a horrible scene. The tone depends, too, on the reader's recognition of an astonishing choice the poet has made, the adaptation of the old toe-counting exercise:

> This little pig went to market,
> This little pig stayed home,
> This little pig had roast beef,
> This little pig had none,
> And this little pig cried, Wee-wee-wee
>   All the way home.

Counting the Mad

This one was put in a jacket,
This one was sent home,
This one was given bread and meat
But would eat none,
And this one cried No No No No   5
All day long.

This one looked at the window
As though it were a wall,
This one saw things that were not there,
This one things that were,   10
And this one cried No No No No
All day long.

This one thought himself a bird,
This one a dog,
And this one thought himself a man,   15
An ordinary man,
And cried and cried No No No No
All day long.

Donald Justice (b. 1925)

The possible variations of tone to be found in poems are as diverse as the personalities and attitudes of the poets writing, and in fact no two poems are exactly alike in tone or emotional texture. It is partly in this diversity that we find both the challenge and the pleasure of reading poetry.

EXERCISES

I. In the following poem, Hugh MacDiarmid adapts Siegfried Sassoon's "Does It Matter?" (p. 213) for his own purposes. Explain the difference in situations and then compare the poems for tonal effect, noting especially the role played by the speaker in each.

In the Children's Hospital

> *"Does it matter? Losing your legs?"*
> SIEGFRIED SASSOON

Now let the legless boy show the great lady
How well he can manage his crutches.
It doesn't matter though the Sister° objects,   *nurse*
"He's not used to them yet," when such is
The will of the Princess. Come, Tommy,   5
Try a few desperate steps through the ward.
Then the hand of Royalty will pat your head
And life suddenly cease to be hard.
For a couple of legs are surely no miss
When the loss leads to such an honour as this!   10
One knows, when one sees how jealous the rest
Of the children are, it's been all for the best!—
But would the sound of your sticks on the floor
Thundered in her skull for evermore!

Hugh MacDiarmid (1892–1978)

II. The poems below all deal with the same motif, the end of the world. Distinguish among the tones you hear and show in each instance how the poet's attitude to the event may be inferred from the dominant tone.

The End of the World

Quite unexpectedly as Vasserot
The armless ambidextrian was lighting
A match between his great and second toe
And Ralph the lion was engaged in biting
The neck of Madame Sossman while the drum   5
Pointed, and Teeny was about to cough
In waltz-time swinging Jocko by the thumb—
Quite unexpectedly the top blew off:

And there, there overhead, there, there, hung over
Those thousands of white faces, those dazed eyes,   10
There in the starless dark the poise, the hover,
There with vast wings across the canceled skies,
There in the sudden blackness the black pall
Of nothing, nothing, nothing—nothing at all.

Archibald MacLeish (b. 1892)

Seven Days

Thunder moved in sleep,
Birds dropped from the sky, white-eyed,
Every animal died
The evening of the first day.
Fish curdled the sea   5
Whales panting on their side
Clogged the uneven tide
The evening of the second day.
On the third day the stars
Darkened, sun and moon   10
Ended their alternate reign.
The fourth day the last leaf
Perished, herb and seed
Shrivelled from the flayed
Earth. Water and land   15
Merged on the fifth day, on the sixth
Darkness and light. The seventh
Became a thousand aeons without word.

J. R. Rowland (b. 1925)

Ordinary People in the Last Days

My mother was taken up to heaven in a pink cloud.
She was talking to a friend on the telephone
When we saw her depart through the ceiling
Still murmuring about bridge.

My father prophesied.   5
He looked out from behind his newspaper
And said, "Johnny-Boy will win the Derby."
The odds against were fifteen to one, and he won.

The unicorn yielded to my sweetheart.
She was giggling with some girls
When the unicorn walked carefully up to her
And laid his head in her lap.

The white bull ran away with my sister.
My father sent me to find her
But the oracle maundered on about a cow
And I came home disgruntled.

The dove descended on my brother.
He was working in the garden
When the air became too bright for comfort
And the glory of the bird scorched his roses.

A mouse ran away in my wainscot.
I study all day and pray all night.
My God, send me a sign of Thy coming
Or let me die.

My mother was taken up to heaven in a pink cloud,
My father prophesied,
The unicorn yielded to my sweetheart,
The white bull ran away with my sister,
The dove descended on my brother,
And a mouse ran away in my wainscot.

Jay MacPherson (b. 1931)

Ordinary People in the Last Days. l. 13: In Greek legend, Zeus in the form of a white bull first attracted and then ran off with the beautiful Europa, promising her that a continent would be named after her. l. 17 *dove:* i.e., the Holy Spirit. l. 23 *sign:* echoes the request made of Jesus by the Pharisees (see p. 420*n*).

Tired

I am tired of work; I am tired of building up somebody else's civilization.
Let us take a rest, M'Lissy Jane.
I will go down to the Last Chance Saloon, drink a gallon or two of gin,
    shoot a game or two of dice and sleep the rest of the night on one of
    Mike's barrels.
You will let the old shanty go to rot, the white people's clothes turn to
    dust, and the Calvary Baptist Church sink to the bottomless pit.
You will spend your days forgetting you married me and your nights
    hunting the warm gin Mike serves the ladies in the rear of the Last
    Chance Saloon.

Throw the children into the river; civilization has given us too many. It is
    better to die than it is to grow up and find out that you are colored.
Pluck the stars out of the heavens. The stars mark our destiny. The stars
    marked my destiny.
I am tired of civilization.

Fenton Johnson (1888–1958)

III.   The three poems that follow are centered on the poets' responses to the
same object. Consider the usual connotations attached to "snake" and then
analyze the differences in tone and attitude of each poem.

A Narrow Fellow in the Grass

A narrow Fellow in the Grass
Occasionally rides—
You may have met Him—did you not
His notice sudden is—

The Grass divides as with a Comb—   5
A spotted shaft is seen—
And then it closes at your feet
And opens further on—

He likes a Boggy Acre
A Floor too cool for Corn—   10
Yet when a Boy, and Barefoot—
I more than once at Noon
Have passed, I thought, a Whip lash
Unbraiding in the Sun
When stooping to secure it   15
It wrinkled, and was gone—

Several of Nature's People
I know, and they know me—
I feel for them a transport
Of cordiality—   20

But never met this Fellow
Attended, or alone
Without a tighter breathing
And Zero at the Bone—

Emily Dickinson (1830–1886)

Snake

A snake came to my water-trough
On a hot, hot day, and I in pajamas for the heat,
To drink there.

In the deep, strange-scented shade of the great dark carob-tree
I came down the steps with my pitcher   5
And must wait, must stand and wait, for there he was at the trough before
   me.

He reached down from a fissure in the earth-wall in the gloom
And trailed his yellow-brown slackness soft-bellied down, over the edge of
   the stone trough
And rested his throat upon the stone bottom,
And where the water had dripped from the tap, in a small clearness,   10
He sipped with his straight mouth,
Softly drank through his straight gums, into his slack long body,
Silently.

Someone was before me at my water-trough,
And I, like a second comer, waiting.   15

He lifted his head from his drinking, as cattle do,
And looked at me vaguely, as drinking cattle do,
And flickered his two-forked tongue from his lips, and mused a moment,
And stooped and drank a little more,
Being earth-brown, earth-golden from the burning bowels of the earth   20
On the day of Sicilian July, with Etna° smoking.   *Mount Etna,*
                                        volcano in Sicily

The voice of my education said to me
He must be killed,
For in Sicily the black, black snakes are innocent, the gold are venomous.

And voices in me said, If you were a man   25
You would take a stick and break him now, and finish him off.

But must I confess how I liked him,
How glad I was he had come like a guest in quiet, to drink at my water-
   trough
And depart peaceful, pacified, and thankless,
Into the burning bowels of this earth?   30

Was it cowardice, that I dared not kill him?
Was it perversity, that I longed to talk to him?
Was it humility, to feel so honoured?
I felt so honoured.

And yet those voices: 35
If you were not afraid, you would kill him!

And truly I was afraid, I was most afraid,
But even so, honoured still more
That he should seek my hospitality
From out the dark door of the secret earth.   40

He drank enough
And lifted his head, dreamily, as one who has drunken,
And flickered his tongue like a forked night on the air, so black,
Seeming to lick his lips,
And looked around like a god, unseeing, into the air,   45
And slowly turned his head,
And slowly, very slowly, as if thrice adream,
Proceeded to draw his slow length curving round
And climb again the broken bank of my wall-face.

And as he put his head into that dreadful hole,   50
And as he slowly drew up, snake-easing his shoulders, and entered
    farther,
A sort of horror, a sort of protest against his withdrawing into that horrid
    black hole,
Deliberately going into the blackness, and slowly drawing himself after,
Overcame me now his back was turned.

I looked round, I put down my pitcher,   55
I picked up a clumsy log
And threw it at the water-trough with a clatter.

I think it did not hit him,
But suddenly that part of him that was left behind convulsed in
    undignified haste,
Writhed like lightning, and was gone   60
Into the black hole, the earth-lipped fissure in the wall-front,
At which, in the intense still noon, I stared with fascination.

And immediately I regretted it.
I thought how paltry, how vulgar, what a mean act!
I despised myself and the voices of my accursed human education.   65

And I thought of the albatross,
And I wished he would come back, my snake.

For he seemed to me again like a king,
Like a king in exile, uncrowned in the underworld,
Now due to be crowned again.   70

Tone and Attitude   227

And so, I missed my chance with one of the lords
Of life.
And I have something to expiate;
A pettiness.

D. H. Lawrence (1885–1930)

To the Snake

Green Snake, when I hung you round my neck
and stroked your cold, pulsing throat
    as you hissed to me, glinting
arrowy gold scales, and I felt
    the weight of you on my shoulders,   5
and the whispering silver of your dryness
    sounded close at my ears—

Green Snake—I swore to my companions that certainly
    you were harmless! But truly
I had no certainty, and no hope, only desiring   10
    to hold you, for that joy,
                    which left
a long wake of pleasure, as the leaves moved
and you faded into the pattern
of grass and shadows, and I returned   15
smiling and haunted, to a dark morning.

Denise Levertov (b. 1923)

IV.   The poems that follow offer a variety of instances of hyperbole, meiosis, paradox, and irony. Show how these devices are used to reveal the poet's attitude toward the subject matter of the poem.

The Ruined Maid

"O 'Melia, my dear, this does everything crown!
Who could have supposed I should meet you in Town?
And whence such fair garments, such prosperi-ty?"
"O didn't you know I'd been ruined?" said she.

"You left us in tatters, without shoes or socks,   5
Tired of digging potatoes, and spudding up docks°;   *weeds*
And now you've gay bracelets and bright feathers three!"
"Yes: that's how we dress when we're ruined," said she.

"At home in the barton° you said 'thee' and 'thou,'   *farmyard*
And 'thik oon,' and 'theäs oon,' and 't'other'; but now   10
Your talking quite fits'ee for high compa-ny!"
"Some polish is gained with one's ruin," said she.

"Your hands were like paws then; your face blue and bleak
But now I'm bewitched by your delicate cheek,
And your little gloves fit as on any la-dy!"   15
"We never do work when we're ruined," said she.

"You used to call home-life a hag-ridden dream,
And you'd sigh, and you'd sock; but at present you seem
To know not of megrims° or melancho-ly!"   *migraine headaches*
"True. One's pretty lively when ruined," said she.   20

"I wish I had feathers, a fine sweeping gown,
And a delicate face, and could strut about Town!"
"My dear—a raw country girl, such as you be,
Cannot quite expect that. You ain't ruined," said she.

Thomas Hardy (1840–1928)

The Fish

I caught a tremendous fish
and held him beside the boat
half out of water, with my hook
fast in a corner of his mouth.
He didn't fight.   5
He hadn't fought at all.
He hung a grunting weight,
battered and venerable
and homely. Here and there
his brown skin hung in strips   10
like ancient wall-paper,
and its pattern of darker brown
was like wall-paper:
shapes like full-blown roses
stained and lost through age.   15
He was speckled with barnacles,
fine rosettes of lime,
and infested
with tiny white sea-lice,
and underneath two or three   20
rags of green weed hung down.

While his gills were breathing in
the terrible oxygen
—the frightening gills,
fresh and crisp with blood,   25
that can cut so badly—
I thought of the coarse white flesh
packed in like feathers,
the big bones and the little bones,
the dramatic reds and blacks   30
of his shiny entrails,
and the pink swim-bladder
like a big peony.
I looked into his eyes
which were far larger than mine   35
but shallower, and yellowed,
the irises backed and packed
with tarnished tinfoil
seen through the lenses
of old scratched isinglass.   40
They shifted a little, but not
to return my stare.
—It was more like the tipping
of an object toward the light.
I admired his sullen face,   45
the mechanism of his jaw,
and then I saw
that from his lower lip
—if you could call it a lip—
grim, wet, and weapon-like,   50
hung five old pieces of fish-line,
or four and a wire leader
with the swivel still attached,
with all their five big hooks
grown firmly in his mouth.   55
A green line, frayed at the end
where he broke it, two heavier lines,
and a fine black thread
still crimped from the strain and snap
when it broke and he got away.   60
Like medals with their ribbons
frayed and wavering,
a five-haired beard of wisdom
trailing from his aching jaw.
I stared and stared   65
and victory filled up
the little rented boat,
from the pool of bilge

where oil had spread a rainbow
around the rusted engine   70
to the bailer rusted orange,
the sun-cracked thwarts,
the oarlocks on their strings,
the gunnels—until everything
was rainbow, rainbow, rainbow!   75
And I let the fish go.

Elizabeth Bishop (1911–1979)

beware   :   do not read this poem

tonite ,   thriller was
abt an ol woman   , so vain she
surrounded herself w/
        many mirrors
it got so bad that finally she   5
locked herself indoors & her
whole life became the
        mirrors

one day the villagers broke
into her house ,   but she was too   10
swift for them .   she disappeared
        into a mirror

each tenant who bought the house
after that ,   lost a loved one to
        the ol woman in the mirror :   15
        first a little girl
        then a young woman
        then the young woman/s husband

the hunger of this poem is legendary
it has taken in many victims   20
back off from this poem
it has drawn in yr feet
back off from this poem
it has drawn in yr legs

back off from this poem   25
it is a greedy mirror
you are into this poem   from
        the waist down

nobody can hear you can they   ?
this poem has had you up to here   30
    belch
this poem aint got no manners
you cant call out frm this poem
relax now & go w/ this poem
move & roll on to this poem   35
do not resist this poem
this poem has yr eyes
this poem has his head
this poem has his arms
this poem has his fingers   40
this poem has his fingertips

this poem is the reader & the
reader this poem

statistic   :   the us bureau of missing persons reports
                that in 1968 over 100,000 people disappeared   45
                leaving no solid clues
                        nor trace   only
    a space   in the lives of their friends

Ishmael Reed (b. 1938)

V.   Below are two poems by Robert Frost. "Stopping by Woods on a Snowy
Evening" was written early in the 1920s; "The Draft Horse" was written shortly
before Frost's death. There are evident resemblances in situation. Compare the
poems in terms of their tone and attitude.

Stopping by Woods on a Snowy Evening

Whose woods these are I think I know.
His house is in the village though;
He will not see me stopping here
To watch his woods fill up with snow.

My little horse must think it queer   5
To stop without a farmhouse near
Between the woods and frozen lake
The darkest evening of the year.

He gives his harness bells a shake
To ask if there is some mistake.   10
The only other sound's the sweep
Of easy wind and downy flake.

The woods are lovely, dark and deep,
But I have promises to keep,
And miles to go before I sleep,   15
And miles to go before I sleep.

Robert Frost (1874–1963)

The Draft Horse

With a lantern that wouldn't burn
In too frail a buggy we drove
Behind too heavy a horse
Through a pitch-dark limitless grove.

And a man came out of the trees   5
And took our horse by the head
And reaching back to his ribs
Deliberately stabbed him dead.

The ponderous beast went down
With a crack of a broken shaft.   10
And the night drew through the trees
In one long invidious draft.

The most unquestioning pair
That ever accepted fate
And the least disposed to ascribe   15
Any more than we had to to hate,

We assumed that the man himself
Or someone he had to obey
Wanted us to get down
And walk the rest of the way.   20

Robert Frost (1874–1963)

Part Two
Perspectives

Poems are complex. As we have seen in Part One, they are unique and self-contained wholes. At the same time, they are also transactions with a reader, involving the reader's interests, the reader's world. We turn in the chapters of Part Two to a consideration of various points of view from which poems may be appreciated. Different readers—or one reader in different circumstances—may discover different values and meanings in the same poem. For instance, a reader with some knowledge of psychology may be able to point out in a poem revelations of personality, or perhaps re-creations of sensory experience, of extraordinary psychological interest. Meanwhile, the student of history, in reading the very same poem, may be able to show the rest of us meanings perceptible only to someone acquainted with historical events at the time in which the poem is set, or perhaps at the time when the poem was written. Other readers—or we ourselves for various reasons—may be especially interested in a poem's philosophical assumptions, or in what it seems to suggest about the poet, or in the critique of society it offers—and many other emphases are possible. The point is that, as long as we are careful to respect the integrity of the poem, each new way of looking at it may show us a new dimension. Each perspective provides potentially an access, a way of discerning implications, of arriving at meanings.

10
Poetry and Biography

When we read a poem by, let us say, John Milton or Emily Dickinson or William Wordsworth, we know there is a person behind the words, a poet whose experiences in life contributed to the choice of subject matter, the imagery, the attitude, or other aspects of the poem. Although we can never know precisely how the poet's experiences come together to inform a poem, some biographical knowledge may often be helpful, and occasionally crucial, to our understanding of the poem.

The following poem by Adrienne Rich speaks both of her own experience and that of an entire generation coming to maturity, as she says, "in those days" (line 2). Much of this becomes evident on a close reading without our knowing that Rich was born in 1929 and married in 1953 and that her husband committed suicide not long before the poem was written. But having these facts at hand makes certain of the references less obscure, more particular.

From a Survivor

The pact that we made was the ordinary pact
of men & women in those days

I don't know who we thought we were
that our personalities
could resist the failures of the race   5

Lucky or unlucky, we didn't know
the race had failures of that order
and that we were going to share them

Like everybody else, we thought of ourselves as special

Your body is as vivid to me   10
as it ever was: even more

since my feeling for it is clearer:
I know what it could do and could not do

it is no longer
the body of a god   15
or anything with power over my life

Next year it would have been 20 years
and you are wastefully dead
who might have made the leap
we talked, too late, of making   20
which I live now
not as a leap
but a succession of brief, amazing movements

each one making possible the next

Adrienne Rich (b. 1929)

QUESTIONS

1. Explain what is meant by "the ordinary pact/of men & women in those days"
   (lines 1–2). How does the biographical information enable you to determine
   when "those days" occurred?
2. How do the biographical facts clarify lines 17–18? lines 19–24?
3. Explain the significance of the speaker's changed awareness of the man's
   body in lines 10–16.

The following poem, which evokes the Salem witchcraft trials of 1692,
is by a contemporary black woman. How does this information about
the poet help illuminate the meaning of the poem? Consider whether
it helps further to know that the poem is prompted by a particular
experience: while Clifton was on a visit with her friend Jeanette Amidon,
a white woman living in Waltham, Massachusetts, the two made a tour
of the modern town of Salem.

In Salem

to Jeanette

Weird sister
the Black witches know that
the terror is not in the moon
choreographing the dance of wereladies
and the terror is not in the broom   5
swinging around to the hum of cat music
nor the wild clock face grinning from the wall,
the terror is in the plain pink
at the window
and the hedges moral as fire   10
and the plain face of the white woman watching us
as she beats her ordinary bread.

Lucille Clifton (b. 1936)

The poem sets up a contrast between two groups of images, the first associated with witchcraft as it was perceived in seventeenth-century Salem, the second a set of contemporary images (lines 8–12) that reflect the poet's perceptions on her recent visit. Clifton is "In Salem," then, in two senses, one historical, the other immediate, and she manages to bring the two worlds into relationship in the poem.

To turn to an earlier period, biographical information is no less important in coming to terms with one of the most remarkable of eighteenth-century works, Christopher Smart's *Jubilate Agno* (Rejoice in the Lamb). The poem was written, generally a line or two a day, while its author was locked away in a madhouse because of his inability or unwillingness to restrain his religious impulses. Smart, according to contemporary accounts, would burst into sudden prayer, shocking, amusing, or irritating those in his company. His "preternatural excitement," as one observer called it, culminated in a seven-year confinement, separating him from family and friends. Though he seems to have had occasional visitors, his sole companion for much of the time was his cat Jeoffry, who is celebrated along with God and the Creation in this excerpt:

from *Jubilate Agno*

For I will consider my Cat Jeoffry.
For he is the servant of the Living God, duly and daily serving him.
For at the first glance of the glory of God in the East he worships in his
  way.

For is this done by wreathing his body seven times round with elegant
 quickness.
For then he leaps up to catch the musk, which is the blessing of God
 upon his prayer.   5
For he rolls upon prank to work it in.
For having done duty and received blessing he begins to consider himself.
For this he performs in ten degrees.
For first he looks upon his fore-paws to see if they are clean.
For secondly he kicks up behind to clear away there.   10
For thirdly he works it upon stretch with the fore-paws extended.
For fourthly he sharpens his paws by wood.
For fifthly he washes himself.
For sixthly he rolls upon wash.
For seventhly he fleas himself, that he may not be interrupted upon the
 beat.   15
For eighthly he rubs himself against a post.
For ninthly he looks up for his instructions.
For tenthly he goes in quest of food.
For having considered God and himself he will consider his neighbor.
For if he meets another cat he will kiss her in kindness.   20
For when he takes his prey he plays with it to give it a chance.
For one mouse in seven escapes by his dallying.
For when his day's work is done his business more properly begins.
For he keeps the Lord's watch in the night against the Adversary.
For he counteracts the powers of darkness by his electrical skin and
 glaring eyes.   25
For he counteracts the Devil, who is death, by brisking about the life.
For in his morning orisons he loves the sun and the sun loves him.
For he is of the tribe of Tiger.
For the Cherub Cat is a term of the Angel Tiger.
For he has the subtlety and hissing of a serpent, which in goodness he
 suppresses.   30
For he will not do destruction if he is well-fed, neither will he spit without
 provocation.
For he purrs in thankfulness when God tells him he's a good Cat.
For he is an instrument for the children to learn benevolence upon.
For every house is incomplete without him, and a blessing is lacking in
 the spirit.
For the Lord commanded Moses concerning the cats at the departure of
 the Children of Israel from Egypt.   35
For every family had one cat at least in the bag.
For the English Cats are the best in Europe.
For he is the cleanest in the use of his fore-paws of any quadruped.
For the dexterity of his defense is an instance of the love of God to him
 exceedingly.
For he is the quickest to his mark of any creature.   40
For he is tenacious of his point.

For he is a mixture of gravity and waggery.
For he knows that God is his Savior.
For there is nothing sweeter than his peace when at rest.
For there is nothing brisker than his life when in motion. 45
For he is of the Lord's poor, and so indeed is he called by benevolence
    perpetually—Poor Jeoffry! poor Jeoffry! the rat has bit thy throat.
For I bless the name of the Lord Jesus that Jeoffry is better.
For the divine spirit comes about his body to sustain it in complete cat.
For his tongue is exceeding pure so that it has in purity what it wants in
    music.
For he is docile and can learn certain things. 50
For he can sit up with gravity which is patience upon approbation.
For he can fetch and carry, which is patience in employment.
For he can jump over a stick which is patience upon proof positive.
For he can spraggle upon waggle at the word of command.
For he can jump from an eminence into his master's bosom. 55
For he can catch the cork and toss it again.
For he is hated by the hypocrite and miser.
For the former is afraid of detection.
For the latter refuses the charge.
For he camels his back to bear the first notion of business. 60
For he is good to think on, if a man would express himself neatly.
For he made a great figure in Egypt for his signal services.
For he killed the Icneumon-rat, very pernicious by land.
For his ears are so acute that they sting again.
For from this proceeds the passing quickness of his attention. 65
For by stroking of him I have found out electricity.
For I perceived God's light about him both wax and fire.
For the electrical fire is the spiritual substance which God sends from
    heaven to sustain the bodies both of man and beast.
For God has blessed him in the variety of his movements.
For, though he cannot fly, he is an excellent clamberer. 70
For his motions upon the face of the earth are more than any other
    quadruped.
For he can tread to all the measures upon the music.
For he can swim for life.
For he can creep.

Christopher Smart (1722–1771)

QUESTIONS

1. What details indicate that Jeoffry is a real cat, closely observed?
2. Explain how your knowledge of Smart's confinement affects your sense of
    the poet's relation to Jeoffry; to God.
3. Show that a coherent vision is being affirmed throughout the poem, or argue
    that the poem is the work of a madman.

Poets occasionally supply their own biographical information in notes accompanying their poems. Read the following poem, "The Lake Isle of Innisfree," by William Butler Yeats and then judge the usefulness of the information he appends. Innisfree is a small island in a lake near Sligo, where Yeats spent periods of his youth. Henry David Thoreau, mentioned in Yeats's note, went to live at Walden Pond (not far from Boston) in 1845, building his own cabin, growing his food, and immersing himself in observations of nature.

The Lake Isle of Innisfree

I will arise and go now, and go to Innisfree,
And a small cabin build there, of clay and wattles made;
Nine bean rows will I have there, a hive for the honey bee,
And live alone in the bee-loud glade.

And I shall have some peace there, for peace comes dropping slow, 5
Dropping from the veils of the morning to where the cricket sings;
There midnight's all a glimmer, and noon a purple glow,
And evening full of the linnet's wings.

I will arise and go now, for always night and day
I hear lake water lapping with low sounds by the shore; 10
While I stand on the roadway, or on the pavements gray,
I hear it in the deep heart's core.

William Butler Yeats (1865–1939)

Yeats's footnote:

> I had still the ambition, formed in Sligo in my teens, of living in imitation of Thoreau on Innisfree . . . and when walking through Fleet Street [London], very homesick, I heard a little tinkle of water and saw a fountain in a shop window which balanced a little ball upon its jet, and began to remember lake water. From the sudden remembrance came my poem *Innisfree*, my first lyric with anything in it of my own music.

QUESTIONS

1. How does the knowledge supplied in the footnote help you to grasp the value the symbol of Innisfree had for Yeats?
2. Explain other details in the footnote that enrich your reading of the poem, for example, the references to "homesick" and "little tinkle of water."

Not all such appended notes are equally useful. Poets may misre-member, prove evasive, or indeed distort for reasons of their own. For example, William Wordsworth, in old age, dictated a series of comments on his earlier poetry that are frequently useful but sometimes imprecise in fact and misleading in their implications. Fortunately there are other kinds of materials—letters, manuscripts, official documents, journals, recollections of contemporaries—to help constitute a biographical con-text for many poets.

We know a good deal about John Milton. That he became blind at the height of his public career is one of the well-known events of his life. His learning was vast, and he seems, at times, to have read everything that reached print. In addition to his poetry, he wrote a large body of prose, much of it pamphlets and tracts on the political, social, and religious issues of the mid-seventeenth century. He wrote in support of divorce and against what he thought were the corruptions of the church; he wrote in justification of the execution of King Charles I and served in the new Commonwealth government (successor to the mon-archy) as Latin secretary, working closely with its leader, Oliver Crom-well. The strain on his eyesight was severe and led finally, in 1651, to his blindness; but even then, with the aid of subordinates, he managed to fulfill his official duties. Not long after, probably in 1655, he wrote the following sonnet in which the loss of sight is intimately linked to the loss of ability to "serve":

When I Consider How My Light Is Spent

When I consider how my light is spent,
Ere half my days, in this dark world and wide,
And that one talent which is death to hide,
Lodg'd with me useless, though my soul more bent
To serve therewith my Maker, and present   5
My true account, lest he returning chide,
Doth God exact day-labor, light denied,
I fondly ask; but Patience to prevent
That murmur, soon replies, God doth not need
Either man's work or his own gifts, who best   10
Bear his mild yoke, they serve him best, his state
Is kingly. Thousands at his bidding speed
And post o'er land and ocean without rest:
They also serve who only stand and wait.

John Milton (1608–1674)

QUESTIONS

1. What distresses the poet more, his blindness or his inability to pursue his active life?
2. To what does "mild yoke" refer (line 11)? Does it seem an adequate description? Why or why not?
3. "Serve" is used twice in the sestet. Show how the way Milton works out the word's meaning helps him resolve his distress.

A curious thing about Milton's sonnet is that he nowhere specifically mentions physical blindness; if we did not know that Milton lost his sight, we could as readily read the opening lines in purely figurative terms, with the "light" representing spiritual or imaginative vision. Once that is "spent," depleted, the poet contemplates a long life ahead in a world dark and wide. That the poem is not usually interpreted in this way is certainly because Milton's blindness is one of the well-known circumstances of his life.

One of the least known episodes of William Wordsworth's life (not disclosed until the twentieth century) was that in the early 1790s, when in France, he fell in love with a young Frenchwoman, Annette Vallon, who bore him a daughter, Caroline, out of wedlock. He returned to England just prior to the child's birth. In 1802, shortly before his marriage to Mary Hutchinson, he returned to France to clear up the past as best he could, and it was at this time that he viewed his daughter for the first time. Among the sonnets he wrote relating to this journey is one that could not possibly have had the same significance for nineteenth-century readers that it has for us in the twentieth century:

It Is a Beauteous Evening, Calm and Free

It is a beauteous evening, calm and free,
The holy time is quiet as a Nun
Breathless with adoration; the broad sun
Is sinking down in its tranquility;
The gentleness of heaven broods o'er the Sea: 5
Listen! the mighty Being is awake,
And doth with his eternal motion make
A sound like thunder—everlastingly.
Dear Child! dear Girl! that walkest with me here,
If thou appear untouched by solemn thought,   10
Thy nature is not therefore less divine:
Thou liest in Abraham's bosom all the year,
And worship'st at the Temple's inner shrine,
God being with thee when we know it not.

William Wordsworth (1770–1850)

QUESTIONS

1. What is the difference in effect if the child addressed is seen to be not any child but the poet's own child?
2. Children born out of wedlock were also called "natural" children. How does Caroline's "natural" condition take on significance from the poet's religious apprehension of nature (lines 1–8)?
3. Explain the poet's argument in lines 10–14. What sort of reassurances is he providing? (For the allusion to Abraham's bosom, see Luke 16:22.)

As biographical information can deepen and enrich our response to poetry, so poetry, when used judiciously, can sometimes illuminate biography. We gain some sense of how Milton responded to his blindness and Smart to his confinement. In Wordsworth's sonnet we have a unique document relating to an event little known during his lifetime and suppressed, after his death, by his family. The danger, of course, is to assume that these were the sole responses of the poets to their situations. Wordsworth may well have felt other emotions at reuniting with his child, just as Smart presumably experienced less exalted moments during his confinement. Milton's life provides ample evidence that he was not, in fact, content to "stand and wait." With this caution in mind, we may nevertheless turn to a poet's work for biographical clarification. Indeed, for particular aspects or periods of a poet's life we may have no better, more revealing alternative than the poems themselves. Thomas Hardy, for example, was exceptionally reticent about his private life, and much of what we know about his response to the sudden death of his first wife, Emma, is to be inferred from a series of poems written when the poet was in his seventy-third year. The Hardys' marriage, childless and unhappy, had lasted some forty years. As you read the three poems printed here, written soon after Emma's death, consider how this biographical information contributes to your response to the poems and the further illumination the poems give to the Hardys' relationship.

The Going

Why did you give no hint that night
That quickly after the morrow's dawn,
And calmly, as if indifferent quite,
You would close your term here, up and be gone
    Where I could not follow   5
    With wing of swallow
To gain one glimpse of you ever anon!

    Never to bid good-bye,
    Or lip me the softest call,

Or utter a wish for a word, while I
Saw morning harden upon the wall,
    Unmoved, unknowing
    That your great going
Had place that moment, and altered all.

Why do you make me leave the house
And think for a breath it is you I see
At the end of the alley of bending boughs
Where so often at dusk you used to be;
    Till in darkening dankness
    The yawning blankness
Of the perspective sickens me!

    You were she who abode
    By those red-veined rocks far West,
You were the swan-necked one who rode
Along the beetling Beeny Crest,
    And, reining nigh me,
    Would muse and eye me,
While Life unrolled us its very best.

Why, then, latterly did we not speak,
Did we not think of those days long dead,
And ere your vanishing strive to seek
That time's renewal? We might have said,
    "In this bright spring weather
    We'll visit together
Those places that once we visited."

    Well, well! All's past amend,
    Unchangeable. It must go.
I seem but a dead man held on end
To sink down soon. . . . O you could not know
    That such swift fleeing
    No soul foreseeing—
Not even I—would undo me so!

Thomas Hardy (1840–1928)

The Voice

Woman much missed, how you call to me, call to me,
Saying that now you are not as you were

When you had changed from the one who was all to me,
But as at first, when our day was fair.

Can it be you that I hear?   Let me view you, then,   5
Standing as when I drew near to the town
Where you would wait for me: yes, as I knew you then,
Even to the original air-blue gown!

Or is it only the breeze, in its listlessness
Traveling across the wet mead to me here,   10
You being ever dissolved to wan wistlessness,
Heard no more again far or near?

    Thus I; faltering forward,
    Leaves around me falling,
Wind oozing thin through the thorn from norward,   15
    And the woman calling.

Thomas Hardy (1840–1928)

I Found Her Out There

I found her out there
On a slope few see,
That falls westwardly
To the salt-edged air,
Where the ocean breaks   5
On the purple strand,
And the hurricane shakes
The solid land.

I brought her here,
And have laid her to rest   10
In a noiseless nest
No sea beats near.
She will never be stirred
In her loamy cell
By the waves long heard   15
And loved so well.

So she does not sleep
By those haunted heights
The Atlantic smites
And the blind gales sweep,   20

Whence she often would gaze
At Dundagel's famed head,
While the dipping blaze
Dyed her face fire-red;

And would sigh at the tale   25
Of sunk Lyonnesse,
As a wind-tugged tress
Flapped her cheek like a flail;
Or listen at whiles
With a thought-bound brow   30
To the murmuring miles
She is far from now.

Yet her shade, maybe,
Will creep underground
Till it catch the sound   35
Of that western sea
As it swells and sobs
Where she once domiciled,
And joy in its throbs
With the heart of a child.   40

Thomas Hardy (1840–1928)

I Found Her Out There. Hardy first met Emma in her native Cornwall, situated on the Atlantic coast; they settled subsequently in southern England, where she was buried. l. 22 *Dundagel:* a location near the legendary Camelot. l. 26 *Lyonnesse:* a legendary area (supposedly sunk beneath the waters) that is the setting of several tales associated with King Arthur and his Knighthood.

QUESTIONS

1. Which lines point to the marital differences between Hardy and Emma?
2. Which lines indicate the effect of Emma's death on Hardy?
3. What emotions seem to prevail in Hardy's assessment of the past?
4. Describe your own sense of the poet, his wife, and the marriage that emerges from your reading of the poems.

The interconnection of life and poem is especially evident in the work of certain modern poets who feel that their best subject matter lies in their own experiences and emotions. Yeats offers an especially intriguing example. Although he drew heavily upon his personal experience, in many of his poems he presented his materials in metaphors and symbols and exotic episodes that served to distance himself from the reader.

Toward the end of his career, however, Yeats appears to have regretted his caution and his decision to conceal the real self: "I must lay aside the pleasant patter I have built up for years, to seek the brutality, the ill-breeding, the barbarism of truth." In a poem written in his last year, he speaks out in a highly personal voice, lamenting his failing powers as a poet. He presents a capsule autobiography of himself as poet, referring to several of the characters based on Irish legend that he had created over the years, showing them now as participants in a circus parade. In the third section Yeats acknowledges the source of all his metaphors, symbols, masks, and disguises, and he resolves to return to the place where all poetry begins.

The Circus Animals' Desertion

I

I sought a theme and sought for it in vain,
I sought it daily for six weeks or so.
Maybe at last, being but a broken man,
I must be satisfied with my heart, although
Winter and summer till old age began   5
My circus animals were all on show,
Those stilted boys, that burnished chariot,
Lion and woman and the Lord knows what.

II

What can I but enumerate old themes?
First that sea-rider Oisin° led by the nose   *Hero of* The   10
Through three enchanted islands, allegorical dreams,   Wanderings of
Vain gaiety, vain battle, vain repose,   Oisin *(1889)*
Themes of the embittered heart, or so it seems,
That might adorn old songs or courtly shows;
But what cared I that set him on to ride,   15
I, starved for the bosom of his faery bride?

And then a counter-truth filled out its play,
The Countess Cathleen° was the name I gave it;   *Written in 1902*
She, pity-crazed, had given her soul away,   *for Maud Gonne,*
But masterful Heaven had intervened to save it.   *whom Yeats loved*
I thought my dear must her own soul destroy,   20
So did fanaticism and hate enslave it,
And this brought forth a dream and soon enough
This dream itself had all my thought and love.

And when the Fool and Blind Man stole the bread   25
Cuchulain° fought the ungovernable sea;   *Legendary Irish hero who*
Heart-mysteries there, and yet when all is said   *figures in a number of*
It was the dream itself enchanted me: *Yeats's poems*
Character isolated by a deed
To engross the present and dominate memory.   30
Players and painted stage took all my love,
And not those things that they were emblems of.

III

Those masterful images because complete
Grew in pure mind, but out of what began?
A mound of refuse or the sweepings of a street,   35
Old kettles, old bottles, and a broken can,
Old iron, old bones, old rags, that raving slut
Who keeps the till. Now that my ladder's gone,
I must lie down where all the ladders start,
In the foul rag-and-bone shop of the heart.   40

William Butler Yeats (1865–1939)

Yeats's shift to more personal statement had great significance for
some contemporary poets, especially those loosely identified by the
name "confessional." Adrienne Rich's "From a Survivor," read at the
start of this chapter, provides a good instance of this confessional mode,
as do many of Robert Lowell's poems. As you read Lowell's "The Old
Flame," which serves as a kind of memorial to his broken marriage,
note the interplay of past and present and the abundance of detail given
to re-creating the poet's life:

The Old Flame

My old flame, my wife!
Remember our lists of birds?
One morning last summer, I drove
by our house in Maine. It was still
on top of its hill—   5

Now a red ear of Indian maize
was splashed on the door.
Old Glory with thirteen stripes
hung on a pole. The clapboard
was old-red schoolhouse red.   10

Inside, a new landlord,
a new wife, a new broom!

Atlantic seaboard antique shop
pewter and plunder
shone in each room.   15

A new frontier!
No running next door
now to phone the sheriff
for his taxi to Bath
and the State Liquor Store!   20

No one saw your ghostly
imaginary lover
stare through the window,
and tighten
the scarf at his throat.   25

Health to the new people,
health to their flag, to their old
restored house on the hill!
Everything had been swept bare,
furnished, garnished and aired.   30

Everything's changed for the best—
how quivering and fierce we were,
there snowbound together,
simmering like wasps
in our tent of books!   35

Poor ghost, old love, speak
with your old voice
of flaming insight
that kept us awake all night.
In one bed and apart,   40

we heard the plow
groaning up hill—
a red light, then a blue,
as it tossed off the snow
to the side of the road.   45

Robert Lowell (1917–1977)

QUESTIONS

1. Show that the poem utilizes three different moments in time.
2. In what ways has the house been modified? How would you describe Lowell's
   attitude to the changes? to the role he plays in lines 21–25?

3. Explain the aptness of the ghost image (lines 21, 36).
4. At what point does Lowell's thought become engaged primarily by his marriage? What aspects of his marriage does he recall?
5. What is the effect of ending on the plow image (lines 41–45)? In what sense is the image both a remembrance of the past and a commentary on the present?

For poets like Lowell and Rich, as well as Allen Ginsberg and Sylvia Plath, Anne Sexton and John Berryman (all represented elsewhere in this volume), the poem often becomes an extension of private history and invites our use of biographical information. There are, of course, poets who resist all traces of the personal and for whom the biographical perspective is less fruitful. The challenge, finally, is to use what we know and to use it judiciously.

EXERCISES

I. The following poem provides details of a single day in the life of a poet, at the end of which he learns of the death of the great blues singer, Billie Holiday (1915–1959). From the particulars in the poem, make as complete a profile as you can of the poet, his life, and his interests.

The Day Lady Died

It is 12:20 in New York a Friday
three days after Bastille day, yes
it is 1959 and I go get a shoeshine
because I will get off the 4:19 in Easthampton
at 7:15 and then go straight to dinner   5
and I don't know the people who will feed me

I walk up the muggy street beginning to sun
and have a hamburger and a malted and buy
an ugly NEW WORLD WRITING to see what the poets
in Ghana are doing these days   10
                    I go on to the bank
and Miss Stillwagon (first name Linda I once heard)
doesn't even look up my balance for once in her life
and in the GOLDEN GRIFFIN I get a little Verlaine
for Patsy with drawings by Bonnard although I do   15
think of Hesiod, trans. Richmond Lattimore or
Brendan Behan's new play or *Le Balcon* or *Les Nègres*
of Genet, but I don't, I stick with Verlaine
after practically going to sleep with quandariness

and for Mike I just stroll into the PARK LANE   20
Liquor Store and ask for a bottle of Strega and
then I go back where I came from to 6th Avenue
and the tobacconist in the Ziegfeld Theatre and
casually ask for a carton of Gauloises and a carton
of Picayunes, and a NEW YORK POST with her face on it   25
and I am sweating a lot by now and thinking of
leaning on the john door in the 5 SPOT
while she whispered a song along the keyboard
to Mal Waldron and everyone and I stopped breathing

Frank O'Hara (1926–1966)

The Day Lady Died. 1. 2 *Bastille day:* July 14, French national holiday. 1. 4 *Easthampton:* resort on eastern Long Island, New York. 1. 14 *Verlaine:* Paul Verlaine (1844–1896), French poet. 1. 15 *Bonnard:* Pierre Bonnard (1867–1947), French artist and illustrator. 1. 16 *Hesiod:* eighth-century Greek poet. 1. 17 *Brendan Behan:* (1923–1964) Irish playwright. 1. 18 *Genet:* Jean Genet (b. 1910), French playwright. 1. 29 *Mal Waldron:* Billie Holiday's pianist.

II. Walt Whitman, a northerner, was profoundly affected by the American Civil War, and he spent much of his time in Washington hospitals ministering to the wounded. His poems of this period, written, as he noted, "on the field, in the hospitals, as I worked with the soldier boys," and collected in a volume called *Drum-Taps*, suggest much about Whitman's moods, attitudes, and activities as the war progressed and his own emotional involvement deepened.

1. As you read the following poems, selected from *Drum-Taps*, consider what biographical inferences they enable you to draw about Whitman's attitude toward the war, his relationship to the soldiers, and his role generally during the period.
2. In what ways does Whitman's "Reconciliation" (p. 9), written at the close of the war, enlarge the biographical context you have been considering?
3. In what ways do "O Captain! My Captain!" (p. 264) and "When Lilacs Last in the Dooryard Bloom'd" (p. 507), both inspired by the death of Abraham Lincoln, further enlarge the biographical context?

Epigraph to *Drum-Taps*, 1871

Arous'd and angry, I'd thought to beat the alarum, and urge relentless war,
But soon my fingers fail'd me, my face droop'd, and I resign'd myself
To sit by the wounded and soothe them, or silently watch the dead.

Walt Whitman (1819–1892)

Cavalry Crossing a Ford

A line in long array where they wind betwixt green islands,
They take a serpentine course, their arms flash in the sun—hark to the
    musical clank,
Behold the silvery river, in it the splashing horses loitering stop to drink,
Behold the brown-faced men, each group, each person a picture, the
    negligent rest on the saddles,
Some emerge on the opposite bank, others are just entering the ford—
    while,
Scarlet and blue and snowy white,
The guidon flags flutter gayly in the wind.

                                      Walt Whitman (1819–1892)

Year That Trembled and Reel'd Beneath Me

Year that trembled and reel'd beneath me!
Your summer wind was warm enough, yet the air I breathed froze me,
A thick gloom fell through the sunshine and darken'd me,
Must I change my triumphant songs? said I to myself,
Must I indeed learn to chant the cold dirges of the baffled?
And sullen hymns of defeat?

                                      Walt Whitman (1819–1892)

A March in the Ranks Hard-Prest,
and the Road Unknown

A march in the ranks hard-prest, and the road unknown,
A route through a heavy wood with muffled steps in the darkness,
Our army foil'd with loss severe, and the sullen remnant retreating,
Till after midnight glimmer upon us the lights of a dim-lighted building,
We come to an open space in the woods, and halt by the dim-lighted
    building,   5
'Tis a large old church at the crossing roads, now an impromptu hospital,
Entering but for a minute I see a sight beyond all the pictures and poems
    ever made,
Shadows of deepest, deepest black, just lit by moving candles and lamps,
And by one great pitchy torch stationary with wild red flame and clouds
    of smoke,
By these, crowds, groups of forms vaguely I see on the floor, some in the
    pews laid down,   10

At my feet more distinctly a soldier, a mere lad, in danger of bleeding to
    death, (he is shot in the abdomen),
I stanch the blood temporarily, (the youngster's face is white as a lily,)
Then before I depart I sweep my eyes o'er the scene fain to absorb it all,
Faces, varieties, postures beyond description, most in obscurity, some of
    them dead,
Surgeons operating, attendants holding lights, the smell of ether, the odor
    of blood,   15
The crowd, O the crowd of the bloody forms, the yard outside also fill'd,
Some on the bare ground, some on planks or stretchers, some in the
    death-spasm sweating,
An occasional scream or cry, the doctor's shouted orders or calls,
The glisten of the little steel instruments catching the glint of the torches,
These I resume as I chant, I see again the forms, I smell the odor,   20
Then hear outside the orders given, *Fall in, my men, fall in;*
But first I bend to the dying lad, his eyes open, a half-smile gives he me,
Then the eyes close, calmly close, and I speed forth to the darkness,
Resuming, marching, ever in darkness marching, on in the ranks,
The unknown road still marching.   25

Walt Whitman (1819–1892)

A Sight in Camp in the Daybreak Gray and Dim

A sight in camp in the daybreak gray and dim,
As from my tent I emerge so early sleepless,
As slow I walk in the cool fresh air the path near by the hospital tent,
Three forms I see on stretchers lying, brought out there untended lying,
Over each the blanket spread, ample brownish woolen blanket,   5
Gray and heavy blanket, folding, covering all.

Curious I halt and silent stand,
Then with light fingers I from the face of the nearest the first just lift the
    blanket;
Who are you elderly man so gaunt and grim, with well-gray'd hair, and
    flesh all sunken about the eyes?
Who are you my dear comrade?   10

Then to the second I step—and who are you my child and darling?
Who are you sweet boy with cheeks yet blooming?

Then to the third—a face nor child nor old, very calm, as of beautiful
    yellow-white ivory;

Young man I think I know you—I think this face is the face of the Christ himself,

Dead and divine and brother of all, and here again he lies.   15

Walt Whitman (1819–1892)

III.   Read the following poem first, then the biographical sketch of Sylvia Plath that follows it. Reread the poem and see if you better understand the poet's attitude and tone, as well as the literal events that are taking place. Then:

1. Write a paragraph explaining the poet's situation described in the poem.
2. Trace the transformations of color in the poem and the sequence of water imagery. How do they relate to the situation and the poet's mood?
3. Describe the people in the poem and Plath's response to them.
4. The hospital stay may have been for a birth, a surgical procedure, or psychiatric care. What is your guess and what is the basis for your answer?
5. What is the overwhelming wish that pervades the poem?

Tulips

The tulips are too excitable, it is winter here.
Look how white everything is, how quiet, how snowed-in.
I am learning peacefulness, lying by myself quietly
As the light lies on these white walls, this bed, these hands.
I am nobody; I have nothing to do with explosions.   5
I have given my name and my day-clothes up to the nurses
And my history to the anaesthetist and my body to surgeons.

They have propped my head between the pillow and the sheet-cuff
Like an eye between two white lids that will not shut.
Stupid pupil, it has to take everything in.   10
The nurses pass and pass, they are no trouble,
They pass the way gulls pass inland in their white caps,
Doing things with their hands, one just the same as another,
So it is impossible to tell how many there are.

My body is a pebble to them, they tend it as water   15
Tends to the pebbles it must run over, smoothing them gently.
They bring me numbness in their bright needles, they bring me sleep.
Now I have lost myself I am sick of baggage—
My patent leather overnight case like a black pillbox,
My husband and child smiling out of the family photo;   20
Their smiles catch onto my skin, little smiling hooks.

I have let things slip, a thirty-year-old cargo boat
Stubbornly hanging on to my name and address.

They have swabbed me clear of my loving associations.
Scared and bare on the green plastic-pillowed trolley   25
I watched my tea-set, my bureaus of linen, my books
Sink out of sight, and the water went over my head.
I am a nun now, I have never been so pure.

I didn't want any flowers, I only wanted
To lie with my hands turned up and be utterly empty.   30
How free it is, you have no idea how free—
The peacefulness is so big it dazes you,
And it asks nothing, a name tag, a few trinkets.
It is what the dead close on, finally; I imagine them
Shutting their mouths on it, like a Communion tablet.   35

The tulips are too red in the first place, they hurt me.
Even through the gift paper I could hear them breathe
Lightly, through their white swaddlings, like an awful baby.
Their redness talks to my wound, it corresponds.
They are subtle: they seem to float, though they weigh me down,   40
Upsetting me with their sudden tongues and their color,
A dozen red lead sinkers round my neck.

Nobody watched me before, now I am watched.
The tulips turn to me, and the window behind me
Where once a day the light slowly widens and slowly thins,   45
And I see myself, flat, ridiculous, a cut-paper shadow
Between the eye of the sun and the eyes of the tulips,
And I have no face, I have wanted to efface myself.
The vivid tulips eat my oxygen.

Before they came the air was calm enough,   50
Coming and going, breath by breath, without any fuss.
Then the tulips filled it up like a loud noise.
Now the air snags and eddies round them the way a river
Snags and eddies round a sunken rust-red engine.
They concentrate my attention, that was happy   55
Playing and resting without committing itself.

The walls, also, seem to be warming themselves.
The tulips should be behind bars like dangerous animals;
They are opening like the mouth of some great African cat,
And I am aware of my heart: it opens and closes   60
Its bowl of red blooms out of sheer love of me.
The water I taste is warm and salt, like the sea,
And comes from a country far away as health.

Sylvia Plath (1932–1963)

Sylvia Plath was born in 1932 and died by her own hand in 1963. She was brought up in a conventional New England environment; her father, who came as a boy from Germany to America, died when she was eight. She attended Smith College on scholarship; had a nervous collapse in her third year, attempting suicide but recovering; returned to graduate *summa cum laude*. By then several of her stories and poems had been published. A Fulbright award to study at Cambridge University in England led to her marriage to the English poet Ted Hughes, whom she called her male counterpart. To earn money they came to the United States, where she taught briefly at Smith, but Hughes was uncomfortable in America and they returned to Devon, England. Her daughter was born in 1960; a miscarriage and an appendectomy occurred in 1961; her son was born in 1962. Six months later the marriage disintegrated, and Hughes left her and went to London, agreeing to a divorce. Plath tried to settle with her two babies in a London flat. Two months later she was dead. In 1960 her first book of poems, *Colossus*, was published; *Ariel*, consisting of poems written in her last months, appeared in 1966.

IV. Following are additional poems by Sylvia Plath. Read them in the light of the biographical sketch of her and determine how the information provided there increases your understanding of the poems. On the basis of all of Plath's poems in this volume, what sense of the poet do you have? of her husband, Ted Hughes? of her father?

The Rival

If the moon smiled, she would resemble you.
You leave the same impression
Of something beautiful, but annihilating.
Both of you are great light borrowers.
Her O-mouth grieves at the world; yours is unaffected,   5

And your first gift is making stone out of everything.
I wake to a mausoleum; you are here,
Ticking your fingers on the marble table, looking for cigarettes,
Spiteful as a woman, but not so nervous,
And dying to say something unanswerable.   10

The moon, too, abases her subjects,
But in the daytime she is ridiculous.
Your dissatisfactions, on the other hand,
Arrive through the mailslot with loving regularity,
White and blank, expansive as carbon monoxide.   15

No day is safe from news of you,
Walking about in Africa maybe, but thinking of me.

Sylvia Plath (1932–1963)

Daddy

You do not do, you do not do
Any more, black shoe
In which I have lived like a foot
For thirty years, poor and white,
Barely daring to breathe or Achoo.   5

Daddy, I have had to kill you.
You died before I had time——
Marble-heavy, a bag full of God,
Ghastly statue with one grey toe
Big as a Frisco seal   10

And a head in the freakish Atlantic
Where it pours bean green over blue
In the waters off beautiful Nauset.
I used to pray to recover you.
Ach, du.   15

In the German tongue, in the Polish town
Scraped flat by the roller
Of wars, wars, wars.
But the name of the town is common.
My Polack friend   20

Says there are a dozen or two:
So I never could tell where you
Put your foot, your root,
I never could talk to you.
The tongue stuck in my jaw.   25

It stuck in a barb wire snare.
Ich, ich, ich, ich,
I could hardly speak.
I thought every German was you.
And the language obscene   30

An engine, an engine
Chuffing me off like a Jew.
A Jew to Dachau, Auschwitz, Belsen.
I began to talk like a Jew.
I think I may well be a Jew.   35

The snows of the Tyrol, the clear beer of Vienna
Are not very pure or true.
With my gypsy ancestress and my weird luck

And my Taroc pack and my Taroc pack
I may be a bit of a Jew.   40

I have always been scared of *you*,
With your Luftwaffe, your gobbledygoo.
And your neat moustache
And your Aryan eye, bright blue.
Panzer-man, panzer-man, O You—   45

Not God but a swastika
So black no sky could squeak through.
Every woman adores a Fascist,
The boot in the face, the brute
Brute heart of a brute like you.   50

You stand at the blackboard, daddy,
In the picture I have of you,
A cleft in your chin instead of your foot
But no less a devil for that, no not
Any less the black man who   55

Bit my pretty red heart in two.
I was ten when they buried you.
At twenty I tried to die
And get back, back, back at you.
I thought even the bones would do.   60

But they pulled me out of the sack,
And they stuck me together with glue.
And then I knew what to do.
I made a model of you,
A man in black with a Meinkampf look   65

And a love of the rack and the screw.
And I said I do, I do.
So daddy, I'm finally through.
The black telephone's off at the root,
The voices just can't worm through.   70

If I've killed one man, I've killed two—
The vampire who said he was you
And drank my blood for a year,
Seven years, if you want to know.
Daddy, you can lie back now.   75

There's a stake in your fat black heart
And the villagers never liked you.

They are dancing and stamping on you.
They always *knew* it was you.
Daddy, daddy, you bastard, I'm through.   80

Sylvia Plath (1932–1963)

Mirror

I am silver and exact. I have no preconceptions.
Whatever I see I swallow immediately
Just as it is, unmisted by love or dislike.
I am not cruel, only truthful—
The eye of a little god, four-cornered.   5
Most of the time I meditate on the opposite wall.
It is pink, with speckles. I have looked at it so long
I think it is a part of my heart. But it flickers.
Faces and darkness separate us over and over.

Now I am a lake. A woman bends over me,   10
Searching my reaches for what she really is.
Then she turns to those liars, the candles or the moon.
I see her back, and reflect it faithfully.
She rewards me with tears and an agitation of hands.
I am important to her. She comes and goes.   15
Each morning it is her face that replaces the darkness.
In me she has drowned a young girl, and in me an old woman
Rises toward her day after day, like a terrible fish.

Sylvia Plath (1932–1963)

11
Poetry and
History

As the biographical perspective views a poem in its relationship to its author, so the historical sees it in terms of the social, political, and cultural context from which it emerges. Indeed, few poems are likely to be without indications of the period in which they were written, though the evidence—language, theme, allusions—may be more or less prominent in a given work. This slave song, set down by Frederick Douglass in his autobiography *My Bondage and My Freedom*, conveys in its few compressed lines a picture of mid-nineteenth-century plantation life from the point of view of the victim:

Song

We raise de wheat,
Dey gib us de corn;
We bake de bread,
Dey gib us de crust;
We sif de meal,   5
Dey gib us de huss;
We peel de meat,
Dey gib us de skin;
And dat's de way
Dey take us in;   10

We skim de pot,
Dey gib us de liquor,
And say dat's good enough for nigger.

Anonymous

QUESTIONS

1. What occupational roles are alluded to in the song?
2. What do you gather about the slaveowner's attitude toward the slave? about the slave's reaction?
3. Would the overall effect be the same if the language and spelling had been standardized?

An American reader of the foregoing poem has some familiarity with the circumstances of slavery in nineteenth-century America. The corruptions at court in eighteenth-century England are more remote, but even so brief a poem as the following epigram by Alexander Pope can evoke that world for us:

Epigram Engraved on the Collar of a Dog Which I Gave to His Royal Highness

I am his Highness' dog at Kew;
Pray tell me, sir, whose dog are you?

Alexander Pope (1688–1744)

It was a world in which kings, in this instance George II, were at the center of power, surrounded by courtiers who were collared, like Pope's dog, and were expected to perform and give pleasure in return for favors and status. Compare Pope's epigram with the following "impromptu," written some fifty years before about another king:

Impromptu on Charles II

God bless our good and gracious King,
  Whose promise none relies on;
Who never said a foolish thing,
  Nor ever did a wise one.

John Wilmot, Earl of Rochester (1647–1680)

Historians generally view Charles II as a shrewd, self-indulgent, and not always scrupulous king who reigned in a difficult time (1660–1685) and whose political skills enabled him to survive a variety of challenges to his power. Rochester's quatrain manages to convey certain of Charles's qualities while giving them a clearly negative cast. Assuming the manner of a loyal courtier, he opens with a toast to the king, but it is a toast that turns, by the second line, into a devastating assessment.

Pope and Rochester are obviously contemptuous of their subjects, and as readers we respond most fully if we have a grasp of the particulars to which they refer. But neither poem is locked into its immediate historical context. Pope's target is both particular—George II's court at Kew—and universal—any situation in which power leads to the courting of favor, the fawning and dependence reducing humans to the status of pet dogs. Rochester's lines extend similarly beyond Charles II, his immediate target, to a type of leader who retains power by neutralizing rather than satisfying the demands made upon him.

For some poems, however, the historical context is so much a part of their texture as to be inseparable from the meaning. Walt Whitman's "O Captain! My Captain!" written in 1865, a few months after the close of the Civil War, is an instance of a poem that can be properly understood only when the historical background is known.

O Captain! My Captain!

O Captain! my Captain! our fearful trip is done,
The ship has weather'd every rack, the prize we sought is won,
The port is near, the bells I hear, the people all exulting,
While follow eyes the steady keel, the vessel grim and daring;
    But O heart! heart! heart! 5
     O the bleeding drops of red,
      Where on the deck my Captain lies,
       Fallen cold and dead.

O Captain! my Captain! rise up and hear the bells;
Rise up—for you the flag is flung—for you the bugle trills, 10
For you bouquets and ribbon'd wreaths—for you the shores a-crowding,
For you they call, the swaying mass, their eager faces turning;
    Here Captain! dear father!
     This arm beneath your head!
      It is some dream that on the deck, 15
       You've fallen cold and dead.

My Captain does not answer, his lips are pale and still,
My father does not feel my arm, he has no pulse nor will,
The ship is anchor'd safe and sound, its voyage closed and done,
From fearful trip the victor ship comes in with object won; 20

Exult O shores, and ring O bells!
  But I with mournful tread,
    Walk the deck my Captain lies,
    Fallen cold and dead.

Walt Whitman (1819–1892)

The imagery makes clear that Whitman's speaker is a sailor, and the poem conceivably could be read as the lament of an anonymous seaman for his "fallen" captain. But to read it in this way would be to make too little of its significance. This becomes evident once we are aware that the year is 1865, that the assertion in the opening line, "our fearful trip is done," refers to the end of the long travail of the Civil War, and that the captain represents Abraham Lincoln, assassinated on Good Friday of 1865. These historical facts impose certain constraints on how the poem and its allusions are to be understood. The ship in question becomes metaphorically a Ship of State, which Lincoln, as captain, has guided finally to port. The "prize" (line 2), peace and national unity, has been won; the nation is exultant; but Lincoln lies "cold and dead." The sailor who speaks, and who seems to be identifiable with Whitman himself, has weathered the worst with his captain, only to find himself in despair, incapable of drawing himself away from the fallen body.

QUESTIONS

1. What other allusions or images in "O Captain! My Captain!" seem appropriate to the historical context?
2. Compare this poem with Whitman's "When Lilacs Last in the Dooryard Bloom'd" (p. 507), also about Lincoln. Which has the fuller range? How do they differ in their descriptions of the effects of Lincoln's death?

Andrew Marvell's "Bermudas" employs similar imagery of a ship, a sea journey, a guiding hand, and a safe arrival. For the historical context, however, we must return to seventeenth-century England, in particular to the difficulties experienced by certain nonconformist religious groups forced into exile by the severe policies of the Anglican Church (see lines 7–12). Marvell's sympathy with the exiles' plight is evident, and in creating their song, "holy" and "cheerful" (line 38), he manages to convey not only their idealism but their sense of having penetrated to a realm of new possibilities. The God they praise has overseen their journey, leading them to the lovely and remote Bermudas, a kind of second Eden. Having left the "prelate's rage" (line 12) of the old world behind, they envision (lines 33–36), almost as a fulfillment of the divine plan, the spreading of God's word beyond the Gulf of Mexico to the new world of the Americas.

Bermudas

Where the remote Bermudas ride,
In th' ocean's bosom unespied,
From a small boat that rowed along,
The listening winds received this song:
    "What should we do but sing His praise,   5
That led us through the watery maze
Unto an isle so long unknown,
And yet far kinder than our own?
Where He the huge sea monsters wracks°,   *shipwrecks*
That lift the deep upon their backs;   10
He lands us on a grassy stage,
Safe from the storms, and prelate's rage.
He gave us this eternal spring
Which here enamels everything,
And sends the fowls to us in care,   15
On daily visits through the air;
He hangs in shades the orange bright,
Like golden lamps in a green night,
And does in the pomegranates close
Jewels more rich than Ormus° shows;   *Persian Gulf port* 20
He makes the figs our mouths to meet,
And throws the melons at our feet;
But apples plants of such a price,
No tree could ever bear them twice;
With cedars, chosen by His hand,   25
From Lebanon, He stores the land;
And makes the hollow seas, that roar,
Proclaim the ambergris on shore;
He cast (of which we rather boast)
The Gospel's pearl upon our coast,   30
And in these rocks for us did frame
A temple, where to sound His name.
O! let our voice His praise exalt,
Till it arrive at heaven's vault,
Which, thence (perhaps) rebounding, may   35
Echo beyond the Mexique Bay."
    Thus sung they in the English boat,
An holy and a cheerful note;
And all the way, to guide their chime,
With falling oars they kept the time.   40

Andrew Marvell (1621–1678)

QUESTIONS

1. What do the objects thought to be present on the isles of Bermuda tell us about the expectations of the voyagers?
2. How do the details used to depict the Bermudas convey a sense also of the England left behind?
3. In Whitman's poem, it is the captain who guides the ship; in Marvell's, it is God. What do you make of the distinction?

The historical dimension is even more pronounced in the sonnet "On the Late Massacre in Piedmont," by John Milton, an older contemporary of Marvell. As in "Bermudas," the larger context is religious, but the focus is on the continuing tensions throughout much of the seventeenth century between Catholics and Protestants, tensions that led to outrages on both sides. The particular occasion for Milton's poem was a massacre of the Waldenses, one of the oldest Protestant sects, named after an early leader, Peter Waldo. Officially excommunicated from the Catholic Church in the thirteenth century for heretical beliefs, the Waldenses had a long and troubled history; and although they had been permitted freedom of worship, they lived uneasily among the Catholic Piedmontese and Savoyards on the slopes of the western Alps in northern Italy. To strengthen his foundering ducal power, Charles Emanuel II, the Duke of Savoy, ruler over French Savoie and the Piedmont, acceded to the demands of the Savoyards that all upland Protestant enclaves be destroyed. He offered the Waldenses a choice of embracing the Roman Catholic faith or going into exile. When they refused, the Waldenses were slaughtered by the partisans of the Duke in April 1655. In addition to "On the Late Massacre in Piedmont," Milton composed the official protest issued by the English government, and he played an active role in arousing Protestants both in England and throughout Europe.

On the Late Massacre in Piedmont

Avenge, O Lord, thy slaughtered saints, whose bones
   Lie scattered on the Alpine mountains cold,
   Even them who kept thy truth so pure of old
   When all our fathers worshiped stocks and stones,
Forget not: in thy book record their groans   5
   Who were thy sheep and in their ancient fold
   Slain by the bloody Piedmontese that rolled
   Mother with infant down the rocks. Their moans
The vales redoubled to the hills, and they
   To Heaven. Their martyred blood and ashes sow   10
   O'er all th' Italian fields where still doth sway

The triple tyrant°: that from these may grow   *the Pope*
    A hundredfold, who having learnt thy way
    Early may fly the Babylonian woe°.   *Catholic rule*

John Milton (1608–1674)

QUESTIONS

1. To whom is the sonnet formally addressed? What exactly is Milton's request?
2. In light of the historical information provided prior to the poem, how do you interpret lines 3–4? the "ancient fold" of line 6?
3. What is the consequence Milton hopes for from the martyrdom of the Waldenses (lines 10–14)?

Milton's sonnet is closely tied to the massacre of the Waldenses, but historical events can serve as the impulse to poems that make only indirect reference to the event itself. A century and a half after Milton composed his sonnet, Percy Bysshe Shelley wrote a series of poems also inspired by a massacre, in this instance a political rather than a religious one.

Shelley was in Italy when word came to him, in 1819, of the so-called Manchester Massacre, occasioned by a cavalry charge into a crowd of some 100,000 workers and children gathered in St. Peter's Field, Manchester, to hear a speech on the need for parliamentary reform. In the massive confusion that followed, hundreds were injured and several killed. The event became notorious and the focus of other protests. But the interesting thing about Shelley's poem is that although it was influenced by the massacre, it uses the event only sparingly, making it rather the basis for a more encompassing statement directed at the general condition of the English working class. The impact of the statement was thought so dangerous by Shelley's friends that they held back the poem for more than a decade. Shelley was long dead by the time it appeared.

Song to the Men of England

Men of England, wherefore plough
For the lords who lay ye low?
Wherefore weave with toil and care
The rich robes your tyrants wear?

Wherefore feed, and clothe, and save,   5
From the cradle to the grave,

Those ungrateful drones who would
Drain your sweat—nay, drink your blood?

Wherefore, Bees of England, forge
Many a weapon, chain, and scourge,   10
That these stingless drones may spoil
The forcèd produce of your toil?

Have ye leisure, comfort, calm,
Shelter, food, love's gentle balm?
Or what is it ye buy so dear   15
With your pain and with your fear?

The seed ye sow, another reaps;
The wealth ye find, another keeps;
The robes ye weave, another wears;
The arms ye forge, another bears.   20

Sow seed,—but let no tyrant reap;
Find wealth,—let no impostor heap;
Weave robes,—let not the idle wear;
Forge arms,—in your defence to bear.

Shrink to your cellars, holes, and cells;   25
In halls ye deck, another dwells.
Why shake the chains ye wrought? Ye see
The steel ye tempered glance on ye.

With plough and spade, and hoe and loom,
Trace your grave, and build your tomb,   30
And weave your winding-sheet, till fair
England be your sepulchre.

Percy Bysshe Shelley (1792–1822)

QUESTIONS

1. Which lines seem to refer specifically to the Manchester events?
2. Explain the dominant metaphor in stanzas 2 and 3. How is the metaphor relevant to the theme?
3. How do you interpret Shelley's attitude to the working men of England in the last stanza?

Shelley and Milton, Marvell and Whitman, Rochester and Pope are writing of specific events and personalities of their own time. But poets may also return to an earlier historical period for their materials, with the result that as readers we must be willing to assume a twofold historical awareness, one relating to the poet's own historical moment, the other to that of the period evoked.

Among the most moving of medieval lyrics is the following quatrain, which dates probably from the early thirteenth century; the moment described goes farther back, some 1,200 years:

Now Goeth Sonne Under Wode

Now goeth sonne under wode°:	*forest, wood*
Me reweth°, Marie, thy fair rode°.	*I pity/face*
Now goeth sonne under tree:	
Me reweth, Marie, thy sone and thee.	

Anonymous

The setting is outdoors, the time late afternoon, with the sun descending beyond the woods and trees (lines 1, 3). But it is clear that the poet is punning on the word "sonne," that it can also mean "son," that is, Mary's son, as in the last line. If it is the "son," Jesus, who is "under wode," "under tree," then "wode" and "tree" also refer to the Cross (made of wood) being borne by Jesus on the road to Calvary. The sunset becomes more than a physical, diurnal phenomenon; its spiritual equivalent is the setting, in human time, of Mary's son. Note, too, the powerful effect of the use of the present tense, which creates a sense of immediacy, an illusion that the event is happening "now," before the poet's eyes. The crucifixion becomes not merely an historical event occurring on a particular day in the past, but a continuing reality at which the medieval poet remains present despite the passage of calendar time.

A common mode of re-creating and interpreting the past is through use of the soliloquy or the dramatic monologue, which enables the poet to move back in time by means of a seemingly historical speaker who may or may not have been an actual person. Edgar Lee Masters uses Anne Rutledge, a real person but one about whom little is known, to speculate on the origins of Abraham Lincoln's vision of America. Anne Rutledge died in 1835 at the age of nineteen. Lincoln knew her in New Salem, Illinois, and the poem, factual or not, accepts the view that she was his one true love:

Anne Rutledge

Out of me unworthy and unknown
The vibrations of deathless music;

"With malice toward none, with charity for all."
Out of me the forgiveness of millions toward millions,
And the beneficent face of a nation   5
Shining with justice and truth.
I am Anne Rutledge who sleep beneath these weeds,
Beloved in life of Abraham Lincoln,
Wedded to him, not through union,
But through separation.   10
Bloom forever, O Republic,
From the dust of my bosom!

Edgar Lee Masters (1868–1950)

For other examples of dramatic monologues with interesting historical implications, see Robert Browning's "My Last Duchess" (p. 173), which is set in sixteenth-century Italy, and James Wright's "Saint Judas" (p. 92), which is set in Jerusalem in the year 33 A.D.

In the following poem, a modern poet, W. H. Auden, turns to a profoundly significant religious event, the origins of the Protestant Reformation with Martin Luther in the sixteenth century. However, we have a sense that Auden's purpose is not so much to re-create for us the experience of an historical event as to propose a provocative contemporary reinterpretation of it.

Luther

With conscience cocked to listen for the thunder
He saw the Devil busy in the wind,
Over the chiming steeples and then under
The doors of nuns and doctors° who had sinned.   *theologians*

What apparatus could stave off disaster   5
Or cut the brambles of man's error down?
Flesh was a silent dog that bites its master,
World a still pond in which its children drown.

The fuse of Judgment spluttered in his head:
"Lord, smoke these honeyed insects from their hives;   10
All Works, Great Men, Societies, are bad;
The Just shall live by Faith . . ." he cried in dread.

And men and women of the world were glad
Who never trembled in their useful lives.

W. H. Auden (1907–1973)

QUESTIONS

1. On the basis of the opening quatrain, what can you infer about Luther's attitude to the Catholic Church?
2. What qualities of Luther's character are implied in lines 1–8?
3. What image is implied by "fuse . . . spluttered" (line 9)? Explain the "Judgment" in lines 10–12. Whose judgment is it?
4. What is the tone of the last two lines? How do they explain the phenomenon of the Reformation?

The extent to which we accept Auden's interpretation depends, of course, on how we choose to understand major historical shifts such as the Reformation. The poem seems to interpret history as the result of the characters of individual personages, and we may want to know more about the economic and historical conditions of the fourteenth and fifteenth centuries before we agree with Auden's formulation. In any event, we may well wonder whether the poem's interpretation of Luther's character takes sufficiently into account the complexities of the "Great Reformer."

It is yet another world, that of post–World War I America, that Galway Kinnell reflects upon and ultimately judges in "For the Lost Generation." Although the time Kinnell refers to is closer to us than the era evoked in Auden's "Luther," a number of Kinnell's allusions may require explanation. The "Lost Generation" of the title, for example, refers to those Americans—many of them writers and artists—who settled abroad, primarily in Paris, after World War I. The opening stanza states Albert Einstein's formulation of the theory of relativity, published in 1912. The "crash" (line 22) alludes to the collapse of the stock market in 1930. The parenthetical reference to Hiroshima and the Jews (line 23) evokes two horrors associated with World War II: the dropping of the atomic bomb on Japan in 1945 and the effort by Nazi Germany systematically to destroy the Jews throughout Europe.

For the Lost Generation

Oddities composed the sum of the news.
$E = mc^2$
Was another weird
Evidence of the existence of Jews.

And Paris! All afternoon in someone's attic   5
We raised our glasses
And drank to the asses
Who ran the world and turned neurotic.

Ours was a wonderful party.
Everyone threw rice,   10
The fattest girls were nice,
The world was rich in wisecracks and confetti.

The war was a first wife, somebody's blunder,
Who was right, who lost,
Held nobody's interest,   15
The dog on top was as bad as the dog under.

Sometimes after whisky, at the break of day,
There was a weary look, trace
Of a tear on a face.
Face of the blue nights that were winging away.   20

Look back on it all, the faraway cost—
Crash and sweet blues
(O Hiroshima, O Jews)—
No generation was so gay as the lost.

Galway Kinnell (b. 1927)

QUESTIONS

1. Describe the view of the world held by the members of the Lost Generation,
   as indicated in stanzas 1–4. What shift occurs in stanza 5?
2. How does the last stanza relate to the rest of the poem? What is suggested
   by the idea of "cost" (line 21)?
3. Trace the poem's chronological development. What implications result about
   the stretch of history covered?

To the extent that they are works of art, poems differ from other
historical documents. It is unlikely that anyone will confuse any of the
poems in this chapter with a page of court proceedings or of the
Congressional Record. Yet, undeniably, poetry and history do often illu-
minate each other, and an awareness of their relation may lead us to
a keener appreciation of both.

EXERCISES

I. The modern poet Robert Lowell frequently uses history as a source for his
subject matter. First, read the excerpt from a letter (dated November 6, 1736)
by Jonathan Edwards, a minister in Northampton, Massachusetts, who is writing

to his friend Reverend Colman of Boston, describing the extraordinary religious revival taking place in his parish. The man who cut his throat was Edwards's uncle, Joseph Hawley. Next, read Lowell's poem which treats this event. Then answer the following questions:

1. What details in the letter find their way into the poem? What does Lowell leave out? Speculate on the reasons for his choices.
2. What aspects of eighteenth-century New England life emerge most prominently from the poem?

> In the latter part of May, it began to be very sensible that the Spirit of God was gradually withdrawing from us, and after this time Satan seemed to be more let loose, and raged in a dreadful manner. The first instance wherein it appeared, was a person's putting an end to his life by cutting his throat. He was a gentleman of more than common understanding, of strict morals, religious in his behavior, and a useful, honorable person in the town; but was of a family that are exceeding prone to melancholy, and his mother was killed with it. He had, from the beginning of this extraordinary time, been exceedingly concerned about the state of his soul, and there were some things in his experience, that appeared very hopefully, but he durst entertain no hope concerning his own good estate. Towards the latter end of his time, he grew much discouraged, and melancholy grew amain upon him, till he was wholly overpowered by it, and was, in great measure, past a capacity of receiving advice, or being reasoned with to any purpose: the devil took the advantage, and drove him into despairing thoughts. He was kept awake nights meditating upon terror, so that he had scarce any sleep at all, for a long time together. And it was observable at last, that he was scarcely well capable of managing his ordinary business, and was judged delirious by the coroner's inquest. The news of this extraordinarily affected the minds of people here, and struck them as it were with astonishment. After this, multitudes in this and other towns seemed to have it strongly suggested to them, and pressed upon them, to do as this person had done. And many that seemed to be under no melancholy, some pious persons, that had no special darkness or doubts about the goodness of their state, nor were under any special trouble or concern of mind about any thing spiritual or temporal, yet had it urged upon them, as if somebody had spoken to them, *Cut your own throat, now is a good opportunity.* Now! Now! So that they were obliged to fight with all their might to resist it, and yet no reason suggested to them why they should do it.

After the Surprising Conversions

September twenty-second, Sir: today
I answer. In the latter part of May,
Hard on our Lord's Ascension, it began
To be more sensible°. A gentleman   *apparent*
Of more than common understanding, strict   5
In morals, pious in behavior, kicked

Against our goad. A man of some renown,
An useful, honored person in the town,
He came of melancholy parents; prone
To secret spells, for years they kept alone—   10
His uncle, I believe, was killed of it:
Good people, but of too much or little wit.
I preached one Sabbath on a text from Kings;
He showed concernment for his soul. Some things
In his experience were hopeful. He   15
Would sit and watch the wind knocking a tree
And praise this countryside our Lord has made.
Once when a poor man's heifer died, he laid
A shilling on the doorsill; though a thirst
For loving shook him like a snake, he durst   20
Not entertain much hope of his estate
In heaven. Once we saw him sitting late
Behind his attic window by a light
That guttered on his Bible; through that night
He meditated terror, and he seemed   25
Beyond advice or reason, for he dreamed
That he was called to trumpet Judgment Day
To Concord. In the latter part of May
He cut his throat. And though the coroner
Judged him delirious, soon a noisome stir   30
Palsied our village. At Jehovah's nod
Satan seemed more let loose amongst us: God
Abandoned us to Satan, and he pressed
Us hard, until we thought we could not rest
Till we had done with life. Content was gone.   35
All the good work was quashed. We were undone.
The breath of God had carried out a planned
And sensible withdrawal from this land;
The multitude, once unconcerned with doubt,
Once neither callous, curious nor devout,   40
Jumped at broad noon, as though some peddler groaned
At it in its familiar twang: "My friend,
Cut your own throat. Cut your own throat. Now! Now!"
September twenty-second, Sir, the bough
Cracks with the unpicked apples, and at dawn   45
The small-mouth bass breaks water, gorged with spawn.

Robert Lowell (1917–1977)

II. The poems that follow deal with different military conflicts: Ralph Waldo
Emerson's with the American Revolutionary War; Thomas Hardy's with the

Boer War (1899–1902) between the British and the South African Dutch (Afrikaners); E. E. Cummings's with World War I. After you have read them individually for content, compare them by answering the following questions:

1. How do they differ in tone and attitude toward the subject?
2. Which poem seems most concerned with the historical significance of the military conflict it treats?
3. In which poem are the particulars associated with warfare most sharply evoked?
4. Conjecture about the reasons for the writing of each poem.

Concord Hymn

Sung at the Completion of the Battle Monument, July 4, 1837

By the rude bridge that arched the flood,
   Their flag to April's breeze unfurled,
Here once the embattled farmers stood
   And fired the shot heard round the world.

The foe long since in silence slept: 5
   Alike the conqueror silent sleeps;
And Time the ruined bridge has swept
   Down the dark stream which seaward creeps.

On this green bank, by this soft stream,
   We set to-day a votive stone;   10
That memory may their deed redeem,
   When, like our sires, our sons are gone.

Spirit, that made those heroes dare
   To die, and leave their children free,
Bid Time and Nature gently spare   15
   The shaft we raise to them and thee.

Ralph Waldo Emerson (1803–1882)

Concord Hymn. The monument referred to in the subtitle recalls the battles of Lexington and Concord, fought in April 1775.

Drummer Hodge

1

They throw in drummer Hodge, to rest
   Uncoffined—just as found:

His landmark is a kopje-crest°   *small hill*
  That breaks the veldt° around;   *plain*
And foreign constellations west°   *set* 5
  Each night above his mound.

                    2

Young Hodge the Drummer never knew—
  Fresh from his Wessex home—
The meaning of the broad Karoo°,   *high plateau*
  The Bush, the dusty loam,   10
And why uprose to nightly view
  Strange stars amid the gloam.

                    3

Yet portion of that unknown plain
  Will Hodge forever be;
His homely Northern breast and brain   15
  Grow to some Southern tree,
And strange-eyed constellations reign
  His stars eternally.

                    Thomas Hardy (1840–1928)

my sweet old etcetera

my sweet old etcetera
aunt lucy during the recent

war could and what
is more did tell you just
what everybody was fighting   5

for,
my sister

isabel created hundreds
(and
hundreds) of socks not to   10
mention shirts fleaproof earwarmers

etcetera wristers etcetera, my
mother hoped that

i would die etcetera
bravely of course my father used   15

to become hoarse talking about how it was
a privilege and if only he
could meanwhile my

self etcetera lay quietly
in the deep mud et   20

cetera
(dreaming,
et
   cetera, of
Your smile   25
eyes knees and of your Etcetera)

e. e. cummings (1894–1962)

III. A number of poems considered in previous chapters deal directly with historical matter. Discuss the significance of the historical context for three poems in particular: Robert Browning's "My Last Duchess" (p. 173), William Butler Yeats's "The Second Coming" (p. 96), and William Jay Smith's "American Primitive" (p. 37).

12
Poetry and Society

As we have seen, most poems have signs of the era in which they were written although the poem itself need not be concerned primarily with illuminating the historical period. At the same time, there is a body of poetry that draws upon the historical scene as a means of bringing into focus the failings or injustices of the poet's society.

W. H. Auden's poem "The Unknown Citizen" gives us a good sense of how a poem can reflect the society that is its subject, in this instance mid-century America, while also offering a critique of that society:

The Unknown Citizen

*(To JS/07/M/378
This Marble Monument
Is Erected by the State)*

He was found by the Bureau of Statistics to be
One against whom there was no official complaint,
And all the reports on his conduct agree
That, in the modern sense of an old-fashioned word, he was a saint,
For in everything he did he served the Greater Community.   5

Except for the War till the day he retired
He worked in a factory and never got fired,
But satisfied his employers, Fudge Motors Inc.
Yet he wasn't a scab or odd in his views,
For his Union reports that he paid his dues,   10
(Our report on his Union shows it was sound)
And our Social Psychology workers found
That he was popular with his mates and liked a drink.
The Press are convinced that he bought a paper every day
And that his reactions to advertisements were normal in every way.   15
Policies taken out in his name prove that he was fully insured,
And his Health-card shows he was once in hospital but left it cured.
Both Producers Research and High-Grade Living declare
He was fully sensible to the advantages of the Installment Plan
And had everything necessary to the Modern Man,   20
A phonograph, a radio, a car and a frigidaire.
Our researchers into Public Opinion are content
That he held the proper opinions for the time of year;
When there was peace, he was for peace; when there was war, he went.
He was married and added five children to the population,   25
Which our Eugenist says was the right number for a parent of his
    generation,
And our teachers report that he never interfered with their education.
Was he free? Was he happy? The question is absurd:
Had anything been wrong, we should certainly have heard.

W. H. Auden (1907–1973)

Auden's title suggests that he is playing ironically with the idea of the
Unknown Soldier buried at Arlington Cemetery, just outside Washing-
ton D.C., as if to ask why not also have a monument to an unknown
citizen. But the qualities of the citizen being extolled by the speaker—
passivity, conformity—are far from the ideal qualities in Auden's view.
It is difficult to believe that "everything necessary to the Modern Man"
can be reduced to the possession of a phonograph, a radio, a car, and
a frigidaire (lines 20–21). It is hard to see acquiescence and a lack of
autonomy—"When there was peace, he was for peace; when there was
war, he went" (line 24)—as the attributes of "a saint" (line 4). Auden
obviously does not believe that the question "Was he free? Was he
happy?" (line 28) is absurd.

    Auden's poem, then, is ironical, his speaker—the voice of the state—
commending those qualities that the poet deplores. By contrast, Walt
Whitman, in the poem that follows, is direct in his criticism, presenting
a long and varied catalogue of the ills of society:

I Sit and Look Out

I sit and look out upon all the sorrows of the world, and upon all
    oppression and shame,
I hear secret convulsive sobs from young men at anguish with themselves,
    remorseful after deeds done,
I see in low life the mother misused by her children, dying, neglected,
    gaunt, desperate,
I see the wife misused by her husband, I see the treacherous seducer of
    young women,
I mark the ranklings of jealousy and unrequited love attempted to be hid,
    I see these sights on the earth,   5
I see the working of battle, pestilence, tyranny, I see martyrs and
    prisoners,
I observe a famine at sea, I observe the sailors casting lots who shall be
    kill'd to preserve the lives of the rest,
I observe the slights and degradations cast by arrogant persons upon
    laborers, the poor, and upon negroes, and the like;
All these—all the meanness and agony without end I sitting look out
    upon,
See, hear, and am silent.   10

Walt Whitman (1819–1892)

Whitman is seated alone, isolated, and yet he seems to possess an encompassing awareness almost as if he were an omniscient god. Looking out over land and sea and into the human heart, he contemplates the world's sorrows, ranging from the agony of the heart—shame, anguish, remorse, neglect, jealousy—to the destructive acts of the hand—war, tyranny, seduction. Though he hears, sees, and marks the sufferings of all victims—mothers, wives, lovers, husbands, martyrs, prisoners—he cannot put an end to such sorrows and is, finally, reduced to silence.

In truth, of course, Whitman has not been silent; he has taken the trouble to write the poem and, at a later point, to attend to its publication. Clearly, then, he wishes to communicate his sense of what is wrong with the world he sees and, by confronting society with its failings, to arouse its conscience.

Much the same impulse is evident in William Blake's "London," which envisions, however, a more directly involved poet who is not sitting in dismay far above the scene but is wandering through the "chartered" streets of late-eighteenth-century London. Here, too, we have a series of observations, but where Whitman offers a listing that tends to be inclusive, Blake is highly selective. The way he structures his materials suggests a coherent vision of the society responsible for the oppression and suffering he encounters.

London

I wander through each chartered street,
Near where the chartered Thames does flow,
And mark in every face I meet
Marks of weakness, marks of woe.

In every cry of every man,   5
In every infant's cry of fear,
In every voice, in every ban,
The mind-forged manacles I hear.

How the chimney-sweeper's cry
Every black'ning church appalls;   10
And the hapless soldier's sigh
Runs in blood down palace walls.

But most through midnight streets I hear
How the youthful harlot's curse
Blasts the new born infant's tear,   15
And blights with plagues the marriage hearse.

William Blake (1757–1827)

QUESTIONS

1. Look up the various meanings of "chartered" and "ban" (lines 1–2, 7) and determine which apply in this poem.
2. Trace the speaker's itinerary through the streets of London, taking into account the people and places named.
3. Explain the nature of the harlot's "curse" and its effect on both the newborn infant and the marriage (lines 14–16). What connection is Blake implying between the institutions of harlotry and marriage?
4. Argue from evidence in the poem that Blake is responding to his society as a whole rather than only to conditions in London.

Robert Bly, a contemporary poet, has spoken of the influence of Blake on his own work, and Blake's impact can probably be felt in the following poem by Bly, written more than a century and a half after the composition of "London." As Blake's London is meant to represent his society as a whole, so Bly's New York seems symbolic of the larger society of America. For his title, he draws upon a political slogan used nationwide by Lyndon Johnson during his presidential campaign of 1964; line 4 seems to make reference to the then recent assassination (1963) of Johnson's predecessor, John F. Kennedy.

The Great Society

Dentists continue to water their lawns even in the rain;
Hands developed with terrible labor by apes
Hang from the sleeves of evangelists;
There are murdered kings in the light-bulbs outside movie theaters;
The coffins of the poor are hibernating in piles of new tires.   5

The janitor sits troubled by the boiler,
And the hotel keeper shuffles the cards of insanity.
The President dreams of invading Cuba.
Bushes are growing over the outdoor grills,
Vines over the yachts and the leather seats.   10

The city broods over ash cans and darkening mortar.
On the far shore, at Coney Island, dark children
Play on the chilling beach: a sprig of black seaweed,
Shells, a skyful of birds,
While the mayor sits with his head in his hands.   15

Robert Bly (b. 1926)

QUESTIONS

1. What is the effect of singling out dentists as Bly does in line 1? What have the dentists in common with the evangelists (line 3)?
2. What seems to be bothering the janitor (line 6)? the mayor (line 15)? Explain the activity of the hotel keeper (line 7).
3. Argue from evidence in the poem that Bly has little faith in the political and religious institutions of America.

Though Bly's poem is closer to Blake's in subject and attitude, it shares with Whitman's the same sense of an overview, of the poet looking down upon the scene he contemplates. The perspective shifts freely from the dentist on the lawn to the movie marquees, to the inside of a hotel, culminating in an overview of the Coney Island shore and a sight of the mayor in his office, head in hands. Like Whitman, Bly makes claim to unrestricted vision and can even read the "dreams" of a president far from Bly's vantage point in New York. That we accept such a claim and subdue our skepticism is owing in part to the forcefulness of the poem, achieved here especially through the series of powerful images Bly employs. Were the poem less effective, our consent would be more restrained and perhaps not given at all.

But there is a larger consideration that affects our reading of Blake, Whitman, Bly, and indeed all poets who write of society from an adversary perspective. If we ask why we are moved by Whitman's reference to "the wife misused by her husband" or by Blake's to the "youthful harlot," we discover that we share with the poet some standard of values against which the failings of society are being measured. We share these values even though we are a part of the very society that violates them and may have, at different moments, ourselves participated in their violation. Blake could have stated that harlotry is wrong and youthful harlotry is horrid, but he omits such explicit assertions on the assumption that we agree and moves on to a more interesting implication that may be more difficult for us to acknowledge: that harlotry and marriage are, finally, inseparable, that the harlot's curse has resonance in the marriage. And he seems to go one step further in suggesting that marriage in the kind of repressive society he has been describing creates the institution of harlotry by forcing the sexual instincts into an unnatural expression based upon money rather than love.

Blake elsewhere writes that "Truth can never be told so as to be understood, and not be believ'd," expressing his faith in our power to grasp the truth instinctively when it is made perceptible. Blake's means of truth-telling is the poem, and it is through the impact of the poem that he hopes to break the "mind-forged manacles" and liberate our inner powers of awareness. Did he not assume the presence of these powers, his task would, of course, be hopeless.

Bly seems to be proceeding on a similar assumption, reminding us, for example, how unnatural we have become (watering lawns in the rain). His title is obviously ironical and asks us to measure the "Great Society" of the 1960s against some ideal of a truly great society whose qualities Bly implies but never formally states.

The following poem by Henry Vaughan, a seventeenth-century poet, presents a similar comparison but makes explicit the values of the ideal society against which Vaughan's own is being weighed.

Happy That First White Age When We

Happy that first white age when we
Lived by the Earth's mere charity!
No soft luxurious diet then
Had effeminated men:
No other meat, nor wine had any   5
Than the coarse mast, or simple honey;
And by the parents' care laid up,
Cheap berries did the children sup.
No pompous wear was in those days,
Of gummy silks or scarlet baize.   10
Their beds were on some flow'ry brink,
And clear spring-water was their drink.
The shady pine in the sun's heat
Was their cool and known retreat,
For then 'twas not cut down, but stood   15

The youth and glory of the wood.
The daring sailor with his slaves
Then had not cut the swelling waves,
Nor for desire of foreign store
Seen any but his native shore.   20
No stirring drum scarred that age,
Nor the shrill trumpet's active rage,
No wounds by bitter hatred made
With warm blood soiled the shining blade;
For how could hostile madness arm   25
An age of love to public harm,
When common justice none withstood,
Nor sought rewards for spilling blood?
   O that at length our age would raise
Into the temper of those days!   30
But—worse than Etna's° fires!—debate   *Mt. Etna, volcano in Sicily*
And avarice inflame our State.
Alas! who was it that first found
Gold, hid of purpose under ground,
That sought out pearls, and dived to find   35
Such precious perils for mankind!

Henry Vaughan (1622–1695)

QUESTIONS

1. Identify the different ills Vaughan finds characteristic of his time.
2. What are the principal characteristics he attributes to the "first" age?
3. To what does Vaughan attribute the differences between the two ages? Does the explanation seem adequate?
4. To what extent do you, as a twentieth-century reader, share the values Vaughan assumes?

Most poems of social criticism are more corrosive than Vaughan's and address issues that are more immediate and volatile. The poem that follows was written at the height of a wave of lynchings of blacks that began after World War I, in both North and South, and continued through the Depression years of the 1930s. Richard Wright's desire to arouse his readers leads him to re-create the experience so vividly that the narrator's identification with the victim becomes complete and he is transformed into the lynched man.

Between the World and Me

And one morning while in the woods I stumbled suddenly upon the thing,
Stumbled upon it in a grassy clearing guarded by scaly oaks and elms.

And the sooty details of the scene rose, thrusting themselves between the
    world and me. . . .
There was a design of white bones slumbering forgottenly upon a cushion
    of ashes.
There was a charred stump of a sapling pointing a blunt finger accusingly
    at the sky.   5
There were torn tree limbs, tiny veins of burnt leaves, and a scorched coil
    of greasy hemp;
A vacant shoe, an empty tie, a ripped shirt, a lonely hat, and a pair of
    trousers stiff with black blood.
And upon the trampled grass were buttons, dead matches, butt-ends of
    cigars and cigarettes, peanut shells, a drained gin-flask, and a whore's
    lipstick:
Scattered traces of tar, restless arrays of feathers, and the lingering smell of
    gasoline.
And through the morning air the sun poured yellow surprise into the eye
    sockets of a stony skull. . . .   10
And while I stood my mind was frozen with a cold pity for the life that was
    gone.
The ground gripped my feet and my heart was circled by icy walls of fear—
The sun died in the sky; a night wind muttered in the grass and fumbled the
    leaves in the trees; the woods poured forth the hungry yelping of hounds;
    the darkness screamed with thirsty voices; and the witnesses rose and
    lived:
The dry bones stirred, rattled, lifted, melting themselves into my bones.
The grey ashes formed flesh firm and black, entering into my flesh.   15
The gin-flask passed from mouth to mouth; cigars and cigarettes glowed, the
    whore smeared the lipstick red upon her lips,
And a thousand faces swirled around me, clamoring that my life be
    burned. . . .

And then they had me, stripped me, battering my teeth into my throat till
    I swallowed my own blood.
My voice was drowned in the roar of their voices, and my black wet body
    slipped and rolled in their hands as they bound me to the sapling.
And my skin clung to the bubbling hot tar, falling from me in limp patches. 20
And the down and quills of the white feathers sank into my raw flesh, and
    I moaned in my agony.
Then my blood was cooled mercifully, cooled by a baptism of gasoline.
And in a blaze of red I leaped to the sky as pain rose like water, boiling my
    limbs.
Panting, begging I clutched childlike, clutched to the hot sides of death.
Now I am dry bones and my face a stony skull staring in yellow surprise at
    the sun. . . .   25

Richard Wright (1908–1960)

QUESTIONS

1. What is "the thing" in line 1?
2. What is implied by "a design of white bones" (line 4) as distinct, say, from a "pile" of white bones?
3. What does the list of clothing in line 7 indicate? How is the line related to line 18?
4. Explain as fully as you can the meanings of the "pity" and the "fear" in lines 11 and 12.
5. Comment on the significance of the title. _

Wright's speaker enters into the experience of the victim, reliving it as if it were his own. Randall Jarrell's speaker, below, recalls his own death in a bitter and disillusioned commentary on the "State" and the horror and impersonality of war.

The Death of the Ball Turret Gunner

From my mother's sleep I fell into the State,
And I hunched in its belly till my wet fur froze.
Six miles from earth, loosed from its dream of life,
I woke to black flak and the nightmare fighters.
When I died they washed me out of the turret with a hose.

Randall Jarrell (1914–1965)

In the following poem, a black poet speaks apparently to black readers, assuming the character of all black women who have seen their men destroyed from the time of slavery, through the rebellion, to World War II and the Korean and Vietnam wars. But the history rendered is a shared one, shared by readers black and white, though they may well be moved in different ways.

I Am a Black Woman

I am a black woman
the music of my song
some sweet arpeggio of tears
is written in a minor key
and I   5
can be heard humming in the night
Can be heard
              humming
in the night

I saw my mate leap screaming to the sea   10
and I/with these hands/cupped the lifebreath
from my issue in the canebrake
I lost Nat's swinging body in a rain of tears
and heard my son scream all the way from Anzio
for Peace he never knew. . . . I   15
learned Da Nang and Pork Chop Hill
in anguish
Now my nostrils know the gas
and these trigger tire/d fingers
seek the softness in my warrior's beard   20

I
am a black woman
tall as a cypress
strong
beyond all definition still   25
defying place
and time
and circumstance
  assailed
    impervious   30
      indestructible
Look
  on me and be
renewed

Mari Evans

QUESTIONS

1. What is the vision of black history presented in lines 10–20?
2. The cypress tree is traditionally a symbol of mourning; explain its appropri-
   ateness to the speaker's sense of self in lines 21–30.
3. What does the poet mean by lines 32–34? What course of action is implied?

Kenneth Rexroth, in "The Bad Old Days," gives priority to his own
experiences rather than to those of a group. What begins as autobiog-
raphy enlarges into a social critique, becoming in the end a poem on
the making of a radical sensibility.

The Bad Old Days

The summer of nineteen eighteen
I read *The Jungle* and *The
Research Magnificent*. That fall

My father died and my aunt
Took me to Chicago to live.   5
The first thing I did was to take
A streetcar to the stockyards.
In the winter afternoon,
Gritty and fetid, I walked
Through the filthy snow, through the   10
Squalid streets, looking shyly
Into the people's faces,
Those who were home in the daytime.
Debauched and exhausted faces,
Starved and looted brains, faces   15
Like the faces in the senile
And insane wards of charity
Hospitals. Predatory
Faces of little children.
Then as the soiled twilight darkened,   20
Under the green gas lamps, and the
Sputtering purple arc lamps,
The faces of the men coming
Home from work, some still alive with
The last pulse of hope or courage,   25
Some sly and bitter, some smart and
Silly, most of them, already
Broken and empty, no life,
Only blinding tiredness, worse
Than any tired animal.   30
The sour smells of a thousand
Suppers of fried potatoes and
Fried cabbage bled into the street.
I was giddy and sick, and out
Of my misery I felt rising   35
A terrible anger and out
Of the anger, an absolute vow.
Today the evil is clean
And prosperous, but it is
Everywhere, you don't have to   40
Take a streetcar to find it,
And it is the same evil.
And the misery, and the
Anger, and the vow are the same.

Kenneth Rexroth (b. 1905)

The Bad Old Days. l. 2 *The Jungle:* Upton Sinclair's *The Jungle* (1906) exposed the corrupt
meat-packing industry in Chicago. ll. 2–3 *The Research Magnificent:* H. G. Wells's *The
Research Magnificent* (1915) described the search for a program to rescue a floundering
society.

1. What connections seem to exist between the events referred to in lines 1–5?
2. Trace the speaker's wanderings in lines 7–30. What human types and levels of society does he encounter?
3. To what extent has the poem prepared you for the reaction described in lines 34–37? At what is the speaker angry? Define his "vow" as best you can.
4. Explain the poet's characterization of today's evil (lines 38–42).
5. What do the last seven lines imply of the poet's life as a whole?

We should not close this chapter without taking note of an argument sometimes made against protest poems such as those we have been considering—namely, that the aesthetic quality of a poem is likely to be neglected when poets are motivated by hopes of social improvement. Certainly it is possible to write a bad poem in a good cause, but it hardly follows that poets must choose between fulfilling the aesthetic and technical demands of a poem and giving expression to their, and our, consciences. The impulse to inveigh against injustice, to force a reluctant public to acknowledge its own best ideals, is an ancient one and as proper to poetry as to any other form of human endeavor.

EXERCISES

I.   Study the two poems that follow for the social critique they make and the positive values that underlie the critique. In which of the poems are those values more explicit? Explain.

The Latest Decalogue

Thou shalt have one God only; who
Would be at the expense of two?
No graven images may be
Worshipped, except the currency.
Swear not at all; for, for thy curse   5
Thine enemy is none the worse.
At church on Sunday to attend
Will serve to keep the world thy friend.
Honor thy parents; that is, all
From whom advancement may befall.   10
Thou shalt not kill; but need'st not strive
Officiously to keep alive.
Do not adultery commit;
Advantage rarely comes of it.
Thou shalt not steal; an empty feat,   15

When it's so lucrative to cheat.
Bear not false witness; let the lie
Have time on its own wings to fly.
Thou shalt not covet, but tradition
Approves all forms of competition.   20

Arthur Hugh Clough (1819–1861)

How Beastly the Bourgeois Is

How beastly the bourgeois is
especially the male of the species—

Presentable eminently presentable—
shall I make you a present of him?

Isn't he handsome? isn't he healthy? Isn't he a fine specimen?   5
doesn't he look the fresh clean englishman, outside?

Isn't it god's own image? tramping his thirty miles a day
after partridges, or a little rubber ball?
wouldn't you like to be like that, well off, and quite the thing?

Oh, but wait!   10
Let him meet a new emotion, let him be faced with another man's need,
let him come home to a bit of moral difficulty, let life face him with a new
    demand on his understanding
and then watch him go soggy, like a wet meringue.
Watch him turn into a mess, either a fool or a bully.
Just watch the display of him, confronted with a new demand on his
    intelligence,   15
a new life-demand.

How beastly the bourgeois is
especially the male of the species—

Nicely groomed, like a mushroom
standing there so sleek and erect and eyeable—   20
and like a fungus, living on the remains of bygone life
sucking his life out of the dead leaves of greater life than his own.

And even so, he's stale, he's been there too long.
Touch him, and you'll find he's all gone inside
just like an old mushroom, all wormy inside, and hollow   25
under a smooth skin and an upright appearance.

Full of seething, wormy, hollow feelings
rather nasty—
How beastly the bourgeois is!

Standing in their thousands, these appearances, in damp England   30
what a pity they can't all be kicked over
like sickening toadstools, and left to melt back, swiftly
into the soil of England.

D. H. Lawrence (1885–1930)

II. Following are three poems that use war as their subject matter. As you read them, consider the following issues:

1. Determine in each instance how the poem functions as social criticism.
2. How is the speaker in each poem involved in the action of the poem?
3. Decide which poem makes the most effective protest and justify your choice.

What Were They Like?

(Questions and Answers)

1) Did the people of Viet Nam
    use lanterns of stone?
2) Did they hold ceremonies
    to reverence the opening of buds?
3) Were they inclined to rippling laughter?   5
4) Did they use bone and ivory,
    jade and silver, for ornament?
5) Had they an epic poem?
6) Did they distinguish between speech and singing?

1) Sir, their light hearts turned to stone.   10
    It is not remembered whether in gardens
    stone lanterns illumined pleasant ways.
2) Perhaps they gathered once to delight in blossom,
    but after the children were killed
    there were no more buds.   15
3) Sir, laughter is bitter to the burned mouth.
4) A dream ago, perhaps. Ornament is for joy.
    All the bones were charred.
5) It is not remembered. Remember,
    most were peasants; their life   20
    was in rice and bamboo.
    When peaceful clouds were reflected in the paddies

and the water-buffalo stepped surely along terraces,
maybe fathers told their sons old tales.
When bombs smashed the mirrors   25
there was time only to scream.
6) There is an echo yet, it is said,
of their speech which was like a song.
It is reported their singing resembled
the flight of moths in moonlight.   30
Who can say? It is silent now.

Denise Levertov (b. 1923)

The Fury of Aerial Bombardment

You would think the fury of aerial bombardment
Would rouse God to relent; the infinite spaces
Are still silent. He looks on shock-pried faces.
History, even, does not know what is meant.

You would feel that after so many centuries   5
God would give man to repent; yet he can kill
As Cain could, but with multitudinous will,
No farther advanced than in his ancient furies.

Was man made stupid to see his own stupidity?
Is God by definition indifferent, beyond us all?   10
Is the eternal truth man's fighting soul
Wherein the Beast ravens in its own avidity?

Of Van Wettering I speak, and Averill,
Names on a list, whose faces I do not recall
But they are gone to early death, who late in school   15
Distinguished the belt feed lever from the belt holding pawl.

Richard Eberhart (b. 1904)

Naming of Parts

Today we have naming of parts. Yesterday,
We had daily cleaning. And tomorrow morning,
We shall have what to do after firing. But today,
Today we have naming of parts. Japonica
Glistens like coral in all of the neighboring gardens,   5
    And today we have naming of parts.

This is the lower sling swivel. And this
Is the upper sling swivel, whose use you will see,
When you are given your slings. And this is the piling swivel,
Which in your case you have not got. The branches   10
Hold in the gardens their silent, eloquent gestures,
     Which in our case we have not got.

This is the safety-catch, which is always released
With an easy flick of the thumb. And please do not let me
See anyone using his finger. You can do it quite easy   15
If you have any strength in your thumb. The blossoms
Are fragile and motionless, never letting anyone see
     Any of them using their finger.

And this you can see is the bolt. The purpose of this
Is to open the breech, as you see. We can slide it   20
Rapidly backwards and forwards: we call this
Easing the spring. And rapidly backwards and forwards
The early bees are assaulting and fumbling the flowers:
     They call it easing the Spring.

They call it easing the Spring: it is perfectly easy   25
If you have any strength in your thumb: like the bolt,
And the breech, and the cocking-piece, and the point of balance,
Which in our case we have not got; and the almond-blossom
Silent in all of the gardens and the bees going backwards and forwards,
     For today we have naming of parts.   30

Henry Reed (b. 1914)

III.   The following poem is written from the point of view of Jewish victims
of the Nazi terror during World War II. The narrator speaks as if he were present
at an international conference.

The Permanent Delegate

My name is Jew.
   I come from the land of skeleton.
They beat me in Berlin,
     tortured me in Warsaw,
        shot me in Lublin   5
And I am still here—the ash of my bones
   a glowing monument, a fiery headstone.

I am the scorched hair of a virgin's bright curls
   smoothed and patted by anxious hands
I am a maddened mother's futile tears
   soothing in vain a hundred anguished hurts. 10

I am the spasm of a body convulsed in flames,
   the crumbling of a skeleton,
the boiling of blood, shriveling of flesh,
   smouldering ash of six million— 15
ashes of body, of brain, of vision, of work
   ashes of genius and dreams,
      ashes of God's master stroke—Man

Count the limbs, gentlemen—
   match them if you can in pairs. 20
     It can't be done.
For I am one ghost of six million.
Out of all the ashes I have become one
And the dream lies broken and spit on.

I am here to tell you, gentlemen 25
   it's a lie—the world is not yet Hitler-free.
Millions see it, condemn it,
   cry out my pain and warn you.

But you are moved like a granite statue
   by the prick of a pin. 30
Therefore I have come,
   uninvited, unwelcome
     bringing a message
from the land of skeleton.

I am grafting my ash to your souls. 35
I am hanging my dreams around your necks.
I am blotting out the sun from your day
                with my shadow.
I am tearing the quiet of your night
                with the shrieks of my tortures. 40
I will beat at your conscience
   with the hands of a million dead children and
I will pick at your brains
              with my maggots.

Yea, though you split the atom to infinity 45
   you will see my face before your eyes.
I sit at all the round tables

At every conference I am a delegate,
my credentials signed by six million
   from the land of skeleton
and you will never get rid of me
   until the world is Hitler-free.

50

     Yuri Suhl (b. 1908)
       (Trans. from the Yiddish by Max Rosenfeld and Walter Lowenfels)

1. Explain the implications of both "permanent" and "delegate" as they apply
   to the poem.
2. To whom is the delegate speaking? Explain the message in lines 25–28. What
   in the message might make him "uninvited, unwelcome" (line 32)?
3. The delegate is a Jew speaking directly of the Jewish experience, and yet the
   protest being made seems to extend beyond. Explain the poem's wider
   application.

IV. In the poems that follow, Stanley Kunitz and Gerard Manley Hopkins take
as their subject a similar act of destruction; both also assume that the preservation
of nature is a value they and their readers will agree upon. Despite the parallels,
however, one of the poems is devoted primarily to social protest, the other is
not.

The War Against the Trees

The man who sold his lawn to standard oil
Joked with his neighbors come to watch the show
While the bulldozers, drunk with gasoline,
Tested the virtue of the soil
Under the branchy sky
By overthrowing first the privet-row.

5

Forsythia-forays and hydrangea-raids
Were but preliminaries to a war
Against the great-grandfathers of the town,
So freshly lopped and maimed.
They struck and struck again,
And with each elm a century went down.

10

All day the hireling engines charged the trees,
Subverting them by hacking underground
In grub-dominions, where dark summer's mole
Rampages through his halls,
Till a northern seizure shook
Those crowns, forcing the giants to their knees.

15

I saw the ghosts of children at their games
Racing beyond their childhood in the shade,   20
And while the green world turned its death-foxed page
And a red wagon wheeled,
I watched them disappear
Into the suburbs of their grievous age.

Ripped from the craters much too big for hearts   25
The club-roots bared their amputated coils,
Raw gorgons matted blind, whose pocks and scars
Cried Moon! on a corner lot
One witness-moment, caught
In the rear-view mirrors of the passing cars.   30

Stanley Kunitz (b. 1905)

Binsey Poplars

Felled 1879

My aspens dear, whose airy cages quelled,
Quelled or quenched in leaves the leaping sun,
All felled, felled, are all felled;
    Of a fresh and following folded rank
        Not spared, not one   5
        That dandled and sandalled
     Shadow that swam or sank
On meadow and river and wind-wandering
    weed-winding bank.

O if we but knew what we do   10
      When we delve or hew—
   Hack and rack the growing green!
      Since country is so tender
   To touch, her being só slender,
   That, like this sleek and seeing ball   15
   But a prick will make no eye at all,
   Where we, even where we mean
      To mend her we end her,
    When we hew or delve:
After-comers cannot guess the beauty been.   20
  Ten or twelve, only ten or twelve
    Strokes of havoc únselve°   *destroy the essence of*

The sweet especial scene,
Rural scene, a rural scene,
Sweet especial rural scene.   25

Gerard Manley Hopkins (1844–1889)

1. Hopkins speaks of the loss of "My aspens dear," Kunitz of the loss of "the great-grandfathers of the town." What do the phrasings suggest about the social dimension of each poem?
2. How do the contrasting moods and tones of the poems affect the protest each makes?
3. Which of the two poems might lead the reader to specific action? Which would not? Explain your answer.

13
Poetry and
Philosophy

In the poems discussed in chapter 12, the poets' primary attention was to the failings of society. Richard Wright and Mari Evans dealt with the unhappy history of blacks in America; Kenneth Rexroth with the oppression of the poor; D. H. Lawrence with the moral and emotional failures of the bourgeois male. In each instance, as we saw, a set of positive values suggested the need for social reform. These values, in turn, rest upon fundamental notions about the world that belong to the realm of philosophy. Kenneth Rexroth, for example, conveys his anger at the poverty and stunted lives he has witnessed and vows to fight exploitation. The philosophical notion that underlies his protest is that of the worth, dignity, and equality of individual human beings.

Directly or indirectly, poets have always engaged broad philosophical questions such as the nature of good and evil, the attributes of being, the relation of the individual to the universe, the possibilities and limits of knowledge, the meaning of time. In the following poem, for instance, A. E. Housman offers a justification of certain themes that recur in his poetry, but in the process he speaks to the issue of man's lot in the universal scheme of things:

They Say My Verse Is Sad: No Wonder

They say my verse is sad: no wonder;
  Its narrow measure spans

Tears of eternity, and sorrow,
   Not mine, but man's.

This is for all ill-treated fellows
   Unborn and unbegot,
For them to read when they're in trouble
   And I am not.

A. E. Housman (1859–1936)

The poet's life is embittered by his sense of cosmic injustice, a condition he shares with "all ill-treated fellows" (line 5). His sorrow is not his alone, "but man's" (line 4), and spans generations, reflecting what always has been and always will be. He writes his poems for those still unbegotten, to reassure them that what they will suffer is no more unique to them than it has been to him. The remedy he envisions is death, when his "trouble" will end and theirs, the unborn's, will have begun.

Notice how Housman's sense of the human "trouble"—of the unhappiness and disappointment that must always beset human beings—informs another poem of his that follows. Set presumably in ancient Greece, the poem is sufficiently universal to apply as well to a local English town.

To an Athlete Dying Young

The time you won your town the race
We chaired you through the market-place;
Man and boy stood cheering by,
And home we brought you shoulder-high.

Today, the road all runners come,   5
Shoulder-high we bring you home,
And set you at your threshold down,
Townsman of a stiller town.

Smart lad, to slip betimes away
From fields where glory does not stay,   10
And early though the laurel grows
It withers quicker than the rose.

Eyes the shady night has shut
Cannot see the record cut,
And silence sounds no worse than cheers   15
After earth has stopped the ears.

Now you will not swell the rout
Of lads that wore their honors out,
Runners whom renown outran
And the name died before the man.   20

So set, before its echoes fade,
The fleet foot on the sill of shade,
And hold to the low lintel up
The still-defended challenge-cup.

And round that early-laureled head   25
Will flock to gaze the strengthless dead,
And find unwithered on its curls
The garland briefer than a girl's.

A. E. Housman (1859–1936)

QUESTIONS

1. Explain the argument presented in lines 9–20 to console the athlete. How
   does this argument relate to the speaker's image of the afterlife in lines 21–28?
2. How would you describe Housman's vision of life? Is it essentially the same
   in both poems? How or how not?

Housman's idea of the human being's place in the universe may be
compared with Alexander Pope's formulation in the excerpt below from
An Essay on Man. Like Housman, Pope accepts the frustrations and
peculiarities of the human role but views them as part of a universal
plan of cosmic order. His opening injunction, that his readers study
themselves rather than God, implies limits on what the human mind
can comprehend, for reasons explained in the couplets that follow it:

from *An Essay on Man**

Know then thyself, presume not God to scan;
The proper study of mankind is Man.
Placed on this isthmus of a middle state,
A being darkly wise, and rudely great:
With too much knowledge for the skeptic side,   5
With too much weakness for the Stoic's pride,
He hangs between; in doubt to act, or rest,

* Epistle II, lines 1–18.

In doubt to deem himself a god, or beast;
In doubt his mind or body to prefer,
Born but to die, and reasoning but to err;   10
Alike in ignorance, his reason such,
Whether he thinks too little, or too much:
Chaos of thought and passion, all confused;
Still by himself abused, or disabused;
Created half to rise, and half to fall;   15
Great lord of all things, yet a prey to all;
Sole judge of truth, in endless error hurled:
The glory, jest, and riddle of the world!

Alexander Pope (1688–1744)

Pope envisions human beings as a composite of paradoxes: Born but to die, they reason but to err; trapped in a "middle state," uncertain whether they are god or beast, they "[hang] between" their aspirations and their more humbling reality. Thought pulls them one way, passions another; supposed masters of all things, they are prey to all. Because their contradictions lie within, "all confused" (literally, all fused together), they live in a chaos of awareness, thus justifying, in Pope's eyes, the larger summation of humankind as "The glory, jest, and riddle of the world!"

Pope's metaphors imply a vertical scheme with God above, beast below, and humans in the middle. Mind is associated with God above, body with beast below (lines 8–9); because human beings are a unique composite of both, they can be said "half to rise, and half to fall" (line 15). But these lines are explanations of the world order as well as metaphors; Pope means us to accept a hierarchy of God, human, and beast, and a conception of the self that sees our potential greatness as impeded by the animal part of our nature.

Pope's principal ideas are not original with him but go back through the Renaissance and Middle Ages and have their roots in ancient Greece. Shakespeare gives expression to similar conceptions in the passage given here from his play *Troilus and Cressida*. Order and harmony are presented as the shaping pattern of the universe, and any violation of the social order is seen as a disruption of nature itself. The play is set during the war between the Greeks and the Trojans; Ulysses is explaining that the superior Greek army has not yet succeeded in its conquest of Troy because the great Greek warrior Achilles has defied the authority of the leader Agamemnon. According to Ulysses, the refusal to acknowledge hierarchy of rank causes chaos and thus jeopardizes the victory and the greatness of Greece:

from *Troilus and Cressida**

The heavens themselves, the planets, and this center°	*earth*
Observe degree, priority, and place,	
Insisture°, course, proportion, season, form,	*constancy*
Office, and custom, in all line of order;	
And therefore is the glorious planet Sol°	*the sun* 5
In noble eminence enthron'd and spher'd	
Amidst the other, whose med'cinable eye	
Corrects the ill aspects of planets evil,	
And posts°, like the commandment of a king,	*speeds*
Sans check°, to good and bad. But when the planets	*without hindrance* 10
In evil mixture to disorder wander,	
What plagues and what portents, what mutiny,	
What raging of the sea, shaking of earth,	
Commotion in the winds! Frights, changes, horrors	
Divert and crack, rend and deracinate°	*uproot* 15
The unity and married calm of states	
Quite from their fixure. O, when degree° is shak'd,	*rank, authority*
Which is the ladder to all high designs,	
The enterprise is sick. How could communities,	
Degrees in schools, and brotherhoods in cities,	20
Peaceful commerce from dividable° shores,	*separate*
The primogenitive and due of birth,	
Prerogative of age, crowns, scepters, laurels,	
But by degree, stand in authentic° place?	*true, legal*
Take but degree away, untune that string,	25
And hark, what discord follows! Each thing meets	
In mere oppugnancy°. The bounded waters	*hostility*
Should° lift their bosoms higher than the shores	*would*
And make a sop of all this solid globe.	
Strength should be lord of imbecility,	30
And the rude son should strike his father dead.	
Force should be right; or rather, right and wrong,	
Between whose endless jar justice resides,	
Should lose her° names, and so should justice too.	*their*
Then everything includes itself in power,	35
Power into will, will into appetite,	
And appetite, an universal wolf,	
So doubly seconded with will and power,	
Must make perforce an universal prey	
And last eat up himself.	40

William Shakespeare (1564–1616)

* Act II, Scene 3, lines 85–124.

The idea of a universal order also underlies the following poem by William Wordsworth. The conception, however, is no longer that of a hierarchical structure; in its place Wordsworth offers the idea of an organic interconnectedness that ideally should include humankind.

Lines Written in Early Spring

I heard a thousand blended notes,
While in a grove I sate reclined,
In that sweet mood when pleasant thoughts
Bring sad thoughts to the mind.

To her fair works did Nature link   5
The human soul that through me ran;
And much it grieved my heart to think
What man has made of man.

Through primrose tufts, in that green bower,
The periwinkle trailed its wreaths;   10
And 'tis my faith that every flower
Enjoys the air it breathes.

The birds around me hopped and played,
Their thoughts I cannot measure—
But the least motion which they made,   15
It seemed a thrill of pleasure.

The budding twigs spread out their fan,
To catch the breezy air;
And I must think, do all I can,
That there was pleasure there.   20

If this belief from heaven be sent,
If such be Nature's holy plan,
Have I not reason to lament
What man has made of man?

William Wordsworth (1770–1850)

QUESTIONS

1. What conception of nature seems to be expressed in lines 9–20? How is it prepared for by the "thousand blended notes" of the opening line?
2. Nature seems to exist in one fashion, human beings in another. Explain the difference and then comment on the implications of lines 5–6.
3. Describe the elements that make up "Nature's holy plan" (line 22) as the poem implies them.

Clearly there is nothing "holy" in Herman Melville's conception of nature in "The Maldive Shark." The natural world he describes is coherent but cruel:

The Maldive Shark

About the Shark, phlegmatical one,
Pale sot of the Maldive sea°,   *off the Indian Ocean*
The sleek little pilot-fish, azure and slim,
How alert in attendance be.
From his saw-pit of mouth, from his charnel of maw°,   *death-house of jaw* 5
They have nothing of harm to dread,
But liquidly glide on his ghastly flank
Or before his Gorgonian head;
Or lurk in the port of serrated teeth
In white triple tiers of glittering gates,   10
And there find a haven when peril's abroad,
An asylum in jaws of the Fates!
They are friends; and friendly they guide him to prey,
Yet never partake of the treat—
Eyes and brains to the dotard lethargic and dull,   15
Pale ravener of horrible meat.

Herman Melville (1819–1891)

The complicity of shark and pilot-fish is easy and unselfconscious; by contrast, the speaker's attitude toward the shark is one of revulsion. He begins with words like "phlegmatical" and "sot," but then shifts to still uglier and more dangerous terms—"saw-pit of mouth," "charnel of maw," "ghastly flank"—culminating in "Gorgonian head" (possessing, that is, the powers of the legendary Gorgon whose frightfulness paralyzes the viewer). Even the pilot-fish, described initially as "azure and slim," alert and fearless, are said to "lurk" and hide. Whatever the inner harmonies of nature, from Melville's point of view it is predatory, repugnant, and perhaps evil.

For another view of nature, in no way threatening, almost celebratory, read Elizabeth Jennings's "In Praise of Creation."

In Praise of Creation

That one bird, one star,
The one flash of the tiger's eye
Purely assert what they are,
Without ceremony testify.

Testify to order, to rule— 5
How the birds mate at one time only,
How the sky is, for a certain time, full
Of birds, the moon sometimes cut thinly.

And the tiger trapped in the cage of his skin,
Watchful over creation, rests 10
For the blood to pound, the drums to begin,
Till the tigress' shadow casts

A darkness over him, a passion, a scent,
The world goes turning, turning, the season
Sieves earth to its one sure element 15
And the blood beats beyond reason.

Then quiet, and birds folding their wings,
The new moon waiting for years to be stared at here,
The season sinks to satisfied things—
Man with his mind ajar. 20

Elizabeth Jennings (b. 1926)

QUESTIONS

1. To what order and rule (line 5) do the bird, star, and tiger testify?
2. How do you explain the greater attention given the tiger? What relationship
   is implied between "the blood" and reason?
3. Show how lines 17–19 resolve the poem to that point. What relationship does
   man (line 20) have to the resolution?

Thomas Hardy, confronted with cruel and oppressive forces in nature
(the leaden sky, the North wind) and human afflictions (sickness and
death), explains their action in the universe as the effect of higher laws
that control human destiny. That an order exists, however harsh, proves
consoling.

The Subalterns

I

"Poor wanderer," said the leaden sky,
    "I fain would lighten thee,
But there are laws in force on high
    Which say it must not be."

II

—"I would not freeze thee, shorn one," cried   5
    The North, "knew I but how
To warm my breath, to slack my stride;
    But I am ruled as thou."

III

—"To-morrow I attack thee, wight,"
    Said Sickness. "Yet I swear   10
I bear thy little ark no spite,
    But am bid enter there."

IV

—"Come hither, Son," I heard Death say;
    "I did not will a grave
Should end thy pilgrimage to-day,   15
    But I, too, am a slave!"

V

We smiled upon each other then,
    And life to me had less
Of that fell look it wore ere when
    They owned their passiveness.   20

Thomas Hardy (1840–1928)

QUESTIONS

1. What point of view do the various speakers in the first four stanzas have in common?
2. Describe the kind of universe Hardy's poem is postulating.

Hardy insists on explanations. By contrast, the speaker of Arthur Hugh Clough's "All Is Well" makes no effort to ask questions. Indeed, he counsels against inquiry, and since the reasons for the doubt and pain that pervade human experience cannot be known, he assumes it is useless to ask about the meaning and purpose of life.

All Is Well

Whate'er you dream, with doubt possessed,
Keep, keep it snug within your breast,
And lay you down and take your rest;

Forget in sleep the doubt and pain,
And when you wake, to work again.   5
The wind it blows, the vessel goes,
And where and whither, no one knows.

'Twill all be well—no need of care;
Though how it will, and when, and where,
We cannot see, and can't declare.   10
In spite of dreams, in spite of thought,
'Tis not in vain, and not for naught,
The wind it blows, the ship it goes,
Though where and whither, no one knows.

Arthur Hugh Clough (1819–1861)

QUESTIONS

1. Show how the speaker wavers between the desire for an orderly, intelligible
   world and an inability to believe in one.
2. Explain the title. Is it irony or sheer optimism?

   The poems we have been considering so far have dealt with issues
such as nature, the meaning and purpose of the universe, and the
human place in it. In most instances some notion of systematic structure
or harmony in the world has provided the poem's frame of reference.
In some cases, however, as in Housman's poems, the sense of systematic
structure is lacking, and this absence is characteristic of the work of
many modern and contemporary poets. For these poets, the process of
achieving awareness has become as central an issue as the awareness
achieved. The sense of things, the way the mind perceives, is primary
in the following poem by Wallace Stevens, which focuses on the rela-
tionship between two instruments of knowledge—sense perception and
imagination:

The Plain Sense of Things

After the leaves have fallen, we return
To a plain sense of things. It is as if
We had come to an end of the imagination,
Inanimate in an inert savoir.

It is difficult even to choose the adjective   5
For this blank cold, this sadness without cause.
The great structure has become a minor house.
No turban walks across the lessened floors.

The greenhouse never so badly needed paint.
The chimney is fifty years old and slants to one side.   10
A fantastic effort has failed, a repetition
In a repetitiousness of men and flies.

Yet the absence of the imagination had
Itself to be imagined. The great pond,
The plain sense of it, without reflections, leaves,   15
Mud, water like dirty glass, expressing silence

Of a sort, silence of a rat come out to see,
The great pond and its waste of the lilies, all this
Had to be imagined as an inevitable knowledge,
Required, as a necessity requires.   20

Wallace Stevens (1879–1955)

Although the imagination seems in danger of dwindling away with the
declining season, the danger proves illusory because the imagination
is required to understand (that is, imagine) the nature of decline.

Another sense of the mind in crisis as it strives to understand reality
appears in Thomas Kinsella's "An Old Atheist Pauses by the Sea." The
speaker is aware of his loss of selective powers: "I choose at random";
he is an aging man whose atheism is under duress. His old way is
breaking down in the very presence of a new awareness achieved by
intuition rather than by logic and reason.

An Old Atheist Pauses by the Sea

I choose at random, knowing less and less.
The shambles of the seashore at my feet
Yield a weathered spiral: I confess
—Appalled at how the waves have polished it—
I know that shores are eaten, rocks are split,
Shells ghosted. Something hates unevenness.
The skin turns porcelain, the nerves retreat,
And then the will, and then the consciousness.

Thomas Kinsella (b. 1928)

QUESTIONS

1. To what does "choose at random" (line 1) refer; seashells, for example, or something else? Explain.
2. In what sense is it important that the speaker is old? How is his age relevant to the closing lines?
3. Clarify the "Something" of line 6. To what extent does your clarification come from within the poem? from outside it?

Thomas Hardy, writing on the last evening of the nineteenth century, manages to extract a glimmer of hope for the new century from the least promising of sources, a gaunt and ragged songbird. "The Darkling Thrush" describes the transaction—the means by which he came to his awareness—in considerable detail but tells us virtually nothing of the nature of the hope.

The Darkling Thrush

I leant upon a coppice gate
  When Frost was specter-gray,
And Winter's dregs made desolate
  The weakening eye of day.
The tangled bine-stems scored the sky   5
  Like strings of broken lyres,
And all mankind that haunted nigh
  Had sought their household fires.

The land's sharp features seemed to be
  The Century's corpse outleant,   10
His crypt the cloudy canopy,
  The wind his death-lament.
The ancient pulse of germ and birth
  Was shrunken hard and dry,
And every spirit upon earth   15
  Seemed fervorless as I.

At once a voice arose among
  The bleak twigs overhead
In a full-hearted evensong
  Of joy illimited;   20
An aged thrush, frail, gaunt, and small,
  In blast-beruffled plume,
Had chosen thus to fling his soul
  Upon the growing gloom.

So little cause for carolings   25
   Of such ecstatic sound
Was written on terrestrial things
   Afar or nigh around,
That I could think there trembled through
   His happy good-night air   30
Some blessed Hope, whereof he knew
   And I was unaware.

Thomas Hardy (1840–1928)

QUESTIONS

1. What sense of Hardy's estimate of the nineteenth century do you get from
   the first two stanzas?
2. How does the image of "broken lyres" (line 6) relate to the scene described
   in the opening stanza? What is the quality of that scene?
3. In what sense is the thrush's condition (stanza 3) the basis for the "blessed
   Hope"? Hope in or for what?

Hardy's poem turns to a bedraggled thrush for meaning. W. H. Auden
turns to art, to the great painters of the past. His "Musée des Beaux
Arts" is set in an actual museum of that name located in Brussels. The
speaker has been wandering from painting to painting, contemplating
the Old Masters. As he does so, certain awarenesses come to him; then
everything seems to merge in his reaction to a particular picture, "The
Fall of Icarus," by the sixteenth-century Flemish painter Pieter Brueghel.
According to classical legend, Icarus and his father Daedalus were
imprisoned in a labyrinth and escaped by means of wings that Daedalus
(known throughout Greece for his cunning craftsmanship) devised of
feathers and wax. Despite his father's warning, Icarus flew too close to
the sun, the wax melted, and he fell into the sea. Brueghel shows only
the boy's legs, the rest of his body being already submerged. But it is
not this painting alone that has stimulated the poet's thoughts. Lines
12–13 allude to another Brueghel painting, "The Massacre of the Inno-
cents," also in the museum, and Auden seems to have a specific nativity
painting in mind in lines 5–7. There may be other allusions as well
buried elsewhere in the opening stanza.

Musée des Beaux Arts

About suffering they were never wrong,
The Old Masters: how well they understood

Its human position; how it takes place
While someone else is eating or opening a window or just walking dully
    along;
How, when the aged are reverently, passionately waiting   5
For the miraculous birth, there always must be
Children who did not specially want it to happen, skating
On a pond at the edge of the wood:
They never forgot
That even the dreadful martyrdom must run its course   10
Anyhow in a corner, some untidy spot
Where the dogs go on with their doggy life and the torturer's horse
Scratches its innocent behind on a tree.

In Brueghel's *Icarus*, for instance: how everything turns away
Quite leisurely from the disaster; the ploughman may   15
Have heard the splash, the forsaken cry,
But for him it was not an important failure; the sun shone
As it had to on the white legs disappearing into the green
Water; and the expensive delicate ship that must have seen
Something amazing, a boy falling out of the sky,   20
Had somewhere to get to and sailed calmly on.

W. H. Auden (1907–1973)

QUESTIONS

1. How are the events in the first section related to one another?
2. To what awarenesses has the poet come in his reflections on the Old Masters
   like Brueghel?

Auden might have pointed his poem differently, protesting at the
callousness in human affairs and moralizing on the need for greater
bonds among people. Had his emphasis moved this way, his poem
might have taken on the character of a social critique and warranted
discussion in the preceding chapter. But he avoids such implications,
implying instead the futility of expecting remedy for a condition that
is built into the human situation. Auden's dictum, from his "In Memory
of W. B. Yeats" (p. 180), that "poetry makes nothing happen," seems
as true of this poem as of any of his others.

And yet something does happen. We learn something of ourselves,
of our place in the world, not necessarily by accepting Auden's wisdom
(or Pope's or Hardy's) but by responding to it, much as Auden responds
in his fashion to the Old Masters and makes meaning of what he has
seen.

EXERCISES

I. Robert Frost's "Mending Wall" has elements of both social comment and philosophical statement. What is the social message? In what sense does the poem offer a philosophical formulation?

Mending Wall

Something there is that doesn't love a wall,
That sends the frozen-ground-swell under it
And spills the upper boulders in the sun,
And makes gaps even two can pass abreast.
The work of hunters is another thing: 5
I have come after them and made repair
Where they have left not one stone on a stone,
But they would have the rabbit out of hiding,
To please the yelping dogs. The gaps I mean,
No one has seen them made or heard them made,   10
But at spring mending-time we find them there.
I let my neighbor know beyond the hill;
And on a day we meet to walk the line
And set the wall between us once again.
We keep the wall between us as we go.   15
To each the boulders that have fallen to each.
And some are loaves and some so nearly balls
We have to use a spell to make them balance:
"Stay where you are until our backs are turned!"
We wear our fingers rough with handling them.   20
Oh, just another kind of outdoor game,
One on a side. It comes to little more:
There where it is we do not need the wall:
He is all pine and I am apple orchard.
My apple trees will never get across   25
And eat the cones under his pines, I tell him.
He only says, "Good fences make good neighbors."
Spring is the mischief in me, and I wonder
If I could put a notion in his head:
"*Why* do they make good neighbors? Isn't it   30
Where there are cows? But here there are no cows.
Before I built a wall I'd ask to know
What I was walling in or walling out,
And to whom I was like to give offense.
Something there is that doesn't love a wall,   35
That wants it down." I could say "Elves" to him,
But it's not elves exactly, and I'd rather

He said it for himself. I see him there,
Bringing a stone grasped firmly by the top
In each hand, like an old-stone savage armed.   40
He moves in darkness as it seems to me,
Not of woods only and the shade of trees.
He will not go behind his father's saying,
And he likes having thought of it so well
He says again, "Good fences make good neighbors."   45

Robert Frost (1874–1963)

II.   Many contemporary poets believe there is no outside force directing human endeavor, no ultimate purpose in life, or if there is, it cannot be known. How does each of the following poems render this conception of reality?

The Snow on Saddle Mountain

The only thing that can be relied on
is the snow on Kurakake Mountain.
fields and woods
thawing, freezing, and thawing,
totally untrustworthy.
it's true, a great fuzzy windstorm
like yeast up there today, still
the only faint source of hope
is the snow on Kurakake mountain.

Gary Snyder (b. 1930)

The Snow Man

One must have a mind of winter
To regard the frost and the boughs
Of the pine-trees crusted with snow:

And have been cold a long time
To behold the junipers shagged with ice,   5
The spruces rough in the distant glitter

Of the January sun; and not to think
Of any misery in the sound of the wind,
In the sound of a few leaves,

Which is the sound of the land   10
Full of the same wind
That is blowing in the same bare place

For the listener, who listens in the snow,
And, nothing himself, beholds
Nothing that is not there and the nothing that is.   15

Wallace Stevens (1879–1955)

III.   Matthew Arnold, describing the world as it seems to be and as he feels
it truly is, conveys a sense of failed values and cosmic uncertainty.

Dover Beach

The sea is calm to-night.
The tide is full, the moon lies fair
Upon the straits—on the French coast, the light
Gleams and is gone; the cliffs of England stand,
Glimmering and vast, out in the tranquil bay.   5
Come to the window, sweet is the night air!
Only, from the long line of spray
Where the ebb meets the moon-blanched land,
Listen! you hear the grating roar
Of pebbles which the waves draw back, and fling,   10
At their return, up the high strand,
Begin, and cease, and then again begin,
With tremulous cadence slow, and bring
The eternal note of sadness in.

Sophocles long ago   15
Heard it on the Ægean, and it brought
Into his mind the turbid ebb and flow
Of human misery; we
Find also in the sound a thought,
Hearing it by this distant northern sea.   20

The Sea of Faith
Was once, too, at the full, and round earth's shore
Lay like the folds of a bright girdle furled.
But now I only hear
Its melancholy, long, withdrawing roar,   25
Retreating, to the breath
Of the night wind, down the vast edges drear
And naked shingles of the world.

Ah, love, let us be true
To one another! for the world, which seems   30
To lie before us like a land of dreams,
So various, so beautiful, so new,
Hath really neither joy, nor love, nor light,
Nor certitude, nor peace, nor help for pain;
And we are here as on a darkling plain   35
Swept with confused alarms of struggle and flight,
Where ignorant armies clash by night.

Matthew Arnold (1822–1888)

Dover Beach. l. 15 *Sophocles:* Greek tragic poet (*c.* 496–*c.* 405 B.C.). The reference is probably to *Antigone*, in which Sophocles compares heaven's curse to the ebb and flow of the sea. l. 28 *naked shingles:* gravel beaches.

1. Explain the relationship between the sea at Dover Beach in stanza 1, the Aegean Sea in stanza 2, and the "Sea of Faith" in stanza 3.
2. In your own words, what image of the world is conveyed by the last three lines?
3. Given the speaker's interpretation of reality, what hope, if any, does the poem offer?

14
Poetry and Religion

When poetry and religion meet, the poet contemplates the spirit, the soul, death, fate, purpose, meaning—that is, one or another of the issues we have seen raised in philosophical terms in the previous chapter—but brings to the interpretation of these issues some system that derives from church doctrine or some conception of God or divine principle of human destiny. In the passage below, for example, from the Book of Job, it is not a philosophical system but a religious conception, one envisioning God as an intervener in human affairs, a tester of humans, that gives meaning to the suffering and anxiety that have marked Job's days and nights:

from The Book of Job*

Therefore I will not refrain my mouth;
I will speak in the anguish of my spirit;
I will complain in the bitterness of my soul.
Am I a sea, or a sea-monster,
That Thou settest a watch over me?   5
When I say: "My bed shall comfort me,
My couch shall ease my complaint";
Then Thou scarest me with dreams,

* Job 7:11–21.

And terrifiest me through visions;
So that my soul chooseth strangling,   10
And death rather than these my bones.
I loathe it; I shall not live alway;
Let me alone; for my days are vanity.
What is man, that Thou shouldest magnify him,
And that Thou shouldest set Thy heart upon him,   15
And that Thou shouldest remember him every morning,
And try him every moment?
How long wilt Thou not look away from me,
Nor let me alone till I swallow down my spittle?
If I have sinned, what do I unto Thee, O Thou watcher of men?   20
Why hast Thou set me as a mark for Thee,
So that I am a burden to myself?
And why dost Thou not pardon my transgression,
And take away mine iniquity?
For now shall I lie down in the dust;   25
And Thou wilt seek me, but I shall not be.

God watches incessantly over Job, refusing him rest, trying him at every
turn. "Let me alone," Job cries. "Why hast Thou set me as a mark for
Thee?" From the extremity of his own plight, Job generalizes about the
nature and condition of mankind ("What is man . . ." lines 14–17) and
in his despair even threatens God with a kind of passive giving up of
life (lines 24–25) depriving God, as it were, of this long-suffering "mark."

Though the intensity of passion and pain is not present in the two
poems that follow, it becomes clear as you read that they, too, draw
upon religious themes, commenting in very different ways on the nature
of God and on the relationship of God to the creation:

Bowl

For what emperor
Was this bowl of Earth designed?
Here are more things
Than on any bowl of the Sungs,
Even the rarest: 5
Vines that take
The various obscurities of the moon,
Approaching rain,
And leaves that would be loose upon the wind;
Pears on pointed trees,   10
The dresses of women,

Oxen. . . .
I never tire
To think of this.

Wallace Stevens (1879–1955)

What Tomas Said in a Pub

I saw God!   Do you doubt it?
Do you dare to doubt it?
I saw the Almighty Man!   His hand
Was resting on a mountain!   And
He looked upon the World, and all about it: 5
I saw Him plainer than you see me now
—You mustn't doubt it!

He was not satisfied!
His look was all dissatisfied!
His beard swung on a wind, far out of sight   10
Behind the world's curve!   And there was light
Most fearful from His forehead!   And He sighed—
—That star went always wrong, and from the start
I was dissatisfied!—

He lifted up His hand!   15
I say He heaved a dreadful hand
Over the spinning earth!   Then I said,—Stay,
You must not strike it, God!   I'm in the way!
And I will never move from where I stand!—
He said,—Dear child, I feared that you were dead,—   20
. . . And stayed His hand!

James Stephens (1882–1950)

The speaker in "Bowl" wonders about the creation of the universe as
well as the nature of the creator. For whom, for what kind of creature
has the earth been made? And even more interesting, who designed
the earth, creating a living, changing, natural entity far more entrancing
than the Sung bowl which, for all its exquisite detail, is fixed forever?
"Bowl" speculates, then, about the identity of God and the relationship
between God and nature.

James Stephens's poem—a kind of tall tale told by a drinker in a
pub—comments more directly on the nature of God and on God's
relationship to humankind. Looking down on the world, the deity of

the poem is dismayed by what he sees and is prepared to annihilate his creation even more decisively, it would seem, than did the Hebraic God of Noah's time, who flooded the earth, redeeming only Noah and his family. Tomas is obviously no righteous man of Noah's order, and yet he manages to deflect the god's mood by the simple reminder of his presence—"I'm in the way!"—and his stalwart desire to live (lines 18–19). As the god's judging hand is stayed, another dimension of his being, love and concern, asserts itself: "Dear child, I feared that you were dead" (line 20). The comment is curious for it suggests a limited awareness: god is apparently not all-knowing, lacks the preknowledge that the earth would go wrong, and is unable to comprehend what is immediately present. And there is at least one other implication which suggests that the god of Stephens's poem (or more precisely, of Tomas's rendering) is not the traditional Hebraic-Christian God. Lines 13–14 suggest that earth is but one of his creations, that other "stars" have had other, more satisfactory histories.

To discuss religious poems in a meaningful way, we need to recognize the religious assumptions on which they are based. Knowing something of the underlying doctrine—whether it be Judaism, Catholicism, Calvinism, or some more recent system such as nineteenth-century Transcendentalism—will usually shed light on the poem's action, characterizations, and symbols. Here, for example, are two poems by Colonial Americans, Anne Bradstreet and Edward Taylor. Both were Puritans and Calvinist in orientation. The necessary doctrine for understanding the poems is the idea of divine election, in which God chooses a few to be saved from damnation; Christ is a protector of those who are divinely chosen. Bradstreet examines the implications of calamity, Taylor of temptation.

Salvation as Anne Bradstreet understood it was a gift of God, granted long before birth, when the few were selected to enjoy heaven after death. But how was one to determine who had been selected? One sign was evidence of distress or suffering. Since everything is ordained by God, all afflictions must come from Him. Calamities of a major dimension may therefore be interpreted as a sign that God is reminding the chosen one of his or her special status. So the sufferer in the poem here finds reassurance of God's favoritism, precisely because of the fire that burns her house to the ground:

Upon the Burning of Our House

July 10th, 1666

In silent night when rest I took
For sorrow near I did not look
I wakened was with thund'ring noise
And piteous shrieks of dreadful voice.

That fearful sound of "Fire!" and "Fire!"   5
Let no man know is my desire.

I, starting up, the light did spy,
And to my God my heart did cry
To strengthen me in my distress
And not to leave me succorless.   10
Then, coming out, beheld a space
The flame consume my dwelling place.

And when I could no longer look,
I blest His name that gave and took,
That laid my goods now in the dust.   15
Yea, so it was, and so 'twas just.
It was His own, it was not mine,
Far be it that I should repine;

He might of all justly bereft
But yet sufficient for us left.   20
When by the ruins oft I past
My sorrowing eyes aside did cast,
And here and there the places spy
Where oft I sat and long did lie:

Here stood that trunk, and there that chest,   25
There lay that store I counted best.
My pleasant things in ashes lie,
And them behold no more shall I.
Under thy roof no guest shall sit,
Nor at thy table eat a bit.   30

No pleasant tale shall e'er be told,
Nor things recounted done of old.
No candle e'er shall shine in thee,
Nor bridegroom's voice e'er heard shall be.
In silence ever shall thou lie,   35
Adieu, Adieu, all's vanity.

Then straight I 'gin my heart to chide,
And did thy wealth on earth abide?
Didst fix thy hope on mold'ring dust?
The arm of flesh didst make thy trust?   40
Raise up thy thoughts above the sky
That dunghill mists away may fly.

Thou hast an house on high erect,
Framed by that mighty Architect,
With glory richly furnished,   45

Stands permanent though this be fled.
It's purchased and paid for too
By Him who hath enough to do.

A price so vast as is unknown
Yet by His gift is made thine own;   50
There's wealth enough, I need no more,
Farewell, my pelf, farewell my store.
The world no longer let me love,
My hope and treasure lies above.

Anne Bradstreet (1612?–1672)

Though the poem offers no explanation for the sudden fire, the woman
accepts the loss of house and treasure without bitterness, reasoning that
although God may deprive her of all her earthly possessions, He has
prepared a finer house for her in heaven. Structurally, the poem falls
into three units that demonstrate the Puritan doctrine: stanzas 1–3
describe the fire and fright, or the affliction; stanzas 4–6, the aftermath
of the fire and the wistful sense of loss; stanzas 7–9, the solace that the
doctrine provides.

   Like Bradstreet, Edward Taylor believed that God in His justice con-
demned humankind because of Adam's sin in the Garden of Eden, but
that in His mercy God allowed Christ to sacrifice Himself to save a
portion of humankind—not every man and woman, just those who had
been chosen long before the creation of the world, all part of a divine
plan. Taylor's poem, which seems at times little more than rhymed
doctrine, takes the form of a dialogue between the soul and Christ, with
the soul speaking as a frightened lamb terrified by a fierce dog, the
Devil. Christ answers and the lamb becomes, as it were, a frightened
child, soothed by a gentle, tender, and loving parent who wipes away
the tears of an anguished soul.

The Souls Groan to Christ for Succour

Good Lord, behold this Dreadfull Enemy
   Who makes me tremble with his fierce assaults,
I dare not trust, yet feare to give the ly,
   For in my soul, my soul finds many faults.
   And though I justify myselfe to's face: 5
   I do Condemn myselfe before thy Grace.

He strives to mount° my sins, and them advance   *increase*
   Above thy Merits, Pardons, or Good Will
Thy Grace to lessen, and thy Wrath t'inhance
   As if thou couldst not pay the sinners bill.   10

He Chiefly injures thy rich Grace, I finde
Though I confess my heart to sin inclin'de.

Those Graces which thy Grace enwrought in mee,
  He makes as nothing but a pack of Sins.
He maketh Grace no grace, but Crueltie,   15
  Is Graces Honey Comb, a Comb of Stings?
  This makes me ready leave thy Grace and run.
  Which if I do, I finde I am undone.

I know he is thy Cur, therefore I bee
  Perplexed lest I from thy Pasture stray.   20
He bayghs, and barks so veh'mently at mee.
  Come rate° this Cur, Lord, breake his teeth I pray.   *scourge*
  Remember me I humbly pray thee first.
  Then halter up this Cur that is so Curst.

Christs Reply

Peace, Peace, my Hony, do not Cry,   25
My Little Darling, wipe thine eye,
  Oh Cheer, Cheer up, come see.
Is anything too deare, my Dove,
Is anything too good, my Love
  To get or give for thee?   30

If in the severall thou art
This Yelper fierce will at thee bark:
  That thou art mine this shows.
As Spot barks back the sheep again
Before they to the Pound are ta'ne,   35
  So he and hence 'way goes.

But yet this Cur that bayghs so sore
Is broken tootht, and muzzled sure,
  Fear not, my Pritty Heart.
His barking is to make thee Cling   40
Close underneath thy Saviours Wing.
  Why did my sweeten start?

And if he run an inch too far,
I'le Check his Chain, and rate the Cur.
  My Chick, keep clost to mee.   45
The Poles shall sooner kiss, and greet
And Paralells shall sooner meet
  Than thou shalt harmed bee.

Edward Taylor (1642–1729)

QUESTIONS

1. Explain the doctrine in lines 1–6 by indicating who is responsible for sin and who for forgiveness.
2. Explain lines 11 and 19. Why does the lamb become confused and tempted to run away in line 17? Explain the relationships between lines 2 and 42; lines 20 and 34; and lines 22, 24, and 38.
3. Contrast the tones of the lament and the reply.

Important as the doctrine is, it is finally inseparable from the quality of the poem's feeling. Taylor obviously wishes to convince the reader of the truth of the doctrine, but he wishes too to express the nature of his emotions when he doubts and when he is relieved of doubt. Toward the close of Christ's reply, we begin to hear the soothing words of a gentle and reassuring parent capable of holding the threatening cur at bay. As is Bradstreet's poem, Taylor's is a far cry from the brassy combination of awe and boast we get from Tomas in the local pub.

John Donne was no Puritan, and he possessed no way of convincing himself that he had been chosen to enjoy immortality. Though he died in the service of the Anglican Church and believed in the soul and in the Resurrection, he could not know how he would fare on Judgment Day. Notice in the sonnet that follows how dramatically he renders the approach of death from the beginning of the mortal hour to the split second between living and dying:

This Is My Play's Last Scene, Here Heavens Appoint

This is my play's last scene, here heavens appoint
My pilgrimage's last mile; and my race
Idly, yet quickly run, has this last pace,
My span's last inch, my minute's latest point,
And gluttonous death, will instantly unjoint   5
My body, and soul, and I shall sleep a space,
But my ever-waking part shall see that face,
Whose fear already shakes my every joint:
Then, as my soul, to heaven her first seat, takes flight,
And earth-born body, in the earth shall dwell,   10
So, fall my sins, that all may have their right,
To where they are bred, and would press me, to hell.
Impute me righteous, thus purged of evil,
For thus I leave the world, the flesh, the devil.

John Donne (1572–1631)

1. Explain the relationship between a play, a pilgrimage, and a race (lines 1–4) in the poem; between sleeping and waking (lines 5–8); between ascent, burial, and fall (lines 9–12).
2. What is meant by the "ever-waking part" (line 7)? Whose "face" is referred to in the same line?
3. Explain the meaning of the final couplet. How does it relate to the rest of the poem?

Robert Southwell's poem, below, is similarly imbued with doctrinal meaning. What the poet sees and then hears makes clear that he has encountered no ordinary child:

The Burning Babe

As I in hoary winter's night stood shivering in the snow,
Surprised I was with sudden heat which made my heart to glow;
And lifting up a fearful eye to view what fire was near,
A pretty babe all burning bright did in the air appear;
Who, scorchèd with excessive heat, such floods of tears did shed   5
As though his floods should quench his flames which with his tears
    were fed.
"Alas," quoth he, "but newly born in fiery heats I fry,
Yet none approach to warm their hearts or feel my fire but I!
My faultless breast the furnace is, the fuel wounding thorns,
Love is the fire, and sighs the smoke, the ashes shame and scorns;   10
The fuel justice layeth on, and mercy blows the coals,
The metal in this furnace wrought are men's defilèd souls,
For which, as now on fire I am to work them to their good,
So will I melt into a bath to wash them in my blood."
With this he vanished out of sight and swiftly shrunk away,   15
And straight I callèd unto mind that it was Christmas day.

Robert Southwell (1561–1595)

QUESTIONS

1. Explain the initial tableau. Where and when does the vision occur?
2. How would you explain the reasons for the child's tears (lines 5–6)?
3. Work out the religious significance of the different events the babe alludes to in lines 7–14.

Like Southwell, but some three centuries later, Gerard Manley Hopkins was a member of the Jesuit order, having converted to the Catholic Church in his early twenties. Though he spent his later life variously as parish priest, missionary, and teacher, the larger part of his poetry is not so much didactic as reflective. In the poem that follows, Hopkins can be seen observing a child's reaction to nature and meditating on its significance:

Spring and Fall

To a Young Child

Márgarét, are you gríeving
Over Goldengrove unleaving?
Leáves, líke the things of man, you
With your fresh thoughts care for, can you?
Ah! ás the heart grows older   5
It will come to such sights colder
By and by, nor spare a sigh
Though worlds of wanwood leafmeal lie;
And yet you wíll weep and know why.
Now no matter, child, the name: 10
Sórrow's spríngs áre the same.
Nor mouth had, no nor mind, expressed
What heart heard of, ghost guessed:
It ís the blight man was born for,
It is Margaret you mourn for.   15

Gerard Manley Hopkins (1844–1889)

A paraphrase will help to clarify the difficult passages:

> Margaret, are you weeping at the loss of leaves in this golden grove? In your innocence, you have as much feeling for leaves as you have for man-made objects; but as you grow older, this seasonal change will upset you much less (line 6). Should you in your time see vast worlds of denuded trees stand barren as if a plague had swept across them ("wanwood leafmeal lie"), you will not weep for the trees, but you will not cease to cry. When you grow up and realize that we are transient creatures, mortal creatures, you will understand why you weep. It hardly matters, since whenever we weep, at whatever age, for whatever reasons ("Sórrow's spríngs áre the same"), it all comes to the same thing. Even though death has yet to be named to you, and your mind does not understand its presence or meaning, your heart has intuitions, and your spirit has guessed the truth. You perceive that not only trees die, but people too must experience blight. You sense your own mortality reflected in the sight of autumn's end. You are really mourning for yourself.

Poems are obviously more than their paraphrases, with implications that go beyond surface meaning. Here "Goldengrove" may be associated with the original golden scene, the Garden of Eden, and the unleaving with the fall from grace, which introduced death into the world. Thus Margaret, though a child, may be said to intuit the presence of original sin, which has been the human heritage since the transgression of Adam and Eve. Her "ghost" (spirit, soul) has already "guessed" what at a later point she will know.

The following poem, also by Hopkins, is concerned less with church doctrine than with praise for the miraculous creative power of God, who although changeless and timeless Himself, can yet create beauty that is always in motion, in endless variation.

Pied Beauty

Glory be to God for dappled things—
For skies of couple-color as a brinded° cow; *streaked*
 For rose-moles all in stipple° upon trout that swim; *dots*
Fresh-firecoal chestnut-falls; finches' wings;
 Landscape plotted and pieced—fold, fallow, and plow; 5
  And all trades, their gear and tackle and trim.

All things counter, original, spare, strange;
 Whatever is fickle, freckled (who knows how?)
  With swift, slow; sweet, sour; adazzle, dim;
He fathers-forth whose beauty is past change: 10
    Praise him.

Gerard Manley Hopkins (1844–1889)

As spiritual experiences are not static, so the tone of religious poems written by a single poet may range from exaltation to despair, from fear and trembling to joy and courage. Hopkins himself underwent a serious emotional crisis in the last years of his life and wrote a series of poems, usually referred to as the "Terrible Sonnets," expressing his torment. Notice how the mood and tone shift from poem to poem and within a poem; but notice, too, that although the poems portray Hopkins's anxieties they never suggest a loss of faith.

I Wake and Feel the Fell of Dark, Not Day

I wake and feel the fell° of dark, not day. *fall (autumn); cruel;*
What hours, O what black hoürs we have spent *animal skin*

This night! what sights you, heart, saw; ways you went!
And more must, in yet longer light's delay.
With witness I speak this. But where I say
Hours I mean years, mean life. And my lament   5
Is cries countless, cries like dead letters sent
To dearest him that lives alas! away.
I am gall, I am heartburn. God's most deep decree
Bitter would have me taste: my taste was me;   10
Bones built in me, flesh filled, blood brimmed the curse.
Selfyeast of spirit a dull dough sours. I see
The lost are like this, and their scourge to be
As I am mine, their sweating selves; but worse.

Gerard Manley Hopkins (1844–1889)

Thou Art Indeed Just, Lord, If I Contend

Justus quidem tu es, Domine, si disputem tecum: verumtamen justa loquar ad te: Quare via impiorum prosperatur? &c.

Thou art indeed just, Lord, if I contend
With thee; but, sir, so what I plead is just.
Why do sinners' ways prosper: and why must
Disappointment all I endeavor end?
Wert thou my enemy, O thou my friend,   5
How wouldst thou worse, I wonder, than thou dost
Defeat, thwart me? Oh, the sots and thralls of lust
Do in spare hours more thrive than I that spend,
Sir, life upon thy cause. See, banks and brakes°   *thickets*
Now, leavèd how thick! lacèd they are again   10
With fretty chervil°, look, and fresh wind shakes   *wild parsley*
Them; birds build—but not I build; no, but strain,
Time's eunuch, and not breed one work that wakes.
Mine, O thou lord of life, send my roots rain.

Gerard Manley Hopkins (1844–1889)

Thou Art Indeed Just, Lord. The Latin passage is of Jeremiah 12:1: "Thou indeed, O Lord, art just, if I plead with thee, but yet I will speak what is just to thee: Why doth the way of the wicked prosper: Why is it well with all of them that transgress and do wickedly?"

Compare, for tone, the two poems that follow by another Catholic priest, Richard Crashaw. The subject is the same in both, the slaughter

of the innocents, though the certitude of the first is somewhat under-
mined in the second. But even in doubt, Crashaw sustains the force of
his faith.

To the Infant Martyrs

Go, smiling souls, your new-built cages break,
In heaven you'll learn to sing, ere here to speak,
Nor let the milky fonts that bathe your thirst
                   Be your delay;
The place that calls you hence is, at the worst,
                   Milk all the way.

Richard Crashaw (1613?–1649)

To the Infant Martyrs. *Infant Martyrs* in the title refers to the Holy Innocents, the children
of Bethlehem, two years old and under, slain by Herod in his effort to eliminate the one
that prophecy said would become the ruler of Israel. (See Matthew 2:16.)

Upon the Infant Martyrs

To see both blended in one flood,
The mother's milk, the children's blood,
Make me doubt if heaven will gather
Roses hence, or lilies rather.

Richard Crashaw (1613?–1649)

Religious poets like Crashaw, Southwell, Donne, and Hopkins merge
specific doctrine with the experience of religious faith, though the
balance between the two may vary from poem to poem. For other poets,
the formal doctrinal elements can be of considerably less significance
and may indeed be virtually nonexistent. Emily Dickinson attains some
of her most meaningful religious expression apart from any established
creed. She wrote a large number of poems about immortality and death,
heaven and God. Though her assumptions are often identifiably Chris-
tian, she resisted adherence to a particular church; as early as her student
days at Mount Holyoke, she violated accepted policy by refusing to
make a public declaration of her religious belief. She may be recalling
that event in the following poem, written many years later:

Some Keep the Sabbath Going to Church

Some keep the Sabbath going to Church—
I keep it, staying at Home—
With a Bobolink for a Chorister—
And an Orchard, for a Dome—

Some keep the Sabbath in Surplice—   5
I just wear my Wings—
And instead of tolling the Bell, for Church,
Our little Sexton—sings.

God preaches, a noted Clergyman—
And the sermon is never long,   10
So instead of getting to Heaven, at last—
I'm going, all along.

Emily Dickinson (1830–1886)

QUESTIONS

1. Find the equivalencies Dickinson presents in lines 1–10 and explain how they contribute to the religious meaning.
2. Explain the meaning of the final two lines.

Dickinson's poem presents an argument that has been common, especially in America, for the last two hundred years. Salvation lies in the encounter between the self and God, an encounter that is most directly mediated through nature, that is, God's own creation. For the spirit so disposed, salvation is joyous, immediate, and continuous— "going, all along." The danger, of course, is that nature may not be so encouraging as it is in Dickinson's world. Thomas Hardy also turned to nature for affirmation, a salvation of sorts, but he encountered a direr principle:

In a Wood

Pale beech and pine so blue,
    Set in one clay,
Bough to bough cannot you
    Live out your day?
When the rains skim and skip,   5
Why mar sweet comradeship,
Blighting with poison-drip
    Neighborly spray?

Heart-halt and spirit-lame,
  City-opprest,
Unto this wood I came
  As to a nest;
Dreaming that sylvan peace
Offered the harrowed ease—
Nature a soft release
  From man's unrest.

But, having entered in,
  Great growths and small
Show them to men akin—
  Combatants all!
Sycamore shoulders oak,
Bines the slim sapling yoke,
Ivy-spun halters choke
  Elms stout and tall.

Touches from ash, O wych,
  Sting you like scorn!
You, too, brave hollies, twitch
  Sidelong from thorn.
Even the rank poplars bear
Lothly a rival's air,
Cankering in black despair
  If overborne.

Since, then, no grace I find
  Taught me of trees,
Turn I back to my kind,
  Worthy as these.
There at least smiles abound,
There discourse trills around,
There, now and then, are found
Life-loyalties.

Thomas Hardy (1840–1928)

QUESTIONS

1. From what is the poet escaping? What is his mood on arrival? To what does
   he return? Why is it preferable?
2. Explain the final phrase.

Dickinson is joyous, Hardy dismayed at what is to be inferred from
the evidences of nature. Alfred, Lord Tennyson, by contrast, is bewil-

dered, as is suggested by the following excerpt from his long poem *In Memoriam*. Written in response to the death of a dear friend, *In Memoriam* offers a faith in immortality apart from established church doctrine:

from *In Memoriam**

The wish, that of the living whole
  No life may fail beyond the grave,
  Derives it not from what we have
The likest God within the soul?

Are God and Nature then at strife,   5
  That Nature lends such evil dreams?
  So careful of the type she seems,
So careless of the single life,

That I, considering everywhere
  Her secret meaning in her deeds,   10
  And finding that of fifty seeds
She often brings but one to bear,

I falter where I firmly trod,
  And falling with my weight of cares
  Upon the great world's altar-stairs   15
That slope thro' darkness up to God,

I stretch lame hands of faith, and grope,
  And gather dust and chaff, and call
  To what I feel is Lord of all,
And faintly trust the larger hope.   20

Alfred, Lord Tennyson (1809–1892)

QUESTIONS

1. Explain the "wish" in the first stanza. How does it relate to the presence of God in the human soul?
2. What sense of nature is conveyed in stanzas 2 and 3? In what way do God and nature seem "at strife"?
3. Explain the image, "the great world's altar-stairs" (line 15) as it is developed in the last two stanzas.

* Lyric LV.

Though *In Memoriam* manages to resolve most of the issues it raises, the answers come neither from nature nor from theological speculation:

> I found Him not in world or sun,
>   Or eagle's wing, or insect's eye,
>   Nor through the questions men may try,
> The petty cobwebs we have spun.

It comes from within, the felt experience of God in the soul, where Tennyson chooses "to dwell/And dream my dream, and hold it true."

In Memoriam is a far cry from the doctrinal controls and implied systems of Southwell, Donne, and Hopkins. But religious need and impulse can inform poetry in innumerable ways. William Wordsworth's heart leaps up at the sight of a rainbow and he avows his "natural piety" (p. 51). Ralph Waldo Emerson, writing in Boston, avows an aspect of his faith through the Hindu deity Brahma (p. 36). Walt Whitman images himself as Adam in a pristine world (p. 21). George Herbert takes steps to arrive within reach of God (p. 107), while Christopher Smart apprehends God through the behavior of his cat Jeoffry (p. 239).

In the following poem, a dramatic monologue by T. S. Eliot, the speaker is one of the wise men, or Magi, who arrived at Bethlehem at the time of the birth of Jesus. Eliot re-creates the experience in order to communicate how it feels to become aware of the significance of Christianity. Nowhere in the poem or in the Gospel is it stated that the Magi were converts.

Journey of the Magi

"A cold coming we had of it,
Just the worst time of the year
For a journey, and such a long journey:
The ways deep and the weather sharp,
The very dead of winter."   5
And the camels galled, sore-footed, refractory,
Lying down in the melting snow.
There were times we regretted
The summer palaces on slopes, the terraces,
And the silken girls bringing sherbet.   10
Then the camel men cursing and grumbling
And running away, and wanting their liquor and women,
And the night-fires going out, and the lack of shelters,
And the cities hostile and the towns unfriendly
And the villages dirty and charging high prices: 15

A hard time we had of it.
At the end we preferred to travel all night,
Sleeping in snatches,
With the voices singing in our ears, saying
That this was all folly.   20

Then at dawn we came down to a temperate valley,
Wet, below the snow line, smelling of vegetation;
With a running stream and a water-mill beating the darkness,
And three trees on the low sky,
And an old white horse galloped away in the meadow.   25
Then we came to a tavern with vine-leaves over the lintel,
Six hands at an open door dicing for pieces of silver,
And feet kicking the empty wine-skins.
But there was no information, and so we continued
And arrived at evening, not a moment too soon   30
Finding the place; it was (you may say) satisfactory.

All this was a long time ago, I remember,
And I would do it again, but set down
This set down
This: were we led all that way for   35
Birth or Death? There was a Birth, certainly,
We had evidence and no doubt. I had seen birth and death,
But had thought they were different; this Birth was
Hard and bitter agony for us, like Death, our death.
We returned to our places, these Kingdoms,   40
But no longer at ease here, in the old dispensation,
With an alien people clutching their gods.
I should be glad of another death.

T. S. Eliot (1888–1965)

Journey of the Magi. ll. 1–5 are a paraphrase of part of a sermon preached on Christmas Day, in 1622, by the Anglican Bishop Lancelot Andrewes: "Last, we consider the time of their coming, the season of the year. It was no summer progress. A cold coming they had of it at this time of the year, just the worst time of the year to take a journey, and specially a long journey in. The ways deep, the weather sharp, the days short, the sun farthest off . . . the very dead of winter."

QUESTIONS

1. The first section describes the slow hard journey to Bethlehem, the second the arrival at the birthplace on Christmas Eve; the third section occurs many years later. Why the time lapse between sections 2 and 3? What is the effect of this time scheme?
2. Find in the poem all the references to the subsequent history of Christ.

3. What is meant by "the old dispensation" (line 41)? Why is the birth likened to a death?
4. Lines 9–10 suggest what life had been before the knowledge of Christ. Which lines show what it was like afterward?

Edwin Muir goes farther back in time, to the moment of the Annunciation, when the angel of God announces to Mary that she will bear Jesus. Muir renders the communion between the angel and the girl as if it were a present moment fixed forever in time:

The Annunciation

The angel and the girl are met.
Earth was the only meeting place.
For the embodied never yet
Travelled beyond the shore of space.
The eternal spirits in freedom go.   5
See, they have come together, see,
While the destroying minutes flow,
Each reflects the other's face
Till heaven in hers and earth in his
Shine steady there. He's come to her   10
From far beyond the farthest star,
Feathered through time. Immediacy
Of strangest strangeness is the bliss
That from their limbs all movement takes.
Yet the increasing rapture brings   15
So great a wonder that it makes
Each feather tremble on his wings.

Outside the window footsteps fall
Into the ordinary day
And with the sun along the wall   20
Pursue their unreturning way
That was ordained in eternity.
Sound's perpetual roundabout
Rolls its numbered octaves out
And hoarsely grinds its battered tune.   25

But through the endless afternoon
These neither speak nor movement make,
But stare into their deepening trance
As if their gaze would never break.

Edwin Muir (1887–1959)

We may close on a poem set more immediately in the present, one of John Berryman's "Eleven Addresses to the Lord." Berryman moves between doubts and appeals, apprehension and joy, and concludes with a declaration of trust. The Lord he addresses is not the powerful adversary to whom Job complains, but the "Master of insight & beauty." As you read the poem, consider how it may be compared or contrasted with the passage from Job with which we began this chapter.

from Eleven Addresses to the Lord

1

Master of beauty, craftsman of the snowflake,
inimitable contriver,
endower of Earth so gorgeous & different from the boring Moon,
thank you for such as it is my gift.

I have made up a morning prayer to you   5
containing with precision everything that most matters.
'According to Thy will' the thing begins.
It took me off & on two days. It does not aim at eloquence.

You have come to my rescue again & again
in my impassable, sometimes despairing years.   10
You have allowed my brilliant friends to destroy themselves
and I am still here, severely damaged, but functioning.

Unknowable, as I am unknown to my guinea pigs:
how can I 'love' you?
I only as far as gratitude & awe   15
confidently & absolutely go.

I have no idea whether we live again.
It doesn't seem likely
from either the scientific or the philosophical point of view
but certainly all things are possible to you,   20

and I believe as fixedly in the Resurrection-appearances to Peter & to Paul
as I believe I sit in this blue chair.
Only that may have been a special case
to establish their initiatory faith.

Whatever your end may be, accept my amazement.   25
May I stand until death forever at attention
for any your least instruction or enlightenment.
I even feel sure you will assist me again, Master of insight & beauty.

John Berryman (1914–1972)

EXERCISES

I. The three poems that follow bring different points of view to bear on the same event, the fall from grace in the Garden of Eden. Compare them for tone and indicate how the tone relates to the different interpretations given to the event.

Adam Lay Bounden

Adam lay bounden, bounden in a bond,
Four thousand winters thought he not too long,
And all was for an apple, an apple that he took,
As clerks° finden written, written in their book.   *scholars*
Nor had the apple taken been, the apple taken been,
Nor had never Our Lady have been heaven Queen.
Blessed be the time that apple taken was:
Therefore we may singen *Deo Gratias*°.   *Give thanks to God*

Anonymous (c. 1450)

A Reflection

When Eve upon the first of Men
    The apple press'd with specious cant,
Oh! what a thousand pities then
    That Adam was not adamant!

Thomas Hood (1799–1845)

Theology

No, the serpent did not
Seduce Eve to the apple.
All that's simply
Corruption of the facts.

Adam ate the apple.   5
Eve ate Adam.
The serpent ate Eve.
This is the dark intestine.

The serpent, meanwhile,
Sleeps his meal off in Paradise—   10
Smiling to hear
God's querulous calling.

Ted Hughes (b. 1930)

II.   The two poems by William Blake that follow are companion pieces, written in the order given but some two or three years apart.

The Lamb

Dost thou know who made thee?
Little Lamb, who made thee?
Gave thee life, and bid thee feed
By the stream and o'er the mead;
Gave thee clothing of delight,   5
Softest clothing, woolly, bright;
Gave thee such a tender voice,
Making all the vales rejoice?
   Little Lamb, who made thee?
   Dost thou know who made thee?   10

   Little Lamb, I'll tell thee,
   Little Lamb, I'll tell thee:
He is callèd by thy name,
For he calls himself a Lamb.
He is meek, and he is mild;   15
He became a little child.
I a child, and thou a lamb,
We are callèd by his name.
   Little Lamb, God bless thee!
   Little Lamb, God bless thee!   20

William Blake (1757–1827)

The Tiger

Tiger, tiger, burning bright
In the forests of the night,
What immortal hand or eye
Could frame thy fearful symmetry?

In what distant deeps or skies   5
Burnt the fire of thine eyes?
On what wings dare he aspire?
What the hand dare seize the fire?

And what shoulder and what art
Could twist the sinews of thy heart?   10
And, when thy heart began to beat,
What dread hand and what dread feet?

What the hammer? What the chain?
In what furnace was thy brain?
What the anvil? What dread grasp   15
Dare its deadly terrors clasp?

When the stars threw down their spears,
And water'd heaven with their tears,
Did He smile His work to see?
Did He who made the lamb make thee?   20

Tiger, tiger, burning bright
In the forests of the night,
What immortal hand or eye
Dare frame thy fearful symmetry?

William Blake (1757–1827)

1. Explain the series of connections made in lines 13–17 of "The Lamb."
2. What is implied about the tiger in lines 1–2 of "The Tiger"? in the phrase "fearful symmetry" (lines 4 and 24)?
3. Characterize the speaker of each poem. What seem to be their essential differences?
4. What aspects of God are emphasized in each poem? Do they seem reconcilable?

III. George Herbert's "Discipline" makes a direct address to God, much as do Gerard Manley Hopkins's "Thou Art Indeed Just, Lord, If I Contend" (p. 328), John Donne's "At the Round Earth's Imagined Corners Blow" (p. 154), and the passage from Job at the beginning of the chapter. Determine in each instance (1) the issue that seems to provoke the poem; (2) the tone of the address; and (3) the qualities of God that are emphasized.

Discipline

Throw away thy rod,
Throw away thy wrath:
            O my God,
Take the gentle path.

For my heart's desire   5
Unto thine is bent:
            I aspire
To a full consent.

Not a word or look
I affect to own,   10

But by book,
And thy book alone.

Though I fail, I weep:
Though I halt in pace,
       Yet I creep   15
To the throne of grace.

Then let wrath remove;
Love will do the deed:
       For with love
Stony hearts will bleed.   20

Love is swift of foot;
Love's a man of war,
       And can shoot,
And can hit from far.

Who can 'scape his bow?   25
That which wrought on thee,
       Brought thee low,
Needs must work on me.

Throw away thy rod;
Though man frailties hath,   30
       Thou art God:
Throw away thy wrath.

George Herbert (1593–1633)

IV. The first poem that follows, by St. John of the Cross, praises God by means of an allegory of sexual union. The second, by St. Francis of Assisi, praises God by means of a description of nature, God's creation. Explain which seems to you to convey the more personal experience.

O Living Flame of Love

O living flame of love,
  how tenderly you wound
my soul in her profoundest core!
  You are no longer shy.
  Do it now, I ask you: 5
break the membrane of our sweet union.

  O soothing cautery!
  O wound that is a joy!

O gentle hand! O delicate touch
  tasting of eternity,   10
  repaying every debt.
Killing, you turn my death to life.

  O lamps of human fire,
  in deep transparency
the lowest caverns of the senses,   15
  once shadowy and blind,
  flare in light and warmth
and wake the lover with amazing joy!

  How lovingly and soft
  you make my breasts recall   20
where you alone lie secretly;
  and with your honeyed breath,
  replete with grace and glory,
how tenderly you make me love!

St. John of the Cross (1542–1591)
(Trans. from the Spanish by Willis Barnstone)

1. Explain the paradoxes in stanza 2.
2. Compare the use of allegorical devices here with their use in St. John's "Songs
   of the Soul in Rapture . . . " (p. 99).

The Canticle of the Sun

*Here begin the praises of the creatures which the Blessed Francis made to the praise and
honour of God while he was ill at St. Damian's:*

Most high, omnipotent, good Lord,
Praise, glory, and honour and benediction all, are Thine.
To Thee alone do they belong, most High,
And there is no man fit to mention Thee.

Praise be to Thee, my Lord, with all Thy creatures,   5
Especially to my worshipful brother sun,
The which lights up the day, and through him dost Thou brightness give;
And beautiful is he and radiant with splendour great;
Of Thee, most High, signification gives.

Praised be my Lord, for sister moon and for the stars,   10
In heaven Thou hast formed them clear and precious and fair.

Praised be my Lord for brother wind
And for the air and clouds and fair and every kind of weather,
By the which Thou givest to Thy creatures nourishment.

Praised be my Lord for sister water,   15
The which is greatly helpful and humble and precious and pure.

Praised be my Lord for brother fire,
By the which Thou lightest up the dark.
And fair is he and gay and mighty and strong.

Praised be my Lord for our sister, mother earth,   20
The which sustains and keeps us
And brings forth diverse fruits with grass and flowers bright.

Praised be my Lord for those who for Thy love forgive
And weakness bear and tribulation.
Blessed those who shall in peace endure,   25
And by Thee, most High, shall they be crowned.

Praised be my Lord for our sister, the bodily death,
From the which no living man can flee.
Woe to them who die in mortal sin;
Blessed those who shall find themselves in Thy most holy will,   30
For the second death shall do them no ill.

Praise ye and bless ye my Lord, and give Him thanks,
And be subject unto Him with great humility.

St. Francis of Assisi (1182–1226)
(Trans. from the Italian by Father P. Robinson)

1. What relationship underlies the various personifications employed by St.
   Francis?
2. What sense of the creation dominates the poem?
3. What qualities of tone distinguish St. Francis's poem from St. John's?
4. Show how the personifications used by St. Francis fall short of true allegory.

15

Poetry and Psychology

Interest in the psychological effect of poetry is certainly not a new phenomenon. It is traceable back to the first-century Greek writer Longinus, who emphasized the power of poetry to arouse and gratify the emotions of the audience, and farther back still, to Aristotle (fourth century B.C.), who explained the overwhelming impact of tragic drama as the purging of emotions of pity and fear. Both assumed what all subsequent critics concerned with poetry and psychology do: that when we respond to poetry, it is not simply at the intellectual level; a full response draws upon depths of self that we may not, as readers, fully understand or significantly control. Poetry is obviously not alone among the arts in eliciting such response, but it seems especially empowered in that direction.

In our own century, the psychological awareness of poets and critics has been influenced primarily by theories of psychoanalysis, deriving from the work of Sigmund Freud. These theories focus attention on the unconscious, seeking in its operations a way to explain aspects of human behavior that seem otherwise inexplicable. Accordingly, we speak of inner drives that are not rational, not generated by any apparent external cause; of an inner self that seems to live apart from, and often in conflict with, the public self and that remains unappeased by the job, the family, the material goods and services of our public lives. Older formulations that once served to explain inner reality—for example, the idea that the sins of the father are visited upon the children—are now interpreted differently: it is not the sins (such as they may be) but the very presence of the father (and mother) that has shaped the child's psychic life and so too, ultimately, the adult's.

For his chart of the human psyche, Freud arrived at a three-part division—id, ego, and superego—each part corresponding to a different aspect and indicating a different function. The *id* he associated with the passions, especially the sexual passions, and, in their relentless impulse to fulfillment, with what he called the Pleasure Principle. Opposed to the id, and constantly challenging it, is the *superego*, which represents moral restraint, conscience, all the values that society in its need to survive esteems and attempts to enforce. As agent of the Ethical Principle, the superego exists to repress or inhibit the id at every turn and force its presence back to the realm of the unconscious. Finally, there is the *ego*, caught as it were between the id and the superego and seeking, for its survival, to mediate between the two. With the aid of the superego the ego seeks to resist the more outlandish pressures of the id; by drawing upon the id, it hopes to hold in check the incessantly repressive demands of the superego. Of the three, the ego is the most conscious and rational, and upon it lies the burden of coping with the third of Freud's postulates, the Reality Principle, by which he meant the frequently harsh realities of the world outside the self. Thus, as Freud wrote in his *New Introductory Lectures on Psychoanalysis*, "The ego stands for reason and circumspection . . . the id stands for the untamed passions," while the superego is "representative of all moral restrictions."

So far as we know, Freud never read any of the following limericks by Edward Lear, but had he done so we can assume that he would immediately have recognized the psychic conflicts they enact. The drawings are by Lear himself, intended, as here, to accompany the text.

There was an Old Person of Buda,
Whose conduct grew ruder and ruder;

Till at last, with a hammer,
They silenced his clamour,
By smashing that Person of Buda.

Edward Lear (1812–1888)

There was an Old Man of Hong Kong,
Who never did anything wrong;
   He lay on his back,
   With his head in a sack,
That innocuous Old Man of Hong Kong.

· *Edward Lear (1812–1888)*

Read in Freudian terms, the two limericks can be said to show aspects of the same problem. The ruder the Old Person of Buda becomes—the more he gives way to the pressures of the id—the more dangerous he seems to the superego, represented here by the collective "They," leading in turn to certain inevitable consequences. In the second limerick, the Old Man of Hong Kong has lived an admirable life from society's · point of view, posing no threat; but to do no "wrong" is entirely to frustrate the id, a condition that is tantamount to the ego's death (head in a sack, body supine).

    Lear's fantasy of happiness in other of his limericks typically consists of a flight from the oppressive superego:

There was an Old Person of Basing,
Whose presence of mind was amazing;
    He purchased a steed,
    Which he rode at full speed,
And escaped from the people of Basing.

Edward Lear (1812–1888)

There was an Old Man of Bohemia,
Whose daughter was christened Euphemia;
    Till one day, to his grief,
    She married a thief,
Which grieved that Old Man of Bohemia.

Edward Lear (1812–1888)

The Old Person of Basing harnesses himself to energy and speed as a way of escaping the "people." His reasons are left unspecified, but the steed certainly seems suggestive of runaway passion, perhaps sexuality, as a Freudian critic might well say the drawing implies. Nor does the journey have a destination; the goal is in the flight itself.

The second limerick is perhaps more interesting in its identification of the superego with the father, who christens his daughter Euphemia, which in Greek means "use of good words." It is more generally cognate to "euphemism," a process of roundabout discourse that substitutes inoffensive terms for offensive ones. The implication is that the father has raised his daughter with such values foremost, but his hopes come to grief as she allies with a thief, an outlaw, the underworld—categories suggestive of the id—in defiance of the ethical order the father represents.

Of Lear's imaginative world in general, we can note that it is characteristically lacking in images of sound egos capable of mediating between the libidinous and the ethical. Either the superego smashes the id or, more rarely, the id breaks free. When they meet in a kind of suspended conflict, as in the following self-portrait, the results can be strange. Which of the two seems to dominate, and with what consequences?

How Pleasant to Know Mr. Lear!

How pleasant to know Mr. Lear!
  Who has written such volumes of stuff!
Some think him ill-tempered and queer,
  But a few think him pleasant enough.

His mind is concrete and fastidious, 5
  His nose is remarkably big;
His visage is more or less hideous,
  His beard it resembles a wig.

He has ears, and two eyes, and ten fingers,
  Leastways if you reckon two thumbs; 10
Long ago he was one of the singers,
  But now he is one of the dumbs.

He sits in a beautiful parlour,
  With hundreds of books on the wall;
He drinks a great deal of Marsala, 15
  But never gets tipsy at all.

He has many friends, laymen and clerical;
  Old Foss is the name of his cat;
His body is perfectly spherical,
  He weareth a runcible hat. 20

When he walks in a waterproof white,
  The children run after him so!

Calling out, 'He's come out in his night-
   Gown, that crazy old Englishman, oh!'

He weeps by the side of the ocean,   25
   He weeps on the top of the hill;
He purchases pancakes and lotion,
   And chocolate shrimps from the mill.

He reads but he cannot speak Spanish,
   He cannot abide ginger-beer: 30
Ere the days of his pilgrimage vanish,
   How pleasant to know Mr. Lear!

Edward Lear (1812–1888)

But rather than trying to work out the complexities of a particular psychoanalytical theory, even one so influential as Freud's, and then imposing it on the poem, we can better proceed inductively, seeking in the poetry itself the kinds of psychological awarenesses that Freud and most analysts assure us are there. A poem like Ann Darr's "The Gift," for example, tells us little about issues of class consciousness or of wars between nations, but much about the conflict between mothers and daughters:

The Gift

Daughter, this small stiletto which I found
sticking in my ribs, I have wiped clean
and given back to you. You will need it.

I had hoped there was some other way.
Some way for you to take your self from me   5
without the violence.

I deluded myself, of course, until now
I am hardly prepared for these scenes
we play. I have forgotten,
if I ever knew, how to repair   10
my face.

       Can't I engage
some Fury to play my part with me, so that
in the climax when you leave my house
"forever" I can defy you, as I must if   15
I would pass the prompt-book, nay the old stiletto
which belonged to my mother's mother's mother's . . .

Ann Darr (b. 1920)

The Gift. l. 13 *Fury:* In Greek and Roman mythology an avenging female entity that punishes transgressions.

The mother is angry at the outset of the poem; we do not know what the daughter has said or done, only that to the mother it has had the effect of being stabbed. By the end of the poem the mother acknowledges that such anger is a condition of life, for though she had wished for a separation without violence, she knows that she has deluded herself, that separation cannot be peaceful. They must defy each other, and she must give back the knife—almost a second gift of life—which "belonged to [her] mother's mother's mother's . . ."

Though the poem opens and closes on the image of the stiletto, another key image is introduced in the third stanza: that of a play being enacted, with "scenes" and "parts" allotted to the two women. The "climax" is yet to come, but when it does it will consist of the daughter's final departure (lines 14–15), in her hands both the knife and a "prompt-book" (line 16)—a theatrical cue-book—that will help her learn her future role as mother. The roles are inevitable, seemingly predetermined; the poem suggests that no change in the scenario is possible.

A similar fatedness pervades the next poem, by Donald Finkel, which approaches the parental role from the point of view of the father. Here, too, there is anger, but the poem's wit tends to defuse the intensity that informs Darr's poem:

The Father

When I am walking with the children, and a girl
still hard in the buttocks bends to them with a laugh,
my heart bangs where it hangs in my empty carcass.
But you knew that. It has already passed
the stage of neighbor's gossip and attained   5

the clarity of an historical fact.
A myth comes down your street: here on my right
toddles my twinkling daughter, who loves me, while
on my left marches my son, who does not.

It is all true, but it does not matter;   10
in twenty years my son and I will have reached
a silent understanding, whereas (poor fool,
already growing hollow) some pimply bastard
will have made off with my blessings and my daughter.

Donald Finkel (b. 1929)

Structurally, the poem separates into three parts, each providing a perspective on the speaker's emotional life. In the first part (lines 1–6) he is a young man (who happens also to be a father), his sexual energies directed outward to the passing girl; in the second (lines 7–9) he is primarily the young father, loved by his daughter and resented by his son; in the third (lines 10–14) he has come to a tacit reconciliation with his grown son but must, contrary to his desire, give up the daughter he loves. Though this last stage is some twenty years away, the father foresees the event, knows it must be, hates the idea of it, and yet has already accepted its inevitability. He is powerless before imperatives such as "historical fact" (line 6) or the "myth" of fatherhood that "comes down [the] street" (line 7) to greet and envelop him.

In both poems we get the sense of characters driven by buried and irrepressible forces that nevertheless correspond to an established pattern. Finkel's speaker may be ironical, almost flip, in ways that Darr's is not, but for all his wit and foreknowledge, in the end he is as submissive.

We have yet, however, to consider the *child's* perspective on what Freud termed the first and most important love story, the "family romance":

Bears

Wonderful bears that walked my room all night,
Where have you gone, your sleek and fairy fur,
Your eyes' veiled and imperious light?

Brown bears as rich as mocha or as musk,
White opalescent bears whose fur stood out   5
Electric in the deepening dusk,

And great black bears that seemed more blue than black,
More violet than blue against the dark—
Where are you now? Upon what track

Mutter your muffled paws that used to tread   10
So softly, surely, up the creakless stair
While I lay listening in bed?

When did I lose you? Whose have you become?
Why do I wait and wait and never hear
Your thick nocturnal pacing in my room?   15
My bears, who keeps you now, in pride and fear?

Adrienne Rich (b. 1929)

Adrienne Rich's adult speaker laments the loss of a recurrent childhood fantasy associated with night, bed, and sleep, and she seems indeed desirous of returning to her childhood to retrieve it. The fantasy centers upon bears, but the bears seem to evoke other meanings, attached perhaps to the nursery tale of Goldilocks and the Three Bears (mommy, daddy, and baby bears). Of the three types enumerated in the poem, the "great black bears" (line 7) may suggest the father; the "white opalescent" ones (line 5), the mother; and the "brown" (line 4), the child that the speaker once was. The three types live harmoniously in the room, coming at night to the waiting child as she "lay listening in bed" (line 12). But the child has matured, the fantasy has been lost; when, exactly, is beyond her determination (line 13). And yet the speaker, older and forlorn, waits and waits in vain, and expresses her longing (in a poem dominated, perhaps not incidentally, by a three-line stanzaic pattern).

So much the poem tells us, but it tells us nothing of the child's actual relationship with her parents or why now, as an adult, the sense of loss is so great. Were the parents hostile, or seemingly so to the child, and was the nighttime fantasy a way of compensating for what reality failed to provide? Has the speaker's subsequent life been oppressive, forcing her back to happier moments, themselves fantasies? And what are we to make of the poem's last word, "fear," in a poem that has seemingly excluded that emotion? Fear of what or of whom? Tempting as they are, speculations of this kind take us well beyond the poem, the strength of which is primarily in its evocation of what has been lost rather than in its explanation of it.

D. H. Lawrence's poem "Piano" is similarly evocative, but here the memories imply the essence of a relationship that remains with him still and is ever capable of reasserting its power:

Piano

Softly, in the dusk, a woman is singing to me;
Taking me back down the vista of years, till I see
A child sitting under the piano, in the boom of the tingling strings
And pressing the small, poised feet of a mother who smiles as she sings.

In spite of myself, the insidious mastery of song   5
Betrays me back, till the heart of me weeps to belong
To the old Sunday evenings at home, with winter outside
And hymns in the cozy parlor, the tinkling piano our guide.

So now it is vain for the singer to burst into clamor
With the great black piano appassionato. The glamor   10

Of childish days is upon me, my manhood is cast
Down in the flood of remembrance, I weep like a child for the past.

D. H. Lawrence (1885–1930)

QUESTIONS

1. What set of associations causes Lawrence's return "down the vista of years"
   (line 2)? How willingly does he go?
2. What relationship is implied between mother and son in lines 3–4? To what
   extent is it modified or reinforced in lines 5–8?
3. In what sense is Lawrence's "manhood . . . cast/Down" (lines 11–12)? What
   are the implications of the tears in the last line?

Whatever their differences, Lawrence and Rich seem to agree that within the adult there resides still the child with all its longings, desires, and remembered gratifications. The final line of Rich's poem reaffirms the idea of possession, "My bears," in tones that recall childhood; whoever their new keepers, the bears remain hers. Lawrence "weep[s] like a child" (line 12) and is able literally to see himself, "A child sitting under the piano . . . pressing the small, poised feet" (lines 3–4). The mother "smiles as she sings," a phrase that leaves ambiguous the precise reasons for her smile. Is it caused by the pleasure of song? of the child's touch? of both? What matters, of course, is not the mother's state (we can never know that), but Lawrence's memory, how he envisions her in relationship to himself.

"Piano" is amenable in other ways to a psychological approach. In a poem so centered on family, there is, for example, no reference to the presence of a father, not even in the strongly domestic scene re-created in the second stanza:

> . . . till the heart of me weeps to belong
> To the old Sunday evenings at home, with winter outside
> And hymns in the cozy parlor, the tinkling piano our guide.

The cozy parlor may well include the father, but guidance comes from the piano, which is associated with the mother. The sense, too, of "cozy," of warmth, in contrast to the "winter outside," returns us to the mother as the center of the household. And it seems reasonable at least to wonder about the worshipful quality of this scene and the one preceding: hymn-singing under the mother's guidance in the enclosure of the parlor proves as pleasurable to the child as worshiping at her feet in the sanctuary under the piano.

In contrast to Rich's speaker, Lawrence's has easy access to his childhood, at least to its pleasures, and is both indulgent and protective of it. What this means for the adult seems several times intimated—"insidious," "Betrays," "manhood is cast/Down" (lines 5, 6, 11–12)—but it is never really examined, certainly not in the manner of the speaker of Robert Duncan's poem that follows, which details the speaker's long struggle to assume his own identity against the will of his mother. As he sees the relationship, she represents the force in his life that "curbs"—inhibits and controls—him, and despite his apparent success in breaking loose from her, and her subsequent death, his anger and fear remain, intensified now by an access of adult guilt.

My Mother Would Be a Falconress

My mother would be a falconress,
And I, her gay falcon treading her wrist,
would fly to bring back
from the blue of the sky to her, bleeding, a prize,
where I dream in my little hood with many bells   5
jangling when I'd turn my head.

My mother would be a falconress,
and she sends me as far as her will goes.
She lets me ride to the end of her curb
where I fall back in anguish.   10
I dread that she will cast me away,
for I fall, I mis-take, I fail in her mission.

She would bring down the little birds.
And I would bring down the little birds.
When will she let me bring down the little birds,   15
pierced from their flight with their necks broken,
their heads like flowers limp from the stem?

I tread my mother's wrist and would draw blood.
Behind the little hood my eyes are hooded.
I have gone back into my hooded silence,   20
talking to myself and dropping off to sleep.

For she has muffled my dreams in the hood she has made me,
sewn round with bells, jangling when I move.
She rides with her little falcon upon her wrist.
She uses a barb that brings me to cower.   25

She sends me abroad to try my wings
and I come back to her.   I would bring down

the little birds to her
I may not tear into, I must bring back perfectly.

I tear at her wrist with my beak to draw blood,   30
and her eye holds me, anguisht, terrifying.
She draws a limit to my flight.
Never beyond my sight, she says.

She trains me to fetch and to limit myself in fetching.
She rewards me with meat for my dinner.   35
But I must never eat what she sends me to bring her.

Yet it would have been beautiful, if she would have carried me,
always, in a little hood with the bells ringing,
at her wrist, and her riding
to the great falcon hunt, and me   40
flying up to the curb of my heart from her heart
to bring down the skylark from the blue to her feet,
straining, and then released for the flight.

My mother would be a falconress,
and I her gerfalcon, raised at her will,   45
from her wrist sent flying, as if I were her own
pride, as if her pride
knew no limits, as if her mind
sought in me flight beyond the horizon.

Ah, but high, high in the air I flew.   50
And far, far beyond the curb of her will,
were the blue hills where the falcons nest.
And then I saw west to the dying sun—
it seemd my human soul went down in flames.

I tore at her wrist, at the hold she had for me,   55
until the blood ran hot and I heard her cry out,
far, far beyond the curb of her will

to horizons of stars beyond the ringing hills of the world where the
    falcons nest
I saw, and I tore at her wrist with my savage beak.
I flew, as if sight flew from the anguish in her eye beyond her sight,   60
sent from my striking loose, from the cruel strike at her wrist,
striking out from the blood to be free of her.

My mother would be a falconress,
and even now, years after this,
when the wounds I left her had surely heald,   65

and the woman is dead,
her fierce eyes closed, and if her heart
were broken, it is stilld

I would be a falcon and go free.
I tread her wrist and wear the hood,   70
talking to myself, and would draw blood.

Robert Duncan (b. 1919)

My Mother Would Be a Falconress. The falcon, or hawk, was trained to hunt birds; it was kept hooded until released for flight. The falcon was tied to the wrist of the falconer, hopefully trained to rest there. l. 45 *gerfalcon:* among the largest of the species.

QUESTIONS

1. Trace the development of feeling, stanza by stanza, beginning with the relatively content youth of the first stanza and ending with the bitter adult of the final stanza.
2. Explain the apparent contradiction in attitude in lines 30–43. How is that contradiction reflected in both the speaker's escape (lines 50–62) and his subsequent attitude (lines 63–71)?
3. What are the effects of developing the poem through an extended metaphor taken from the ancient art of falconry?

Poems that seem less centrally concerned with psychological issues can nonetheless bear interesting meanings when considered from a psychological perspective. William Blake's "A Little Boy Lost" makes, certainly, a political statement about autocratic societies, but as you read the poem consider its psychological implications and the ways in which the political and the psychological seem to mesh to make a unified, comprehensive statement.

A Little Boy Lost

Nought loves another as itself
Nor venerates another so.
Nor is it possible to Thought
A greater than itself to know:

And Father, how can I love you,   5
Or any of my brothers more?
I love you like the little bird
That picks up crumbs around the door.

The Priest sat by and heard the child.
In trembling zeal he seiz'd his hair: 10
He led him by his little coat:
And all admir'd the Priestly care.

And standing on the altar high,
Lo what a fiend is here! said he:
One who sets reason up for judge   15
Of our most holy Mystery.

The weeping child could not be heard.
The weeping parents wept in vain:
They strip'd him to his little shirt.
And bound him in an iron chain.   20

And burn'd him in a holy place,
Where many had been burn'd before:
The weeping parents wept in vain.
Are such things done on Albion's° shore?   *England's*

William Blake (1757–1827)

QUESTIONS

1. Paraphrase the boy's argument (lines 1–8) to show what in it proves so threatening to the priest.
2. What is the priest's relationship to the people? In what sense do they share a common interest?
3. Explain the role of the parents. How do you interpret their tears and their apparent helplessness (lines 18, 23)?
4. To what extent does the punishment fit the crime? Explain.
5. How do you interpret line 22?
6. On what basis can you argue that the political and the psychological implications enforce each other?

William Shakespeare's sonnet defines the effects of lust, one of the seven cardinal sins, and can obviously be read in Christian terms of heaven, hell, and original sin. But the poem is no less a dramatization of the conflict of psychic forces, especially comprehensible in psychoanalytical terms:

Th' Expense of Spirit in a Waste of Shame

Th' expense of spirit in a waste of shame
Is lust in action; and, till action, lust

Is perjured, murd'rous, bloody, full of blame,
Savage, extreme, rude, cruel, not to trust;
Enjoyed no sooner but despiséd straight;   5
Past reason hunted, and no sooner had,
Past reason hated, as a swallowed bait
On purpose laid to make the taker mad;
Mad in pursuit, and in possession so;
Had, having, and in quest to have, extreme;   10
A bliss in proof—and proved, a very woe;
Before, a joy proposed; behind, a dream.
   All this the world well knows; yet none knows well
   To shun the heaven that leads men to this hell.

William Shakespeare (1564–1616)

QUESTIONS

1. How do the language and sentence patterns reflect the presence of conflict?
2. Argue that "lust in action" (line 2) is identifiable with the id and the Pleasure Principle.
3. Where is there evidence of the play of the superego and the Ethical Principle? Explain.
4. Explain the plight of the ego in the concluding couplet.
5. To what extent is it possible to reconcile the Christian and psychological readings?

   Not all poems invite a psychological reading, and even for those that do the question is often one of degree or emphasis. We can say, for example, of the resolution of Robert Frost's "Stopping by Woods on a Snowy Evening" (p. 232) that it contains a powerful assertion of the Ethical Principle in its acknowledgment of the "promises" (line 14) or responsibilities that must be met. But the impulses that are being defeated are hardly those of the untamed passions that Freud associated with the id. If anything, they may be tied to a later stage of Freud's own thought, when he formulated the presence of a death wish deep in our psychic beings. The woods that draw Frost's speaker are "lovely, dark and deep" (line 13) and seem to offer peace, envelopment, a return to and absorption back into nature. Though the delicacy of the mood and its effect are not dependent on our knowing this aspect of Freud's thought, such recognition helps to clarify the nature of the speaker's response as well as our own.

   As to why poets write as they do ("What drove Frost to write such a poem?"), psychoanalytical criticism has offered only tentative answers.* The poem seems to have its source in inner conflict and to represent the poet's way of expressing and managing that conflict. As Emily Dickinson, writing well before Freud, remarked, "I felt a palsy, here—the Verses just relieve." The poem is therapeutic, offering the poet relief from, though not a cure for, the conflict that produces it. It does so by objectifying the conflict, giving it symbolic expression within a poetic structure that is logical, coherent, and—perhaps above all—public. The problem has been externalized and communicated and has found resolution, if only for the moment. To quote Alfred, Lord Tennyson, "for the unquiet heart and brain,/A use in measured language lies." Or in Louise Bogan's words:

To an Artist, To Take Heart

Slipping in blood, by his own hand, through pride,
Hamlet, Othello, Coriolanus fall.
Upon his bed, however, Shakespeare died,
Having endured them all.

Louise Bogan (1897–1970)

Hamlet, Othello, and Coriolanus are characters in Shakespeare's plays who all died violently, as line 1 tells us. Shakespeare himself, on the other hand, died peacefully in bed, "Having endured them all," through them perhaps having dealt with his own impulses to destruction. That is the encouraging counsel the poet offers her colleagues.

Poets may or may not be more neurotic than the rest of us, but if the psychoanalytical approach to creativity is at all accurate they are surely the more blessed in possessing the means of shaping and expressing impulses that might otherwise prove crippling or totally destructive.

EXERCISES

I. Although the two poems below differ in tone and approach, they suggest similar psychological awarenesses on the part of the poets. Outline the similarities and then account for the factors within the poems that make for the major differences.

---

* Freud himself warned of the difficulties in seeking to account for "the nature of the artistic gift," in seeking to "explain the means by which the artist works—artistic technique" (*An Autobiographical Study*).

From a Correct Address in a Suburb of a Major City

She wears her middle age like a cowled
gown, sleeved in it, folded high
at the breast,

charming, proper at cocktails
but the inner one raging   5
and how to hide her,

how to keep her leashed, contain
the heat of her, the soaring cry
never yet loosed,

demanding a chance before the years devour her,   10
before the marrow of her fine long legs
congeals and she

settles forever for this street, this house,
her face set to the world
sweet, sweet   15

above the shocked, astonished
hunger.

Helen Sorrells (b. 1908)

The Temperaments

Nine adulteries, 12 liaisons, 64 fornications and something approaching a
      rape
   Rest nightly upon the soul of our delicate friend Florialis,
And yet the man is so quiet and reserved in demeanour
That he passes for both bloodless and sexless.
Bastidides, on the contrary, who both talks and writes of nothing save
      copulation,
Has become the father of twins,
But he accomplished this feat at some cost;
   He had to be four times cuckold.

Ezra Pound (1885–1972)

II. The three poems that follow focus on the child-father relationship. Determine in each instance the speaker's response to the parent, taking into account imagery, tone, and attitude. Then compare the poems in terms of the degree of self-revelation they contain and the kind of resolution they achieve.

Silence

My father used to say,
"Superior people never make long visits,
have to be shown Longfellow's° grave   *Henry Wadsworth Longfellow*
or the glass flowers at Harvard.   *(1807–1882), American poet*
Self-reliant like the cat—   5
that takes its prey to privacy,
the mouse's limp tail hanging like a shoelace from its mouth—
they sometimes enjoy solitude,
and can be robbed of speech
by speech which has delighted them.   10
The deepest feeling always shows itself in silence;
not in silence, but restraint."
Nor was he insincere in saying, "Make my house your inn."
Inns are not residences.

Marianne Moore (1887–1972)

Middle Age

Now the midwinter grind
is on me, New York
drills through my nerves,
as I walk
the chewed-up streets.   5

At forty-five,
what next, what next?
At every corner,
I meet my Father,
my age, still alive.   10

Father, forgive me
my injuries,
as I forgive
those I
have injured!   15

You never climbed
Mount Sion, yet left
dinosaur
death-steps on the crust,
where I must walk.   20

Robert Lowell (1917–1977)

The Revelation

Stress of his anger set me back
To musing over time and space.
The apple branches dripping black
Divided light across his face.
Towering beneath the broken tree,   5
He seemed a stony shade to me.
He spoke no language I could hear
For long with my distracted ear.

Between his lips and my delight
In blowing wind, a bird-song rose.   10
And soon in fierce, blockading light
The planet's shadow hid his face.
And all that strongly molded bone
Of chest and shoulder soon were gone,
Devoured among the solid shade.   15
Assured his angry voice was dead,

And satisfied his judging eyes
Had given over plaguing me,
I stood to let the darkness rise—
My darkness, gathering in the tree,   20
The field, the swollen shock of hay,
Bank of the creek half washed away.
Lost in my self, and unaware
Of love, I took the evening air.

I blighted, for a moment's length,   25
My father out of sight and sound;
Prayed to annihilate his strength,
The proud legs planted on the ground.
Why should I hear his angry cry
Or bear the damning of his eye?   30
Anger for anger I could give,
And murder for my right to live.

The moon rose. Lucidly the moon
Ran skimming shadows off the trees.
To strip all shadow but its own   35
Down to the perfect mindlessness.
Yet suddenly the moonlight caught
My father's fingers reaching out,
The strong arm begging me for love,
Loneliness I knew nothing of.   40

And weeping in the nakedness
Of moonlight and of agony,
His blue eyes lost their barrenness
And bore a blossom out to me.
And as I ran to give it back,   45
The apple branches, dripping black,
Trembled across the lunar air
And dropped white petals on his hair.

James Wright (1927–1980)

III.   At the center of each of the following three poems is an act of violence.
Compare the psychological states of the perpetrators in each poem. Then
consider your own response. Which of the poems affects you most directly and
immediately? Why?

A Poison Tree

I was angry with my friend,
I told my wrath, my wrath did end;
I was angry with my foe,
I told it not, my wrath did grow.

And I water'd it in fears,   5
Night and morning with my tears;
And I sunned it with smiles,
And with soft deceitful wiles.

And it grew both day and night,
Till it bore an apple bright;   10
And my foe beheld it shine,
And he knew that it was mine,

And into my garden stole
When the night had veil'd the pole:
In the morning glad I see   15
My foe outstretch'd beneath the tree.

William Blake (1757–1827)

The Whipping

The old woman across the way
    is whipping the boy again
and shouting to the neighborhood
    her goodness and his wrongs.

Wildly he crashes through elephant ears,   5
    pleads in dusty zinnias,
while she in spite of crippling fat
    pursues and corners him.

She strikes and strikes the shrilly circling
    boy till the stick breaks   10
in her hand. His tears are rainy weather
    to woundlike memories:

My head gripped in bony vise
    of knees, the writhing struggle
to wrench free, the blows, the fear   15
    worse than blows that hateful

Words could bring, the face that I
    no longer knew or loved . . .
Well, it is over now, it is over,
    and the boy sobs in his room,   20

And the woman leans muttering against
    a tree, exhausted, purged—
avenged in part for lifelong hidings
    she has had to bear.

Robert Hayden (1913–1980)

The Ballad of a Barber

Here is the tale of Carrousel,
The barber of Meridian Street.
He cut, and coiffed, and shaved so well,
That all the world was at his feet.

The King, the Queen, and all the Court,   5
To no one else would trust their hair,
And reigning belles of every sort
Owed their successes to his care.

With carriage and with cabriolet°   *one-horse, two-wheeled carriage*
Daily Meridian Street was blocked,   10
Like bees about a bright bouquet
The beaux about his doorway flocked.

Such was his art he could with ease
Curl wit into the dullest face;
Or to a goddess of old Greece   15
Add a new wonder and a grace.

All powders, paints, and subtle dyes,
And costliest scents that men distil,
And rare pomades, forgot their price
And marvelled at his splendid skill.   20

The curling irons in his hand
Almost grew quick enough to speak,
The razor was a magic wand
That understood the softest cheek.

Yet with no pride his heart was moved;   25
He was so modest in his ways!
His daily task was all he loved,
And now and then a little praise.

An equal care he would bestow
On problems simple or complex;   30
And nobody had seen him show
A preference for either sex.

How came it then one summer day,
Coiffing the daughter of the King,
He lengthened out the least delay   35
And loitered in his hairdressing?

The Princess was a pretty child,
Thirteen years old, or thereabout.
She was as joyous and as wild
As spring flowers when the sun is out.   40

Her gold hair fell down to her feet
And hung about her pretty eyes;
She was as lyrical and sweet
As one of Schubert's° melodies.   *Franz Schubert (1797–1828),*
                                        Austrian composer

Three times the barber curled a lock,   45
And thrice he straightened it again;

And twice the irons scorched her frock,
And twice he stumbled in her train.

His fingers lost their cunning quite,
His ivory combs obeyed no more;   50
Something or other dimmed his sight,
And moved mysteriously the floor.

He leant upon the toilet table,
His fingers fumbled in his breast;
He felt as foolish as a fable,   55
And feeble as a pointless jest.

He snatched a bottle of Cologne,
And broke the neck between his hands;
He felt as if he was alone,
And mighty as a king's commands.   60

The Princess gave a little scream,
Carrousel's cut was sharp and deep;
He left her softly as a dream
That leaves a sleeper to his sleep.

He left the room on pointed feet;   65
Smiling that things had gone so well.
They hanged him in Meridian Street.
You pray in vain for Carrousel.

Aubrey Beardsley (1872–1898)

IV.   Though religious in theme, George Herbert's "The Collar" is psychological
in emphasis and echoes secular patterns. Read it with both its religious and
secular possibilities in mind, noting especially the reasons for the speaker's
rebelliousness. Then answer the questions that follow the poem.

The Collar

I struck the board° and cried, "No more;   *table*
        I will abroad!
What? shall I ever sigh and pine?
My lines and life are free, free as the road,
    Loose as the wind, as large as store°.   *abundant* 5
        Shall I be still in suit°?   *waiting for favors*
Have I no harvest but a thorn

To let me blood, and not restore
What I have lost with cordial° fruit?   *life-sustaining*
        Sure there was wine   10
    Before my sighs did dry it; there was corn
      Before my tears did drown it.
    Is the year only lost to me?
      Have I no bays° to crown it,   *laurel wreath*
No flowers, no garlands gay? All blasted?   15
        All wasted?
    Not so, my heart; but there is fruit,
      And thou hast hands.
    Recover all thy sigh-blown age
On double pleasures: leave thy cold dispute   20
Of what is fit and not. Forsake thy cage,
      Thy rope of sands,
Which petty thoughts have made, and made to thee
    Good cable, to enforce and draw,
      And be thy law,   25
While thou didst wink° and wouldst not see.   *closed your eyes*
      Away! take heed;
      I will abroad.
Call in thy death's-head° there; tie up thy fears.   *skull recalling one's mortal lot*
      He that forbears   30
    To suit and serve his need,
      Deserves his load."
But as I raved and grew more fierce and wild
      At every word,
Methought I heard one calling, *Child!*   35
    And I replied, *My Lord.*

George Herbert (1593–1633)

1. What is the nature of the speaker's reaction at the start? What does it imply
   about his past behavior? How does it prepare for what follows?
2. Explain the speaker's grievances in lines 3–16. What is his emotional state?
3. How does the speaker hope to find remedy, "serve his need" (line 31),
   according to lines 17–32?
4. What is the effect of introducing God only at the end of the poem (lines
   33–36)? What relationship is implied here between the speaker and God?
   How does your answer account for the word "Methought"?
5. Argue that the poem is built by analogy, drawing on a young man's relations
   with his father, and that its psychological center lies in the tension between
   rebellion and submission.

V.   A number of poems in this volume bring psychological issues into focus, among them William Blake's "The Garden of Love" (p. 134), Sylvia Plath's "Daddy" (p. 259), Theodore Roethke's "My Papa's Waltz" (p. 480), and Anne Sexton's "The Moss of His Skin" (p. 199). Discuss the central issue in each instance. Which poem seems to you most moving? Describe your response.

16
Poetry, Mythology, and Myth

Countless stories from classical and other MYTHOLOGIES describe gods, goddesses, and other immortals who interact among themselves but also participate in the lives of mortals, directing or interfering with events, engaging in battles, plots, love affairs, and countless quarrels. In their original contexts, stories of this order often carried the impact of religious truth and seemed to explain or comment upon such phenomena as the Creation, the origins of ritual and law, or the functioning of natural processes. Thus, the legend of Demeter (goddess of grain and fertility) and her daughter Persephone, the latter abducted by Hades to the underworld, became for the Greeks a means of reflecting on changes in the seasonal cycle.* Other stories, such as that of Prometheus who brought fire and light to humans in defiance of the god Zeus, touched upon other aspects of reality. The interesting thing is that the legends are so vivid, compelling, and imaginatively suggestive that they have

---

* Learning of Persephone's disappearance, Demeter sought her throughout the land, laying aside her responsibilities as fertility goddess. The earth lay unproductive and the gods were deprived of their sacrifices and tribute, until at last Hades was forced to relent and Persephone was allowed to rejoin her mother. But since she had been tricked into tasting of the food of the underworld (pomegranate seeds), Persephone was obliged to return to Hades's realm for a third of each year, reemerging each spring to the joy of Demeter.

survived and remain significant for us as legends long after they have lost their religious impact. Traces of the gods can even be found embedded in certain of our common words: *cereal* derives from the goddess Ceres (the Roman name for Demeter); *mercury* from the Roman god of that name known for his fleetness; *martial* from Mars, the Roman god of war; and *venereal* from Venus, the Roman goddess of love. Other words of similar derivation include *vulcanize, psychic, erotic, olympian,* and *titanic;* behind each is a specific story or character.

Later poets have been fascinated by the figures and tales of past mythologies and frequently use them, sometimes in a full retelling, sometimes more briefly by allusion, to shed light on some aspect of the poet's mood or thought. (See our discussion of the uses of allusion in poetry in chapter 3.) In the sonnet that follows, William Wordsworth draws upon classical mythology to point up the failings of his own time:

The World Is Too Much with Us; Late and Soon

The world is too much with us; late and soon,
Getting and spending, we lay waste our powers:
Little we see in Nature that is ours;
We have given our hearts away, a sordid boon!
The sea that bares her bosom to the moon;   5
The winds that will be howling at all hours,
And are up-gathered now like sleeping flowers;
For this, for everything, we are out of tune;
It moves us not.—Great God! I'd rather be
A pagan suckled in a creed outworn;   10
So might I, standing on this pleasant lea,
Have glimpses that would make me less forlorn;
Have sight of Proteus rising from the sea;
Or hear old Triton blow his wreathèd horn.

William Wordsworth (1770–1850)

Writing in the early nineteenth century, Wordsworth laments the loss of powers of the imagination, the ability to respond to the natural world—a world far different from that alluded to in the opening line, where busy materialism wastes people's best energies, blinding them to the beauty and force of sea and wind. Had he been a Greek, standing in the same place and capable of believing in a "creed" no longer tenable, his imagination would have been invigorated by visions of Proteus, a sea god, and echoes of Triton, the god of storms.

Similarly, Alfred, Lord Tennyson uses mythological allusions to reflect on a loss of imagination, but it is with his personal loss, not that of his society, that he is concerned. The references in lines 3–4 are to the Trojan Wars, fought between Greece and Troy ("Ilion") and recounted in Homer's epic *The Iliad:*

Lines

Here often, when a child, I lay reclined,
I took delight in this locality.
Here stood the infant Ilion of the mind,
And here the Grecian ships did seem to be.
And here again I come, and only find
The drain-cut levels of the marshy lea,—
Grey sandbanks, and pale sunsets,—dreary wind,
Dim shores, dense rains, and heavy-clouded sea.

Alfred, Lord Tennyson (1809–1892)

QUESTIONS

1. How do you explain the many particulars the poet gives of the revisited scene and the lack of them in his description of the scene when first visited?
2. Describe the transformation that has occurred.

Allusions to classical mythology such as those we have seen in the two previous poems by Wordsworth and Tennyson contribute to the effect of countless poems. In this text see, for instance, Edgar Allan Poe's "To Helen" and H. D.'s "Helen" in Exercise I at the end of this chapter, Walter Savage Landor's "Dirce" (p. 59), John Keats's "Ode on a Grecian Urn" (p. 201), and William Butler Yeats's "Long-Legged Fly" (p. 60). But it is the possibilities of reinterpretation, not merely allusion, that have especially interested later poets. Robert Graves, not only a poet and novelist but an authority on classical myths, brings a cool and precise wit to the legend of Pygmalion, a sculptor who created a marble statue of a young woman and then fell in love with it. In the classical story, his prayers to the goddess Aphrodite that she find him a wife similar to the statue he had created are more than answered: the statue comes to life and the sculptor and his creation wed. But Graves adds a chapter to the story:

Galatea and Pygmalion

Galatea, whom his furious chisel
From Parian stone had by greed enchanted,

Fulfilled, so they say, Pygmalion's longings:
  Stepped from the pedestal on which she stood,
Bare in his bed laid her down, lubricious,
With low responses to his drunken raptures,   5
  Enroyalled his body with her demon blood.

Alas, Pygmalion had so well plotted
The articulation of his woman monster
That schools of eager connoisseurs beset   10
  Her single person with perennial suit;
Whom she (a judgement on the jealous artist)
Admitted rankly to a comprehension
  Of themes that crowned her own, not his repute.

Robert Graves (b. 1895)

QUESTIONS

1. Describe Galatea's character and behavior and the kind of "judgement" (line 12) Pygmalion suffers.
2. You may have noticed that the poem is a variation on the sonnet form. Analyze its structure.
3. On the basis of this poem, what would you suppose to be Graves's attitude toward the use of mythological materials?

    Although the Pygmalion-Galatea legend is also the subject of George Bernard Shaw's play *Pygmalion* (written well before Graves's poem), it has otherwise remained in the background of literary usage. Certain other mythological figures, however, like Helen of Troy and Odysseus (also called Ulysses), have proved especially appealing, and a considerable body of literature has grown up about them. The original document on Odysseus is the rendering of his experiences in the two Greek epics, *The Iliad* and *The Odyssey*. A Greek hero in the defeat of Troy, known for his cunning and courage, Odysseus underwent a variety of adventures in his ten-year effort to return home to Ithaca after the Trojan Wars. In the following poem, the exiled Russian poet Joseph Brodsky envisions Odysseus writing to his son Telemachus from the domain of Circe, a sorceress Odysseus and his crew encountered who tempts men and then transforms them into swine. Two further notes are useful: (1) forewarned that if he went to Troy he would be gone for twenty years and return destitute, Odysseus had originally resisted going on the expedition, pretending madness, a ruse that was uncovered by Palamedes (line 24); (2) Odysseus's efforts to return from Troy were thwarted by the sea god Poseidon (lines 7–8) in revenge for the hero's blinding of Poseidon's son, the giant Polyphemus.

Odysseus to Telemachus

My dear Telemachus,
                    The Trojan War
is over now; I don't recall who won it.
The Greeks, no doubt, for only they would leave
so many dead so far from their own homeland.   5
But still, my homeward way has proved too long.
While we were wasting time there, old Poseidon,
it almost seems, stretched and extended space.

I don't know where I am or what this place
can be. It would appear some filthy island,   10
with bushes, buildings, and great grunting pigs.
A garden choked with weeds; some queen or other.
Grass and huge stones . . . Telemachus, my son!
To a wanderer the faces of all islands
resemble one another. And the mind   15
trips, numbering waves; eyes, sore from sea horizons,
run; and the flesh of water stuffs the ears.
I can't remember how the war came out;
even how old you are—I can't remember.

Grow up, then, my Telemachus, grow strong.   20
Only the gods know if we'll see each other
again. You've long since ceased to be that babe
before whom I reined in the plowing bullocks.
Had it not been for Palamedes' trick
we two would still be living in one household.   25
But maybe he was right; away from me
you are quite safe from all Oedipal passions,
and your dreams, my Telemachus, are blameless.

Joseph Brodsky (b. 1940)
(Trans. from the Russian by George L. Kline)

Compare with Brodsky's version that of Alfred, Lord Tennyson, which picks up Odysseus's history several years later, after his return and his reunion with Telemachus and with his wife Penelope, who had remained faithful to him, despite the most dire pressures, for the twenty years of his absence:

Ulysses

It little profits that an idle king,
By this still hearth, among these barren crags,
Matched with an aged wife, I mete and dole
Unequal laws unto a savage race,
That hoard, and sleep, and feed, and know not me.   5
I cannot rest from travel: I will drink
Life to the lees: all times I have enjoyed
Greatly, have suffered greatly, both with those
That loved me, and alone; on shore, and when
Through scudding drifts the rainy Hyades°   *stars whose appearance*   10
Vext the dim sea. I am become a name;   *predicted rain*
For always roaming with a hungry heart
Much have I seen and known: cities of men
And manners, climates, councils, governments,
Myself not least, but honored of them all,—   15
And drunk delight of battle with my peers,
Far on the ringing plains of windy Troy.
I am a part of all that I have met;
Yet all experience is an arch wherethrough
Gleams that untraveled world, whose margin fades   20
For ever and for ever when I move.
How dull it is to pause, to make an end,
To rust unburnished, not to shine in use!
As though to breathe were life. Life piled on life
Were all too little, and of one to me   25
Little remains: but every hour is saved
From that eternal silence, something more,
A bringer of new things; and vile it were
For some three suns to store and hoard myself,
And this gray spirit yearning in desire   30
To follow knowledge, like a sinking star,
Beyond the utmost bound of human thought.
    This is my son, mine own Telemachus,
To whom I leave the scepter and the isle—
Well-loved of me, discerning to fulfill   35
This labor, by slow prudence to make mild
A rugged people, and through soft degrees
Subdue them to the useful and the good.
Most blameless is he, centered in the sphere
Of common duties, decent not to fail   40
In offices of tenderness, and pay
Meet adoration to my household gods,
When I am gone. He works his work, I mine.
    There lies the port: the vessel puffs her sail:

There gloom the dark broad seas. My mariners,   45
Souls that have toiled, and wrought, and thought with me—
That ever with a frolic welcome took
The thunder and the sunshine, and opposed
Free hearts, free foreheads—you and I are old;
Old age hath yet his honor and his toil.   50
Death closes all; but something ere the end,
Some work of noble note, may yet be done,
Not unbecoming men that strove with gods.
The lights begin to twinkle from the rocks;
The long day wanes; the slow moon climbs; the deep   55
Moans round with many voices. Come, my friends,
'Tis not too late to seek a newer world.
Push off, and sitting well in order smite
The sounding furrows; for my purpose holds
To sail beyond the sunset, and the baths   60
Of all the western stars, until I die.
It may be that the gulfs will wash us down;
It may be we shall touch the Happy Isles°,   *the final resting place of Greek heroes*
And see the great Achilles, whom we knew.
Though much is taken, much abides; and though   65
We are not now that strength which in old days
Moved earth and heaven, that which we are, we are,
One equal temper of heroic hearts,
Made weak by time and fate, but strong in will
To strive, to seek, to find, and not to yield.   70

Alfred, Lord Tennyson (1809–1892)

QUESTIONS

1. In which of the two versions, Brodsky's or Tennyson's, would you say
   Odysseus (Ulysses) is more heroic? Explain.
2. Describe the nature of the hero's discontent in each version.
3. What attitude does each speaker take toward Telemachus?
4. How do Tennyson and Brodsky differ in their interpretations of the hero's
   character? To what extent can the two interpretations be reconciled?

The two poems that follow invoke another figure from Greek my-
thology, Medusa, a beautiful mortal maiden transformed by the goddess
Athena into a hideous winged monster, a Gorgon, with hair of writhing
serpents. All who gaze upon her are transfixed to stone—all, that is,
except young Perseus, son of Zeus and Danaë, who kills her by use of
an unbreakable sickle given him by the god Hermes and a polished

shield provided by Athena. Gazing not on Medusa but on her reflection in the shield, Perseus cuts off her head as she sleeps. The first of the poems, by Louise Bogan, re-creates an encounter with Medusa told from the point of view of one of Medusa's victims, now turned to stone. Although the poem is modern, the event is imagined within the terms of the original legend. In contrast, the second poem, by Vincent O'Sullivan, presents a contemporary encounter between a woman and a man by reconstituting the classical legend in thoroughly modern terms.

Medusa

I had come to the house, in a cave of trees,
Facing a sheer sky.
Everything moved,—a bell hung ready to strike,
Sun and reflection wheeled by.

When the bare eyes were before me   5
And the hissing hair,
Held up at a window, seen through a door.
The stiff bald eyes, the serpents on the forehead
Formed in the air.

This is a dead scene forever now.   10
Nothing will ever stir.
The end will never brighten it more than this,
Nor the rain blur.

The water will always fall, and will not fall,
And the tipped bell make no sound.   15
The grass will always be growing for hay
Deep on the ground.

And I shall stand here like a shadow
Under the great balanced day,
My eyes on the yellow dust that was lifting in the wind,   20
And does not drift away.

Louise Bogan (1897–1970)

Medusa

Sits at the window, waits the threatened steel
as any common housewife waits near dark
for groceries that should have come at four,

when it's too late to phone to hear they're certain,
to know the boy is pedalling up the hill   5
and not gone home. A boy who's late—
it could be simply that, so still her hands.

Two or three birds. Bare branches.
A thrush taps on the gravel, tilts its head.
Her eyes, she thinks, could hold it if she wanted,   10
could make it come up close, think this is home.
Sits there, her hands folded, her lips cold,
the expected blade already on her skin.

A piece of wind no bigger than a man
moves the dead leaves, bends the sopping grass.   15
A blind cord knocks the window like a drum.
"Perseus, stalwart, honest, comes his way,
his footstep nicks the corners of the day,
like something hard against a grey, chipped stone."
The stone he says she makes with those grey eyes.   20
Jade in the dusk. Heavier than grey.

And when he comes, how talk moves like a mirror,
a polished shield, in shadows, then in light,
always his care to stay behind its hurt.
Talks of her greatest gift—to deck out men   25
in stone: stone heart, stone limbs, the lot.
Turns men to stone, turns them to herself.
"The only way to end, for both our good."
And like a man who shows off coins or gems
he lets his words fall in the room by ones,   30
and twos, or if in piles, it's when
their rushing sounds and feels a streaming sword.
Edges in close with that, to do his work.
And all her strength, to keep her eyes from his.

Vincent O'Sullivan (b. 1937)

QUESTIONS

1. What is the effect of the domestic details used in lines 1–7 of O'Sullivan's
   poem?
2. How would you characterize the relationship between the woman and the
   man?
3. Explain the weaponry the man uses in the encounter.

At this point we are ready to make a distinction between mythology and MYTH. Whereas in mythology we encounter particular characters enacting particular stories, in myth we recognize patterns and types—that is, ways in which stories and characters *recur* in various forms in many literatures over long periods of time. In myth criticism we refer to the Medusa, for example, not as a unique phenomenon, but as a type that may include female figures as different in detail as Circe, Medusa herself, Eve, and the seductress in the latest Hollywood film. Taken as a group, they can be said to exemplify the myth of the *femme fatale* whose influence represents danger and perhaps death. A poem such as John Keats's "La Belle Dame sans Merci" (p. 164) offers yet another variation on the motif, as do several of the ballads ("Lord Randal," p. 161; "Bonny Barbara Allen," p. 391).

In the same way, Perseus's slaying of the Medusa can be related to a broader pattern generally termed an *Initiation myth,* in which a young hero earns his manhood by undertaking a seemingly impossible task, or more often a series of such tasks, in the process of which he displays his prowess and gains knowledge and wisdom. In the Perseus myth, after slaying the Medusa and securing her head in a container, he begins his journey home, but on the way discovers a young maiden, Andromeda, chained to a rock and about to be ravaged by a sea monster. Quick-wittedly, Perseus produces the decapitated head, petrifies the monster, liberates Andromeda, and returns home with her. Once there, he also liberates his mother, Danaë, who has been kept captive during his absence; marries Andromeda and again leaves home with her and Danaë; has several other adventures (using the Medusa's head as his prime weapon); and ends his life the wise and honored king of Argos, a land he inherits (and has dutifully earned) from his wicked grandfather, Acrisius. These are the particulars of the Perseus story, but the mythical pattern is one of departure, challenge and conquest, and triumphant return—a pattern that can be found to recur in many stories focusing on other heroic characters experiencing other adventures.

The Initiation myth sometimes shades into the *Quest myth,* as in the medieval legend of Perceval, a young knight at King Arthur's court who leaves Camelot and undergoes a series of adventures and temptations in his search for the Holy Grail (the mystical chalice that Christ is reputed to have drunk from during the Last Supper). The following sonnet, loosely adapted from the French of Paul Verlaine, condenses the Perceval (here Parsifal) legend, much as Richard Wagner's opera *Parsifal* expands on it.

Parsifal

Conquered the flower-maidens, and the wide embrace
Of their round proffered arms, that tempt the virgin boy;
Conquered the trickling of their babbling tongues; the coy

Back glances, and the mobile breasts of subtle grace;
Conquered the Woman Beautiful, the fatal charm   5
Of her hot breast, the music of her babbling tongue;
Conquered the gate of Hell, into the gate the young
Man passes, with the heavy trophy at his arm,

The holy Javelin that pierced the Heart of God.
He heals the dying king, he sits upon the throne,   10
King, and high priest of that great gift, the living Blood.
In robe of gold the youth adores the glorious Sign
Of the green goblet, worships the mysterious Wine.
And oh! the chime of children's voices in the dome.

Paul Verlaine (1844–1896)
(Trans. from the French by John Gray)

QUESTIONS

1. Distinguish among the kinds of challenges Parsifal encounters in the octet.
2. Explain Parsifal's new status (lines 9–11) and the reason for it.
3. Specify the resemblances between this story and the Perseus myth described above.

   As certain plot and character types seem to recur in myth, so certain images also seem constant. That of the sun rising usually suggests birth, resurrection, an increase of knowledge, while the sun's setting implies decline, death, a state of unawareness. Colors, too, seem to have certain recurrent associations: green tends to be linked with growth, hope, natural processes; red with blood, violence, passion, chaos; white with innocence, coldness, death. Poets may, of course, choose to invert such usages, but a critic would argue that when they do they are implicitly acknowledging the prevalent type. (Consider in light of this discussion two poems studied earlier: Robert Frost's "Design," p. 47, and Wallace Stevens's "Disillusionment of Ten O'Clock," p. 94.)
   We have spoken above of types and motifs, but the more common term in myth criticism is *archetype,* a term drawn from the work of the Swiss psychologist Carl Gustav Jung (1875–1961), who thought of an archetype as a "primordial image" deeply implanted in the "collective unconscious" of the human race. Originally a follower of Sigmund Freud, Jung later moved in a contrary direction, in the process depersonalizing Freud's view of the unconscious by substituting for individual memory the idea of a "racial memory," that is, one shared by all human beings. The archetypes embedded there transcend distinctions of time

and place, correspond as it were to certain "world molds," and can find expression in many different forms (dreams, religion, folklore) as well as in literature. The particulars may vary, depending on the form or the cultural coloration the archetypes take, but not the underlying pattern. Their presence in literature is especially evident, according to Jung, because the artist is provisioned with an exceptionally powerful "primordial vision" that is capable of drawing upon the unconscious and returning its images to the conscious realm in the form of the literary work.

Though myth criticism is commonly identified with Jung's theories, it has managed to thrive apart from the specific archetypes he formulated and often apart from any explicit acknowledgment of a shared racial memory. Without recourse to such concepts, the critic may find enough recurrent patterns to justify (if somewhat loosely) the designation of archetype or myth. In this less restrictive sense, we can recognize the interaction of two archetypes in the poem that follows by Judith Wright. The speaker is not simply a woman, but the image of woman as bearer and protector, a kind of beneficent Earth Mother (as Jung might name her). At the same time, the awareness she has of what lies ahead for the unborn child evokes an archetypal pattern whose phases—birth, growth, maturity, death—we readily acknowledge for their universality.

Woman's Song

O move in me, my darling,
for now the sun must rise;
the sun that will draw open
the lids upon your eyes.

O wake in me, my darling.   5
The knife of day is bright
to cut the thread that binds you
within the flesh of night.

Today I lose and find you
whom yet my blood would keep—   10
would weave and sing around you
the spells and songs of sleep.

None but I shall know you
as none but I have known;
yet there's a death and a maiden   15
who wait for you alone;

so move in me, my darling,
whose debt I cannot pay.
Pain and the dark must claim you,
and passion and the day.   20

Judith Wright (b. 1915)

QUESTIONS

1. What evidence suggests that the speaker is not to be understood simply as
   the poet herself?
2. Explain the image of the knife in the second stanza as well as the contrast
   between "bright" and "night."
3. The word "must" in line 2 suggests a certain inevitability at work. Where
   else is this sense of inevitability implied in the poem?

The allusions in James Dickey's poem to both a garden and a snake
should be sufficient to activate thoughts of the Garden of Eden and the
unhappy events that occurred there:

The Poisoned Man

When the rattlesnake bit, I lay
In a dream of the country, and dreamed
Day after day of the river,

Where I sat with a jackknife and quickly
Opened my sole to the water.   5
Blood shed for the sake of one's life

Takes on the hid shape of the channel,
Disappearing under logs and through boulders.
The freezing river poured on

And, as it took hold of my blood,   10
Leapt up round the rocks and boiled over.
I felt that my heart's blood could flow

Unendingly out of the mountain,
Splitting bedrock apart upon redness,
And the current of life at my instep   15

Give deathlessly as a spring.

Some leaves fell from trees and whirled under.
I saw my struck bloodstream assume,

Inside the cold path of the river,
The inmost routes of a serpent   20
Through grass, through branches and leaves.

When I rose, the live oaks were ashen
And the wild grass was dead without flame.
Through the blasted cornfield I hobbled,

My foot tied up in my shirt,   25
And met my old wife in the garden,
Where she reached for a withering apple.

I lay in the country and dreamed
Of the substance and course of the river
While the different colors of fever   30

Like quilt patches flickered upon me.
At last I arose, with the poison
Gone out of the seam of the scar,

And brought my wife eastward and weeping
Through the copper fields springing alive   35
With the promise of harvest for no one.

James Dickey (b. 1923)

QUESTIONS

1. What evidence enables you to identify the speaker with Adam and his wife (line 26) with Eve?
2. In what significant ways does Dickey's poem differ from the version of the Fall in Genesis?
3. How would you characterize the archetype common to both the biblical version and this poem?

Myth criticism, as we have seen, draws attention to the presence of underlying patterns and enables us to see thematic continuities. The fact that these patterns and continuities do persist, that they are not limited by time periods or national boundaries, seems to point to certain constants in human behavior and awareness and to buttress the claim of myth critics that their approach leads toward universal truths and insights. At the same time, there is an obvious danger in this approach:

that too exclusive an emphasis on patterns and continuities will tend to obscure differences and lead to neglect of the texture and particularity of individual poems. The difference in quality between, let us say, Dickey's "The Poisoned Man" and another poem that employs the same archetype will be found in other realms—for instance, in language, tone, rhythm, form, imaginative intensity—and we must bring an awareness of all these to our reading of a poem if we are to see it whole.

EXERCISES

I. Compare the images of Helen of Troy in the two poems below by Edgar Allan Poe and H. D. (Hilda Doolittle) and in the middle stanza of William Butler Yeats's "Long-Legged Fly" (p. 60). In what ways do the three versions differ? To what extent are they reconcilable? (You may find it helpful to know that according to classical legend Helen, a woman of surpassing beauty born of the union of Zeus and a mortal, Leda, was married to the Greek king Menelaus but fled with the young prince Paris to his home at Troy. Their flight provoked a ten-year war between Greece and Troy that ended in the destruction of Troy.)

To Helen

Helen, thy beauty is to me
  Like those Nicèan barks of yore,
That gently, o'er a perfumed sea,
  The weary, way-worn wanderer bore
  To his own native shore.   5

On desperate seas long wont to roam,
  Thy hyacinth hair, thy classic face,
Thy Naiad airs have brought me home
  To the glory that was Greece
And the grandeur that was Rome.   10

Lo! in yon brilliant window-niche
  How statue-like I see thee stand,
  The agate lamp within thy hand!
Ah, Psyche, from the regions which
  Are Holy Land!   15

Edgar Allan Poe (1809–1849)

To Helen. l. 2 *Nicèan:* Nicaea was an ancient city of the Byzantine Empire. l. 7 *hyacinth hair:* curled in the manner of the hyacinth flower. l. 8 *Naiad:* a freshwater nymph believed by Greeks and Romans to inhabit rivers, lakes, and springs, giving life to the waters. l. 14 *Psyche:* the soul (Greek); also, in mythology, the beloved of Cupid (Eros), whose identity she was forbidden to know and who deserted her when she lit a lamp to see him.

Helen

All Greece hates
the still eyes in the white face,
the luster as of olives
where she stands,
And the white hands.   5

All Greece reviles
the wan face when she smiles,
hating it deeper still
when it grows wan and white,
remembering past enchantments   10
and past ills.

Greece sees unmoved,
God's daughter, born of love,
the beauty of cool feet
and slenderest knees,   15
could love indeed the maid,
only if she were laid,
white ash amid funereal cypresses.

H. D. (Hilda Doolittle) (1886–1961)

II. Interpret the following poem as expressive of the archetype of the Earth
Mother; then answer the questions that follow the poem.

Bog Queen

I lay waiting
between turf-face and demesne wall,
between heathery levels
and glass-toothed stone.

My body was braille   5
for the creeping influences:
dawn suns groped over my head
and cooled at my feet,

through my fabrics and skins
the seeps of winter   10
digested me,
the illiterate roots

pondered and died
in the cavings

of stomach and socket.   15
I lay waiting

on the gravel bottom,
my brain darkening,
a jar of spawn
fermenting underground   20

dreams of Baltic amber.
Bruised berries under my nails,
the vital hoard reducing
in the crock of the pelvis.

My diadem grew carious,   25
gemstones dropped
in the peat floe
like the bearings of history.

My sash was a black glacier
wrinkling, dyed weaves   30
and phoenician stitchwork
retted° on my breasts'   *rotted*

soft moraines°.   *glacial deposits of earth and stones*
I knew winter cold
like the nuzzle of fjords   35
at my thighs—

the soaked fledge°, the heavy   *feathery growth*
swaddle of hides.
My skull hibernated
in the wet nest of my hair.   40

Which they robbed.
I was barbered
and stripped
by a turfcutter's spade

who veiled me again   45
and packed coomb° softly   *soot, coal dust*
between the stone jambs
at my head and my feet.

Till a peer's wife bribed him.
The plait of my hair,   50
a slimy birth-cord
of bog, had been cut

and I rose from the dark,
hacked bone, skull-ware,

frayed stitches, tufts,   55
small gleams on the bank.

Seamus Heaney (b. 1939)

1. What details seem especially relevant to the Irish landscape? To what extent, if any, do such details restrict the poem's implications?
2. Exactly what happens to the speaker beginning at line 41? How does your answer help determine the theme of the poem?
3. Compare Heaney's use of the Earth Mother archetype with Judith Wright's in "Woman's Song" (p. 379).

III. Interpret the following poem as an archetype of the Quest myth; then answer the questions that follow the poem.

Choice

Idling through the mean space dozing,
blurred by indirection, I came upon a
stairwell and steadied a moment to
think against the stem:
upward turned golden steps   5
and downward dark steps entered the dark:

unused to other than even ground I
spurned the airless heights though bright
and the rigor to lift an immaterial soul
and sank   10
sliding in a smooth rail whirl and fell
asleep in the inundating dark
but waking said god abhors me
but went on down obeying at least
the universal law of gravity: 15

millenniums later waking in a lightened air
I shivered in high purity
and still descending grappled with
the god that
rolls up circles of our linear   20
sight in crippling disciplines
tighter than any climb.

A. R. Ammons (b. 1926)

1. Paraphrase the action that occurs in the poem.
2. Explain the basis for the speaker's decision in lines 5–10.
3. To what extent is it possible to identify the god of line 19 with any particular religion?
4. Would you characterize the final stanza as a triumph or a defeat? Explain.

Part Three
Anthology

The Road

Three then came forward out of darkness, one
An old man bearded, his old eyes red with weeping,
A peasant, with hard hands. "Come now," he said,
"And see the road, for which our people die.
Twelve miles of road we've made, a little only,   5
Westward winding. Of human blood and stone
We build; and in a thousand years will come
Beyond the hills to sea."

                   I went with them,
Taking a lantern, which upon their faces   10
Showed years and grief; and in a time we came
To the wild road which wound among wild hills
Westward; and so along this road we stooped,
Silent, thinking of all the dead men, there
Compounded with sad clay. Slowly we moved: 15
For they were old and weak, had given all
Their life, to build this twelve poor miles of road,
Muddy, under the rain. And in my hand
Turning the lantern, here or there, I saw
Deep holes of water where the raindrop splashed,   20
And rainfilled footprints in the grass, and heaps
Of broken stone, and rusted spades and picks,
And helves° of axes. And the old man spoke,   *handles*
Holding my wrist: "Three hundred years it took
To build these miles of road: three hundred years;   25
And human lives unnumbered. But the day
Will come when it is done." Then spoke another,
One not so old, but old, whose face was wrinkled:
"And when it comes, our people will all sing
For joy, passing from east to west, or west   30
To east, returning, with the light behind them;
All meeting in the road and singing there."
And the third said: "The road will be their life;
A heritage of blood. Grief will be in it,
And beauty out of grief. And I can see   35
How all the women's faces will be bright.
In that time, laughing, they will remember us.
Blow out your lantern now, for day is coming."
My lantern blown out, in a little while
We climbed in long light up a hill, where climbed   40
The dwindling road, and ended in a field.
Peasants were working in the field, bowed down
With unrewarded work, and grief, and years
Of pain. And as we passed them, one man fell

Into a furrow that was bright with water   45
And gave a cry that was half cry half song—
"The road . . . the road . . . the road . . ." And all then fell
Upon their knees and sang.

                     We four passed on
Over the hill, to westward. Then I felt   50
How tears ran down my face, tears without number;
And knew that all my life henceforth was weeping,
Weeping, thinking of human grief, and human
Endeavour fruitless in a world of pain.
And when I held my hands up they were old;   55
I knew my face would not be young again.

Conrad Aiken (b. 1889)

Address

address
occupation
age
marital status
—perdone . . .   5
         yo me llamo pedro
telephone
height
hobbies
previous employers   10
—perdone . . .
         yo me llamo pedro
         pedro ortega
zip code   15
i.d. number
classification
rank
—perdone mi padre era
         el señor ortega   20
         (a veces don josé)
race

Alurista (b. 1947)

Address. ll. 5–6 *perdone . . . pedro:* pardon, my name is Pedro. ll. 19–21 *perdone . . .(a veces don josé):* pardon, my father was señor Ortega (sometimes called don José).

Bonny Barbara Allan

1

It was in and about the Martinmas° time,
   When the green leaves were a falling,
That Sir John Græme, in the West Country,
   Fell in love with Barbara Allan.

November 11

2

He sent his man down through the town,
   To the place where she was dwelling:
"O haste and come to my master dear,
   Gin° ye be Barbara Allan."

5

if

3

O hooly°, hooly rose she up,
   To the place where he was lying,
And when she drew the curtain by:
   "Young man, I think you're dying."

slowly

10

4

"O it's I'm sick, and very, very sick,
   And 'tis a' for Barbara Allan."
"O the better for me ye s'° never be,
   Though your heart's blood were a-spilling."

shall 15

5

"O dinna ye mind°, young man," said she,
   "When ye was in the tavern a drinking,
That ye made the healths gae round and round,
   And slighted Barbara Allan?"

don't you recall

20

6

He turned his face unto the wall,
   And death was with him dealing:
"Adieu, adieu, my dear friends all,
   And be kind to Barbara Allan."

7

And slowly, slowly raise she up,
   And slowly, slowly left him,
And sighing said, she could not stay,
   Since death of life had reft him.

25

8

She had not gane a mile but twa,
   When she heard the dead-bell ringing,

30

And every jow° that the dead-bell geid, *stroke*
  It cried, "Woe to Barbara Allan!"

9

"O mother, mother, make my bed!
  O make it saft and narrow!
Since my love died for me to-day, 35
  I'll die for him to-morrow."

Anonymous

The Silver Swan

The silver swan, who living had no note,
When death approached, unlocked her silent throat;
Leaning her breast against the reedy shore,
Thus sung her first and last, and sung no more:
"Farewell, all joys; Oh death, come close mine eyes;
More geese than swans now live, more fools than wise."

Anonymous (17th century)

We Are Standing Facing Each Other

We are standing facing each other
in an eighteenth century room
with fragile tables and mirrors
in carved frames; the curtains,
red brocade, are drawn 5

the doors are shut, you aren't talking,
the chandeliers aren't talking, the carpets

also remain silent.
You stay closed, your skin
is buttoned firmly around you, 10
your mouth is a tin decoration,
you are in the worst possible taste.

You are fake as the marble trim
around the fireplace, there is nothing
I wouldn't do to be away 15
from here.   I do nothing

because the light changes, the tables
and mirrors radiate from around you,
you step backwards away from me
the length of the room   20

holding cupped in your hands
behind your back
                    an offering
a gold word   a signal

I need more than   25
air, blood, it would open
everything

which you won't let me see.

Margaret Atwood (b. 1939)

The Cultural Presupposition

Happy the hare at morning, for she cannot read
The Hunter's waking thoughts, lucky the leaf
Unable to predict the fall, lucky indeed
The rampant suffering suffocating jelly
Burgeoning in pools, lapping the grits of the desert,   5
But what shall man do, who can whistle tunes by heart,
Knows to the bar when death shall cut him short like the cry of the
    shearwater,
What can he do but defend himself from his knowledge?

How comely are his places of refuge and the tabernacles of his peace,
The new books upon the morning table, the lawns and the afternoon
    terraces!   10
Here are the playing-fields where he may forget his ignorance
To operate within a gentleman's agreement: twenty-two sins have here a
    certain licence.

Here are the thickets where accosted lovers combatant
May warm each other with their wicked hands,
Here are the avenues for incantation and workshops for the cunning
    engravers.   15
The galleries are full of music, the pianist is storming the keys, the great
    cellist is crucified over his instrument,
That none may hear the ejaculations of the sentinels

Nor the sigh of the most numerous and the most poor; the thud of their
  falling bodies
Who with their lives have banished hence the serpent and the faceless
  insect.

W. H. Auden (1907–1973)

W. W.

Back home the black women are all beautiful,
and the white ones fall back, cutoff from 1000
years stacked booty, and Charles of the Ritz
where jooshladies turn into billy burke in blueglass
kicks. With wings, and jingly bew-teeful things.   5
The black women in Newark are fine. Even with all that grease
in their heads. I mean even the ones where the wigs
slide around, and they coming at you 75 degrees off course.
I could talk to them. Bring them around. To something.
Some kind of quick course, on the sidewalk, like Hey baby   10
why don't you take that thing off yo' haid. You look like
Miss Muffett in a runaway ugly machine. I mean. Like that.

Imamu Amiri Baraka (b. 1934)

As Firmly Cemented Clam-Shells

As firmly cemented clam-shells
Fall apart in autumn,
So I must take to the road again,
Farewell, my friends.

Bashō (1644–1694)
(Trans. from the Japanese by Nobuyuki Yuasa)

Only for Morning Glories

Only for morning glories
I open my door—
During the daytime I keep it
Tightly barred.

Bashō (1644–1694)
(Trans. from the Japanese by Nobuyuki Yuasa)

Song

Love Arm'd

Love in fantastic triumph sat
  Whilst bleeding hearts around him flow'd,
For whom fresh paines he did create,
  And strange tyrannic power he show'd;

From thy bright eyes he took his fire,   5
  Which round about in sport he hurl'd;
But 'twas from mine he took desire,
  Enough to undo the amorous world.

From me he took his sighs and tears,
  From thee his pride and cruelty;   10
From me his languishments and fears,
  And every killing dart from thee.

Thus thou and I the god have arm'd,
  And set him up a deity;
But my poor heart alone is harm'd,   15
  Whilst thine the victor is, and free.

Aphra Behn (1640–1689)

Indian Children Speak

People said, "Indian children are hard to teach.
Don't expect them to talk."
One day stubby little Boy said,
"Last night the moon went all the way with me,
When I went out to walk."   5
People said, "Indian children are very silent.
Their only words are no and yes."
But, ragged Pansy confided softly,
"My dress is old, but at night the moon is kind;
Then I wear a beautiful moon-colored dress."   10
People said, "Indian children are dumb.
They seldom make a reply."
Clearly I hear Delores answer,
"Yes, the sunset is so good, I think God is throwing
A bright shawl around the shoulders of the sky."   15
People said, "Indian children have no affection.
They just don't care for anyone."

Then I feel Ramon's hand and hear him whisper,
"A wild animal races in me since my mother sleeps
under the ground. Will it always run and run?"   20
People said, "Indian children are rude.
They don't seem very bright."
Then I remember Joe Henry's remark,
"The tree is hanging down her head because the sun
is staring at her. White people always stare.   25
They do not know it is not polite."
People said, "Indian children never take you in,
Outside their thoughts you'll always stand."
I have forgotten the idle words that People said,
But treasure the day when iron doors swung wide,   30
And I slipped into the heart of Indian Land.

Juanita Bell

Life, Friends, Is Boring. We Must Not Say So

Life, friends, is boring. We must not say so.
After all, the sky flashes, the great sea yearns,
we ourselves flash and yearn,
and moreover my mother told me as a boy
(repeatedly) "Ever to confess you're bored   5
means you have no

Inner Resources." I conclude now I have no
inner resources, because I am heavy bored.
Peoples bore me,
literature bores me, especially great literature,   10
Henry bores me, with his plights & gripes
as bad as achilles,

who loves people and valiant art, which bores me.
And the tranquil hills, & gin, look like a drag
and somehow a dog   15
has taken itself & its tail considerably away
into mountains or sea or sky, leaving
behind: me, wag.

John Berryman (1914–1972)

Life, Friends, Is Boring. We Must Not Say So. l. 11 *Henry:* an imagined character who
figures in a cycle of Berryman's poems. l. 12 *achilles:* Greek hero of the Trojan War who
temporarily withdrew from battle complaining of ill-treatment.

North Haven

(In Memoriam: Robert Lowell)

I can make out the rigging of a schooner
a mile off; I can count
the new cones on the spruce. It is so still
the pale bay wears a milky skin; the sky
no clouds except for one long, carded horse's tail.   5

The islands haven't shifted since last summer,
even if I like to pretend they have—
drifting, in a dreamy sort of way,
a little north, a little south, or sidewise—
and that they're free within the blue frontiers of bay.   10

This month our favorite one is full of flowers:
buttercups, red clover, purple vetch,
hawkweed still burning, daisies pied, eyebright,
the fragrant bedstraw's incandescent stars,
and more, returned, to paint the meadows with delight.   15

The goldfinches are back, or others like them,
and the white-throated sparrow's five-note song,
pleading and pleading, brings tears to the eyes.
Nature repeats herself, or almost does:
repeat, repeat, repeat; revise, revise, revise.   20

Years ago, you told me it was here
(in 1932?) you first "discovered *girls*"
and learned to sail, and learned to kiss.
You had "such fun," you said, that classic summer.
("Fun"—it always seemed to leave you at a loss . . .)   25

You left North Haven, anchored in its rock,
afloat in mystic blue . . . And now—you've left
for good. You can't derange, or rearrange,
your poems again. (But the sparrows can their song.)
The words won't change again. Sad friend, you cannot change.   30

Elizabeth Bishop (1911–1979)

North Haven. Robert Lowell (1917–1977), in whose memory this poem was written, was an American poet and a friend of Elizabeth Bishop.

And Did Those Feet in Ancient Time*

And did those feet in ancient time
Walk upon England's mountains green?
And was the holy Lamb of God
On England's pleasant pastures seen?

And did the Countenance Divine   5
Shine forth upon our clouded hills?
And was Jerusalem builded here,
Among these dark Satanic Mills?

Bring me my Bow of burning gold!
Bring me my Arrows of desire: 10
Bring me my Spear: O clouds unfold!
Bring me my Chariot of fire!

I will not cease from Mental Fight,
Nor shall my Sword sleep in my hand,
Till we have built Jerusalem   15
In England's green & pleasant Land.

William Blake (1757–1827)

The Chimney Sweeper

When my mother died I was very young,
And my father sold me while yet my tongue
Could scarcely cry " 'weep! 'weep! 'weep! 'weep!"
So your chimneys I sweep, and in soot I sleep.

There's little Tom Dacre, who cried when his head,   5
That curled like a lamb's back, was shaved; so I said,
"Hush, Tom! never mind it, for, when your head's bare,
You know that the soot cannot spoil your white hair."

And so he was quiet, and that very night,
As Tom was asleeping, he had such a sight!   10
That thousands of sweepers, Dick, Joe, Ned, and Jack,
Were all of them locked up in coffins of black.

And by came an Angel who had a bright key,
And he opened the coffins and set them all free;
Then down a green plain leaping, laughing, they run,   15
And wash in a river, and shine in the sun.

* From the Preface to Blake's *Milton* (1804).

Then naked and white, all their bags left behind,
They rise upon clouds and sport in the wind;
And the Angel told Tom, if he'd be a good boy,
He'd have God for his father, and never want joy.   20

And so Tom awoke, and we rose in the dark,
And got with our bags and our brushes to work.
Though the morning was cold, Tom was happy and warm;
So if all do their duty they need not fear harm.

William Blake (1757–1827)

The Crystal Cabinet

The Maiden caught me in the Wild
Where I was dancing merrily
She put me into her Cabinet
And Lockd me up with a golden Key

This Cabinet is formd of Gold   5
And Pearl & Crystal shining bright
And within it opens into a World
And a little lovely Moony Night

Another England there I saw
Another London with its Tower   10
Another Thames & other Hills
And another pleasant Surrey° Bower   *county in southern England*

Another Maiden like herself
Translucent lovely shining clear
Threefold each in the other closd   15
O what a pleasant trembling fear

O what a smile a threefold Smile
Filld me that like a flame I burnd
I bent to Kiss the lovely Maid
And found a Threefold Kiss returnd   20

I strove to sieze the inmost Form
With ardor fierce & hands of flame
But burst the Crystal Cabinet
And like a Weeping Babe became
A weeping Babe upon the wild   25
And Weeping Woman pale reclind

And in the outward air again
I filld with woes the passing Wind

William Blake (1757–1827)

Before the Birth of One of Her Children

All things within this fading world hath end,
Adversity doth still our joys attend;
No ties so strong, no friends so dear and sweet,
But with death's parting blow is sure to meet.
The sentence past is most irrevocable,   5
A common thing, yet oh, inevitable.
How soon, my Dear, death may my steps attend,
How soon't may be thy lot to lose thy friend,
We both are ignorant, yet love bids me
These farewell lines to recommend to thee,   10
That when that knot's untied that made us one,
I may seem thine, who in effect am none.
And if I see not half my days that's due,
What nature would, God grant to yours and you;
The many faults that well you know I have   15
Let be interred in my oblivious grave;
If any worth or virtue were in me,
Let that live freshly in thy memory
And when thou feel'st no grief, as I no harms,
Yet love thy dead, who long lay in thine arms.   20
And when thy loss shall be repaid with gains
Look to my little babes, my dear remains.
And if thou love thyself, or loved'st me,
These O protect from step-dame's injury.
And if chance to thine eyes shall bring this verse,   25
With some sad sighs honour my absent hearse;
And kiss this paper for thy love's dear sake,
Who with salt tears this last farewell did take.

Anne Bradstreet (1612?–1672)

An Aspect of Love, Alive in the Ice and Fire
LaBohem Brown

It is the morning of our love.

In a package of minutes there is this We.

How beautiful.
Merry foreigners in our morning,
we laugh, we touch each other,   5
are responsible props and posts.

A physical light is in the room.

Because the world is at the window
we cannot wonder very long.

You rise. Although   10
genial, you are in yourself again.
I observe
your direct and respectable stride.
You are direct and self-accepting as a lion
in African velvet. You are level, lean,   15
remote.

There is a moment in Camaraderie
when interruption is not to be understood.
I cannot bear an interruption.
This is the shining joy;   20
the time of not-to-end.

On the street we smile.
We go
in different directions
down the imperturbable street.   25

Gwendolyn Brooks (b. 1917)

Soliloquy of the Spanish Cloister

Gr-r-r—there go, my heart's abhorrence!
  Water your damned flower-pots, do!
If hate killed men, Brother Lawrence,
  God's blood, would not mine kill you!
What? your myrtle-bush wants trimming?   5
  Oh, that rose has prior claims—
Needs its leaden vase filled brimming?
  Hell dry you up with its flames!

At the meal we sit together;
  Salve tibi!° I must hear   *Hail to thee!* 10
Wise talk of the kind of weather,

Sort of season, time of year:
Not a plenteous cork-crop: scarcely
  Dare we hope oak-galls, I doubt;
What's the Latin name for "parsley"?   15
  What's the Greek name for "swine's snout"?

Whew! We'll have our platter burnished,
  Laid with care on our own shelf!
With a fire-new spoon we're furnished,
  And a goblet for ourself,   20
Rinsed like something sacrificial
  Ere 'tis fit to touch our chaps°—   jaws
Marked with L. for our initial!
  (He-he! There his lily snaps!)

Saint, forsooth! While brown Dolores   25
  Squats outside the Convent bank
With Sanchicha, telling stories,
  Steeping tresses in the tank,
Blue-black, lustrous, thick like horsehairs,
  —Can't I see his dead eye glow,   30
Bright as 'twere a Barbary corsair's?
  (That is, if he'd let it show!)

When he finishes refection,
  Knife and fork he never lays
Cross-wise, to my recollection,   35
  As do I, in Jesu's praise.
I, the Trinity illustrate,
  Drinking watered orange-pulp—
In three sips the Arian frustrate;
  While he drains his at one gulp!   40

Oh, those melons! if he's able
  We're to have a feast; so nice!
One goes to the Abbot's table,
  All of us get each a slice.
How go on your flowers? None double?   45
  Not one fruit-sort can you spy?
Strange!—And I, too, at such trouble,
  Keep them close-nipped on the sly!

There's a great text in Galatians,
  Once you trip on it, entails   50
Twenty-nine distinct damnations,
  One sure, if another fails;
If I trip him just a-dying,

402 Anthology

Sure of heaven as sure can be,
Spin him round and send him flying   55
   Off to hell, a Manichee?

Or, my scrofulous French novel
   On grey paper with blunt type!
Simply glance at it, you grovel
   Hand and foot in Belial's gripe;   60
If I double down its pages
   At the woeful sixteenth print,
When he gathers his greengages,
   Ope a sieve and slip it in't?

Or, there's Satan!—one might venture   65
   Pledge one's soul to him, yet leave
Such a flaw in the indenture
   As he'd miss till, past retrieve,
Blasted lay that rose-acacia
   We're so proud of! *Hy, Zy, Hine.* . . .   70
'St, there's Vespers! *Plena gratia*
   Ave, Virgo! Gr-r-r—you swine!

Robert Browning (1812–1889)

Soliloquy of the Spanish Cloister. l. 31 *Barbary corsair:* Barbary Coast pirate. l. 39 *Arian:*
adherent of Arius, who denied the doctrine of the Trinity. l. 49 *text in Galatians:* a New
Testament passage, possibly Galatians 15:23, whose complexity of interpretation may lead
Brother Lawrence into heresy. l. 56 *Manichee:* heretical follower of Mani, third-century
Persian who saw the world as a constant struggle between forces of good and evil. l. 60
Belial: Old Testament personification of evil. l. 70 *Hy, Zy, Hine:* perhaps the bell announcing
vespers, or the opening words of an esoteric curse. ll. 71–72 *Plena gratia/Ave, Virgo!:*
distortion of "*Ave, Maria, gratia plena*" (Hail Mary, full of grace).

Hymn

Now we should praise   Heaven-kingdom's Guard,
the Measurer's might   and His mind-thought,
the work of the Glory-Father,   since He, the eternal Prince,
established the beginning   of every wonder.
First He shaped   for the sons of earth
heaven as a roof,   the holy Shaper;
then mankind's Guard,   the eternal Prince,
afterwards drew out   Middle-Earth,
the land for men,   the Ruler almighty.

Cædmon (d. 680?)
(Trans. from the Old English by D. K. Fry)

Hymn. Cædmon, a cowherd who lived in the seventh century in northern England, learned to sing when a figure in a dream inspired him.

There Is a Garden in Her Face

There is a garden in her face
Where roses and white lilies grow;
   A heav'nly paradise is that place
Wherein all pleasant fruits do flow.
     There cherries grow which none may buy   5
     Till "Cherry-ripe" themselves do cry.

Those cherries fairly do enclose
Of orient pearl a double row,
   Which when her lovely laughter shows,
They look like rose-buds filled with snow;   10
     Yet them nor peer nor prince can buy,
     Till "Cherry-ripe" themselves do cry.

Her eyes like angels watch them still;
Her brows like bended bows do stand,
   Threat'ning with piercing frowns to kill   15
All that attempt, with eye or hand
     Those sacred cherries to come nigh
     Till "Cherry-ripe" themselves do cry.

Thomas Campion (1567–1620)

Mediocrity in Love Rejected

Give me more love, or more disdain;
   The torrid or the frozen zone
Bring equal ease unto my pain;
   The temperate affords me none:
Either extreme, of love or hate,   5
Is sweeter than a calm estate.

Give me a storm; if it be love,
   Like Danaë in that golden shower,
I swim in pleasure; if it prove
   Disdain, that torrent will devour   10
My vulture hopes; and he's possessed
Of heaven that's but from hell released.
     Then crown my joys, or cure my pain;
     Give me more love or more disdain.

Thomas Carew (1594?–1640?)

Mediocrity in Love Rejected. l.8 *Danaë*: locked away in a bronze tower by her father, Danaë was visited by Zeus, who poured himself through a roof opening as a shower of gold.

A Song

Ask me no more where Jove bestows,
When June is past, the fading rose;
For in your beauty's orient deep
These flowers, as in their causes, sleep.

Ask me no more whither do stray   5
The golden atoms of the day;
For, in pure love, heaven did prepare
Those powders to enrich your hair.

Ask me no more whither doth haste
The nightingale, when May is past;   10
For in your sweet dividing° throat   *harmonious*
She winters, and keeps warm her note.

Ask me no more where those stars light
That downwards fall in dead of night;
For in your eyes they sit, and there   15
Fixed become, as in their sphere.

Ask me no more if east or west
The phoenix builds her spicy nest;
For unto you at last she flies,
And in your fragrant bosom dies.   20

Thomas Carew (1594?–1640?)

A Song. l. 18 *phoenix*: legendary bird that dies in flames each thousand years, only to arise anew from its own ashes.

A Good Man Was Ther of Religioun*

A good man was ther of religioun,
And was a poure PERSON° of a toun;   *parson*
But riche he was of hooly thoght and werk.
He was also a lerned man, a clerk°   *scholar*
That Cristes gospel trewely wolde preche.   5
Hise parisshens° devoutly wolde he teche;   *parishioners*
Benygne he was, and wonder° diligent,   *wonderfully*

*From "The Prologue" to *The Canterbury Tales.*

And in adversitee ful pacient,
And swich° he was ypreved° ofte sithes°.   *so/proved/times*
Ful looth were hym to cursen for hise tithes,   10
But rather wolde he yeven°, out of doute°,   *give/without doubt*
Unto his poure parisshens aboute
Of his offrying and eek° of his substaunce;   *also*
He koude in litel thyng have suffisaunce°.   *sufficiency*
Wyd was his parisshe, and houses fer asonder,   15
But he ne lafte nat°, for reyn ne thonder,   *neglected not*
In siknesse nor in meschief° to visite   *misfortune*
The ferreste° in his parisshe, muche and lite°,   *farthest/high and low*
Upon his feet, and in his hand a staf.
This noble ensample to his sheepe he yaf,   20
That 'firste he wroghte° and afterward that he taughte.'   *did, performed*
Out of the gospel he tho wordes caughte,
And this figure he added eek therto:
That 'if gold ruste, what shal iren doo?'
For if a preest be foul, on whom we truste,   25
No wonder is a lewed° man to ruste;   *uneducated*
And shame it is—if a prest take keep°—   *heed*
A shiten° shepherde and a clene sheep.   *filthy, corrupt*
Wel oghte a preest ensample for to yive
By his clennesse how that his sheep sholde lyve.   30
He sette nat his benefice to hyre,
And leet° his sheepe encombred in the myre°   *abandoned/mud*
And ran to London, unto Seint Poules°,   *St. Paul's Cathedral*
To seken hym a chaunterie for soules;
Or with a bretherhed to been withholde;   35
But dwelleth at hoom and kepte wel his folde,
So that the wolf ne made it nat myscarie.
He was a shepherde and noght a mercenarie.
And though he hooly were and vertuous,
He was to synful man nat despitous°,   *scornful* 40
Ne of his speche daungerous° ne digne°,   *disdainful/arrogant*
But in his techying discreet and benygne;
To drawen folk to hevene by fairnesse,
By good ensample, this was his bisynesse.
But it were° any persone obstinat,   *if there were* 45
What-so he were, of heigh or lough estat,
Hym wolde he snybben° sharply for the nonys°.   *scold/occasion*
A bettre preest I trowe° that nowher noon ys.   *believe*
He waitede after° no pompe and reverence,   *looked for*
Ne maked him a spiced conscience;   50
But Cristes loore° and his apostles twelve   *teachings*
He taughte, but first he folwed it hymselve.

Geoffrey Chaucer (1343?–1400)

A Good Man Was Ther of Religioun. l. 10: He was loath to excommunicate to collect his tithes. l. 13: Of the congregation's offerings and also of his own property. l. 31: He didn't set his parish out to rent. l. 34: To seek a position singing masses for departed souls. l. 50: Nor pretended to an overly delicate conscience.

Mouse's Nest

I found a ball of grass among the hay
And progged it as I passed and went away;
And when I looked I fancied something stirred,
And turned again and hoped to catch the bird—
When out an old mouse bolted in the wheats   5
With all her young ones hanging at her teats;
She looked so odd and so grotesque to me,
I ran and wondered what the thing could be,
And pushed the knapweed bunches where I stood;
Then the mouse hurried from the craking° brood.   *crying*   10
The young ones squeaked, and as I went away
She found her nest again among the hay.
The water o'er the pebbles scarce could run
And broad old cesspools glittered in the sun.

John Clare (1793–1864)

Kubla Khan

Or a Vision in a Dream. A Fragment

In Xanadu did Kubla Khan
A stately pleasure dome decree:
Where Alph, the sacred river, ran
Through caverns measureless to man
  Down to a sunless sea.   5
So twice five miles of fertile ground
With walls and towers were girdled round:
And there were gardens bright with sinuous rills,
Where blossomed many an incense-bearing tree;
And here were forests ancient as the hills,   10
Enfolding sunny spots of greenery.

But oh! that deep romantic chasm which slanted
Down the green hill athwart a cedarn cover°!   *across a cedar forest*
A savage place! as holy and enchanted

As e'er beneath a waning moon was haunted   15
By woman wailing for her demon lover!
And from this chasm, with ceaseless turmoil seething,
As if this earth in fast thick pants were breathing,
A mighty fountain momently° was forced: *moment by moment*
Amid whose swift half-intermitted burst   20

Huge fragments vaulted like rebounding hail,
Or chaffy grain beneath the thresher's flail:
And 'mid these dancing rocks at once and ever
It flung up momently the sacred river.
Five miles meandering with a mazy motion   25
Through wood and dale the sacred river ran,
Then reached the caverns measureless to man,
And sank in tumult to a lifeless ocean:
And 'mid this tumult Kubla heard from far
Ancestral voices prophesying war!   30
   The shadow of the dome of pleasure
   Floated midway on the waves;
   Where was heard the mingled measure
   From the fountain and the caves.
It was a miracle of rare device,   35
A sunny pleasure dome with caves of ice!

   A damsel with a dulcimer
   In a vision once I saw:
   It was an Abyssinian maid,
   And on her dulcimer she played,   40
   Singing of Mount Abora.
Could I revive within me
Her symphony and song,
To such a deep delight 'twould win me,
That with music loud and long,   45
I would build that dome in air,
That sunny dome! those caves of ice!
And all who heard should see them there,
And all should cry, Beware! Beware!
His flashing eyes, his floating hair!   50
Weave a circle round him thrice,
And close your eyes with holy dread,
For he on honey-dew hath fed,
And drunk the milk of Paradise.

Samuel Taylor Coleridge (1772–1834)

Kubla Khan. *Kubla Khan* was a thirteenth-century warrior and founder of the vast Mongol Empire. l. 41 *Mount Abora:* perhaps Mt. Amara in Abyssinia where, according to legend, true Paradise had been.

On Donne's° Poetry

John Donne (1572–1631)

With Donne, whose muse on dromedary° trots,   *camel*
Wreathe iron pokers into true-love knots;
Rhyme's sturdy cripple, fancy's maze and clue,
Wit's forge and fire-blast, meaning's press and screw.

Samuel Taylor Coleridge (1772–1834)

Work Without Hope

Lines Composed 21st February 1825

All Nature seems at work. Slugs leave their lair—
The bees are stirring—birds are on the wing—
And Winter slumbering in the open air
Wears on his smiling face a dream of Spring!
And I the while, the sole unbusy thing,   5
Nor honey make, nor pair, nor build, nor sing.

   Yet well I ken the banks where amaranths° blow,   *eternal flowers*
Have traced the fount whence streams of nectar flow.
Bloom, O ye amaranths! bloom for whom ye may,
For me ye bloom not! Glide, rich streams, away!   10
With lips unbrightened, wreathless brow, I stroll:
And would you learn the spells that drowse my soul?
Work without Hope draws nectar in a sieve,
And Hope without an object cannot live.

Samuel Taylor Coleridge (1772–1834)

Pious Celinda Goes to Prayers

Pious Celinda goes to prayers
   If I but ask the favor,
And yet the tender fool's in tears
   When she believes I'll leave her.

Would I were free from this restraint,
   Or else had hopes to win her;
Would she could make of me a saint,
   Or I of her a sinner.

William Congreve (1670–1729)

The Air Plant

Grand Cayman

This tuft that thrives on saline° nothingness   *salty*
Inverted octopus with heavenward arms
Thrust parching from a palm-bole° hard by the cove—   *palm-tree trunk*
A bird almost—of almost bird alarms,

Is pulmonary to the wind that jars   5
Its tentacles, horrific in their lurch.
The lizard's throat, held bloated for a fly,
Balloons but warily from this throbbing perch.

The needles and hack-saws of cactus bleed
A milk of earth when stricken off the stalk;   10
But this,—defenseless, thornless, sheds no blood,
Almost no shadow—but the air's thin talk.

Angelic Dynamo! Ventriloquist of the Blue!
While beachward creeps the shark-swept Spanish Main
By what conjunctions do the winds appoint   15
Its apotheosis, at last—the hurricane!

Hart Crane (1899–1932)

The Air Plant. *Grand Cayman,* the poem's subtitle, is a small island in the Caribbean Sea, south of Cuba, northwest of Jamaica.

The Flower

I think I grow tensions
like flowers
in a wood where
nobody goes.

Each wound is perfect,   5
encloses itself in a tiny
imperceptible blossom,
making pain.

Pain is a flower like that one,
like this one,
like that one,   10
like this one.

Robert Creeley (b. 1926)

Saturday's Child

Some are teethed on a silver spoon,
With the stars strung for a rattle;
I cut my teeth as the black racoon——
For implements of battle.

Some are swaddled in silk and down,   5
And heralded by a star;
They swathed my limbs in a sackcloth gown
On a night that was black as tar.

For some, godfather and goddame
The opulent fairies be;   10
Dame Poverty gave me my name,
And Pain godfathered me.

For I was born on Saturday——
"Bad time for planting a seed,"
Was all my father had to say,   15
And, "One mouth more to feed."

Death cut the strings that gave me life,
And handed me to Sorrow,
The only kind of middle wife
My folks could beg or borrow.   20

Countee Cullen (1903–1946)

After Great Pain, a Formal Feeling Comes

After great pain, a formal feeling comes—
The Nerves sit ceremonious, like Tombs—
The stiff Heart questions was it He°, that bore,   *Christ*
And Yesterday, or Centuries before?

The Feet, mechanical, go round—   5
A Wooden way
Of Ground, or Air, or Ought—
Regardless grown,
A Quartz contentment, like a stone—

This is the Hour of Lead—   10
Remembered, if outlived,
As Freezing persons, recollect the Snow—
First—Chill—then Stupor—then the letting go—

Emily Dickinson (1830–1886)

I Heard a Fly Buzz—When I Died

I heard a Fly buzz—when I died—
The Stillness in the Room
Was like the Stillness in the Air—
Between the Heaves of Storm—

The Eyes around—had wrung them dry—
And Breaths were gathering firm
For that last Onset—when the King
Be witnessed—in the Room—

I willed my Keepsakes—Signed away
What portion of me be
Assignable—and then it was
There interposed a Fly—

With Blue—uncertain stumbling Buzz—
Between the light—and me—
And then the Windows failed—and then
I could not see to see—

5

10

15

Emily Dickinson (1830–1886)

The Soul Selects Her Own Society

The Soul selects her own Society—
Then—shuts the Door—
To her divine Majority—
Present no more—

Unmoved—she notes the Chariots—pausing—
At her low Gate—
Unmoved—an Emperor be kneeling
Upon her Mat—

I've known her—from an ample nation—
Choose One—
Then—close the Valves of her attention—
Like Stone—

5

10

Emily Dickinson (1830–1886)

Batter My Heart, Three-Personed God, for You

Batter my heart, three-personed God°, for You   *the Trinity*
As yet but knock, breathe, shine, and seek to mend.
That I may rise and stand, o'erthrow me, and bend
Your force to break, blow, burn, and make me new.
I, like an usurped town to another due,   5
Labor to admit You, but Oh! to no end.
Reason, Your viceroy in me, me should defend,
But is captived, and proves weak or untrue.
Yet dearly I love You, and would be lovèd fain,
But am betrothed unto Your enemy;   10
Divorce me, untie or break that knot again;
Take me to You, imprison me, for I,
Except You enthrall° me, never shall be free,   *imprison*
Nor ever chaste, except You ravish me.

John Donne (1572–1631)

Song: Go and Catch a Falling Star

Go and catch a falling star,
   Get with child a mandrake root,
Tell me where all past years are,
   Or who cleft the devil's foot,
Teach me to hear mermaids singing,   5
   Or to keep off envy's stinging,
         And find
         What wind
Serves to advance an honest mind.

If thou be'st born to strange sights,   10
   Things invisible to see,
Ride ten thousand days and nights,
   Till age snow white hairs on thee,
Thou, when thou return'st, wilt tell me
   All strange wonders that befell thee,   15
         And swear
         No where
Lives a woman true and fair.

If thou find'st one, let me know;
   Such a pilgrimage were sweet.   20
Yet do not; I would not go,

Though at next door we might meet.
Though she were true when you met her,
  And last till you write your letter,
      Yet she
      Will be
False, ere I come, to two or three.

John Donne (1572–1631)

Song. l. 2 *mandrake root:* the mandragora, a forked root that resembles the lower portion of the human torso; it was famed as an aphrodisiac and an aid to fertility.

The Sun Rising

  Busy old fool, unruly sun,
    Why dost thou thus,
Through windows and through curtains call on us?
Must to thy motions lovers' seasons run?
    Saucy, pedantic wretch, go chide
    Late schoolboys and sour 'prentices,
  Go tell court huntsmen that the king will ride,
  Call country ants to harvest offices°.   *duties*
Love, all alike, no season knows nor clime°,   *climate*
Nor hours, days, months, which are the rags of time.

  Thy beams, so reverend and strong
    Why shouldst thou think?
I could eclipse and cloud them with a wink,
But that I would not lose her sight so long.
    If her eyes have not blinded thine,
    Look, and tomorrow late tell me
  Whether both th' Indias of spice and mine
  Be where thou left'st them, or lie here with me;
Ask for those kings whom thou saw'st yesterday,
And thou shalt hear: All here in one bed lay.

  She's all states, and all princes I;
    Nothing else is.
Princes do but play us; compared to this,
All honor's mimic°, all wealth alchemy°.   *imitation/fraud*
    Thou, sun, art half as happy's we,
    In that the world's contracted thus;
  Thine age asks ease, and since thy duties be
  To warm the world, that's done in warming us.

Shine here to us, and thou art everywhere;
This bed thy center is, these walls thy sphere. 30

John Donne (1572–1631)

The Sun Rising. l. 17 *both th' Indias:* the East India of spices, the West Indies of mined
treasure.

A Valediction: Forbidding Mourning

As virtuous men pass mildly away,
   And whisper to their souls to go,
Whilst some of their sad friends do say
   The breath goes now, and some say, No;

So let us melt, and make no noise, 5
   No tear-floods, nor sigh-tempests move,
'Twere profanation of our joys
   To tell the laity our love.

Moving of th' earth° brings harms and fears,   *earthquake*
   Men reckon what it did and meant; 10
But trepidation° of the spheres°,   *shuddering/planetary spheres*
   Though greater far, is innocent.

Dull sublunary° lovers' love   *earthly, mundane*
   (Whose soul is sense) cannot admit
Absence, because it doth remove 15
   Those things which elemented° it.   *composed*

But we by a love so much refined
   That our selves know not what it is,
Inter-assuréd of the mind,
   Care less, eyes, lips, and hands to miss. 20

Our two souls therefore, which are one,
   Though I must go, endure not yet
A breach°, but an expansion,   *break*
   Like gold to airy thinness beat.

If they be two, they are two so 25
   As stiff twin compasses are two;
Thy soul, the fixed foot, makes no show
   To move, but doth, if th' other do.

And though it in the center sit,
   Yet when the other far doth roam,   30
It leans and hearkens after it,
   And grows erect, as that comes home.

Such wilt thou be to me, who must
   Like th' other foot, obliquely run;
Thy firmness makes my circle just,   35
   And makes me end where I begun.

John Donne (1572–1631)

To the Memory of Mr. Oldham

Fare well, too little and too lately known,
Whom I began to think and call my own:
For sure our souls were near allied, and thine
Cast in the same poetic mold with mine.
One common note on either lyre did strike,   5
And knaves and fools we both abhorred alike.
To the same goal did both our studies drive:
The last set out the soonest did arrive.
Thus Nisus fell upon the slippery place,
Whilst his young friend performed and won the race.   10
O early ripe! to thy abundant store
What could advancing age have added more?
It might (what nature never gives the young)
Have taught the numbers° of thy native tongue.   *metrics*
But satire needs not those, and wit will shine   15
Through the harsh cadence° of a rugged line.   *meter*
A noble error, and but seldom made,
When poets are by too much force betrayed.
Thy gen'rous fruits, though gathered ere their prime,
Still showed a quickness°; and maturing time   *tartness, life* 20
But mellows what we write to the dull sweets of rhyme.
Once more, hail, and farewell! farewell, thou young,
But ah! too short, Marcellus of our tongue!
Thy brows with ivy and with laurels° bound;   *poet's wreath*
But fate and gloomy night encompass thee around.   25

John Dryden (1631–1700)

To the Memory of Mr. Oldham. John Oldham, a poet whose satires gave promise of a successful career, died suddenly at the age of thirty. ll. 9–10 *Nisus*: a character in Virgil's *Aeneid* who was about to win a race when he slipped, allowing his friend to arrive first. l. 23 *Marcellus*: nephew to Augustus, was to succeed him as emperor of Rome but died prematurely, aged twenty.

The Groundhog

In June, amid the golden fields,
I saw a groundhog lying dead.
Dead lay he; my senses shook,
And mind outshot our naked frailty.
There lowly in the vigorous summer   5
His form began its senseless change,
And made my senses waver dim
Seeing nature ferocious in him.
Inspecting close his maggots' might
And seething cauldron of his being,   10
Half with loathing, half with a strange love,
I poked him with an angry stick.
The fever arose, became a flame
And Vigour circumscribed the skies,
Immense energy in the sun,   15
And through my frame a sunless trembling.
My stick had done nor good nor harm.
Then stood I silent in the day
Watching the object, as before;
And kept my reverence for knowledge   20
Trying for control, to be still,
To quell the passion of the blood;
Until I had bent down on my knees
Praying for joy in the sight of decay.
And so I left; and I returned   25
In Autumn strict of eye, to see
The sap gone out of the groundhog,
But the bony sodden hulk remained.
But the year had lost its meaning,
And in intellectual chains   30
I lost both love and loathing,
Mured up in the wall of wisdom.
Another summer took the fields again
Massive and burning, full of life,
But when I chanced upon the spot   35
There was only a little hair left,
And bones bleaching in the sunlight
Beautiful as architecture;
I watched them like a geometer,
And cut a walking stick from a birch.   40
It has been three years, now.
There is no sign of the groundhog.
I stood there in the whirling summer,
My hand capped a withered heart,
And thought of China and of Greece,   45

Of Alexander in his tent;
Of Montaigne in his tower,
Of Saint Theresa in her wild lament.

Richard Eberhart (b. 1904)

The Groundhog. ll. 46–48 *Alexander, Montaigne, Saint Theresa:* The speaker contemplates successively Alexander the Great, conqueror of the ancient world; Michel de Montaigne, sixteenth-century French essayist and skeptical philosopher; and Saint Theresa of Ávila, sixteenth-century Christian mystic.

Gerontion

Thou hast nor youth nor age
But as it were an after dinner sleep
Dreaming of both.

Here I am, an old man in a dry month,
Being read to by a boy, waiting for rain.
I was neither at the hot gates
Nor fought in the warm rain
Nor knee deep in the salt marsh, heaving a cutlass,   5
Bitten by flies, fought.
My house is a decayed house,
And the jew squats on the window sill, the owner,
Spawned in some estaminet° of Antwerp,   *cheap café*
Blistered in Brussels, patched and peeled in London.   10
The goat coughs at night in the field overhead;
Rocks, moss, stonecrop, iron, merds.
The woman keeps the kitchen, makes tea,
Sneezes at evening, poking the peevish gutter°.   *drain*
                 I an old man,   15
A dull head among windy spaces.

Signs are taken for wonders. "We would see a sign!"
The word within a word, unable to speak a word,
Swaddled with darkness. In the juvescence° of the year   *youth, spring*
Came Christ the tiger   20
In depraved May, dogwood and chestnut, flowering judas,
To be eaten, to be divided, to be drunk
Among whispers; by Mr. Silvero
With caressing hands, at Limoges
Who walked all night in the next room;   25

By Hakagawa, bowing among the Titians;
By Madame de Tornquist, in the dark room

Shifting the candles; Fräulein von Kulp
Who turned in the hall, one hand on the door. Vacant shuttles
Weave the wind. I have no ghosts,   30
An old man in a draughty house
Under a windy knob.

After such knowledge, what forgiveness? Think now
History has many cunning passages, contrived corridors
And issues, deceives with whispering ambitions,   35
Guides us by vanities. Think now
She gives when our attention is distracted
And what she gives, gives with such supple confusions
That the giving famishes the craving. Gives too late
What's not believed in, or if still believed,   40
In memory only, reconsidered passion. Gives too soon
Into weak hands, what's thought can be dispensed with
Till the refusal propagates a fear. Think
Neither fear nor courage saves us. Unnatural vices
Are fathered by our heroism. Virtues   45
Are forced upon us by our impudent crimes.
These tears are shaken from the wrath-bearing tree.

The tiger springs in the new year. Us he devours. Think at last
We have not reached conclusion, when I
Stiffen° in a rented house. Think at last   *die* 50
I have not made this show purposelessly
And it is not by any concitation°   *stirrings*
Of the backward devils.
I would meet you upon this honestly.
I that was near your heart was removed therefrom   55
To lose beauty in terror, terror in inquisition.
I have lost my passion; why should I need to keep it
Since what is kept must be adulterated?
I have lost my sight, smell, hearing, taste and touch:
How should I use them for your closer contact?   60

These° with a thousand small deliberations   *other people*
Protract the profit of their chilled delirium,
Excite the membrane, when the sense has cooled,
With pungent sauces, multiply variety
In a wilderness of mirrors. What will the spider do,   65
Suspend its operations, will the weevil
Delay? De Bailhache, Fresca, Mrs. Cammel, whirled
Beyond the circuit of the shuddering Bear
In fractured atoms. Gull against the wind, in the windy straits
Of Belle Isle, or running on the Horn.   70
White feathers in the snow, the Gulf claims,

And an old man driven by the Trades
To a sleepy corner.

Tenants of the house,
Thoughts of a dry brain in a dry season.

T. S. Eliot (1888–1965)

Gerontion. *Gerontion* means "little old man." The epigraph is from William Shakespeare's *Measure for Measure*, Act III, Scene 1, lines 32–34. l. 3 *hot gates:* a translation of the Greek "Thermopylae," where the Persians and Greeks fought a decisive battle in 480 B.C. l. 17 *"We would see a sign!":* the words of the Pharisees, asking evidence of Jesus's divinity (Matthew 12:38–39). ll. 23–28: The names Silvero, Hakagawa, Tornquist, and Von Kulp are fictional, Eliot's creation, as are those in l. 67; *Limoges:* a city in France noted for its fine chinaware; *Titians:* paintings by Titian, the great sixteenth-century Italian artist. ll. 29–32 *Vacant shuttles/Weave the wind:* cf. "My days are swifter than a weaver's shuttle . . . spent without hope . . . my life is wind" (Job 7: 6–7). ll. 67–68: Their remains are whirled beyond the constellation of the Great Bear, "shuddering" in the cold north. l. 70 *Belle Isle:* a strait in the North Atlantic between Labrador and Newfoundland; *Horn:* Cape Horn, at the southernmost end of South America. l. 72: *Trades:* Gulf Stream trade winds.

The Love Song of J. Alfred Prufrock

S'io credessi che mia risposta fosse
a persona che mai tornasse al mondo,
questa fiamma staria senza più scosse.
Ma per ciò che giammai di questo fondo
non tornò vivo alcun, s'i'odo il vero,
senza tema d'infamia ti rispondo.

Let us go then, you and I,
When the evening is spread out against the sky
Like a patient etherized upon a table;
Let us go, through certain half-deserted streets,
The muttering retreats   5
Of restless nights in one-night cheap hotels
And sawdust restaurants with oyster-shells:
Streets that follow like a tedious argument
Of insidious intent
To lead you to an overwhelming question . . .   10
Oh, do not ask, "What is it?"
Let us go and make our visit.

In the room the women come and go
Talking of Michelangelo.

The yellow fog that rubs its back upon the window-panes,   15
The yellow smoke that rubs its muzzle on the window-panes,

Licked its tongue into the corners of the evening,
Lingered upon the pools that stand in drains,
Let fall upon its back the soot that falls from chimneys,
Slipped by the terrace, made a sudden leap,   20
And seeing that it was a soft October night,
Curled once about the house, and fell asleep.

And indeed there will be time
For the yellow smoke that slides along the street
Rubbing its back upon the window-panes;   25
There will be time, there will be time
To prepare a face to meet the faces that you meet;
There will be time to murder and create,
And time for all the works and days of hands
That lift and drop a question on your plate;   30
Time for you and time for me,
And time yet for a hundred indecisions,
And for a hundred visions and revisions,
Before the taking of a toast and tea.

In the room the women come and go   35
Talking of Michelangelo.

And indeed there will be time
To wonder, "Do I dare?" and, "Do I dare?"
Time to turn back and descend the stair,
With a bald spot in the middle of my hair—   40
(They will say: "How his hair is growing thin!")
My morning coat, my collar mounting firmly to the chin,
My necktie rich and modest, but asserted by a simple pin—
(They will say: "But how his arms and legs are thin!")
Do I dare   45
Disturb the universe?
In a minute there is time
For decisions and revisions which a minute will reverse.

For I have known them all already, known them all—
Have known the evenings, mornings, afternoons,   50
I have measured out my life with coffee spoons;
I know the voices dying with a dying fall
Beneath the music from a farther room.
   So how should I presume?

And I have known the eyes already, known them all—   55
The eyes that fix you in a formulated phrase,
And when I am formulated, sprawling on a pin,
When I am pinned and wriggling on the wall,

Then how should I begin
To spit out all the butt-ends of my days and ways?   60
      And how should I presume?

And I have known the arms already, known them all—
Arms that are braceleted and white and bare
(But in the lamplight, downed with light brown hair!)
Is it perfume from a dress   65
That makes me so digress?
Arms that lie along a table, or wrap about a shawl.
      And should I then presume?
      And how should I begin?

                    .   .   .   .   .

Shall I say, I have gone at dusk through narrow streets   70
And watched the smoke that rises from the pipes
Of lonely men in shirt-sleeves, leaning out of windows? . . .

I should have been a pair of ragged claws
Scuttling across the floors of silent seas.

                    .   .   .   .   .

And the afternoon, the evening, sleeps so peacefully!   75
Smoothed by long fingers,
Asleep . . . tired . . . or it malingers,
Stretched on the floor, here beside you and me.
Should I, after tea and cakes and ices,
Have the strength to force the moment to its crisis?   80
But though I have wept and fasted, wept and prayed,
Though I have seen my head (grown slightly bald) brought in upon a
      platter,
I am no prophet—and here's no great matter;
I have seen the moment of my greatness flicker,
And I have seen the eternal Footman hold my coat, and snicker,   85
And in short, I was afraid.

And would it have been worth it, after all,
After the cups, the marmalade, the tea,
Among the porcelain, among some talk of you and me,
Would it have been worth while,   90
To have bitten off the matter with a smile,
To have squeezed the universe into a ball
To roll it toward some overwhelming question,
To say: "I am Lazarus, come from the dead,
Come back to tell you all, I shall tell you all"—   95
If one, settling a pillow by her head,
      Should say: "That is not what I meant at all.
      That is not it, at all."

And would it have been worth it, after all,
Would it have been worth while,   100
After the sunsets and the dooryards and the sprinkled streets,
After the novels, after the teacups, after the skirts that trail along the
    floor—
And this, and so much more?—
It is impossible to say just what I mean!
But as if a magic lantern threw the nerves in patterns on a screen: 105
Would it have been worth while
If one, settling a pillow or throwing off a shawl,
And turning toward the window, should say:
    "That is not it at all,
    That is not what I meant, at all."   110

                    •   •   •   •   •

No! I am not Prince Hamlet, nor was meant to be;
Am an attendant lord, one that will do
To swell a progress, start a scene or two,
Advise the prince; no doubt, an easy tool,
Deferential, glad to be of use,   115
Politic, cautious, and meticulous;
Full of high sentence°, but a bit obtuse;   *stately (pompous) meanings*
At times, indeed, almost ridiculous—
Almost, at times, the Fool.

I grow old . . . I grow old . . .   120
I shall wear the bottoms of my trousers rolled.

Shall I part my hair behind? Do I dare to eat a peach?
I shall wear white flannel trousers, and walk upon the beach.
I have heard the mermaids singing, each to each.

I do not think that they will sing to me.   125

I have seen them riding seaward on the waves
Combing the white hair of the waves blown back
When the wind blows the water white and black.

We have lingered in the chambers of the sea
By sea-girls wreathed with seaweed red and brown   130
Till human voices wake us, and we drown.

T. S. Eliot (1888–1965)

The Love Song of J. Alfred Prufrock. The epigraph is from Dante's *Inferno* 27, lines 61–66.
Dante and Virgil, descending to the chasm of evil counselors, hear the voice of Guido da
Montefeltro. The spirit is imprisoned in a flame that sways as the voice speaks. Dante has
asked the spirit, "Who art thou?"

If I thought my answer were given
to anyone who would ever return to the world,
this flame would stand still without moving any further.
But since never from this abyss
has anyone ever returned alive, if what I hear is true,
without fear of infamy I answer thee.

In the passage that follows, Guido admits his sinful, deceitful, and fraudulent behavior while on earth. l. 14 *Michelangelo:* great Italian painter and sculptor of the sixteenth century. l. 29: Ironical echo of *Works and Days,* a lengthy work by the ancient Greek poet Hesiod, dealing with productive agricultural labor. l. 82 *platter:* referring to the beheading of John the Baptist, who had come to prophesy Jesus's arrival (see Mark 6:17–28). l. 94 *Lazarus:* for his return from the dead see John 11:1–44.

In Golden Gate Park That Day

In Golden Gate Park° that day   *in San Francisco*
        a man and his wife were coming along
  thru the enormous meadow
      which was the meadow of the world
He was wearing green suspenders   5
     and carrying an old beat-up flute
        in one hand
 while his wife had a bunch of grapes
     which she kept handing out
         individually   10
     to various squirrels
        as if each
     were a little joke

And then the two of them came on
      thru the enormous meadow   15
which was the meadow of the world
     and then
  at a very still spot where the trees dreamed
 and seemed to have been waiting thru all time
       for them   20
  they sat down together on the grass
      without looking at each other
  and ate oranges
     without looking at each other
       and put the peels   25
 in a basket which they seemed
      to have brought for that purpose
  without looking at each other

And then
   he took his shirt and undershirt off   30

but kept his hat on
                        sideways
                                and without saying anything
       fell asleep under it
                        And his wife just sat there looking   35
at the birds which flew about
    calling to each other
                in the stilly air
      as if they were questioning existence
                    or trying to recall something forgotten   40

But then finally
           she too lay down flat
                   and just lay there looking up
                            at nothing
        yet fingering the old flute   45
                   which nobody played
     and finally looking over
                at him
without any particular expression
                      except a certain awful look   50
     of terrible depression

Lawrence Ferlinghetti (b. 1919)

Birches

When I see birches bend to left and right
Across the lines of straighter darker trees,
I like to think some boy's been swinging them.
But swinging doesn't bend them down to stay.
Ice-storms do that. Often you must have seen them   5
Loaded with ice a sunny winter morning
After a rain. They click upon themselves
As the breeze rises, and turn many-colored
As the stir cracks and crazes their enamel.
Soon the sun's warmth makes them shed crystal shells   10
Shattering and avalanching on the snow-crust—
Such heaps of broken glass to sweep away
You'd think the inner dome of heaven had fallen.
They are dragged to the withered bracken by the load,
And they seem not to break; though once they are bowed   15
So low for long, they never right themselves:
You may see their trunks arching in the woods
Years afterwards, trailing their leaves on the ground
Like girls on hands and knees that throw their hair
Before them over their heads to dry in the sun.   20

But I was going to say when Truth broke in
With all her matter-of-fact about the ice-storm
I should prefer to have some boy bend them
As he went out and in to fetch the cows—
Some boy too far from town to learn baseball,   25
Whose only play was what he found himself,
Summer or winter, and could play alone.
One by one he subdued his father's trees
By riding them down over and over again
Until he took the stiffness out of them,   30
And not one but hung limp, not one was left
For him to conquer. He learned all there was
To learn about not launching out too soon
And so not carrying the tree away
Clear to the ground. He always kept his poise   35
To the top branches, climbing carefully
With the same pains you use to fill a cup
Up to the brim, and even above the brim.
Then he flung outward, feet first, with a swish,
Kicking his way down through the air to the ground.   40
So was I once myself a swinger of birches.
And so I dream of going back to be.
It's when I'm weary of considerations,
And life is too much like a pathless wood
Where your face burns and tickles with the cobwebs   45
Broken across it, and one eye is weeping
From a twig's having lashed across it open.
I'd like to get away from earth awhile
And then come back to it and begin over.
May no fate willfully misunderstand me   50
And half grant what I wish and snatch me away
Not to return. Earth's the right place for love:
I don't know where it's likely to go better.
I'd like to go by climbing a birch tree,
And climb black branches up a snow-white trunk   55
Toward heaven, till the tree could bear no more,
But dipped its top and set me down again.
That would be good both going and coming back.
One could do worse than be a swinger of birches.

Robert Frost (1874–1963)

The Wild Boar and the Ram

Against an elm a sheep was tied,
The butcher's knife in blood was dyed;

The patient flock, in silent fright,
From far beheld the horrid sight;
A savage boar, who near them stood,   5
Thus mocked to scorn the fleecy brood.
    "All cowards should be served like you.
See, see, your murd'rer is in view;
With purple hands and reeking knife
He strips the skin yet warm with life: 10
Your quartered sires, your bleeding dams°,   *mothers*
The dying bleat of harmless lambs
Call for revenge. O stupid race!
The heart that wants° revenge is base."   *lacks*
    "I grant," an ancient ram replies,   15
"We bear no terror in our eyes,
Yet think us not of soul so tame,
Which no repeated wrongs inflame,
Insensible of ev'ry ill,
Because we want thy tusks to kill.   20
Know, those who violence pursue
Give to themselves the vengeance due,
For in these massacres they find
The two chief plagues that waste mankind.
Our skin supplies the wrangling bar°,   *law courts* 25
It wakes their slumb'ring sons to war,
And well revenge may rest contented,
Since drums and parchment were invented."

                    John Gay (1685–1732)

To Aunt Rose

Aunt Rose—now—might I see you
with your thin face and buck tooth smile and pain
          of rheumatism—and a long black heavy shoe
               for your bony left leg
     limping down the long hall in Newark on the running carpet   5
          past the black grand piano
               in the day room
                    where the parties were
          and I sang Spanish loyalist songs
               in a high squeaky voice   10
                    (hysterical) the committee listening
               while you limped around the room
                    collected the money—

Aunt Honey, Uncle Sam, a stranger with a cloth arm
      in his pocket
         and huge young bald head
           of Abraham Lincoln Brigade

—your long sad face
     your tears of sexual frustration
        (what smothered sobs and bony hips
           under the pillows of Osborne Terrace)
    —the time I stood on the toilet seat naked
      and you powdered my thighs with Calomine
         against the poison ivy—my tender
           and shamed first black curled hairs
  what were you thinking in secret heart then
        knowing me a man already—
and I an ignorant girl of family silence on the thin pedestal
        of my legs in the bathroom—Museum of Newark.
            Aunt Rose
Hitler is dead, Hitler is in Eternity; Hitler is with
      Tamburlane and Emily Brontë

Though I see you walking still, a ghost on Osborne Terrace
      down the long dark hall to the front door
    limping a little with a pinched smile
      in what must have been a silken
         flower dress
  welcoming my father, the Poet, on his visit to Newark
      —see you arriving in the living room
         dancing on your crippled leg
        and clapping hands his book
         had been accepted by Liveright

Hitler is dead and Liveright's gone out of business
The Attic of the Past and *Everlasting Minute* are out of print
        Uncle Harry sold his last silk stocking
      Claire quit interpretive dancing school
        Buba sits a wrinkled monument in Old
          Ladies Home blinking at new babies
last time I saw you was the hospital
      pale skull protruding under ashen skin
         blue veined unconscious girl
          in an oxygen tent
    the war in Spain has ended long ago
        Aunt Rose

Allen Ginsberg (b. 1926)

l. 9 *loyalist:* the first of several references to the Spanish Civil War (1937–1939) between the republican-loyalist forces and the fascists led by General Francisco Franco. l. 17 *Abraham Lincoln Brigade:* volunteers from the United States who went to Spain to fight against the fascists. ll. 31–32 *Hitler:* Adolf Hitler (1889–1945), leader of Nazi Germany from 1933 to 1945. *Tamburlane* (1336?–1405), Mongol conqueror. *Emily Brontë* (1818–1848), English novelist. l. 42 *Liveright:* the Boni-Liveright publishing firm.

Nikki-Rosa

childhood remembrances are always a drag
if you're Black
you always remember things like living in Woodlawn
with no inside toilet
and if you become famous or something   5
they never talk about how happy you were to have your mother
all to your self and
how good the water felt when you got your bath from one of those
big tubs that folk in chicago barbecue in
and somehow when you talk about home   10
it never gets across how much you
understood their feelings
as the whole family attended meetings about Hollydale
and even though you remember
your biographers never understand   15
your father's pain as he sells his stock
and another dream goes
and though you're poor it isn't poverty that
concerns you
and though they fought a lot   20
it isn't your father's drinking that makes any difference
but only that everybody is together and you
and your sister have happy birthdays and very good christmasses
and I really hope no white person ever has cause to write about me
because they never understand Black love is Black wealth and they'll   25
probably talk about my hard childhood and never understand that
all the while I was quite happy.

Nikki Giovanni (b. 1943)

Winter Poem

once a snowflake fell
on my brow and i loved
it so much and i kissed

it and it was happy and called its cousins
and brothers and a web   5
of snow engulfed me then
i reached to love them all
and i squeezed them and they became
a spring rain and i stood perfectly
still and was a flower   10

Nikki Giovanni (b. 1943)

Elegy Written in a Country Churchyard

The curfew tolls the knell of parting day,
    The lowing herd wind slowly o'er the lea,
The plowman homeward plods his weary way,
    And leaves the world to darkness and to me.

Now fades the glimmering landscape on the sight,   5
    And all the air a solemn stillness holds,
Save where the beetle wheels his droning flight,
    And drowsy tinklings lull the distant folds;

Save that from yonder ivy-mantled tower
    The moping owl does to the moon complain   10
Of such, as wandering near her secret bower,
    Molest her ancient solitary reign.

Beneath those rugged elms, that yew tree's shade,
    Where heaves the turf in many a moldering heap,
Each in his narrow cell forever laid,   15
    The rude° forefathers of the hamlet sleep.   *untaught*

The breezy call of incense-breathing morn,
    The swallow twittering from the straw-built shed,
The cock's shrill clarion, or the echoing horn°,   *of the hunters*
    No more shall rouse them from their lowly bed.   20

For them no more the blazing hearth shall burn,
    Or busy housewife ply her evening care;
No children run to lisp their sire's return,
    Or climb his knees the envied kiss to share.

Oft did the harvest to their sickle yield,   25
    Their furrow oft the stubborn glebe° has broke;   *soil*
How jocund did they drive their team afield!
    How bowed the woods beneath their sturdy stroke!

Let not Ambition mock their useful toil,
   Their homely joys, and destiny obscure;   30
Nor Grandeur hear with a disdainful smile
   The short and simple annals° of the poor.   *history, records*

The boast of heraldry°, the pomp of power,   *high birth*
   And all that beauty, all that wealth e'er gave,
Awaits alike the inevitable hour.   35
   The paths of glory lead but to the grave.

Nor you, ye proud, impute to these the fault,
   If Memory o'er their tomb no trophies raise,
Where through the long-drawn aisle and fretted° vault   *ornamented*
   The pealing anthem swells the note of praise.   40

Can storied urn or animated° bust   *lifelike*
   Back to its mansion call the fleeting breath?
Can Honor's voice provoke the silent dust,
   Or Flattery soothe the dull cold ear of Death?

Perhaps in this neglected spot is laid   45
   Some heart once pregnant with celestial fire;
Hands that the rod of empire might have swayed,
   Or waked to ecstasy the living lyre.

But Knowledge to their eyes her ample page
   Rich with the spoils of time did ne'er unroll;   50
Chill Penury repressed their noble rage,
   And froze the genial current of the soul.

Full many a gem of purest ray serene,
   The dark unfathomed caves of ocean bear:
Full many a flower is born to blush unseen,   55
   And waste its sweetness on the desert air.

Some village Hampden, that with dauntless breast
   The little tyrant of his fields withstood;
Some mute inglorious Milton here may rest,
   Some Cromwell guiltless of his country's blood.   60

The applause of listening senates to command,
   The threats of pain and ruin to despise,
To scatter plenty o'er a smiling land,
   And read their history in a nation's eyes,

Their lot forbade: nor circumscribed alone   65
   Their growing virtues, but their crimes confined;

Forbade to wade through slaughter to a throne,
  And shut the gates of mercy on mankind,

The struggling pangs of conscious truth to hide,
  To quench the blushes of ingenuous shame,   70
Or heap the shrine of Luxury and Pride
  With incense kindled at the Muse's flame.

Far from the madding° crowd's ignoble strife,   *frenzied*
  Their sober wishes never learned to stray;
Along the cool sequestered vale of life   75
  They kept the noiseless tenor of their way.

Yet even these bones from insult to protect
  Some frail memorial still erected nigh,
With uncouth° rhymes and shapeless sculpture decked,   *untaught*
  Implores the passing tribute of a sigh.   80

Their name, their years, spelt by the unlettered Muse,
  The place of fame and elegy supply:
And many a holy text around she strews,
  That teach the rustic moralist to die.

For who to dumb Forgetfulness a prey,   85
  This pleasing anxious being e'er resigned,
Left the warm precincts of the cheerful day,
  Nor cast one longing lingering look behind?

On some fond breast the parting soul relies,
  Some pious drops the closing eye requires;   90
Even from the tomb the voice of Nature cries,
  Even in our ashes live their wonted fires.

For thee, who mindful of the unhonored dead
  Dost in these lines their artless tale relate;
If chance, by lonely contemplation led,   95
  Some kindred spirit shall inquire thy fate,

Haply° some hoary-headed swain may say,   *perhaps*
  "Oft have we seen him at the peep of dawn
Brushing with hasty steps the dews away
  To meet the sun upon the upland lawn.   100

"There at the foot of yonder nodding beech
  That wreathes its old fantastic roots so high,
His listless length at noontide would he stretch,
  And pore upon the brook that babbles by.

"Hard by yon wood, now smiling as in scorn,   105
    Muttering his wayward fancies he would rove,
Now drooping, woeful wan, like one forlorn,
    Or crazed with care, or crossed in hopeless love.

"One morn I missed him on the customed hill,
    Along the heath and near his favorite tree;   110
Another came; nor yet beside the rill,
    Nor up the lawn, nor at the wood was he;

"The next with dirges due in sad array
    Slow through the churchway path we saw him borne.
Approach and read (for thou canst read) the lay°,   *tale* 115
    Graved on the stone beneath yon aged thorn."

  The Epitaph

Here rests his head upon the lap of Earth
 A youth to Fortune and to Fame unknown.
Fair Science° frowned not on his humble birth,   *formal learning*
 And Melancholy marked him for her own.   120

Large was his bounty, and his soul sincere,
 Heaven did a recompense as largely send:
He gave to Misery all he had, a tear,
 He gained from Heaven ('twas all he wished) a friend.

No farther seek his merits to disclose,   125
 Or draw his frailties from their dread abode
(There they alike in trembling hope repose),
 The bosom of his Father and his God.

Thomas Gray (1716–1771)

Elegy Written in a Country Churchyard. ll. 57–60: Gray refers to three significant seventeenth-century figures who opposed monarchial privilege: John *Hampden* (1594–1643), member of Parliament and defender of people's rights against King Charles I; John *Milton* (1608–1674), great poet and pamphleteer, also Latin secretary to Oliver *Cromwell* (1599–1658), Puritan leader who governed after the monarchy was overthrown and Charles I executed.

The Sleeping Giant

(A Hill, so Named, in Hamden, Connecticut)

The whole day long, under the walking sun
That poised an eye on me from its high floor,

Holding my toy beside the clapboard house
I looked for him, the summer I was four.

I was afraid the waking arm would break   5
From the loose earth and rub against his eyes
A fist of trees, and the whole country tremble
In the exultant labor of his rise;

Then he with giant steps in the small streets
Would stagger, cutting off the sky, to seize   10
The roofs from house and home because we had
Covered his shape with dirt and planted trees;

And then kneel down and rip with fingernails
A trench to pour the enemy Atlantic
Into our basin, and the water rush,   15
With the streets full and all the voices frantic.

That was the summer I expected him.
Later the high and watchful sun instead
Walked low behind the house, and school began,
And winter pulled a sheet over his head.   20

Donald Hall (b. 1928)

The Convergence of the Twain

(Lines on the loss of the "Titanic")

I

In a solitude of the sea
Deep from human vanity,
And the Pride of Life that planned her, stilly couches she.

II

Steel chambers, late the pyres
Of her salamandrine fires,   5
Cold currents thrid°, and turn to rhythmic tidal lyres.   *thread*

III

Over the mirrors meant
To glass the opulent
The sea-worm crawls—grotesque, slimed, dumb, indifferent.

IV

Jewels in joy designed
To ravish the sensuous mind
Lie lightless, all their sparkles bleared and black and blind.

10

V

Dim moon-eyed fishes near
Gaze at the gilded gear
And query: "What does this vaingloriousness down here?"

15

VI

Well: while was fashioning
This creature of cleaving wing,
The Immanent Will that stirs and urges everything

VII

Prepared a sinister mate
For her—so gaily great—
A Shape of Ice, for the time far and dissociate.

20

VIII

And as the smart ship grew
In stature, grace, and hue,
In shadowy silent distance grew the Iceberg too.

IX

Alien they seemed to be:
No mortal eye could see
The intimate welding of their later history,

25

X

Or sign that they were bent
By paths coincident
On being anon twin halves of one august event.

30

XI

Till the Spinner of the Years
Said "Now!" And each one hears,
And consummation comes, and jars two hemispheres.

Thomas Hardy (1840–1928)

The Convergence of the Twain. Subtitle: The *Titanic*, elegant and supposedly impregnable,
sank (April 14, 1912) on its initial voyage from England to America, with great loss of life.

Witch Doctor

I

He dines alone surrounded by reflections
of himself. Then after sleep and benzedrine
descends the Cinquecento stair° his magic   *ornate Renaissance staircase*
wrought from hypochondria of the well-
to-do and nagging deathwish of the poor;   5
swirls on smiling genuflections of
his liveried chauffeur into a crested
lilac limousine, the cynosure
of mousey neighbors tittering behind
Venetian blinds and half afraid of him   10
and half admiring his outrageous flair.

II

Meanwhile his mother, priestess in gold lamé,
precedes him to the quondam theater
now Israel Temple of the Highest Alpha,
where the bored, the sick, the alien, the tired   15
await euphoria. With deadly vigor
she prepares the way for mystery
and lucre. Shouts in blues-contralto, "He's
God's dictaphone of all-redeeming truth.
Oh he's the holyweight champeen who's come   20
to give the knockout lick to your bad luck;
say he's the holyweight champeen who's here
to deal a knockout punch to your hard luck."

III

Reposing on cushions of black leopard skin,
he telephones instructions for a long   25
slow drive across the park that burgeons now
with spring and sailors. Peers questingly
into the green fountainous twilight, sighs
and turns the gold-plate dial to Music For
Your Dining-Dancing Pleasure. Smoking Egyptian   30
cigarettes rehearses in his mind
a new device that he must use tonight.

IV

Approaching Israel Temple, mask in place,
he hears ragtime allegros of a "Song
of Zion" that becomes when he appears   35
a hallelujah wave for him to walk.

His mother and a rainbow-surpliced cordon
conduct him choiring to the altar-stage,
and there he kneels and seems to pray before
a lighted Jesus painted sealskin-brown.   40
Then with a glittering flourish he arises,
turns, gracefully extends his draperied arms:
"Israelites, true Jews, O found lost tribe
of Israel, receive my blessing now.
Selah, selah°." He feels them yearn toward him   *hallelujah* 45
as toward a lover, exults before the image
of himself their trust gives back. Stands as though
in meditation, letting their eyes caress
his garments jewelled and chatoyant°, cut   *undulating color*
to fall, to flow from his tall figure   50
dramatically just so. Then all at once
he sways, quivers, gesticulates as if
to ward off blows or kisses, and when he speaks
again he utters wildering vocables,
hypnotic no-words planned (and never failing)   55
to enmesh his flock in theopathic° tension.   *religious*
Cries of eudaemonic° pain attest   *happiness-producing*
his artistry. Behind the mask he smiles.
And now in subtly altering light he chants
and sinuously trembles, chants and trembles   60
while convulsive energies of eager faith
surcharge the theater with power of
their own, a power he has counted on
and for a space allows to carry him.
Dishevelled antiphons° proclaim the moment   *answering chant* 65
his followers all day have hungered for,
but which is his alone.
He signals: tambourines begin, frenetic
drumbeat and glissando. He dances from the altar,
robes hissing, flaring, shimmering; down aisles   70
where mantled guardsmen intercept wild hands
that arduously strain to clutch his vestments,
he dances, dances, ensorcelled and aloof,
the fervid juba of God as lover, healer,
conjurer. And of himself as God.   75

Robert Hayden (1913–1980)

Witch Doctor. l. 14 *Israel Temple of the Highest Alpha:* the name of the church, now housed
in the former theater. l. 45 *Selah:* Hebrew word, probably meaning "hallelujah" or "lift
up your voices."

Easter Wings

Lord, who createdst man in wealth and store°,   *fullness*
  Though foolishly he lost the same,
    Decaying more and more
     Till he became
      Most poor: 5
      With thee
     O let me rise,
    As larks, harmoniously,
  And sing this day thy victories;
Then shall the fall further the flight in me.   10

My tender age in sorrow did begin;
  And still with sicknesses and shame
    Thou didst so punish sin,
     That I became
      Most thin.   15
      With thee
     Let me combine
    And feel this day thy victory;
  For, if I imp° my wing on thine,   *graft (attach)*
Affliction shall advance the flight in me.   20

George Herbert (1593–1633)

The Pulley

  When God at first made man,
Having a glass of blessings standing by,
Let us, said he, pour on him all we can.
Let the world's riches, which dispersèd lie,
  Contract into a span.   5

  So strength first made a way,
Then beauty flowed, then wisdom, honor, pleasure.
When almost all was out, God made a stay°,   *pause*
Perceiving that alone of all his treasure
  Rest in the bottom lay.   10

  For if I should, said he,
Bestow this jewel also on my creature,
He would adore my gifts instead of me,
And rest in nature, not the God of nature:
  So both should losers be.   15

Yet let him keep the rest,
But keep them with repining restlessness.
Let him be rich and weary, that at least
If goodness lead him not, yet weariness
    May toss him to my breast.   20

George Herbert (1593–1633)

Virtue

Sweet day, so cool, so calm, so bright,
The bridal of the earth and sky;
The dew shall weep thy fall to-night,
    For thou must die.

Sweet rose, whose hue angry and brave   5
Bids the rash gazer wipe his eye;
Thy root is ever in its grave,
    And thou must die.

Sweet spring, full of sweet days and roses,
A box where sweets compacted lie;   10
My music shows ye have your closes,
    And all must die.

Only a sweet and virtuous soul,
Like seasoned timber, never gives;
But though the whole world turn to coal,   15
    Then chiefly lives.

George Herbert (1593–1633)

Delight in Disorder

A sweet disorder in the dress
Kindles in clothes a wantonness.
A lawn° about the shoulders thrown   *fine linen scarf*
Into a fine distractión;
An erring° lace, which here and there   *wandering* 5
Enthralls the crimson stomacher°;   *bodice, frontpiece*
A cuff neglectful, and thereby
Ribbons to flow confusedly;

A winning wave, deserving note,
In the tempestuous petticoat;
A careless shoestring, in whose tie
I see a wild civility;
Do more bewitch me than when art
Is too precise in every part.

Robert Herrick (1591–1674)

To the Virgins, to Make Much of Time

Gather ye rosebuds while ye may,
  Old time is still a-flying;
And this same flower that smiles today
  Tomorrow will be dying.

The glorious lamp of heaven, the sun,
  The higher he's a-getting,
The sooner will his race be run,
  And nearer he's to setting.

That age is best which is the first,
  When youth and blood are warmer;
But being spent, the worse, and worst
  Times still succeed the former.

Then be not coy, but use your time;
  And while ye may, go marry;
For having lost but once your prime,
  You may forever tarry.

Robert Herrick (1591–1674)

Upon Julia's Clothes

Whenas in silks my Julia goes,
Then, then, methinks, how sweetly flows
That liquefaction of her clothes.

Next, when I cast mine eyes and see
That brave vibration each way free,
O how that glittering taketh me!

Robert Herrick (1591–1674)

The Brides

Down the assembly line they roll and pass
Complete at last, a miracle of design;
Their chromium fenders, the unbreakable glass,
The fashionable curve, the air-flow line.

Grease to the elbows Mum and Dad enthuse,   5
Pocket their spanners° and survey the bride;   *wrenches*
Murmur: 'A sweet job! All she needs is juice!
Built for a life-time—sleek as a fish. Inside

'He will find every comfort: the full set
Of gadgets; knobs that answer to the touch   10
For light or music; a place for his cigarette;
Room for his knees; a honey of a clutch.'

Now slowly through the show-room's flattering glare
See her wheeled in to love, console, obey,
Shining and silent! Parson with a prayer   15
Blesses the number-plate, she rolls away

To write her numerals in his book of life;
And now, at last, stands on the open road,
Triumphant, perfect, every inch a wife,
While the corks pop, the flash-light bulbs explode.   20

Her heavenly bowser-boy assumes his seat;
She prints the soft dust with her brand-new treads,
Swings towards the future, purring with a sweet
Concatenation° of the poppet heads°.   *coupling/valve heads*

A. D. Hope (b. 1907)

The Brides. l. 21 *bowser-boy:* British and Australian slang for gas-station attendant. l. 24
poppet: may also mean "puppet" or "small person."

God's Grandeur

The world is charged with the grandeur of God.
  It will flame out, like shining from shook foil°;   *tinsel, goldfoil*
  It gathers to a greatness, like the ooze of oil
Crushed. Why do men then now not reck his rod°?   *acknowledge his discipline*
Generations have trod, have trod, have trod;   5
  And all is seared with trade; bleared, smeared with toil;

And wears man's smudge and shares man's smell: the soil
Is bare now, nor can foot feel, being shod.

And for all this, nature is never spent;
   There lives the dearest freshness deep down things;   10
And though the last lights off the black West went
   Oh, morning, at the brown brink eastward, springs—
Because the Holy Ghost over the bent
   World broods with warm breast and with ah! bright wings.

Gerard Manley Hopkins (1844–1889)

The Windhover

To Christ Our Lord

I caught this morning morning's minion°, kingdom of daylight's   *darling*
   dauphin, dapple-dawn-drawn Falcon, in his riding
   Of the rolling level underneath him steady air, and striding
High there, how he rung upon the rein of a wimpling° wing   *rippling*
In his ecstasy! then off, off forth on swing,
   As a skate's heel sweeps smooth on a bow-bend: the hurl and gliding   5
   Rebuffed the big wind. My heart in hiding
Stirred for a bird,—the achieve of, the mastery of the thing!

Brute beauty and valour and act, oh, air, pride, plume here
   Buckle! *and* the fire that breaks from thee° then, a billion   *Christ*
Times told lovelier, more dangerous, O my chevalier!   10

   No wonder of it: shéer plód makes plough down sillion°   *furrow*
Shine, and blue-bleak embers, ah my dear,
   Fall, gall° themselves, and gash gold-vermilion.   *break*

Gerard Manley Hopkins (1844–1889)

The Windhover. The kestrel, or *windhover,* is a small falcon capable of hovering in the air much as Hopkins describes its behavior in the octet. l. 1 *dauphin:* in France, the king's eldest son and hence heir to the throne. l. 9 *Buckle:* probably meaning "come together," fuse into a totality. l. 10 *chevalier:* knight, master (from the French).

Eight O'Clock

He stood, and heard the steeple
   Sprinkle the quarters on the morning town.
One, two, three, four, to market-place and people
   It tossed them down.

Strapped, noosed, nighing his hour,
  He stood and counted them and cursed his luck;
And then the clock collected in the tower
  Its strength, and struck.

A. E. Housman (1859–1936)

With Rue My Heart Is Laden

With rue my heart is laden
  For golden friends I had,
For many a rose-lipt maiden
  And many a lightfoot lad.

By brooks too broad for leaping
  The lightfoot boys are laid;
The rose-lipt girls are sleeping
  In fields where roses fade.

A. E. Housman (1859–1936)

The Negro Speaks of Rivers
(To W. E. B. Du Bois)

I've known rivers:
I've known rivers ancient as the world and older than the
    flow of human blood in human veins.

My soul has grown deep like the rivers.

I bathed in the Euphrates when dawns were young.   5
I built my hut near the Congo and it lulled me to sleep.
I looked upon the Nile and raised the pyramids above it.
I heard the singing of the Mississippi when Abe Lincoln
    went down to New Orleans, and I've seen its muddy
    bosom turn all golden in the sunset.   10

I've known rivers:
Ancient, dusky rivers.

My soul has grown deep like the rivers.

Langston Hughes (1902–1967)

The Negro Speaks of Rivers. W. E. B. Du Bois (1868–1963), to whom the poem is dedicated,
was a black American historian and leader.

Oedipus

My hands shook as I bargained for passage,
my hands shook because by his face I could tell
he was not one I could bargain with; death only
was his price. And when he lashed out at me
from his preeminence, his chariot, my hand   5
leapt to my sword, my throat ached.
I had no head then to consider I was killing
one who like myself had not been brought up
to countenance such manners, as to bargain.
Only against my grain I had wanted to.   10
I killed him, I felt myself cut off;
I heard myself inwardly go mad,
I had destroyed an image I hated:
I was destroyed.

David Ignatow (b. 1914)

Oedipus. In Greek legend, *Oedipus,* unaware of his adversary's identity, killed his father,
King Laius, in a violent encounter at a crossroads, thus fulfilling an earlier prophecy that
he would do so.

Hurt Hawks

The broken pillar of the wing jags from the clotted shoulder,
The wing trails like a banner in defeat,
No more to use the sky forever but live with famine
And pain a few days: cat nor coyote
Will shorten the week of waiting for death, there is game without talons.   5
He stands under the oak-bush and waits
The lame feet of salvation: at night he remembers freedom
And flies in a dream, the dawns ruin it.
He is strong and pain is worse to the strong, incapacity is worse.
The curs of the day come and torment him   10
At distance, no one but death the redeemer will humble that head,
The intrepid readiness, the terrible eyes.
The wild God of the world is sometimes merciful to those
That ask mercy, not often to the arrogant.
You do not know him, you communal people, or you have forgotten him;   15
Intemperate and savage, the hawk remembers him;
Beautiful and wild, the hawks, and men that are dying, remember him.

I'd sooner, except the penalties, kill a man than a hawk; but the great
   redtail

Had nothing left but unable misery
From the bone too shattered for mending, the wing that trailed under his
    talons when he moved.   20
We had fed him six weeks, I gave him freedom,
He wandered over the foreland hill and returned in the evening, asking
    for death,
Not like a begger, still eyed with the old
Implacable arrogance. I gave him the lead gift in the twilight. What fell
    was relaxed,
Owl-downy, soft feminine feathers; but what   25
Soared: the fierce rush: the night-herons by the flooded river cried fear at
    its rising
Before it was quite unsheathed from reality.

Robinson Jeffers (1887–1962)

To the Stone-Cutters

Stone-cutters fighting time with marble, you foredefeated°   *defeated*
Challengers of oblivion,   *beforehand*
Eat cynical earnings, knowing rock splits, records fall down,
The square-limbed Roman letters
Scale in the thaws, wear in the rain. The poet as well   5
Builds his monument mockingly;
For man will be blotted out, the blithe earth die, the brave sun
Die blind, his heart blackening:
Yet stones have stood for a thousand years, and pained thoughts found
The honey of peace in old poems.   10

Robinson Jeffers (1887–1962)

Inviting a Friend to Supper

Tonight, grave sir, both my poor house, and I
Do equally desire your company;
Not that we think us worthy such a guest,
But that your worth will dignify our feast
With those that come, whose grace may make that seem   5
Something, which else could hope for no esteem.
It is the fair acceptance, sir, creates
The entertainment perfect, not the cates°.   *food*
Yet shall you have, to rectify your palate,
An olive, capers, or some better salad   10

Ushering the mutton; with a short-legged hen,
If we can get her, full of eggs, and then
Lemons, and wine for sauce; to these a cony°   *rabbit*
Is not to be despaired of, for our money;
And, though fowl now be scarce, yet there are clerks°,   *learned friends* 15
The sky not falling, think we may have larks.
I'll tell you of more, and lie, so you will come:
Of partridge, pheasant, woodcock, of which some
May yet be there, and godwit, if we can;
Knot, rail, and ruff too. Howsoe'er, my man   20
Shall read a piece of Virgil, Tacitus,
Livy, or of some better book to us,
Of which we'll speak our minds, amidst our meat;
And I'll profess no verses to repeat.
To this, if aught appear which I not know of,   25
That will the pastry, not my paper, show of.
Digestive cheese and fruit there sure will be;
But that which most doth take my Muse and me,
Is a pure cup of rich Canary wine,
Which is the Mermaid's now, but shall be mine;   30
Of which had Horace, or Anacreon tasted,
Their lives, as do their lines, till now had lasted.
Tobacco, nectar, or the Thespian spring,
Are all but Luther's beer° to this I sing.   *weak German beer*
Of this we will sup free, but moderately,   35
And we will have no Pooley°, or Parrot° by,   *government informers*
Nor shall our cups make any guilty men;
But, at our parting we will be as when
We innocently met. No simple word
That shall be uttered at our mirthful board,   40
Shall make us sad next morning or affright
The liberty that we'll enjoy tonight.

Ben Jonson (1573?–1637)

Inviting a Friend to Supper. l. 16: cf. the proverb "When the sky falls, we shall have larks." ll. 18–19 *partridge, pheasant, woodcock . . . godwit:* varieties of birds, eaten as delicacies. ll. 21–22 *Virgil, Tacitus, Livy:* great Latin classical writers. ll. 29–30 *rich Canary wine/Which is the Mermaid's now:* wine to be sent from the famous Mermaid Tavern. l. 31 *Horace:* Roman lyric poet; *Anacreon:* Greek lyric poet.

Still to Be Neat, Still to Be Dressed

Still to be neat, still to be dressed
As you were going to a feast:
Still to be powdered, still perfumed:

Lady, it is to be presumed,
Though art's hid causes are not found,
All is not sweet, all is not sound.

Give me a look, give me a face
That makes simplicity a grace;
Robes loosely flowing, hair as free:
Such sweet neglect more taketh me,
Than all the adulteries° of art,   *sophistications*
That strike mine eyes, but not my heart.

Ben Jonson (1573?–1637)

A Poem About Intelligence for My Brothers and Sisters

A few year back and they told me Black
means a hole where other folks
got brain/it was like the cells in the heads
of Black children was out to every hour on the hour naps
Scientists called the phenomenon the Notorious   5
Jensen Lapse, remember?
Anyway I was thinking
about how to devise
a test for the wise
like a Stanford-Binet   10
for the C.I.A.
you know?
Take Einstein
being the most the unquestionable the outstanding
the maximal mind of the century   15
right?
And I'm struggling against this lapse leftover
from my Black childhood to fathom why
anybody should say so:
$E = mc$ *squared?*   20
I try that on this old lady live on my block:
She sweeping away Saturday night from the stoop
and mad as can be because some absolute
jackass have left a kingsize mattress where
she have to sweep around it stains and all she   25
don't want to know nothing about in the first place
"Mrs. Johnson!" I say, leaning on the gate
between us: "What you think about somebody come up
with an E equals $M C$ 2?"

"How you doin," she answer me, sideways, like she don't   30
want to let on she know I ain
combed my hair yet and here it is
Sunday morning but still I have the nerve
to be bothering serious work with these crazy
questions about   35
"E equals what you say again, dear?"
Then I tell her, "Well
also this same guy? I think
he was undisputed Father of the Atom Bomb!"
"That right." She mumbles or grumbles, not too politely   40
"And dint remember to wear socks when he put on
his shoes!" I add on (getting desperate)
at which point Mrs. Johnson take herself and her broom
a very big step down the stoop away from me
"And never did nothing for nobody in particular   45
lessen it was a committee
and
used to say, 'What time is it?'
and
you'd say, 'Six o'clock.'   50
and
he'd say, 'Day or night?'
and
and he never made nobody a cup a tea
in his whole brilliant life!"   55
"and
(my voice rises slightly)
and
he dint never boogie neither: never!"

"Well," say Mrs. Johnson, "Well, honey,   60
I do guess
that's genius for you."

June Jordan (b. 1936)

Ode to a Nightingale

1

My heart aches, and a drowsy numbness pains
  My sense, as though of hemlock° I had drunk,   *poisonous herb*
Or emptied some dull opiate to the drains
  One minute past, and Lethe-wards had sunk:
'Tis not through envy of thy happy lot,   5

But being too happy in thy happiness,—
   That thou, light-winged Dryad of the trees,
      In some melodious plot
Of beechen green, and shadows numberless,
   Singest of summer in full-throated ease.   10

2

O, for a draught of vintage! that hath been
   Cooled a long age in the deep-delved earth,
Tasting of Flora and the country green,
   Dance, and Provençal song, and sunburnt mirth!
O for a beaker full of the warm South,   15
   Full of the true, the blushful Hippocrene,
      With beaded bubbles winking at the brim,
         And purple-stained mouth;
   That I might drink, and leave the world unseen,
   And with thee fade away into the forest dim: 20

3

Fade far away, dissolve, and quite forget
   What thou among the leaves hast never known,
The weariness, the fever, and the fret
   Here, where men sit and hear each other groan;
Where palsy shakes a few, sad, last gray hairs,   25
   Where youth grows pale, and specter-thin, and dies;
      Where but to think is to be full of sorrow
         And leaden-eyed despairs,
   Where Beauty cannot keep her lustrous eyes,
   Or new Love pine at them beyond tomorrow.   30

4

Away! away! for I will fly to thee,
   Not charioted by Bacchus and his pards,
But on the viewless wings of Poesy,
   Though the dull brain perplexes and retards:
Already with thee! tender is the night,   35
   And haply the Queen-Moon is on her throne,
      Clustered around by all her starry Fays°;   *fairies*
        But here there is no light,
   Save what from heaven is with the breezes blown
      Through verdurous glooms and winding mossy ways.   40

5

I cannot see what flowers are at my feet,
   Nor what soft incense hangs upon the boughs,
But, in embalmed darkness, guess each sweet
   Wherewith the seasonable month endows

The grass, the thicket, and the fruit-tree wild;   45
  White hawthorn, and the pastoral eglantine;
    Fast fading violets covered up in leaves;
      And mid-May's eldest child,
  The coming musk-rose, full of dewy wine,
    The murmurous haunt of flies on summer eves.   50

6

Darkling° I listen; and, for many a time   *in darkness*
  I have been half in love with easeful Death,
Called him soft names in many a muséd rhyme,
  To take into the air my quiet breath;
Now more than ever seems it rich to die,   55
  To cease upon the midnight with no pain,
    While thou art pouring forth thy soul abroad
      In such an ecstasy!
  Still wouldst thou sing, and I have ears in vain—
    To thy high requiem° become a sod.   *music for the dead* 60

7

Thou wast not born for death, immortal Bird!
  No hungry generations tread thee down;
The voice I hear this passing night was heard
  In ancient days by emperor and clown:
Perhaps the self-same song that found a path   65
  Through the sad heart of Ruth, when, sick for home,
    She stood in tears amid the alien corn;
      The same that oft-times hath
  Charmed magic casements°, opening on the foam   *windows*
    Of perilous seas, in faery lands forlorn.   70

8

Forlorn! the very word is like a bell
  To toll me back from thee to my sole self!
Adieu! the fancy cannot cheat so well
  As she is famed to do, deceiving elf.
Adieu! adieu! thy plaintive anthem fades   75
  Past the near meadows, over the still stream,
    Up the hill-side; and now 'tis buried deep
      In the next valley-glades:
  Was it a vision, or a waking dream?
    Fled is that music:—Do I wake or sleep?   80

John Keats (1795–1821)

Ode to a Nightingale. l. 4 *Lethe-wards:* in Greek legend, the underworld river Lethe;
crossing its waters caused forgetfulness. l. 7 *Dryad:* creature of the woods. l. 13 *Flora:*

Roman goddess of flowers. l. 14 *Provençal song:* medieval troubadours were centered in Provence, in the south of France. l. 16 *Hippocrene:* fountain of the Muses and of poetic inspiration. l. 32 *Bacchus:* Greek god of wine whose chariot was pulled by leopards (*pards*). l. 66 *Ruth:* see the Old Testament Book of Ruth for the story of her sojourn in a foreign land.

This Living Hand

This living hand, now warm and capable
Of earnest grasping, would, if it were cold
And in the icy silence of the tomb,
So haunt thy days and chill thy dreaming nights
That thou wouldst wish thine own heart dry of blood
So in my veins red life might stream again,
And thou be conscience-calmed—see here it is—
I hold it towards you.

John Keats (1795–1821)

Last Songs

1

What do they sing, the last birds
coasting down the twilight,
banking
across woods filled with darkness, their
frayed wings
curved on the world like a lover's arms
which form, night after night, in sleep,
an irremediable absence?

2

Silence. Ashes
in the grate. Whatever it is
that keeps us from heaven,
sloth, wrath, greed, fear, could we only
reinvent it on earth
as song.

Galway Kinnell (b. 1927)

The Absent Ones

The two foals sleep back to back
in the sun like one butterfly.
Their mothers, the mares, have weaned them,
have bitten them loose like button thread.

The beavers have forced their kit   5
out of the stick house; he waddles
like a hairy beetle across the bottom land
in search of other arrangements.

My mother has begun to grow down,
tucking her head like a turtle.   10
She is pasting everyone's name
on the undersides of her silver tea service.

Our daughters and sons have burst
from the marionette show
leaving a tangle of strings   15
and gone into the unlit audience.

Alone I water the puffball patch.
I exhort the mushrooms to put up.
Alone I visit the hayfield.
I fork up last summer's horse-apples   20
to let the seeds back in the furrow.

Someone comes toward me—a shadow.
Two parts of a butterfly flicker
in false sun and knit together.
A thigh brushes my thigh.   25
The stones are talking in code.

I will braid up the absent ones like onions.
The missing I will wrap like green tomatoes.
I will split seventy logs for winter,
seven times seven times seven.   30

This is the life I came with.

Maxine Kumin (b. 1925)

Church Going

Once I am sure there's nothing going on
I step inside, letting the door thud shut.

Another church: matting, seats, and stone,
And little books; sprawlings of flowers, cut
For Sunday, brownish now; some brass and stuff   5
Up at the holy end; the small neat organ;
And a tense, musty, unignorable silence,
Brewed God knows how long. Hatless, I take off
My cycle-clips in awkward reverence,

Move forward, run my hand around the font.   10
From where I stand, the roof looks almost new—
Cleaned, or restored? Someone would know: I don't.
Mounting the lectern, I peruse a few
Hectoring large-scale verses, and pronounce
"Here endeth" much more loudly than I'd meant.   15
The echoes snigger briefly. Back at the door
I sign the book, donate an Irish sixpence,
Reflect the place was not worth stopping for.

Yet stop I did: in fact I often do,
And always end much at a loss like this,   20
Wondering what to look for; wondering, too,
When churches fall completely out of use
What we shall turn them into, if we shall keep
A few cathedrals chronically on show,
Their parchment, plate and pyx in locked cases,   25
And let the rest rent-free to rain and sheep.
Shall we avoid them as unlucky places?

Or, after dark, will dubious women come
To make their children touch a particular stone;
Pick simples° for a cancer; or on some   *herbs* 30
Advised night see walking a dead one?
Power of some sort or other will go on
In games, in riddles, seemingly at random;
But superstition, like belief, must die,
And what remains when disbelief has gone?   35
Grass, weedy pavement, brambles, buttress, sky,

A shape less recognizable each week,
A purpose more obscure. I wonder who
Will be the last, the very last, to seek
This place for what it was; one of the crew   40
That tap and jot and know what rood-lofts were?
Some ruin-bibber, randy for antique,
Or Christmas-addict, counting on a whiff
Of gown-and-bands and organ-pipes and myrrh?
Or will he be my representative,   45

Bored, uninformed, knowing the ghostly silt
Dispersed, yet tending to this cross of ground
Through suburb scrub because it held unspilt
So long and equably what since is found
Only in separation—marriage, and birth, 50
And death, and thoughts of these—for which was built
This special shell? For, though I've no idea
What this accoutred frowsty° barn is worth, *dowdily dressed*
It pleases me to stand in silence here;

A serious house on serious earth it is, 55
In whose blent air all our compulsions meet,
Are recognized, and robed as destinies.
And that much never can be obsolete,
Since someone will forever be surprising
A hunger in himself to be more serious, 60
And gravitating with it to this ground,
Which, he once heard, was proper to grow wise in,
If only that so many dead lie round.

Philip Larkin (b. 1922)

Church Going. l. 15 *"Here endeth"*: from the phrase "Here endeth the Lesson," said at the conclusion of Scripture reading. l. 25 *plate*: for offerings; *pyx*: a container housing the Communion wafers. l. 41 *rood-lofts*: screened galleries separating the nave of a church from the choir.

Toads

Why should I let the toad *work*
 Squat on my life?
Can't I use my wit as a pitchfork
 And drive the brute off?

Six days of the week it soils 5
 With its sickening poison—
Just for paying a few bills!
 That's out of proportion.

Lots of folk live on their wits:
 Lecturers, lispers, 10
Losels°, loblolly-men°, louts— *loafers/con men*
 They don't end as paupers;

Lots of folk live up lanes
 With fires in a bucket,

Eat windfalls and tinned sardines—   15
   They seem to like it.

Their nippers have got bare feet,
   Their unspeakable wives
Are skinny as whippets—and yet
   No one actually *starves*.   20

Ah, were I courageous enough
   To shout *Stuff your pension!*
But I know, all too well, that's the stuff
   That dreams are made on:

For something sufficiently toad-like   25
   Squats in me, too;
Its hunkers are heavy as hard luck,
   And cold as snow,

And will never allow me to blarney
   My way to getting   30
The fame and the girl and the money
   All at one sitting.

I don't say, one bodies the other
   One's spiritual truth;
But I do say it's hard to lose either,   35
   When you have both.

Philip Larkin (b. 1922)

Bavarian Gentians

Not every man has gentians in his house
in Soft September, at slow, sad Michaelmas.

Bavarian gentians, big and dark, only dark
darkening the daytime, torch-like with the smoking blueness of Pluto's
   gloom,
ribbed and torch-like, with their blaze of darkness spread blue   5
down flattening into points, flattened under the sweep of white day
torch-flower of the blue-smoking darkness, Pluto's dark-blue daze,
black lamps from the halls of Dis, burning dark blue,
giving off darkness, blue darkness, as Demeter's pale lamps give off light,
lead me then, lead the way.   10

Reach me a gentian, give me a torch!
let me guide myself with the blue, forked torch of this flower
down the darker and darker stairs, where blue is darkened on blueness
even where Persephone goes, just now, from the frosted September
to the sightless realm where darkness is awake upon the dark   15
and Persephone herself is but a voice
or a darkness invisible enfolded in the deeper dark
of the arms Plutonic, and pierced with the passion of dense gloom,
among the splendor of torches of darkness, shedding darkness on the lost
    bride and her groom.

D. H. Lawrence (1885–1930)

Bavarian Gentians. l. 2 *Michaelmas:* feast of St. Michael, September 29. l. 4 *Pluto's gloom:* for the legend of Hades's abduction of Persephone, daughter of Demeter, see p. 368. Lawrence refers to Hades by his Roman names, Dis and Pluto.

Gloire de Dijon

When she rises in the morning
I linger to watch her;
She spreads the bath-cloth underneath the window
And the sunbeams catch her
Glistening white on the shoulders,   5
While down her sides the mellow
Golden shadow glows as
She stoops to the sponge, and her swung breasts
Sway like full-blown yellow
Gloire de Dijon roses.   10

She drips herself with water, and her shoulders
Glisten as silver, they crumple up
Like wet and falling roses, and I listen
For the sluicing of their rain-dishevelled petals.
In the window full of sunlight   15
Concentrates her golden shadow
Fold on fold, until it glows as
Mellow as the glory roses.

D. H. Lawrence (1885–1930)

Man Thinking About Woman

some thing is lost in me,
like

the way you lose old thoughts   that
somehow seemed unlost at the right time.

i've not known it or you many days;   5
we met as friends with an absence of strangeness.
it was the month
that my lines got longer & my metaphors softer.

it was the week   that
i felt the city's narrow breezes rush about   10
me
looking for a place to disappear
as   i walked the clearway,
sure footed in used sandals screaming to be replaced

your empty shoes (except for used stockings)   15
partially hidden beneath the dresser
looked at me,
as i sat thoughtlessly   waiting
for your touch.

that day,   20
as your body rested upon my chest
i saw the shadow of the
window blinds   beam
across the unpainted ceiling
going somewhere   25
like the somewhere i was going
when
the clearness of yr/teeth,
& the scars on yr/legs stopped me.

your beauty: un-noticed by regular eyes   is   30
like   a blackbird resting
on a telephone wire   that moves
quietly with the wind.

a southwind.

Don L. Lee (b. 1942)

To a Child Trapped in a Barber Shop

You've gotten in through the transom
    and you can't get out
till Monday morning or, worse,
    till the cops come.

That six-year-old red face   5
        calling for mama
is yours; it won't help you
        because your case

is closed forever, hopeless.
        So don't drink   10
the Lucky Tiger°, don't   *hairdressing*
        fill up on grease

because that makes it a lot worse,
        that makes it a crime
against property and the state   15
        and that costs time.

We've all been here before,
        we took our turn
under the electric storm
        of the vibrator   20

and stiffened our wills to meet
        the close clippers
and heard the true blade mowing
        back and forth

on a strip of dead skin,   25
        and we stopped crying.
You think your life is over?
        It's just begun.

                          Philip Levine (b. 1928)

Abraham Lincoln Walks at Midnight

In Springfield, Illinois

It is portentous, and a thing of state
That here at midnight in our little town,
A mourning figure walks, and will not rest,
Near the old court-house pacing up and down.

Or by his homestead, or in shadowed yards,   5
He lingers where his children used to play;
Or through the market, on the well-worn stones,
He stalks until the dawn-stars burn away.

A bronzed lank man! His suit of ancient black,
A famous high top-hat and plain worn shawl,   10
Make his the quaint great figure that men love,
The prairie lawyer, master of us all.

He cannot sleep upon his hillside now.
He is among us—as in times before!
And we who toss and lie awake for long   15
Breathe deep, and start, to see him pass the door.

His head is bowed. He thinks on men and kings.
Yea, when the sick world cries, how can he sleep?
Too many peasants fight, they know not why;
Too many homesteads in black terror weep.   20

The sins of all the war-lords burn his heart.
He sees the dreadnaughts scouring every main.
He carries on his shawl-wrapped shoulders now
The bitterness, the folly and the pain.

He cannot rest until a spirit-dawn   25
Shall come—the shining hope of Europe free:
The league of sober folk, the Workers' Earth,
Bringing long peace to Cornland, Alp and Sea.

It breaks his heart that kings must murder still,
That all his hours of travail here for men   30
Seem yet in vain. And who will bring white peace
That he may sleep upon his hill again?

Vachel Lindsay (1879–1931)

Wind and Silver

Greatly shining,
The Autumn moon floats in the thin sky;
And the fish-ponds shake their backs and flash their dragon scales
As she passes over them.

Amy Lowell (1874–1925)

Skunk Hour

For Elizabeth Bishop

Nautilus Island's hermit
heiress still lives through winter in her Spartan cottage;
her sheep still graze above the sea.
Her son's a bishop. Her farmer
is first selectman in our village;   5
she's in her dotage.

Thirsting for
the hierarchic privacy
of Queen Victoria's century°,   *the nineteenth century*
she buys up all   10
the eyesores facing her shore,
and lets them fall.

The season's ill—
we've lost our summer millionaire,
who seemed to leap from an L. L. Bean   15
catalogue. His nine-knot yawl
was auctioned off to lobstermen.
A red fox stain covers Blue Hill.

And now our fairy
decorator brightens his shop for fall;   20
his fishnet's filled with orange cork,
orange, his cobbler's bench and awl;
there is no money in his work,
he'd rather marry.

One dark night,   25
my Tudor Ford climbed the hill's skull;
I watched for love-cars. Lights turned down,
they lay together, hull to hull,
where the graveyard shelves on the town. . . .
My mind's not right.   30

A car radio bleats,
"Love, O careless Love. . . ." I hear
my ill-spirit sob in each blood cell,
as if my hand were at its throat. . . .
I myself am hell;   35
nobody's here—

only skunks, that search
in the moonlight for a bite to eat.

They march on their soles up Main Street:
white stripes, moonstruck eyes' red fire   40
under the chalk-dry and spar spire
of the Trinitarian Church.

I stand on top
of our back steps and breathe the rich air—
a mother skunk with her column of kittens swills the garbage pail.   45
She jabs her wedge-head in a cup
of sour cream, drops her ostrich tail,
and will not scare.

Robert Lowell (1917–1977)

Skunk Hour. The poem is set in Maine, the location of Lowell's summer house. Elizabeth
Bishop, for whom the poem was written, was an American poet (1911–1979). l. 15 *L. L.
Bean:* Maine mail-order firm specializing in outdoor goods and sporting clothes.

Ars Poetica

A poem should be palpable and mute
As a globed fruit,

Dumb
As old medallions to the thumb,

Silent as the sleeve-worn stone   5
Of casement° ledges where the moss has grown—   *window*

A poem should be wordless
As the flight of birds.
                            *

A poem should be motionless in time
As the moon climbs,   10

Leaving, as the moon releases
Twig by twig the night-entangled trees,

Leaving, as the moon behind the winter leaves,
Memory by memory the mind—

A poem should be motionless in time   15
As the moon climbs.
                            *

A poem should be equal to:
Not true.

For all the history of grief
An empty doorway and a maple leaf.   20

For love
The leaning grasses and two lights above the sea—

A poem should not mean
But be.

Archibald MacLeish (b. 1892)

Ars Poetica. The title, *Ars Poetica*, means "Art of Poetry."

The Passionate Shepherd to His Love*

Come live with me and be my love,
And we will all the pleasures prove°   *try, experience*
That valleys, groves, hills, and fields,
Woods, or steepy mountain yields.

And we will sit upon the rocks,   5
Seeing the shepherds feed their flocks,
By shallow rivers to whose falls
Melodious birds sing madrigals.

And I will make thee beds of roses
And a thousand fragrant posies,   10
A cap of flowers, and a kirtle°   *robe*
Embroidered all with leaves of myrtle;

A gown made of the finest wool
Which from our pretty lambs we pull;
Fair lined slippers for the cold,   15
With buckles of the purest gold;

A belt of straw and ivy buds,
With coral clasps and amber studs:
And if these pleasures may thee move,
Come live with me, and be my love.   20

The shepherds' swains shall dance and sing
For thy delight each May morning:
If these delights thy mind may move,
Then live with me and be my love.

Christopher Marlowe (1564–1593)

* See Sir Walter Raleigh's "The Nymph's Reply to the Shepherd" on p. 477.

To His Coy Mistress

Had we but world enough, and time,
This coyness, lady, were no crime.
We would sit down and think which way
To walk, and pass our long love's day.
Thou by the Indian Ganges' side   5
Should'st rubies find; I by the tide
Of Humber would complain. I would
Love you ten years before the Flood,
And you should, if you please, refuse
Till the conversion of the Jews.   10
My vegetable love should grow
Vaster than empires, and more slow.
An hundred years should go to praise
Thine eyes, and on thy forehead gaze,
Two hundred to adore each breast,   15
But thirty thousand to the rest.
An age at least to every part,
And the last age should show your heart.
For, lady, you deserve this state,
Nor would I love at lower rate.   20
    But at my back I always hear
Time's winged chariot hurrying near;
And yonder all before us lie
Deserts of vast eternity.
Thy beauty shall no more be found,   25
Nor in thy marble vault shall sound
My echoing song; then worms shall try
That long preserved virginity,
And your quaint honor turn to dust,
And into ashes all my lust.   30
The grave's a fine and private place,
But none, I think, do there embrace.
    Now therefore, while the youthful hue
Sits on thy skin like morning glew°,   *glow*
And while thy willing soul transpires   35
At every pore with instant fires,
Now let us sport us while we may;
And now, like am'rous birds of prey,
Rather at once our time devour,
Than languish in his slow-chapped power,   40
Let us roll all our strength, and all
Our sweetness, up into one ball;
And tear our pleasures with rough strife
Thorough° the iron gates of life.   *through*

Thus, though we cannot make our sun
Stand still, yet we will make him run.

Andrew Marvell (1621–1678)

To His Coy Mistress. l. 5 *Ganges' side:* the Ganges River is in India. l. 7 *Humber:* a river flowing by the town of Hull, England, where Marvell was born. l. 10 *conversion of the Jews:* an event that, according to St. John, will take place at the end of the world.

Another Year Come

I have nothing new to ask of you,
Future, heaven of the poor.
I am still wearing the same things.

I am still begging the same question
By the same light,
Eating the same stone,

And the hands of the clock still knock without entering.

W. S. Merwin (b. 1927)

For the Anniversary of My Death

Every year without knowing it I have passed the day
When the last fires will wave to me
And the silence will set out
Tireless traveller
Like the beam of a lightless star   5

Then I will no longer
Find myself in life as in a strange garment
Surprised at the earth
And the love of one woman
And the shamelessness of men   10
As today writing after three days of rain
Hearing the wren sing and the falling cease
And bowing not knowing to what

W. S. Merwin (b. 1927)

How Soon Hath Time

How soon hath Time, the subtle thief of youth,
    Stol'n on his wing my three and twentieth year!

My hasting days fly on with full career,
But my late spring no bud or blossom shew'th.
Perhaps my semblance might deceive the truth,   5
   That I to manhood am arrived so near,
   And inward ripeness doth much less appear,
That some more timely-happy spirits endu'th°.   *endoweth*
Yet be it less or more, or soon or slow,
   It shall be still in strictest measure ev'n°   *equal*   10
      To that same lot, however mean, or high,
   Toward which Time leads me, and the will of Heav'n;
All is, if I have grace to use it so,
      As ever in my great task-Master's eye.

John Milton (1608–1674)

Lycidas

*In this monody the author bewails a learned friend, unfortunately drowned in his passage
from Chester on the Irish seas, 1637. And by occasion foretells the ruin of our corrupted
clergy, then in their height.*

Yet once more, O ye laurels, and once more,
Ye myrtles brown, with ivy never sear,
I come to pluck your berries harsh and crude°,   *unripe*
And with forced fingers rude
Shatter your leaves before the mellowing year.   5
Bitter constraint and sad occasion dear
Compels me to disturb your season due;
For Lycidas is dead, dead ere his prime,
Young Lycidas, and hath not left his peer.
Who would not sing for Lycidas? He knew   10
Himself to sing, and build the lofty rime.
He must not float upon his watery bier°   *coffin*
Unwept, and welter to the parching wind,
Without the meed° of some melodious tear.   *benefit*
   Begin, then, Sisters° of the sacred well°,   *Muses/of inspiration*   15
That from beneath the seat of Jove doth spring;
Begin, and somewhat loudly sweep the string.
Hence with° denial vain and coy excuse;   *away with*
So may some gentle muse
With lucky words favor my destined urn,   20
And as he passes turn
And bid fair peace be to my sable shroud!
   For we were nursed upon the selfsame hill,
Fed the same flock, by fountain, shade, and rill;
Together both, ere the high lawns appeared   25

Under the opening eyelids of the Morn,
We drove afield, and both together heard
What time the gray-fly winds her sultry horn,
Battening° our flocks with the fresh dews of night,   *feeding*
Oft till the star that rose at evening, bright,   30
Toward heaven's descent had sloped his westering wheel.
Meanwhile the rural ditties were not mute,
Tempered to the oaten flute°;   *shepherd's pipe*
Rough Satyrs° danced, and Fauns° with cloven heel   *woodland creatures*
From the glad sound would not be absent long;   35
And old Damoetas loved to hear our song.
   But, oh! the heavy change, now thou art gone,
Now thou art gone, and never must return!
Thee, Shepherd, thee the woods and desert caves,
With wild thyme and the gadding vine o'ergrown,   40
And all their echoes, mourn.
The willows, and the hazel copses green,
Shall now no more be seen
Fanning their joyous leaves to thy soft lays°.   *songs*
As killing as the canker° to the rose,   *cankerworm* 45
Or taint-worm to the weanling herds that graze,
Or frost to flowers, that their gay wardrobe wear,
When first the white-thorn blows°—   *blooms*
Such, Lycidas, thy loss to shepherd's ear.
   Where were ye, Nymphs°, when the remorseless deep   *minor divinities* 50
Closed o'er the head of your loved Lycidas?   *of nature*
For neither were ye playing on the steep
Where your old bards, the famous Druids, lie,
Nor on the shaggy top of Mona high,
Nor yet where Deva spreads her wizard stream.   55
Aye me! I fondly dream
"Had ye been there"—for what could that have done?
What could the Muse° herself that Orpheus bore,   *Calliope*
The Muse herself, for her enchanting son,
Whom universal nature did lament,   60
When, by the rout that made the hideous roar,
His gory visage down the stream was sent,
Down the swift Hebrus to the Lesbian shore?
   Alas! what boots° it with uncessant care   *profits*
To tend the homely, slighted shepherd's trade,   65
And strictly meditate the thankless Muse?
Were it not better done as others use,
To sport with Amaryllis in the shade,
Or with the tangles of Neaera's hair?
Fame is the spur that the clear spirit doth raise   70
(That last infirmity of noble mind)
To scorn delights, and live laborious days;

But, the fair guerdon° when we hope to find,   *reward*
And think to burst out into sudden blaze,
Comes the blind Fury with the abhorréd shears,   75
And slits the thin-spun life. "But not the praise,"
Phoebus replied, and touched my trembling ears;
"Fame is no plant that grows on mortal soil,
Nor in the glistering foil°   *glittering metal*
Set off to the world, nor in broad rumor lies,   80
But lives and spreads aloft by those pure eyes
And perfect witness of all-judging Jove;
As he pronounces lastly on each deed,
Of so much fame in heaven expect thy meed°."   *reward*
   O fountain Arethuse, and thou honored flood,   85
Smooth-sliding Mincius, crowned with vocal reeds,
That strain I heard was of a higher mood.
But now my oat° proceeds,   *flute*
And listens to the Herald of the Sea°   *Triton*
That came in Neptune's plea.   90
He asked the waves, and asked the felon winds,
What hard mishap hath doomed this gentle swain!
And questioned every gust of rugged wings
That blows from off each beakéd promontory.
They knew not of his story;   95
And sage Hippotades° their answer brings,   *god of winds*
That not a blast was from his dungeon strayed;
The air was calm, and on the level brine
Sleek Panope° with all her sisters played.   *sea nymph*
It was that fatal and perfidious bark°,   *ship* 100
Built in the eclipse, and rigged with curses dark,
That sunk so low that sacred head of thine.
   Next, Camus, reverend sire, went footing slow,ˎ
His mantle hairy, and his bonnet sedge,
Inwrought with figures dim, and on the edge   105
Like to that sanguine flower inscribed with woe.
"Ah! who hath reft," quoth he, "my dearest pledge?"
Last came, and last did go,
The Pilot° of the Galilean Lake;   *St. Peter*
Two massy keys° he bore of metals twain   *to heaven's gates* 110
(The golden opes, the iron shuts amain).
He shook his mitered locks, and stern bespake:
"How well could I have spared for thee, young swain,
Enow° of such as, for their bellies' sake,   *enough*
Creep, and intrude, and climb into the fold!   115
Of other care they little reckoning make
Than how to scramble at the shearers' feast,
And shove away the worthy bidden guest.
Blind mouths! that scarce themselves know how to hold

A sheep-hook, or have learned aught else the least   120
That to the faithful herdman's art belongs!
What recks it them? What need they? They are sped;
And, when they list°, their lean and flashy songs   *choose*
Grate on their scrannel° pipes of wretched straw;   *rough, thin*
The hungry sheep look up, and are not fed,   125
But, swoln with wind and the rank mist they draw,
Rot inwardly, and foul contagion spread;
Besides what the grim wolf° with privy° paw   *Catholic Church/secret*
Daily devours apace, and nothing said.
But that two-handed engine at the door   130
Stands ready to smite once, and smite no more."
   Return, Alpheus, the dread voice° is past   *of St. Peter*
That shrunk thy streams; return, Sicilian Muse,
And call the vales, and bid them hither cast
Their bells and flowerets of a thousand hues.   135
Ye valleys low, where the mild whispers use
Of shades, and wanton winds, and gushing brooks,
On whose fresh lap the swart star sparely looks,
Throw hither all your quaint enameled eyes,
That on the green turf suck the honeyed showers,   140
And purple all the ground with vernal flowers.
Bring the rathe° primrose that forsaken dies,   *early*
The tufted crow-toe, and pale jessamine,
The white pink, and the pansy freaked with jet,
The glowing violet,   145
The musk-rose, and the well-attired woodbine,
With cowslips wan that hang the pensive head,
And every flower that sad embroidery wears;
Bid amaranthus° all his beauty shed,   *eternal flower*
And daffadillies fill their cups with tears,   150
To strew the laureate hearse° where Lycid lies.   *laureled coffin*
For so, to interpose a little ease,
Let our frail thoughts dally with false surmise.
Aye me! Whilst thee the shores and sounding seas
Wash far away, where'er thy bones are hurled,   155
Whether beyond the stormy Hebrides,
Where thou perhaps under the whelming tide
Visit'st the bottom of the monstrous world;
Or whether thou, to our moist vows denied
Sleep'st by the fable of Bellerus old,   160
Where the great Vision° of the guarded mount   *of the angel Michael*
Looks toward Namancos and Bayona's° hold.   *northern Spain*
Look homeward, Angel, now, and melt with ruth°;   *pity*
And, O ye dolphins, waft the hapless youth.
   Weep no more, woeful shepherds, weep no more,   165
For Lycidas, your sorrow, is not dead,

Sunk though he be beneath the watery floor;
So sinks the day-star° in the ocean bed,   *the sun*
And yet anon repairs his drooping head,
And tricks° his beams, and with new-spangled ore   *dresses up* 170
Flames in the forehead of the morning sky.
So Lycidas sunk low, but mounted high,
Through the dear might of Him that walked the waves,
Where, other groves and other streams along,
With nectar pure his oozy locks he laves°,   *washes* 175
And hears the unexpressive° nuptial song,   *inexpressible*
In the blest kingdoms meek of joy and love.
There entertain him all the Saints above,
In solemn troops, and sweet societies,
That sing, and singing in their glory move,   180
And wipe the tears forever from his eyes.
Now, Lycidas, the shepherds weep no more;
Henceforth thou art the Genius° of the shore,   *spirit, protector*
In thy large recompense, and shalt be good
To all that wander in that perilous flood°.   *dangerous sea* 185
    Thus sang the uncouth swain° to the oaks and rills,   *untaught shepherd*
While the still morn went out with sandals gray;
He touched the tender stops of various quills°,   *flutes, pipes*
With eager thought warbling his Doric lay°.   *simple country song*
And now the sun had stretched out all the hills,   190
And now was dropped into the western bay.
At last he rose, and twitched his mantle blue;
Tomorrow to fresh woods and pastures new.

John Milton (1608–1674)

Lycidas. *Headnote:* The friend whose death Milton laments, Edward King, was a former fellow student at Cambridge University. A *monody* is a poem sung in a single voice. The corruptions of the clergy are denounced by St. Peter in 11:108–131. ll. 1–2 *laurels, myrtles, ivy:* plants associated with the Greek gods Apollo, Venus, and Bacchus (that is, with poetry, love, and ecstatic inspiration). l. 28: When the gray-fly buzzes. l. 36 *Damoetas:* a classical name for a shepherd. l. 53 *Druids:* Celtic poet-priests of ancient Britain. ll. 58–63 *Orpheus:* son of Calliope and Apollo, noted for his song and mastery of nature, was torn apart by a mob of women from Thrace; his severed head, thrown into the Hebrus River, was carried to the isle of Lesbos in the Aegean Sea. ll. 68–69 *Amaryllis, Neaera:* classical names for country nymphs. ll. 75–76 *Fury:* refers to Atropos, one of the Three Fates, who cuts the thread of life. l. 77 *Phoebus:* Apollo, god of poetry. l. 85 *Arethuse:* fountain in Sicily. l. 86 *Mincius:* river in Lombardy. l. 103 *Camus:* god of the river Cam, which flows through Cambridge. l. 106 *sanguine flower:* the hyacinth, which grew from the blood of a youth mistakenly killed by Apollo. l. 130 *engine:* may refer to St. Peter's keys, or to the authority of Parliament or some other means of swift justice. ll. 152–153: Pretend that the dead body is present, has not been lost to the waters. ll. 154–160: Speculation on where the body has drifted; perhaps to the Hebrides Islands off the coast of Scotland, or to Cornwall, in southwest England, where the giant *Bellerus* is supposedly buried. l. 164 *dolphins:* in legend, dolphins are beneficent creatures and often transport souls from one sphere of existence to another.

Poetry

I, too, dislike it: there are things that are important beyond
      all this fiddle.
  Reading it, however, with a perfect contempt for it, one
      discovers in
  it after all, a place for the genuine.
      Hands that can grasp, eyes
      that can dilate, hair that can rise
        if it must, these things are important not because a

high-sounding interpretation can be put upon them but be-
      cause they are
  useful. When they become so derivative as to become
      unintelligible,
  the same thing may be said for all of us, that we
      do not admire what
      we cannot understand: the bat
        holding on upside down or in quest of something to

eat, elephants pushing, a wild horse taking a roll, a tireless
      wolf under
  a tree, the immovable critic twitching his skin like a horse
      that feels a flea, the base-
  ball fan, the statistician—
      nor is it valid
        to discriminate against "business documents and

school-books"; all these phenomena are important. One
      must make a distinction
  however: when dragged into prominence by half poets,
      the result is not poetry,
  nor till the poets among us can be
      "literalists of
      the imagination"—above
        insolence and triviality and can present

for inspection, "imaginary gardens with real toads in them,"
      shall we have
  it. In the meantime, if you demand on the one hand,
  the raw material of poetry in
      all its rawness and
      that which is on the other hand
        genuine, you are interested in poetry.

Marianne Moore (1887–1972)

Poetry. ll. 23–24: The quotation refers to a passage from the *Diaries of Tolstoi:* "Where the boundary between prose and poetry lies, I shall never be able to understand. The question is raised in manuals of style, yet the answer to it lies beyond me. Poetry is verse: prose is not verse. Or else poetry is everything with the exception of business documents and school books." [Moore's note.] ll. 29–30: The quotation refers to a passage in an essay by T. S. Eliot on William Blake: "The limitation of his [Blake's] view was from the very intensity of his vision; he was a too literal realist of imagination as others are of nature: and because he believed that the figures seen by the mind's eye, when exalted by inspiration, were 'eternal existences,' symbols of divine essences, he hated every grace of style that might obscure their lineaments." [Moore's note.]

from The Songs of Maximus

Song 3

This morning of the small snow
I count the blessings, the leak in the faucet
which makes of the sink time, the drop
of the water on water as sweet
as the Seth Thomas°   *brand name of clock* 5
in the old kitchen
my father stood in his drawers to wind (always
he forgot the 30th day, as I don't want to remember
the rent
      a house these days   10
so much somebody else's,
especially,
Congoleum's°   *brand name of linoleum*

     Or the plumbing,
that it doesn't work, this I like, have even used paper clips   15
as well as string to hold the ball° up And flush it   *ball valve*
with my hand
     But that the car doesn't, that no moving thing moves
without that song I'd void my ear of, the musickracket
of all ownership . . .   20
      Holes
in my shoes, that's all right, my fly
gaping, me out
at the elbows, the blessing
      that difficulties are once more   25

  "In the midst of plenty, walk
  as close to
  bare
    In the face of sweetness,
  piss   30

In the time of goodness,
go side, go
smashing, beat them, go as
(as near as you can

tear   35

In the land of plenty, have
nothing to do with it
                              take the way of
the lowest,
including   40
your legs, go
contrary, go

sing

Song 4

I know a house made of mud & wattles,
I know a dress just sewed
                              (saw the wind
blow its cotton
against her body   5
from the ankle
                    so!
it was Nike

                    And her feet: such bones
I could have had the tears   10
that lovely pedant had
who couldn't unwrap it himself, had to ask them to,
                              on the schooner's deck

and he looked,
the first human eyes to look again   15
at the start of human motion (just last week
300,000,000 years ago

                    She
was going fast
across the square, the water   20
this time of year, that
scarce

And the fish

Song 5

I have seen faces of want,
and have not wanted the FAO: Appleseed
's gone back to
what any of us
New England

Song 6

you sing, you

who also

wants

Charles Olson (1910–1970)

from The Songs of Maximus. Song 4, l. 8 *Nike:* goddess of victory; the reference here is
to the beautifully draped statue of Nike loosening her sandal straps. Song 5, l. 2 *FAO:* F.
A. O. Schwarz, a famous New York City department store for toys.

À Terre

(Being the Philosophy of Many Soldiers)

Sit on the bed. I'm blind, and three parts shell.
Be careful; can't shake hands now; never shall.
Both arms have mutinied against me,—brutes.
My fingers fidget like ten idle brats.

I tried to peg out soldierly,—no use!   5
One dies of war like any old disease.
This bandage feels like pennies on my eyes.
I have my medals?—Discs to make eyes close.
My glorious ribbons?—Ripped from my own back
In scarlet shreds. (That's for your poetry book.)   10

A short life and a merry one, my buck!
We used to say we'd hate to live dead-old,—
Yet now . . . I'd willingly be puffy, bald,
And patriotic. Buffers catch from boys
At least the jokes hurled at them. I suppose   15
Little I'd ever teach a son, but hitting,
Shooting, war, hunting, all the arts of hurting.
Well, that's what I learnt,—that, and making money.

Your fifty years ahead seem none too many?
Tell me how long I've got? God! For one year   20
To help myself to nothing more than air!
One Spring! Is one too good to spare, too long?
Spring wind would work its own way to my lung,
And grow me legs as quick as lilac-shoots.

My servant's lamed, but listen how he shouts!   25
When I'm lugged out, he'll still be good for that.
Here in this mummy-case, you know, I've thought
How well I might have swept his floors for ever.
I'd ask no nights off when the bustle's over,
Enjoying so the dirt. Who's prejudiced   30
Against a grimed hand when his own's quite dust,
Less live than specks that in the sun-shafts turn,
Less warm than dust that mixes with arms' tan?
I'd love to be a sweep°, now, black as Town,   *chimney sweep*
Yes; or a muckman. Must I be his load?   35

O Life, Life, let me breathe,—a dug-out rat!
Not worse than ours the existences rats lead—
Nosing along at night down some safe rut,
They find a shell-proof home before they rot.
Dead men may envy living mites in cheese,   40
Or good germs even. Microbes have their joys,
And subdivide, and never come to death.
Certainly flowers have the easiest time on earth.
"I shall be one with nature, herb, and stone,"
Shelley would tell me. Shelley would be stunned: 45
The dullest Tommy hugs that fancy now.
"Pushing up daisies" is their creed, you know.
To grain, then, go my fat, to buds my sap,
For all the usefulness there is in soap.
D'you think the Boche° will ever stew man-soup?   *World War I slang* 50
Some day, no doubt, if . . .   *for Germans*

                    Friend, be very sure
I shall be better off with plants that share
More peaceably the meadow and the shower.
Soft rains will touch me,—as they could touch once,
And nothing but the sun shall make me ware.   55
Your guns may crash around me. I'll not hear;
Or, if I wince, I shall not know I wince.
Don't take my soul's poor comfort for your jest.
Soldiers may grow a soul when turned to fronds,
But here the thing's best left at home with friends.   60
My soul's a little grief, grappling your chest,

To climb your throat on sobs; easily chased
On other sighs and wiped by fresher winds.

Carry my crying spirit till it's weaned
To do without what blood remained these wounds.   65

Wilfred Owen (1893–1918)

À **Terre.** *À Terre* (French) means "To the Ground" or "To Earth." l. 7: It was an ancient
custom to place a coin on a dead person's eyelids as a fee for Charon who ferried the dead
across the river Styx to Hades. l. 45 *Shelley:* the English poet Percy Bysshe Shelley
(1792–1822).

Futility

Move him into the sun—
Gently its touch awoke him once,
At home, whispering of fields unsown.
Always it woke him, even in France,
Until this morning and this snow.   5
If anything might rouse him now
The kind old sun will know.

Think how it wakes the seeds—
Woke, once, the clays of a cold star.
Are limbs, so dear-achieved, are sides,   10
Full-nerved—still warm—too hard to stir?
Was it for this the clay grew tall?
—O what made fatuous sunbeams toil
To break earth's sleep at all?

Wilfred Owen (1893–1918)

Most Souls, 'Tis True, but Peep Out
Once an Age

Most souls, 'tis true, but peep out once an age,
Dull sullen pris'ners in the body's cage:
Dim lights of life, that burn a length of years
Useless, unseen, as lamps in sepulchres:
Like Eastern Kings a lazy state they keep,
And, close confin'd to their own palace, sleep.

Alexander Pope (1688–1744)

In a Station of the Metro

The apparition of these faces in the crowd;
Petals on a wet, black bough.

Ezra Pound (1885–1972)

A Pact

I make a pact with you, Walt Whitman——
I have detested you long enough.
I come to you as a grown child
Who has had a pig-headed father;
I am old enough now to make friends.
It was you that broke the new wood,
Now is a time for carving.
We have one sap and one root——
Let there be commerce between us.

Ezra Pound (1885–1972)

A Pact. l. 1 *Walt Whitman*: the American poet (1819–1892). Although born and schooled in America, Pound spent most of his adult life abroad.

Portrait d'une Femme

Your mind and you are our Sargasso Sea,
London has swept about you this score years
And bright ships left you this or that in fee:
Ideas, old gossip, oddments of all things,
Strange spars of knowledge and dimmed wares of price.   5
Great minds have sought you—lacking someone else.
You have been second always. Tragical?
No. You preferred it to the usual thing:
One dull man, dulling and uxorious,
One average mind—with one thought less, each year.   10
Oh, you are patient, I have seen you sit
Hours, where something might have floated up.
And now you pay one. Yes, you richly pay.
You are a person of some interest, one comes to you
And takes strange gain away: 15
Trophies fished up; some curious suggestion;
Fact that leads nowhere; and a tale or two,

Pregnant with mandrakes, or with something else
That might prove useful and yet never proves,
That never fits a corner or shows use,   20
Or finds its hour upon the loom of days:
The tarnished, gaudy, wonderful old work;
Idols and ambergris and rare inlays,
These are your riches, your great store; and yet
For all this sea-hoard of deciduous things,   25
Strange woods half-sodden, and new brighter stuff:
In the slow float of differing light and deep,
No! there is nothing! in the whole and all,
Nothing that's quite your own.
            Yet this is you.   30

Ezra Pound (1885–1972)

Portait d'une Femme. *Portrait d'une Femme* (French) means "Portrait of a Woman." l. 1
Sargasso Sea: a sea in the North Atlantic, legendary for its overgrowth of seaweed and
dangers to passing ships. l. 18 *mandrakes:* the mandragora, whose forked roots resemble
the human torso, was thought to have aphrodisiacal and fertility properties.

The Nymph's Reply to the Shepherd*

If all the world and love were young,
And truth in every shepherd's tongue,
These pretty pleasures might me move
To live with thee and be thy love.

Time drives the flocks from field to fold   5
When rivers rage and rocks grow cold,
And Philomel° becometh dumb;   *the nightingale*
The rest complains of cares to come.

The flowers do fade, and wanton fields
To wayward winter reckoning yields;   10
A honey tongue, a heart of gall,
Is fancy's spring, but sorrow's fall.

Thy gowns, thy shoes, thy beds of roses,
Thy cap, thy kirtle°, and thy posies   *robe*
Soon break, soon wither, soon forgotten—   15
In folly ripe, in reason rotten.

*See Christopher Marlowe's "The Passionate Shepherd to His Love" (p. 462), which
provoked a number of replies, including this one.

Thy belt of straw and ivy buds,
Thy coral clasps and amber studs,
All these in me no means can move
To come to thee and be thy love. 20

But could youth last and love still breed,
Had joys no date° nor age no need, *ending*
Then these delights my mind might move
To live with thee and be thy love.

Sir Walter Raleigh (1552–1618)

Miniver Cheevy

Miniver Cheevy, child of scorn,
   Grew lean while he assailed the seasons;
He wept that he was ever born,
   And he had reasons.

Miniver loved the days of old 5
   When swords were bright and steeds were prancing;
The vision of a warrior bold
   Would set him dancing.

Miniver sighed for what was not,
   And dreamed, and rested from his labors; 10
He dreamed of Thebes and Camelot,
   And Priam's neighbors.

Miniver mourned the ripe renown
   That made so many a name so fragrant;
He mourned Romance, now on the town, 15
   And Art, a vagrant.

Miniver loved the Medici,
   Albeit he had never seen one;
He would have sinned incessantly
   Could he have been one. 20

Miniver cursed the commonplace
   And eyed a khaki suit with loathing;
He missed the mediæval grace
   Of iron clothing.

Miniver scorned the gold he sought, 25
   But sore annoyed was he without it;

Miniver thought, and thought, and thought,
   And thought about it.

Miniver Cheevy, born too late,
   Scratched his head and kept on thinking;   30
Miniver coughed, and called it fate,
   And kept on drinking.

Edwin Arlington Robinson (1869–1935)

Miniver Cheevy. l. 11 *Thebes:* famous city in ancient Greece. l. 11 *Camelot:* legendary capital of King Arthur's court. l. 12 *Priam:* king of Troy at the time of the wars between Greece and Troy, celebrated in Homer's *Iliad.* l. 17 *Medici:* powerful Italian Renaissance family dominant in Florence.

The Meadow Mouse

1

In a shoe box stuffed in an old nylon stocking
Sleeps the baby mouse I found in the meadow,
Where he trembled and shook beneath a stick
Till I caught him up by the tail and brought him in,
Cradled in my hand,   5
A little quaker, the whole body of him trembling,
His absurd whiskers sticking out like a cartoon-mouse,
His feet like small leaves,
Little lizard-feet,
Whitish and spread wide when he tried to struggle away,   10
Wriggling like a miniscule puppy.

Now he's eaten his three kinds of cheese and drunk from his bottle-cap
   watering-trough—
So much he just lies in one corner,
His tail curled under him, his belly big
As his head; his bat-like ears   15
Twitching, tilting toward the least sound.

Do I imagine he no longer trembles
When I come close to him?
He seems no longer to tremble.

2

But this morning the shoe-box house on the back porch is empty.   20
Where has he gone, my meadow mouse,
My thumb of a child that nuzzled in my palm?—
To run under the hawk's wing,

Under the eye of the great owl watching from the elm-tree,
To live by courtesy of the shrike, the snake, the tom-cat.   25

I think of the nestling fallen into the deep grass,
The turtle gasping in the dusty rubble of the highway,
The paralytic stunned in the tub, and the water rising,—
All things innocent, hapless, forsaken.

Theodore Roethke (1908–1963)

My Papa's Waltz

The whiskey on your breath
Could make a small boy dizzy;
But I hung on like death:
Such waltzing was not easy.

We romped until the pans   5
Slid from the kitchen shelf;
My mother's countenance
Could not unfrown itself.

The hand that held my wrist
Was battered on one knuckle;   10
At every step you missed
My right ear scraped a buckle.

You beat time on my head
With a palm caked hard by dirt,
Then waltzed me off to bed   15
Still clinging to your shirt.

Theodore Roethke (1908–1963)

In an Artist's Studio

One face looks out from all his canvases,
    One selfsame figure sits or walks or leans:
    We found her hidden just behind those screens,
That mirror gave back all her loveliness.
A queen in opal or in ruby dress,   5
    A nameless girl in freshest summer-greens,
    A saint, an angel—every canvas means

The same one meaning, neither more nor less.
He feeds upon her face by day and night,
    And she with true kind eyes looks back on him,   10
Fair as the moon and joyful as the light:
    Not wan with waiting, not with sorrow dim;
Not as she is, but was when hope shone bright;
    Not as she is, but as she fills his dream.

Christina Rossetti (1830–1894)

Effort at Speech Between Two People

Speak to me.   Take my hand.   What are you now?
I will tell you all.   I will conceal nothing.
When I was three, a little child read a story about a rabbit
who died, in the story, and I crawled under a chair:
a pink rabbit: it was my birthday, and a candle   5
burnt a sore spot on my finger, and I was told to be happy.

Oh, grow to know me.   I am not happy.   I will be open:
Now I am thinking of white sails against a sky like music,
like glad horns blowing, and birds tilting, and an arm about me.
There was one I loved, who wanted to live, sailing.   10

Speak to me.   Take my hand.   What are you now?
When I was nine, I was fruitily sentimental,
fluid: and my widowed aunt played Chopin,
and I bent my head on the painted woodwork, and wept.
I want now to be close to you.   I would   15
link the minutes of my days close, somehow, to your days.

I am not happy.   I will be open.
I have liked lamps in evening corners, and quiet poems.
There has been fear in my life.   Sometimes I speculate
On what a tragedy his life was, really.   20

Take my hand.   Fist my mind in your hand.   What are you now?
When I was fourteen, I had dreams of suicide,
and I stood at a steep window, at sunset, hoping toward death:
if the light had not melted clouds and plains to beauty,
if light had not transformed that day, I would have leapt,   25
I am unhappy.   I am lonely.   Speak to me.

I will be open.   I think he never loved me:
he loved the bright beaches, the little lips of foam

that ride small waves, he loved the veer of gulls:
he said with a gay mouth: I love you.   Grow to know me.   30

What are you now?   If we could touch one another,
if these our separate entities could come to grips,
clenched like a Chinese puzzle . . . yesterday
I stood in a crowded street that was live with people,
and no one spoke a word, and the morning shone.   35
Everyone silent, moving. . . . Take my hand.   Speak to me.

Muriel Rukeyser (1913–1980)

Effort at Speech Between Two People. l. 13 *Chopin:* Frédéric Chopin (1810–1849), French-
Polish composer and pianist.

IF You Hear that a Thousand People Love You

IF you hear that a thousand people love you
remember . . . saavedra is among them.

IF you hear that a hundred people love you
remember . . . saavedra is either in the first
                or very last row   5

IF you hear that seven people love you
remember . . . saavedra is among them,
like a wednesday in the middle of the week

IF you hear that two people love you
remember . . . one of them is saavedra   10

IF you hear that only one person loves you
remember . . . he is saavedra

AND when you see no one else around you,
        and you find out,
        that no one loves you anymore,   15
        then you will know for certain
        that . . . saavedra is dead

Guadalupe de Saavedra (b. 1936)

Welcome Morning

There is joy
in all:
in the hair I brush each morning,
in the Cannon towel, newly washed,
that I rub my body with each morning,   5
in the chapel of eggs I cook
each morning,
in the outcry from the kettle
that heats my coffee,
each morning,   10
in the spoon and the chair,
that cry "hello there, Anne"
each morning,
in the godhead of the table
that I set my silver, plate, cup upon,   15
each morning.

All this is God,
right here in my pea green house,
each morning
and I mean,   20
though often forget,
to give thanks,
to faint down by the kitchen table
in a prayer of rejoicing
as the holy birds at the kitchen window   25
peck into their marriage of seeds.

So while I think of it,
let me paint a thank you on my palm
for this God, this laughter of the morning,
lest it go unspoken.   30

The Joy that isn't shared, I've heard,
dies young.

Anne Sexton (1928–1974)

Fear No More the Heat o' the Sun*

Fear no more the heat o' the sun,
    Nor the furious winter's rages;

* From *Cymbeline*, Act IV, Scene 2, lines 258–281.

Thou thy worldly task hast done,
   Home art gone, and ta'en thy wages;
Golden lads and girls all must,   5
As chimney-sweepers, come to dust.

Fear no more the frown o' the great,
   Thou art past the tyrant's stroke;
Care no more to clothe and eat,
   To thee the reed is as the oak.   10
The scepter°, learning, physic°, must   king's staff/medicine
All follow this and come to dust.

Fear no more the lightning flash,
   Nor the all-dreaded thunder-stone°;   meteorites
Fear not slander, censure rash;   15
   Thou hast finished joy and moan.
All lovers young, all lovers must
Consign to thee and come to dust.

No exorciser harm thee!
   Nor no witchcraft charm thee!   20
Ghost unlaid forbear thee!
   Nothing ill come near thee!
Quiet consummation have;
And renownéd be thy grave!

William Shakespeare (1564–1616)

Full Fathom Five Thy Father Lies*

Full fathom five thy father lies;
   Of his bones are coral made;
Those are pearls that were his eyes;
   Nothing of him that doth fade
But doth suffer a sea-change
Into something rich and strange.
Sea-nymphs hourly ring his knell:
   Ding-dong.
   Hark! Now I hear them—
   Ding-dong, bell.

William Shakespeare (1564–1616)

* From *The Tempest*, Act I, Scene 2, lines 396–402.

Let Me Not to the Marriage of True Minds

Let me not to the marriage of true minds
Admit impediments. Love is not love
Which alters when it alteration finds,
Or bends with the remover to remove.
O no! it is an ever-fixèd mark   5
That looks on tempests and is never shaken;
It is the star to every wandering bark°,   *ship*
Whose worth's unknown, although his height be taken.
Love's not Time's fool, though rosy lips and cheeks
Within his bending sickle's compass come°;   *reach* 10
Love alters not with his brief hours and weeks,
But bears it out even to the edge of doom°.   *Judgment Day*
　　If this be error and upon me proved,
　　I never writ, nor no man ever loved.

William Shakespeare (1564–1616)

No Longer Mourn for Me When I Am Dead

No longer mourn for me when I am dead
Than you shall hear the surly sullen bell
Give warning to the world that I am fled
From this vile world, with vilest worms to dwell.
Nay, if you read this line, remember not   5
The hand that writ it, for I love you so,
That I in your sweet thoughts would be forgot,
If thinking on me then should make you woe.
O, if, I say, you look upon this verse
When I perhaps compounded am with clay,   10
Do not so much as my poor name rehearse°,   *repeat*
But let your love even with my life decay,
　　Lest the wise world should look into your moan
　　And mock you with me after I am gone.

William Shakespeare (1564–1616)

Spring*

When daisies pied and violets blue,
  And lady-smocks all silver-white,
And cuckoo-buds of yellow hue
  Do paint the meadows with delight,
The cuckoo then, on every tree,   5
Mocks married men; for thus sings he,
          "Cuckoo!
Cuckoo, cuckoo!" O word of fear,
Unpleasing to a married ear!

When shepherds pipe on oaten straws,   10
  And merry larks are ploughmen's clocks,
When turtles tread, and rooks, and daws,
  And maidens bleach their summer smocks,
The cuckoo then, on every tree,
Mocks married men; for thus sings he,   15
          "Cuckoo!
Cuckoo, cuckoo!" O word of fear,
Unpleasing to a married ear!

William Shakespeare (1564–1616)

Spring. l. 7 *Cuckoo:* a play on the word "cuckold." l. 12 *turtles tread:* turtledoves copulate.

When My Love Swears That She Is Made Of Truth

When my love swears that she is made of truth,
I do believe her, though I know she lies,
That she might think me some untutored youth,
Unlearnèd in the world's false subtleties.
Thus vainly thinking that she thinks me young,   5
Although she knows my days are past the best,
Simply° I credit her false-speaking tongue;   *innocently*
On both sides thus is simple truth supprest.
But wherefore says she not she is unjust°?   *faithless*
And wherefore say not I that I am old?   10
Oh, love's best habit° is in seeming trust,   *appearance, attire*
And age in love loves not to have years told:
  Therefore I lie with her and she with me,
  And in our faults by lies we flattered be.

William Shakespeare (1564–1616)

*From *Love's Labour's Lost*, Act V, Scene 2, lines 902–919.

When to the Sessions of Sweet Silent Thought

When to the sessions° of sweet silent thought   *court sessions*
I summon up remembrance of things past,
I sigh the lack of many a thing I sought
And with old woes new wail my dear time's waste.
Then can I drown an eye (unused to flow)   5
For precious friends hid in death's dateless° night,   *endless*
And weep afresh love's long since canceled woe,
And moan th' expense° of many a vanished sight.   *loss*
Then can I grieve at grievances foregone,
And heavily from woe to woe tell o'er   10
The sad account of fore-bemoanéd moan,
Which I new pay as if not paid before.
    But if the while I think on thee, dear friend,
    All losses are restored and sorrows end.

William Shakespeare (1564–1616)

Winter*

When icicles hang by the wall,
    And Dick the shepherd blows his nail°,   *warms his fingers*
And Tom bears logs into the hall,
    And milk comes frozen home in pail,
When blood is nipped and ways be foul,   5
Then nightly sings the staring owl,
                "Tu-whit, tu-who!"
A merry note,
While greasy Joan doth keel° the pot.   *stir, skim*

When all aloud the wind doth blow,   10
    And coughing drowns the parson's saw°,   *old saying*
And birds sit brooding in the snow,
    And Marian's nose looks red and raw,
When roasted crabs° hiss in the bowl,   *crab apples*
Then nightly sings the staring owl,   15
                "Tu-whit, tu-who!"
A merry note,
While greasy Joan doth keel the pot.

William Shakespeare (1564–1616)

*From *Love's Labour's Lost*, Act V, Scene 2, lines 920–937.

My Father in the Night Commanding No

My father in the night commanding No
Has work to do. Smoke issues from his lips;
    He reads in silence.
The frogs are croaking and the streetlamps glow.

And then my mother winds the gramophone;   5
The Bride of Lammermoor begins to shriek—
    Or reads a story
About a prince, a castle, and a dragon.

The moon is glittering above the hill.
I stand before the gateposts of the King—   10
    So runs the story—
Of Thule, at midnight when the mice are still.

And I have been in Thule! It has come true—
The journey and the danger of the world,
    All that there is   15
To bear and to enjoy, endure and do.

Landscapes, seascapes . . . where have I been led?
The names of cities—Paris, Venice, Rome—
    Held out their arms.
A feathered god, seductive, went ahead.   20

Here is my house. Under a red rose tree
A child is swinging; another gravely plays.
    They are not surprised
That I am here; they were expecting me.

And yet my father sits and reads in silence,   25
My mother sheds a tear, the moon is still,
    And the dark wind
Is murmuring that nothing ever happens.

Beyond his jurisdiction as I move
Do I not prove him wrong? And yet, it's true   30
    They will not change
There, on the stage of terror and of love.

The actors in that playhouse always sit
In fixed positions—father, mother, child
    With painted eyes.   35
How sad it is to be a little puppet!

Their heads are wooden. And you once pretended
To understand them! Shake them as you will,
    They cannot speak.
Do what you will, the comedy is ended.   40

Father, why did you work? Why did you weep,
Mother? Was the story so important?
    "Listen!" the wind
Said to the children, and they fell asleep.

Louis Simpson (b. 1923)

My Father in the Night Commanding No. l. 6. *Bride of Lammermoor:* Gaetano Donizetti's opera *Lucia di Lammermoor* (1835), based on a novel by Sir Walter Scott. l. 12 *Thule:* the ancient name of an island, well north of Britain, once thought to be the outer limits of the world. l. 20 *feathered god:* perhaps Icarus; for the legend of his feathered flight and death see p. 311.

April Inventory

The green catalpa tree has turned
All white; the cherry blooms once more.
In one whole year I haven't learned
A blessed thing they pay you for.
The blossoms snow down in my hair;   5
The trees and I will soon be bare.

The trees have more than I to spare.
The sleek, expensive girls I teach,
Younger and pinker every year,
Bloom gradually out of reach.   10
The pear tree lets its petals drop
Like dandruff on a tabletop.

The girls have grown so young by now
I have to nudge myself to stare.
This year they smile and mind me how   15
My teeth are falling with my hair.
In thirty years I may not get
Younger, shrewder, or out of debt.

The tenth time, just a year ago,
I made myself a little list   20
Of all the things I'd ought to know,
Then told my parents, analyst,

And everyone who's trusted me
I'd be substantial, presently.

I haven't read one book about   25
A book or memorized one plot.
Or found a mind I did not doubt.
I learned one date. And then forgot.
And one by one the solid scholars
Get the degrees, the jobs, the dollars.   30

And smile above their starchy collars.
I taught my classes Whitehead's notions;
One lovely girl, a song of Mahler's.
Lacking a source-book or promotions,
I showed one child the colors of   35
A 'una moth and how to love.

I taught myself to name my name,
To bark back, loosen love and crying;
To ease my woman so she came,
To ease an old man who was dying.   40
I have not learned how often I
Can win, can love, but choose to die.

I have not learned there is a lie
Love shall be blonder, slimmer, younger;
That my equivocating eye   45
Loves only by my body's hunger;
That I have poems, true to feel,
Or that the lovely world is real.

While scholars speak authority
And wear their ulcers on their sleeves,   50
My eyes in spectacles shall see
These trees procure and spend their leaves.
There is a value underneath
The gold and silver in my teeth.

Though trees turn bare and girls turn wives,   55
We shall afford our costly seasons;
There is a gentleness survives
That will outspeak and has its reasons.
There is a loveliness exists,
Preserves us. Not for specialists.   60

W. D. Snodgrass (b. 1926)

April Inventory. l. 32 *Whitehead:* Alfred North Whitehead (1861–1947), English philosopher.
l. 33 *Mahler:* Gustav Mahler (1860–1911), Austrian composer.

I Think Continually of Those Who Were Truly Great

I think continually of those who were truly great.
Who, from the womb, remembered the soul's history
Through corridors of light where the hours are suns
Endless and singing. Whose lovely ambition
Was that their lips, still touched with fire, 5
Should tell of the Spirit clothed from head to foot in song.
And who hoarded from the Spring branches
The desires falling across their bodies like blossoms.

What is precious is never to forget
The essential delight of the blood drawn from ageless springs 10
Breaking through rocks in worlds before our earth.
Never to deny its pleasure in the morning simple light
Nor its grave evening demand for love.
Never to allow gradually the traffic to smother
With noise and fog the flowering of the spirit. 15

Near the snow, near the sun, in the highest fields
See how these names are fêted by the waving grass
And by the streamers of white cloud
And whispers of wind in the listening sky.
The names of those who in their lives fought for life 20
Who wore at their hearts the fire's centre.
Born of the sun they travelled a short while towards the sun,
And left the vivid air signed with their honour.

Stephen Spender (b. 1909)

My Love Is Like to Ice and I to Fire

My love is like to ice and I to fire;
How comes it then that this her cold great
Is not dissolved through my so hot desire,
But harder grows the more I her entreat?
Or how comes it that my exceeding heat 5
Is not delayed by her heart frozen cold,
But that I burn much more in boiling sweat,
And feel my flames augmented manifold?
What more miraculous thing may be told,
That fire, which all things melts, should harden ice, 10

And ice, which is congealed with senseless cold,
Should kindle fire by wonderful device?
Such is the power of love in gentle mind,
That it can alter all the course of kind°.   *species*

Edmund Spenser (1552?–1599)

One Day I Wrote Her Name upon the Strand

One day I wrote her name upon the strand,
But came the waves, and washed it away:
Again I wrote it with a second hand°,   *a second time*
But came the tide, and made my pains his prey.
Vain man, said she, that dost in vain assay   5
A mortal thing so to immortalize!
For I myself shall like to this decay,
And eek° my name be wiped out likewise.   *also*
Not so (quoth I) let baser things devise
To die in dust, but you shall live by fame: 10
My verse your virtues rare shall eternize,
And in the heavens write your glorious name;
Where, whenas death shall all the world subdue,
Our love shall live, and later life renew.

Edmund Spenser (1552?–1599)

For the Grave of Daniel Boone

The farther he went the farther home grew.
Kentucky became another room;
the mansion arched over the Mississippi;
flowers were spread all over the floor.
He traced ahead a deepening home,   5
and better, with goldenrod:

Leaving the snakeskin of place after place,
going on—after the trees
the grass, a bird flying after a song.
Rifle so level, sighting so well   10
his picture freezes down to now,
a story-picture for children.

They go over the velvet falls
into the tapestry of his time,
heirs to the landscape, feeling no jar: 15
it is like evening; they are the quail
surrounding his fire, coming in for the kill;
their little feet move sacred sand.

Children, we live in a barbwire time
but like to follow the old hands back—   20
the ring in the light, the knuckle, the palm,
all the way to Daniel Boone,
hunting our own kind of deepening home.
From the land that was his I heft this rock.

Here on his grave I put it down.   25

William Stafford (b. 1914)

For the Grave of Daniel Boone. *Daniel Boone* (1734–1820) was a Kentucky frontiersman
and explorer about whom many legends grew.

The Emperor of Ice-Cream

Call the roller of big cigars,
The muscular one, and bid him whip
In kitchen cups concupiscent° curds.   *lustful*
Let the wenches dawdle in such dress
As they are used to wear, and let the boys   5
Bring flowers in last month's newspapers.
Let be be finale of seem.
The only emperor is the emperor of ice-cream.

Take from the dresser of deal°,   *pine or fir wood*
Lacking the three glass knobs, that sheet   10
On which she embroidered fantails° once   *fantail pigeons*
And spread it so as to cover her face.
If her horny feet protrude, they come
To show how cold she is, and dumb.
Let the lamp affix its beam.   15
The only emperor is the emperor of ice-cream.

Wallace Stevens (1879–1955)

The Emperor of Ice-Cream. l. 7: cf. Stevens's comment that "the true sense of Let be be
the finale of seem is let being become the conclusion or denouement of appearing to be:
in short, ice cream is an absolute good. The poem is obviously not about ice cream, but
about being as distinguished from seeming to be."

Peter Quince at the Clavier

I

Just as my fingers on these keys
Make music, so the selfsame sounds
On my spirit make a music, too.

Music is feeling, then, not sound;
And thus it is that what I feel,   5
Here in this room, desiring you,

Thinking of your blue-shadowed silk,
Is music. It is like the strain
Waked in the elders by Susanna.

Of a green evening, clear and warm,   10
She bathed in her still garden, while
The red-eyed elders watching, felt

The basses of their beings throb
In witching chords, and their thin blood
Pulse pizzicati of Hosanna.   15

II

In the green water, clear and warm,
Susanna lay.
She searched
The touch of springs,
And found   20
Concealed imaginings.
She sighed,
For so much melody.

Upon the bank, she stood
In the cool   25
Of spent emotions.
She felt, among the leaves,
The dew
Of old devotions.

She walked upon the grass,   30
Still quavering.
The winds were like her maids,
On timid feet,
Fetching her woven scarves,
Yet wavering.   35

A breath upon her hand
Muted the night.
She turned—
A cymbal crashed,
And roaring horns.   40

III

Soon, with a noise like tambourines,
Came her attendant Byzantines.

They wondered why Susanna cried
Against the elders by her side;

And as they whispered, the refrain   45
Was like a willow swept by rain.

Anon, their lamps' uplifted flame
Revealed Susanna and her shame.

And then, the simpering Byzantines
Fled, with a noise like tambourines.   50

IV

Beauty is momentary in the mind—
The fitful tracing of a portal;
But in the flesh it is immortal.

The body dies; the body's beauty lives.
So evenings die, in their green going,   55
A wave, interminably flowing.
So gardens die, their meek breath scenting
The cowl of winter, done repenting.
So maidens die, to the auroral
Celebration of a maiden's choral.   60

Susanna's music touched the bawdy strings
Of those white elders; but, escaping,
Left only Death's ironic scraping.
Now, in its immortality, it plays
On the clear viol of her memory,   65
And makes a constant sacrament of praise.

Wallace Stevens (1879–1955)

Peter Quince at the Clavier. *Peter Quince* is the buffoonish carpenter who performs in the
mock tragic play in William Shakespeare's *A Midsummer Night's Dream;* a *clavier* is the
keyboard of a musical instrument—here, probably, a small piano. l. 9 *Susanna:* in the Old
Testament story, the beautiful Susanna, while bathing, is spied upon by a few lascivious
old men; she flees their attempts at seduction and they vengefully charge her with adultery
but are themselves put to death for bearing false witness.

Thirteen Ways of Looking at a Blackbird

I

Among twenty snowy mountains,
The only moving thing
Was the eye of the blackbird.

II

I was of three minds,
Like a tree
In which there are three blackbirds.   5

III

The blackbird whirled in the autumn winds.
It was a small part of the pantomime.

IV

A man and a woman
Are one.   10
A man and a woman and a blackbird
Are one.

V

I do not know which to prefer,
The beauty of inflections,
Or the beauty of innuendoes,   15
The blackbird whistling
Or just after.

VI

Icicles filled the long window
With barbaric glass.
The shadow of the blackbird   20
Crossed it, to and fro.
The mood
Traced in the shadow
An indecipherable cause.

VII

O thin men of Haddam°,   *a town in Connecticut*   25
Why do you imagine golden birds?
Do you not see how the blackbird
Walks around the feet
Of the women about you?

VIII

I know noble accents   30
And lucid, inescapable rhythms;

But I know, too,
That the blackbird is involved
In what I know.

IX

When the blackbird flew out of sight,   35
It marked the edge
Of one of many circles.

X

At the sight of blackbirds
Flying in a green light,
Even the bawds of euphony   40
Would cry out sharply.

XI

He rode over Connecticut
In a glass coach.
Once, a fear pierced him,
In that he mistook   45
The shadow of his equipage
For blackbirds.

XII

The river is moving.
The blackbird must be flying.

XIII

It was evening all afternoon.   50
It was snowing
And it was going to snow.
The blackbird sat
In the cedar-limbs.

Wallace Stevens (1879–1955)

Thirteen Ways of Looking at a Blackbird. "This group of poems is not meant to be a
collection of epigrams or of ideas, but sensations." [Stevens's *Letters.*] *Stanza X:* "What
was intended by X was that the bawds of euphony would suddenly cease to be academic
and express themselves sharply: naturally, with pleasure, etc." [Stevens's *Letters.*]

Out upon It!

Out upon it! I have loved
    Three whole days together;

And am like to love three more,
    If it prove fair weather.

Time shall moult away° his wings,   *shed* 5
    Ere he shall discover
In the whole wide world again
    Such a constant lover.

But the spite on 't is, no praise
    Is due at all to me;   10
Love with me had made no stays,
    Had it any been but she.

Had it any been but she,
    And that very face,
There had been at least ere this   15
    A dozen dozen in her place.

Sir John Suckling (1609–1642)

The Secret in the Cat

I took my cat apart
to see what made him purr.
Like an electric clock
or like the snore

of a warming kettle,   5
something fizzed and sizzled in him.
Was he a soft car,
the engine bubbling sound?

Was there a wire beneath his fur,
or humming throttle?   10
I undid his throat.
Within was no stir.

I opened up his chest
as though it were a door:
no whisk or rattle there.   15
I lifted off his skull:

no hiss or murmur.
I halved his little belly
but found no gear,
no cause for static.   20

So I replaced his lid,
laced his little gut.
His heart into his vest I slid
and buttoned up his throat.

His tail rose to a rod   25
and beckoned to the air.
Some voltage made him vibrate
warmer than before.

Whiskers and a tail:
perhaps they caught   30
some radar code
emitted as a pip, a dot-and-dash

of woolen sound.
My cat a kind of tuning fork?—
amplifier?—telegraph?—   35
doing secret signal work?

His eyes elliptic tubes:
there's a message in his stare.
I stroke him
but cannot find the dial.   40

May Swenson (b. 1919)

Tithonus

The woods decay, the woods decay and fall,
The vapours weep their burthen to the ground,
Man comes and tills the field and lies beneath,
And after many a summer dies the swan.
Me only cruel immortality   5
Consumes: I wither slowly in thine arms,
Here at the quiet limit of the world,
A white-hair'd shadow roaming like a dream
The ever-silent spaces of the East,
Far-folded mists, and gleaming halls of morn.   10

   Alas! for this gray shadow, once a man—
So glorious in his beauty and thy choice,
Who madest him thy chosen, that he seem'd
To his great heart none other than a God!
I ask'd thee, "Give me immortality."   15

Then didst thou grant mine asking with a smile,
Like wealthy men who care not how they give.
But thy strong Hours indignant work'd their wills,
And beat me down and marr'd and wasted me,
And tho' they could not end me, left me maim'd   20
To dwell in presence of immortal youth,
Immortal age beside immortal youth,
And all I was, in ashes. Can thy love,
Thy beauty, make amends, tho' even now
Close over us, the silver star, thy guide,   25
Shines in those tremulous eyes that fill with tears
To hear me? Let me go: take back thy gift:
Why should a man desire in any way
To vary from the kindly race of men,
Or pass beyond the goal of ordinance   30
Where all should pause, as is most meet for all?

    A soft air fans the cloud apart: there comes
A glimpse of that dark world where I was born.
Once more the old mysterious glimmer steals
From thy pure brows, and from thy shoulders pure,   35
And bosom beating with a heart renew'd.
Thy cheek begins to redden thro' the gloom,
Thy sweet eyes brighten slowly close to mine,
Ere yet they blind the stars, and the wild team
Which love thee, yearning for thy yoke, arise,   40
And shake the darkness from their loosen'd manes,
And beat the twilight into flakes of fire.

    Lo! ever thus thou growest beautiful
In silence, then before thine answer given
Departest, and thy tears are on my cheek.   45

    Why wilt thou ever scare me with thy tears,
And make me tremble lest a saying learnt,
In days far-off, on that dark earth, be true?
"The Gods themselves cannot recall their gifts."

    Ay me! ay me! with what another heart   50
In days far-off, and with what other eyes
I used to watch—if I be he that watch'd—
The lucid outline forming round thee; saw
The dim curls kindle into sunny rings;
Changed with thy mystic change, and felt my blood   55
Glow with the glow that slowly crimson'd all
Thy presence and thy portals, while I lay,
Mouth, forehead, eyelids, growing dewy-warm

With kisses balmier than half-opening buds
Of April, and could hear the lips that kiss'd   60
Whispering I knew not what of wild and sweet,
Like that strange song I heard Apollo sing,
While Ilion like a mist rose into towers.

    Yet hold me not for ever in thine East:
How can my nature longer mix with thine?   65
Coldly thy rosy shadows bathe me, cold
Are all thy lights, and cold my wrinkled feet
Upon thy glimmering thresholds, when the steam
Floats up from those dim fields about the homes
Of happy men that have the power to die,   70
And grassy barrows of the happier dead.
Release me, and restore me to the ground;
Thou seëst all things, thou wilt see my grave:
Thou wilt renew thy beauty morn by morn;
I earth in earth forget these empty courts,   75
And thee returning on thy silver wheels.

Alfred, Lord Tennyson (1809–1892)

Tithonus. According to legend, *Tithonus* was so beautiful that the goddess of the dawn, Aurora, fell in love with him and granted him immortality. But he forgot to ask for perpetual youth and soon grew old and longed for death. Aurora granted his prayer, returning him to the world in the form of a grasshopper. l. 25 *silver star:* the morning star.

Fern Hill

Now as I was young and easy under the apple boughs
About the lilting house and happy as the grass was green,
    The night above the dingle° starry,   narrow valley
        Time let me hail and climb
    Golden in the heydays of his eyes,   5
And honoured among wagons I was prince of the apple towns
And once below a time I lordly had the trees and leaves
        Trail with daisies and barley
    Down the rivers of the windfall light.

And as I was green and carefree, famous among the barns   10
About the happy yard and singing as the farm was home,
    In the sun that is young once only,
        Time let me play and be
    Golden in the mercy of his means,
And green and golden I was huntsman and herdsman, the calves   15
Sang to my horn, the foxes on the hills barked clear and cold,

And the sabbath rang slowly
In the pebbles of the holy streams.

All the sun long it was running, it was lovely, the hay
Fields high as the house, the tunes from the chimneys, it was air   20
  And playing, lovely and watery
    And fire green as grass.
  And nightly under the simple stars
As I rode to sleep the owls were bearing the farm away,
All the moon long I heard, blessed among stables, the nightjars   25
  Flying with the ricks, and the horses
    Flashing into the dark.

And then to awake, and the farm, like a wanderer white
With the dew, come back, the cock on his shoulder: it was all
  Shining, it was Adam and maiden,   30
    The sky gathered again
  And the sun grew round that very day.
So it must have been after the birth of the simple light
In the first, spinning place, the spellbound horses walking warm
  Out of the whinnying green stable   35
    On to the fields of praise.

And honoured among foxes and pheasants by the gay house
Under the new made clouds and happy as the heart was long,
  In the sun born over and over,
    I ran my heedless ways,   40
  My wishes raced through the house-high hay
And nothing I cared, at my sky blue trades, that time allows
In all his tuneful turning so few and such morning songs
  Before the children green and golden
    Follow him out of grace.   45

Nothing I cared, in the lamb white days, that time would take me
Up to the swallow thronged loft by the shadow of my hand,
  In the moon that is always rising,
    Nor that riding to sleep
  I should hear him fly with the high fields   50
And wake to the farm forever fled from the childless land.
Oh as I was young and easy in the mercy of his means,
  Time held me green and dying
  Though I sang in my chains like the sea.

Dylan Thomas (1914–1953)

Fern Hill. *Fern Hill* was the country house of Thomas's aunt where, as a boy, he spent his summer holidays.

In My Craft or Sullen Art

In my craft or sullen art
Exercised° in the still night   *practiced*
When only the moon rages
And the lovers lie abed
With all their griefs in their arms,   5
I labor by singing light
Not for ambition or bread
Or the strut and trade of charms
On the ivory stages
But for the common wages   10
Of their most secret heart.

Not for the proud man apart
From the raging moon I write
On these spindrift pages
Nor for the towering dead   15
With their nightingales and psalms
But for the lovers, their arms
Round the griefs of the ages,
Who pay no praise or wages
Nor heed my craft or art.   20

Dylan Thomas (1914–1953)

A Refusal to Mourn the Death, by Fire, of a Child in London

Never until the mankind making
Bird beast and flower
Fathering and all humbling darkness
Tells with silence the last light breaking
And the still hour   5
Is come of the sea tumbling in harness

And I must enter again the round
Zion of the water bead
And the synagogue of the ear of corn
Shall I let pray the shadow of a sound   10
Or sow my salt seed
In the least valley of sackcloth to mourn

The majesty and burning of the child's death.
I shall not murder

The mankind of her going with a grave truth   15
Nor blaspheme down the stations of the breath
With any further
Elegy of innocence and youth.

Deep with the first dead lies London's daughter,
Robed in the long friends,   20
The grains beyond age, the dark veins of her mother,
Secret by the unmourning water
Of the riding Thames.
After the first death, there is no other.

Dylan Thomas (1914–1953)

Medicine

Grandma sleeps with
my sick
      grand-
pa so she
can get him   5
during the night
medicine
to stop
  the pain

  In   10
the morning
  clumsily
  I
wake
them   15

Her eyes
look at me
from under-
      neath
his withered   20
arm

  The
medicine
  is all
   in   25

her long
  un-
    braided
        hair.

Alice Walker (b. 1944)

Apology for Domitian

He was not bad, as emperors go, not really—
Not like Tiberius cruel, or poor Nero silly.
The trouble was only that omens said he would die,
So what could he, mortal, do? Not worse, however, than you might, or I.

Suppose from long back you had known the very hour—   5
"Fear the fifth hour"—and yet for all your power
Couldn't strike it out from the day, or the day from the year,
Then wouldn't you have to strike something at least? If you did, would it
    seem so queer?

Suppose you were proud of your beauty, but baldness set in?
Suppose your good leg were dwindling to spindly and thin?   10
Wouldn't you, like Domitian, try the classic bed-stunt
To prove immortality on what was propped to bear the imperial brunt?

Suppose you had dreamed a gold hump sprouted out of your back,
And such a prosperous burden oppressed you to breath-lack;
Suppose lightning scorched the sheets in your own bedroom;   15
And from your own statue a storm yanked the name plate and chucked it
    into a tomb—

Well, it happened to him. Therefore, there's little surprise
That for hours he'd lock himself up to pull wings from flies.
Fly or man, what odds? He would wander his hall of moonstone,
Mirror-bright so he needn't look over his shoulder to see if he was alone. 20

Let's stop horsing around—it's not Domitian, it's you
We mean, and the omens are bad, very bad, and it's true
That virtue comes hard in face of the assiduous clock,
And music, at sunset, faint as a dream, is heard from beyond the
    burdock,

And as for Domitian, the first wound finds the groin,   25
And he claws like a cat, but the blade continues to go in,
And the body is huddled forth meanly, and what ritual
It gets is at night, and from his old nurse, a woman poor, nonpolitical.

Robert Penn Warren (b. 1905)

Apology for Domitian. *Domitian* (51–96 A.D.) was a Roman emperor noted for his cruelty and decadence. l. 2 *Tiberius, Nero:* Roman emperors of the first century, both remembered as despots.

Bearded Oaks

The oaks, how subtle and marine,
Bearded, and all the layered light
Above them swims; and thus the scene,
Recessed, awaits the positive night.

So, waiting, we in the grass now lie   5
Beneath the languorous tread of light:
The grasses, kelp-like, satisfy
The nameless motions of the air.

Upon the floor of light, and time,
Unmurmuring, of polyp made,   10
We rest; we are, as light withdraws,
Twin atolls on a shelf of shade.

Ages to our construction went,
Dim architecture, hour by hour:
And violence, forgot now, lent   15
The present stillness all its power.

The storm of noon above us rolled,
Of light the fury, furious gold,
The long drag troubling us, the depth:
Dark is unrocking, unrippling, still.   20

Passion and slaughter, ruth°, decay   *pity, remorse*
Descend, minutely whispering down,
Silted through swaying streams, to lay
Foundation for our voicelessness.

All our debate is voiceless here,   25
As all our rage, the rage of stone;
If hope is hopeless, then fearless fear,
And history is thus undone.

Our feet once wrought the hollow street
With echo when the lamps were dead   30
At windows; once our headlight glare
Disturbed the doe that, leaping, fled.

I do not love you less that now
The caged heart makes iron stroke,
Or less that all that light once gave
The graduate dark should now revoke.

We live in time so little time
And we learn all so painfully,
That we may spare this hour's term
To practice for eternity.

Robert Penn Warren (b. 1905)

When Lilacs Last in the Dooryard Bloom'd*

1

When lilacs last in the dooryard bloom'd,
And the great star early droop'd in the western sky in the night,
I mourn'd, and yet shall mourn with ever-returning spring.

Ever-returning spring, trinity sure to me you bring,
Lilac blooming perennial and drooping star in the west,
And thought of him I love.

2

O powerful western fallen star!
O shades of night—O moody, tearful night!
O great star disappear'd—O the black murk that hides the star!
O cruel hands that hold me powerless—O helpless soul of me!
O harsh surrounding cloud that will not free my soul.

3

In the dooryard fronting an old farm-house near the white-wash'd palings,
Stands the lilac-bush tall-growing with heart-shaped leaves of rich green,
With many a pointed blossom rising delicate, with the perfume strong I
    love,
With every leaf a miracle—and from this bush in the dooryard,
With delicate-color'd blossoms and heart-shaped leaves of rich green,
A sprig with its flower I break.

4

In the swamp in secluded recesses,
A shy and hidden bird is warbling a song.

* An elegy on the death of Abraham Lincoln, assassinated on April 14, 1865. His body
was taken from Washington, D.C., to Springfield, Illinois, by train—the famous "Lincoln
Train" which made stops at Philadelphia, New York, Chicago, and many small towns
along the way.

Solitary the thrush, 20
The hermit withdrawn to himself, avoiding the settlements,
Sings by himself a song.

Song of the bleeding throat,
Death's outlet song of life, (for well dear brother I know,
If thou wast not granted to sing thou would'st surely die.) 25

5

Over the breast of the spring, the land, amid cities,
Amid lanes and through old woods, where lately the violets peep'd from
the ground, spotting the gray debris,
Amid the grass in the fields each side of the lanes, passing the endless
grass,
Passing the yellow-spear'd wheat, every grain from its shroud in the dark-
brown fields uprisen,
Passing the apple-tree blows of white and pink in the orchards, 30
Carrying a corpse to where it shall rest in the grave,
Night and day journeys a coffin.

6

Coffin that passes through lanes and streets,
Through day and night with the great cloud darkening the land,
With the pomp of the inloop'd flags with the cities draped in black, 35
With the show of the States themselves as of crape-veil'd women
standing,
With processions long and winding and the flambeaus of the night,
With the countless torches lit, with the silent sea of faces and the unbared
heads,
With the waiting depot, the arriving coffin, and the sombre faces,
With dirges through the night, with the thousand voices rising strong and
solemn,
40
With all the mournful voices of the dirges pour'd around the coffin,
The dim-lit churches and the shuddering organs—where amid these you
journey,
With the tolling tolling bells' perpetual clang,
Here, coffin that slowly passes,
I give you my sprig of lilac. 45

7

(Nor for you, for one alone,
Blossoms and branches green to coffins all I bring,
For fresh as the morning, thus would I chant a song for you O sane and
sacred death.

All over bouquets of roses,
O death, I cover you over with roses and early lilies, 50

But mostly and now the lilac that blooms the first,
Copious I break, I break the sprigs from the bushes,
With loaded arms I come, pouring for you,
For you and the coffins all of you O death.)

O western orb sailing the heaven,   55
Now I know what you must have meant as a month since I walk'd,
As I walk'd in silence the transparent shadowy night,
As I saw you had something to tell as you bent to me night after night,
As you droop'd from the sky low down as if to my side, (while the other
    stars all look'd on,)
As we wander'd together the solemn night, (for something I know not
    what kept me from sleep,)   60
As the night advanced, and I saw on the rim of the west how full you
    were of woe,
As I stood on the rising ground in the breeze in the cool transparent
    night,
As I watch'd where you pass'd and was lost in the netherward black of
    the night,
As my soul in its trouble dissatisfied sank, as where you sad orb,
Concluded, dropt in the night, and was gone.   65

Sing on there in the swamp,
O singer bashful and tender, I hear your notes, I hear your call,
I hear, I come presently, I understand you,
But a moment I linger, for the lustrous star has detain'd me,
The star my departing comrade holds and detains me.   70

O how shall I warble myself for the dead one there I loved?
And how shall I deck my song for the large sweet soul that has gone?
And what shall my perfume be for the grave of him I love?

Sea-winds blown from east and west,
Blown from the Eastern sea and blown from the Western sea, till there on
    the prairies meeting,   75
These and with these and the breath of my chant,
I'll perfume the grave of him I love.

11

O what shall I hang on the chamber walls?
And what shall the pictures be that I hang on the walls,
To adorn the burial-house of him I love?   80

Pictures of growing spring and farms and homes,

With the Fourth-month° eve at sundown, and the gray smoke *April*
    lucid and bright,

With floods of the yellow gold of the gorgeous, indolent, sinking sun,
    burning, expanding the air,

With the fresh sweet herbage under foot, and the pale green leaves of the
    trees prolific,

In the distance the flowing glaze, the breast of the river, with a wind-
    dapple here and there, 85

With ranging hills on the banks, with many a line against the sky, and
    shadows,

And the city at hand with dwellings so dense, and stacks of chimneys,

And all the scenes of life and the workshops, and the workmen
    homeward returning.

12

Lo, body and soul—this land,

My own Manhattan with spires, and the sparkling and hurrying tides, and
    the ships, 90

The varied and ample land, the South and the North in the light, Ohio's
    shores and flashing Missouri,

And ever the far-spreading prairies cover'd with grass and corn.

Lo, the most excellent sun so calm and haughty,

The violet and purple morn with just-felt breezes,

The gentle soft-born measureless light, 95

The miracle spreading bathing all, the fulfill'd noon,

The coming eve delicious, the welcome night and the stars,

Over my cities shining all, enveloping man and land.

13

Sing on, sing on you gray-brown bird,

Sing from the swamps, the recesses, pour your chant from the bushes, 100

Limitless out of the dusk, out of the cedars and pines.

Sing on dearest brother, warble your reedy song,

Loud human song, with voice of uttermost woe.

O liquid and free and tender!

O wild and loose to my soul—O wondrous singer! 105

You only I hear—yet the star holds me, (but will soon depart,)

Yet the lilac with mastering odor holds me.

14

Now while I sat in the day and look'd forth,

In the close of the day with its light and the fields of spring, and the
    farmers preparing their crops,

In the large unconscious scenery of my land with its lakes and forests, 110
In the heavenly aerial beauty, (after the perturb'd winds and the storms,)
Under the arching heavens of the afternoon swift passing, and the voices
    of children and women,
The many-moving sea-tides, and I saw the ships how they sail'd,
And the summer approaching with richness, and the fields all busy with
    labor,
And the infinite separate houses, how they all went on, each with its
    meals and minutia of daily usages, 115
And the streets how their throbbings throbb'd, and the cities pent—lo,
    then and there,
Falling upon them all and among them all, enveloping me with the rest,
Appear'd the cloud, appear'd the long black trail,
And I knew death, its thought, and the sacred knowledge of death.

Then with the knowledge of death as walking one side of me, 120
And the thought of death close-walking the other side of me,
And I in the middle as with companions, and as holding the hands of
    companions,
I fled forth to the hiding receiving night that talks not,
Down to the shores of the water, the path by the swamp in the dimness,
To the solemn shadowy cedars and ghostly pines so still. 125

And the singer so shy to the rest receiv'd me,
The gray-brown bird I know receiv'd us comrades three,
And he sang the carol of death, and a verse for him I love.

From deep secluded recesses,
From the fragrant cedars and the ghostly pines so still, 130
Came the carol of the bird.

And the charm of the carol rapt me,
As I held as if by their hands my comrades in the night,
And the voice of my spirit tallied the song of the bird.

Come lovely and soothing death, 135
Undulate round the world, serenely arriving, arriving,
In the day, in the night, to all, to each,
Sooner or later delicate death.

Prais'd be the fathomless universe,
For life and joy, and for objects and knowledge curious, 140
And for love, sweet love—but praise! praise! praise!
For the sure-enwinding arms of cool-enfolding death.

Dark mother always gliding near with soft feet,
Have none chanted for thee a chant of fullest welcome?

Then I chant it for thee, I glorify thee above all,   145
I bring thee a song that when thou must indeed come, come unfalteringly.

Approach strong deliveress,
When it is so, when thou hast taken them I joyously sing the dead,
Lost in the loving floating ocean of thee,
Laved in the flood of thy bliss O death.   150

From me to thee glad serenades,
Dances for thee I propose saluting thee, adornments and feastings for thee,
And the sights of the open landscape and the high-spread sky are fitting,
And life and the fields, and the huge and thoughtful night.

The night in silence under many a star,   155
The ocean shore and the husky whispering wave whose voice I know,
And the soul turning to thee O vast and well-veil'd death,
And the body gratefully nestling close to thee.

Over the tree-tops I float thee a song,
Over the rising and sinking waves, over the myriad fields and the prairies wide,   160
Over the dense-pack'd cities all and the teeming wharves and ways,
I float this carol with joy, with joy to thee O death.

                                    15

To the tally of my soul,
Loud and strong kept up the gray-brown bird,
With pure deliberate notes spreading filling the night.   165

Loud in the pines and cedars dim,
Clear in the freshness moist and the swamp-perfume,
And I with my comrades there in the night.

While my sight that was bound in my eyes unclosed,
As to long panoramas of visions.   170

And I saw askant the armies,
I saw as in noiseless dreams hundreds of battle-flags,
Borne through the smoke of the battles and pierc'd with missiles I saw
   them,
And carried hither and yon through the smoke, and torn and bloody,
And at last but a few shreds left on the staffs, (and all in silence,)   175
And the staffs all splinter'd and broken.

I saw battle-corpses, myriads of them,
And the white skeletons of young men, I saw them,
I saw the debris and debris of all the slain soldiers of the war,
But I saw they were not as was thought,   180
They themselves were fully at rest, they suffer'd not,

The living remain'd and suffer'd, the mother suffer'd,
And the wife and the child and the musing comrade suffer'd,
And the armies that remain'd suffer'd.

16

Passing the visions, passing the night,   185
Passing, unloosing the hold of my comrades' hands,
Passing the song of the hermit bird and the tallying song of my soul,
Victorious song, death's outlet song, yet varying ever-altering song,
As low and wailing, yet clear the notes, rising and falling, flooding the
    night,
Sadly sinking and fainting, as warning and warning, and yet again
    bursting with joy,   190
Covering the earth and filling the spread of the heaven,
As that powerful psalm in the night I heard from recesses,
Passing, I leave thee lilac with heart-shaped leaves,
I leave thee there in the door-yard, blooming, returning with spring.

I cease from my song for thee,   195
From my gaze on thee in the west, fronting the west, communing with
    thee,
O comrade lustrous with silver face in the night.

Yet each to keep and all, retrievements out of the night,
The song, the wondrous chant of the gray-brown bird,
And the tallying chant, the echo arous'd in my soul,   200
With the lustrous and drooping star with the countenance full of woe,
With the holders holding my hand nearing the call of the bird,
Comrades mine and I in the midst, and their memory ever to keep, for the
    dead I loved so well,
For the sweetest, wisest soul of all my days and lands—and this for his
    dear sake,
Lilac and star and bird twined with the chant of my soul,   205
There in the fragrant pines and the cedars dusk and dim.

Walt Whitman (1819–1892)

The Dance

In Breughel's great picture, The Kermess,
the dancers go round, they go round and
around, the squeal and the blare and the
tweedle of bagpipes, a bugle and fiddles
tipping their bellies (round as the thick-   5
sided glasses whose wash they impound)
their hips and bellies off balance
to turn them. Kicking and rolling about

the Fair Grounds, swinging their butts, those
shanks must be sound to bear up under such   10
rollicking measures, prance as they dance
in Breughel's great picture, The Kermess.

William Carlos Williams (1883–1963)

The Dance. l. 1 *Breughel:* Pieter Brueghel (1525?–1569), the Flemish painter whose subjects
were frequently of Dutch rural life; *Kermess:* an outdoor fair held on the saint's day of the
town.

The Red Wheelbarrow

so much depends
upon

a red wheel
barrow

glazed with rain
water

beside the white
chickens.

William Carlos Williams (1883–1963)

This Is Just to Say

I have eaten
the plums
that were in
the icebox

and which   5
you were probably
saving
for breakfast

Forgive me
they were delicious   10
so sweet
and so cold

William Carlos Williams (1883–1963)

To Waken an Old Lady

Old age is
a flight of small
cheeping birds
skimming
bare trees   5
above a snow glaze.
Gaining and failing,
they are buffeted
by a dark wind—
But what?   10
On harsh weedstalks
the flock has rested—
the snow
is covered with broken
seed-husks,   15
and the wind tempered
with a shrill
piping of plenty.

William Carlos Williams (1883–1963)

London, 1802

Milton! thou shouldst be living at this hour:
England hath need of thee: she is a fen
Of stagnant waters: altar, sword, and pen,
Fireside, the heroic wealth of hall and bower,
Have forefeited their ancient English dower°   *dowry* 5
Of inward happiness. We are selfish men;
Oh! raise us up, return to us again;
And give us manners, virtue, freedom, power.
Thy soul was like a Star, and dwelt apart;
Thou hadst a voice whose sound was like the sea: 10
Pure as the naked heavens, majestic, free,
So didst thou travel on life's common way,
In cheerful godliness; and yet thy heart
The lowliest duties on herself did lay.

William Wordsworth (1770–1850)

London, 1802. The Treaty of Amiens was concluded between Britain and France in 1802, with Britain surrendering all its colonial conquests except Ceylon and Trinidad to Napoleon. l. 1 *Milton:* John Milton (1608–1674), English poet and pamphleteer.

Ode

Intimations of Immortality from Recollections of Early Childhood

> *The Child is father of the Man;*
> *And I could wish my days to be*
> *Bound each to each by natural piety.*

1

There was a time when meadow, grove, and stream,
The earth, and every common sight,
    To me did seem
    Appareled in celestial light,
The glory and the freshness of a dream.   5
It is not now as it hath been of yore—
    Turn wheresoe'er I may,
      By night or day,
The things which I have seen I now can see no more.

2

    The rainbow comes and goes,   10
    And lovely is the rose;
    The moon doth with delight
  Look round her when the heavens are bare;
    Waters on a starry night
    Are beautiful and fair;   15
  The sunshine is a glorious birth;
  But yet I know, where'er I go,
That there hath passed away a glory from the earth.

3

Now, while the birds thus sing a joyous song,
  And while the young lambs bound,   20
    As to the tabor's° sound,   *a drum*
To me alone there came a thought of grief;
A timely utterance gave that thought relief,
    And I again am strong.
The cataracts blow their trumpets from the steep;   25
No more shall grief of mine the season wrong;
I hear the echoes through the mountains throng,
The winds come to me from the fields of sleep,
    And all the earth is gay;
      Land and sea   30
    Give themselves up to jollity,
      And with the heart of May
    Doth every beast keep holiday—

Thou child of joy,
Shout round me, let me hear thy shouts, thou happy shepherd boy!   35

4

Ye blessèd Creatures, I have heard the call
    Ye to each other make; I see
The heavens laugh with you in your jubilee;
    My heart is at your festival,
    My head hath its coronal,   40
The fullness of your bliss, I feel—I feel it all.
    Oh evil day! if I were sullen
    While Earth herself is adorning,
      This sweet May-morning,
    And the Children are culling°   *gathering* 45
      On every side,
    In a thousand valleys far and wide,
    Fresh flowers; while the sun shines warm,
And the Babe leaps up on his Mother's arm:—
    I hear, I hear, with joy I hear!   50
    —But there's a Tree, of many, one,
A single Field which I have looked upon,
Both of them speak of something that is gone:
    The Pansy at my feet
    Doth the same tale repeat: 55
Whither is fled the visionary gleam?
Where is it now, the glory and the dream?

5

Our birth is but a sleep and a forgetting:
The Soul that rises with us, our life's Star,
    Hath had elsewhere its setting,   60
      And cometh from afar:
    Not in entire forgetfulness,
    And not in utter nakedness,
But trailing clouds of glory do we come
    From God, who is our home: 65
Heaven lies about us in our infancy!
Shades of the prison-house begin to close
    Upon the growing Boy,
But he beholds the light, and whence it flows,
    He sees it in his joy;   70
The Youth, who daily farther from the east
    Must travel, still is Nature's Priest,
    And by the vision splendid
    Is on his way attended;
At length the Man perceives it die away,   75
And fade into the light of common day.

Earth fills her lap with pleasures of her own;
Yearnings she hath in her own natural kind,
And, even with something of a mother's mind,
    And no unworthy aim,   80
    The homely nurse doth all she can
To make her foster-child, her inmate man,
    Forget the glories he hath known,
And that imperial palace whence he came.

7

Behold the child among his new-born blisses,   85
A six years' darling of a pygmy size!
See, where 'mid work of his own hand he lies,
Fretted by sallies of his mother's kisses,
With light upon him from his father's eyes!
See, at his feet, some little plan or chart,   90
Some fragment from his dream of human life,
Shaped by himself with newly-learnéd art;
    A wedding or a festival,
    A mourning or a funeral;
      And this hath now his heart,   95
    And unto this he frames his song;
      Then will he fit his tongue
To dialogues of business, love, or strife.
    But it will not be long
    Ere this be thrown aside,   100
    And with new joy and pride
The little actor cons another part;
Filling from time to time his "humorous stage"
With all the persons, down to palsied Age,
That Life brings with her in her equipage;   105
    As if his whole vocation
    Were endless imitation.

8

Thou whose exterior semblance doth belie
    Thy soul's immensity;
Thou best philosopher, who yet dost keep   110
Thy heritage, thou eye among the blind,
That, deaf and silent, read'st the eternal deep,
Haunted forever by the eternal mind—
    Mighty prophet! Seer blest!
    On whom those truths do rest,   115
Which we are toiling all our lives to find,
In darkness lost, the darkness of the grave;
Thou, over whom thy immortality
Broods like the day, a master o'er a slave,

A presence which is not to be put by;   120
Thou little child, yet glorious in the might
Of heaven-born freedom on thy being's height,
Why with such earnest pains dost thou provoke
The years to bring the inevitable yoke,
Thus blindly with thy blessedness at strife?   125
Full soon thy soul shall have her earthly freight,
And custom lie upon thee with a weight,
Heavy as frost, and deep almost as life!

9

    O joy! that in our embers
    Is something that doth live,   130
    That Nature yet remembers
    What was so fugitive!
The thought of our past years in me doth breed
Perpetual benediction: not indeed
For that which is most worthy to be blest;   135
Delight and liberty, the simple creed
Of Childhood, whether busy or at rest,
With new-fledged hope still fluttering in his breast:—
    Not for these I raise
    The song of thanks and praise;   140
    But for those obstinate questionings
    Of sense and outward things,
    Fallings from us, vanishings;
    Blank misgivings of a Creature
Moving about in worlds not realized,   145
High instincts before which our mortal Nature
Did tremble like a guilty Thing surprised:
    But for those first affections,
    Those shadowy recollections,
    Which, be they what they may,   150
Are yet the fountain-light of all our day,
Are yet a master-light of all our seeing;
    Uphold us, cherish, and have power to make
Our noisy years seem moments in the being
Of the eternal Silence: truths that wake,   155
    To perish never:
Which neither listlessness, nor mad endeavour,
    Nor Man nor Boy,
Nor all that is at enmity with joy,
Can utterly abolish or destroy!   160
    Hence in a season of calm weather
    Though inland far we be,
Our Souls have sight of that immortal sea
    Which brought us hither,
    Can in a moment travel thither,   165

And see the Children sport upon the shore,
And hear the mighty waters rolling evermore.

10

Then sing, ye Birds, sing, sing a joyous song!
    And let the young Lambs bound
    As to the tabor's sound!   170
We in thought will join your throng,
    Ye that pipe and ye that play,
    Ye that through your hearts to-day
    Feel the gladness of the May!
What though the radiance which was once so bright   175
Be now for ever taken from my sight,
  Though nothing can bring back the hour
Of splendour in the grass, of glory in the flower;
    We will grieve not, rather find
    Strength in what remains behind;   180
    In the primal sympathy
    Which having been must ever be;
    In the soothing thoughts that spring
    Out of human suffering;
    In the faith that looks through death,   185
In years that bring the philosophic mind.

11

And O, ye Fountains, Meadows, Hills, and Groves,
Forebode not any severing of our loves!
Yet in my heart of hearts I feel your might;
I only have relinquished one delight   190
To live beneath your more habitual sway.
I love the Brooks which down their channels fret,
Even more than when I tripped lightly as they;
The innocent brightness of a new-born Day
    Is lovely yet;   195
The Clouds that gather round the setting sun
Do take a sober coloring from an eye
That hath kept watch o'er man's mortality;
Another race hath been, and other palms are won.
Thanks to the human heart by which we live,   200
Thanks to its tenderness, its joys, and fears,
To me the meanest° flower that blows° can give   *most common/blooms*
Thoughts that do often lie too deep for tears.

William Wordsworth (1770–1850)

Ode: Intimations of Immortality. Wordsworth, in the epigraph, is quoting the final lines
of his poem "My Heart Leaps Up When I Behold" (p. 51). l. 103 *"humorous stage"*: stage
for various human types, illustrating the various temperaments, or humors.

She Dwelt Among the Untrodden Ways

She dwelt among the untrodden ways
   Beside the springs of Dove°,   *rural English river*
A maid whom there were none to praise
   And very few to love:

A violet by a mossy stone   5
   Half hidden from the eye!
—Fair as a star, when only one
   Is shining in the sky.

She lived unknown, and few could know
   When Lucy ceased to be;   10
But she is in her grave, and, oh,
   The difference to me!

              William Wordsworth (1770–1850)

Crazy Jane Talks with the Bishop

I met the Bishop on the road
And much said he and I.
"Those breasts are flat and fallen now,
Those veins must soon be dry;
Live in a heavenly mansion   5
Not in some foul sty."

"Fair and foul are near of kin,
And fair needs foul," I cried.
"My friends are gone, but that's a truth
Nor grave nor bed denied,   10
Learned in bodily lowliness
And in the heart's pride.

"A woman can be proud and stiff
When on love intent;
But Love has pitched his mansion in   15
The place of excrement;
For nothing can be sole or whole
That has not been rent."

              William Butler Yeats (1865–1939)

Leda and the Swan

A sudden blow: the great wings beating still
Above the staggering girl, her thighs caressed
By the dark webs, her nape caught in his bill,
He holds her helpless breast upon his breast.

How can those terrified vague fingers push   5
The feathered glory from her loosening thighs?
And how can body, laid in that white rush,
But feel the strange heart beating where it lies?

A shudder in the loins engenders there
The broken wall, the burning roof and tower   10
And Agamemnon dead.
                        Being so caught up,
So mastered by the brute blood of the air,
Did she put on his knowledge with his power
Before the indifferent beak could let her drop?   15

William Butler Yeats (1865–1939)

Leda and the Swan. Zeus, in the form of a swan, violated *Leda,* who gave birth to Helen
and Clytemnestra. Helen's flight with Paris to Troy, leaving her husband Menelaus,
Agamemnon's brother, caused the war between the Greeks and the Trojans. Clytemnestra
murdered her husband Agamemnon on his return from victory at Troy.

Sailing to Byzantium

1

That is no country for old men. The young
In one another's arms, birds in the trees
—Those dying generations—at their song,
The salmon-falls, the mackerel-crowded seas,
Fish, flesh, or fowl, commend all summer long   5
Whatever is begotten, born, and dies.
Caught in that sensual music all neglect
Monuments of unageing intellect.

2

An aged man is but a paltry thing,
A tattered coat upon a stick, unless   10
Soul clap its hands and sing, and louder sing
For every tatter in its mortal dress,
Nor is there singing school but studying

Monuments of its own magnificence;
And therefore I have sailed the seas and come   15
To the holy city of Byzantium.

3

O sages standing in God's holy fire
As in the gold mosaic of a wall,
Come from the holy fire, perne° in a gyre°,   *spiral/cycle (of history)*
And be the singing-masters of my soul.   20
Consume my heart away; sick with desire
And fastened to a dying animal
It knows not what it is; and gather me
Into the artifice of eternity.

4

Once out of nature I shall never take   25
My bodily form from any natural thing,
But such a form as Grecian goldsmiths make
Of hammered gold and gold enameling
To keep a drowsy Emperor awake;
Or set upon a golden bough to sing   30
To lords and ladies of Byzantium
Of what is past, or passing, or to come.

William Butler Yeats (1865–1939)

Sailing to Byzantium. *Byzantium* was an ancient city, later called Constantinople and in present times Istanbul. Yeats said, in *A Vision* (1937), "I think that in early Byzantium, maybe never before or since in recorded history, religious, aesthetic and practical life were one, that architect and artificers . . . spoke to the multitude and the few alike. The painter, the mosaic worker, the worker in gold and silver, the illuminator of sacred books, were almost impersonal, almost perhaps without the consciousness of individual design, absorbed in their subject-matter and that the vision of a whole people. They would copy out of old gospel books those pictures that seemed as sacred as the text, and yet weave all into a vast design, the work of many that seemed the work of one, that made building, picture, pattern, metalwork of rail and lamp, seem but a single image. . . ." l. 18 *gold mosaic:* the mosaics in the Church of St. Sophia in Istanbul.

The Deer on Pine Mountain

The deer on pine mountain,
Where there are no falling leaves,
Knows the coming of autumn
Only by the sound of his own voice.

Onakatomi No Yoshinobu (c. 900)
(Trans. from the Japanese by Kenneth Rexroth)

Writing About Poetry

This book has been devoted to the acts of reading, understanding, and, we hope, enjoying poetry. In this section, we offer a few suggestions about a related process, writing about poems; that is, putting on paper—refining and giving shape to—your responses and perceptions.

Generally speaking, writing about poems is no different from writing about plays or stories or indeed any other subject worthy of your attention. Your instructor, in making the class assignment, will have established some framework within which you are to proceed. The assignment may be quite specific and include particular instructions; for instance, write on the theme of patriotism in Walt Whitman's "When Lilacs Last in the Dooryard Bloom'd." Or the assignment may be more general, leaving to you the choice of poem or poems or, if the poems are determined in advance, then the choice of theme or focus. Assuming for the moment a more open assignment, let us try to visualize several of the steps you are likely to be taking in the preparation of your paper.

To begin with, you should have a clear sense of the implications of the assignment and of the appropriateness of the poem you have chosen or have been assigned. If the choice is yours, work with a poem that is of genuine interest to you, since nothing is so fruitless as writing from boredom or indifference. Involve yourself in the poem, reading it three, four, five times; try reading it aloud; read it pencil in hand, scribbling in the margins or underlining significant words. Listen to the poem's language and rhythm, noting distinctive qualities in the imagery, the tone, the use (or lack) of rhyme. Be sure of who is speaking (the poet? a created persona?) and what the poem's setting is. Consider, even, the degree to which your response is affected by how the poem *looks* on the page—whether the lines are long or short, whether they are set in uniform stanzas, are divided into uneven units, or compose one unbroken block. If a difficulty persists, keep at it, puzzle it out, on the assumption that a resolution will come once you achieve a fuller understanding of the poem.

It is likely that, as you continue to read the poem, the meaning will become increasingly clear and what you want to say will begin to emerge. Your next step will be to start organizing your thoughts, using an outline perhaps or simply putting down terms or key phrases that will help you map out your paper. You may see that some terms and phrases require expanding and reordering to achieve a firmer sense of continuity and logical sequence, for you are now in the process of presenting some argument or proposing some interpretation. And you will next want to gather various kinds of evidence from the poem, including lines and passages to be cited, in order to give force and particularity to your paper. You may find too at this point that your sense of the poem has undergone change and that you need to modify some of your original thoughts, narrowing or enlarging their scope or substantially reformulating them to bring them into line with new perceptions derived from your study of the poem thus far.

Revision is indispensible to all writing assignments. You should work over your paper, treating your first version as an early draft open to rethinking and stylistic improvement. You should challenge, judge, and correct your own writing. In effect, this means finding and eliminating irrelevancies, repetitions, and obscure phrasings; compressing or expanding your materials to increase their effectiveness; making sure that the evidence you offer is truly pertinent to the discussion; checking for overall consistency in the argument; and correcting errors of spelling, punctuation, and grammar. It may help to read your paper aloud, for that can often tell you a good deal about excess verbiage and awkward constructions. Now set your paper aside for a time, in order to gain some distance from it, and then return for a final consideration.

For your final copy use standard 8½" × 11" paper, lined if you are writing by hand or unlined if you are typing. In either case, double space your text, and leave wide enough margins for your instructor's comments. Give some thought to your title, too, since that first alerts the reader to your focus or argument.

We have talked generally about how to prepare your assignment. Now let us consider the kinds of papers you are most likely to be asked to write. One such assignment is the EXPLICATION. Like a summary or a paraphrase, an explication is concerned with a single poem, but it differs from summary or paraphrase in that it affords detailed attention to every noteworthy element in the poem, and it does so line by line, stanza by stanza, beginning with line one and carrying through the concluding line. The purpose of explication is to arrive at a sense of the whole poem by examining all of the parts that contribute to it. When writing an explication you would, for example, point out and explain significant instances of simile and metaphor; clarify the meaning of obscure words and allusions, as well as the use of particular symbols; note not only the dominant metrical pattern but also variations on it as they affect meaning; and explain shifts in setting or tone and such structural effects as turns in the plot or argument.

Another kind of paper is the ANALYSIS, which focuses on one element or aspect of a poem, usually to show its relationship to some other element or aspect or to the poem as a whole. Any of the major elements of poetry discussed in the first nine chapters of this book may serve as a basis for analysis—speaker, setting, rhyme, metrical pattern, figurative language, tone, structure, genre, and so on. Similarly, an analysis paper might take up any one of the perspectives dealt with in chapters ten through sixteen. A poem might be examined for its psychological or historical or biographical significance. Whatever you choose to single out for attention depends on your interest and your purpose. It is often the interplay of elements that is most fascinating to observe, and your task will almost certainly be easier if you take up one aspect of a poem and analyze its relationship to some other aspect. For example, rather than simply describing the rhyme scheme, explain how this rhyme scheme helps to determine the tone; instead of listing the metaphors or similes that appear, explain how such figures of speech help to reveal the attitude of the speaker. You might examine the details of the setting in terms of the historical perspective, or you might look at imagery or symbolism in terms of the religious perspective.

Certain assignments are best satisfied through yet another approach, that of a COMPARISON (finding likenesses) or CONTRAST (finding differences) of two or more poems. Much might be said, for example, about the different designs possible in the sonnet form. Such a paper might begin with an examination of sonnets by William Shakespeare, John Milton, and Edmund Spenser, and then go on to compare and contrast these with an unrhymed modern variation on the sonnet by, say, Robert Lowell or E. E. Cummings. Or you might consider the different effects of understatement by bringing together for comparison poems by modern poets as diverse as Wallace Stevens, Elizabeth Bishop, and W. H. Auden. Or you might examine some theme such as love or war or honor, comparing two or three poems written at different historical moments to show how they express different value systems.

Whatever the approach—explication, analysis, or comparison or contrast—your paper will be most effective if you develop your discussion as specifically and precisely as you can. Take, for example, the two passages below, each a response to the same poem, Richard Wright's "Between the World and Me." Note that the first passage conveys the writer's reaction but tells little about the poem. The second is far more satisfying: as it moves toward the personal reaction at the close, it focuses on specific images and metaphors to give the reader a good sense of the poem and its texture.

Richard Wright's poem "Between the World and Me" made me feel so angry that I realized how intensely I hate lynching. I had a gut response such as I rarely get from life or poetry. I won't ever forget it.

* * * *

The details of the natural setting in "Between the World and Me" by Richard Wright suggest the horror of the lynching that is the subject of the poem. It is not only the "vacant shoe," "empty tie," "ripped shirt," and "trousers stiff with black blood" (line 7), images related to the victim, but phrases such as "scaly oaks," "charred stump of a sapling," "torn tree limbs," and "tiny veins of burnt leaves" (lines 2, 5, 6), images drawn from the world of nature, that prove so affecting. The sun is dying in the sky, the wind is muttering, and there is an angry yelping of hounds that accompanies the fall of the victim. And when the victim and the scene seem to come back to life and enter into the observer——

> The dry bones stirred, rattled, lifted, melting
> themselves into my bones.
> The grey ashes formed flesh firm and black,
> entering into my flesh.
> (lines 14–15)

I felt as if I myself were the lynched man, very much as Richard Wright seems to have felt at the conclusion of his poem:

> Now I am dry bones and my face a stony skull
> staring in yellow surprise at the sun....
> (line 25)

When quoting a poem, always be sure that your quotations are accurate and, as in the instance above, are followed by line numbers in parentheses to show where in the poem the quoted passages may be found. For quotations of less than two complete lines, use quotation marks and run the quotations into the text. For quotations of two lines or more, separate the quoted material from your own text (in which case you do not use quotations marks) and arrange the lines exactly as they appear in the poem. Below are two examples for study.

Marianne Moore begins her description of poetry with a negative assessment, saying "I, too, dislike it: there

are things that are important beyond / all this fiddle"
(lines 1-2). However, by the time Moore reaches her
conclusion she seems to have changed her mind:

> . . . In the meantime if you demand on the one hand,
> the raw material of poetry in
> all its rawness and
> that which is on the other hand
> genuine, you are interested in poetry.
>
> (lines 34-38)

It is interesting to observe what took place in the
intervening thirty lines of the poem. . . .

* * * *

The poem "Welcome Morning" by Anne Sexton is an
altogether unconventional prayer to God, but there can be
no doubt of the poet's sincerity. The unexpected joinings
of conventional religious references with more
unconventional objects such as "chapel of eggs,"
"godhead of the table," "the holy birds at the kitchen
window / peck into their marriage of seeds" (lines 6, 14,
25-26) may lead the reader to be suspicious of Sexton's
attitude toward religion, but there can be no doubt of
her serious, even respectful, attitude toward God when we
read her strophe near the end of the poem:

> So while I think of it,
> let me paint a thank you on my palm
> for this God, this laughter of the morning,
> lest it go unspoken.
>
> (lines 27-30)

Notice in both examples that when a quotation run into the text involves
more than one line of a poem, a slash (/) is used to indicate the break
between lines. Notice too that a full line space is left between the set-off
quotation and the text, and that the quotation is indented from both the
right and left margins, and it is single-spaced.

Whenever feasible, it is a good idea to begin your essay with a copy
of the poem, reproduced exactly as it appears in the book, numbering
the lines for easy reference. Having the poem at hand enables the reader
to check the accuracy and context of all quotations.

A FEW CAUTIONS

Avoid wordy generalizations and vague promises and get right down
to your topic. Resist the temptation to speculate and philosophize at
length, and don't begin your essay with a personal narrative. After all,
you are writing a formal paper, not a letter to the instructor. Here is the
sort of thing you should avoid:

When I was given this assignment, to compare three
poems about snakes, one by Emily Dickinson, one by D. H.
Lawrence, and a third by Denise Levertov, I wondered what
was the best way to begin. Finally I realized I was
afraid of snakes, so I thought I should put myself in
Denise Levertov's place in order to see if I could ever
bring myself to imagine how it felt to hang a snake
around my neck. Well, I couldn't bear the thought, so I
decided to compare Lawrence and Dickinson for I could
relate to those best of all. Here is my interpretation.

If you choose to discuss the excerpt from *Jubilate Agno* by Christopher
Smart as a poem which has no coherence because it was written while
Smart was confined to a madhouse, don't begin with:

It must be terrible to have a nervous breakdown. I
once knew a man who had the misfortune to spend some
months in a mental hospital, and I know it would have
been very hard for him to have written a poem. So I don't
think there is any structure in the poem about Jeoffry
the cat.

Finally, don't explain what you are going to do; do it instead. The
following opening brings us some sixty words into the paper without
having really begun:

I have always been interested in the question of life
after death, and when I read the poem about the buzzing
fly by Emily Dickinson I thought this would be a good
chance to discover what the American poet had to say on
the subject. I will begin with a summary of the poem and
then go on to give my interpretation.

Begin at once:

Emily Dickinson's "I Heard a Fly Buzz--When I Died"
describes the experience of a dying person whose senses
deteriorate as death approaches.

Having established the focus of your paper, you may carry on from
there, advancing your ideas, mustering your evidence. The reader will
be grateful for the directness and clarity of your approach.

Some Groupings of Poems for Comparison

The listings of poems that follow make no pretense to completeness. They are offered, rather, as a guide to some of the connections—thematic or formal—that can be made among the poems included in this volume.

ALIENATION

A. R. Ammons, So I Said I Am Ezra   169
Matthew Arnold, Dover Beach   315
Margaret Atwood, We Are Standing Facing Each Other   392
Aubrey Beardsley, The Ballad of a Barber   363
Emily Dickinson, The Soul Selects Her Own Society   412
Mari Evans, And the Hotel Room Held Only Him   206
Thomas Hardy, The Going   245
Gerard Manley Hopkins, I Wake and Feel the Fell of Dark, Not Day   327
Gerard Manley Hopkins, Thou Art Indeed Just, Lord, If I Contend   328
Ted Hughes, Owl's Song   144
Thomas Kinsella, An Old Atheist Pauses by the Sea   309
Robert Lowell, The Old Flame   250
Robert Lowell, Skunk Hour   460
Sylvia Plath, Tulips   256
Edwin Arlington Robinson, Miniver Cheevy   478
Alfred, Lord Tennyson, Ulysses   373
Shirley Williams, You Know It's Really Cold   17
William Wordsworth, The World Is Too Much With Us; Late and Soon   369
James Wright, Saint Judas   92

THE ARTS

BALLADS

CELEBRATIONS

CHILDREN

CREATURES

DEATH

DREAMS AND VISIONS

ELEGIES

IRONY

JOURNEYS

LOVE

ODES

Some Groupings of Poems for Comparison 539

SONNETS

TIME

YOUTH AND AGE

A Gallery
of Poets

William Shakespeare
(1564-1616)

John Donne
(1572-1631)

Ben Jonson
(1573?-1637)

George Herbert
(1593-1633)

John Milton
(1608-1674)

Jonathan Swift
(1667-1745)

Alexander Pope
(1688-1744)

Christopher Smart
(1722-1771)

William Blake
(1757-1827)

William Wordsworth
(1770-1850)

Samuel Taylor Coleridge
(1772-1834)

George Gordon, Lord Byron
(1788-1824)

Percy Bysshe Shelley
(1792-1822)

John Keats
(1795-1821)

Ralph Waldo Emerson
(1803-1882)

Edgar Allan Poe
(1809-1849)

Alfred, Lord Tennyson
(1809-1892)

Robert Browning
(1812-1889)

Walt Whitman
(1819-1892)

Emily Dickinson
(1830-1886)

Thomas Hardy
(1840-1928)

Gerard Manly Hopkins
(1844-1889)

A. E. Housman
(1859-1936)

Edwin Arlington Robinson
(1869-1935)

Stephen Crane
(1871-1900)

William Butler Yeats
(1865-1939)

Robert Frost
(1874-1963)

Wallace Stevens
(1879-1955)

William Carlos Williams
(1883-1963)

D. H. Lawrence
(1885-1930)

Elinor Wylie
(1885-1928)

Ezra Pound
(1885-1972)

Marianne Moore
(1887-1972)

T. S. Eliot
(1888-1965)

Wilfred Owen
(1893-1918)

E. E. Cummings
(1894-1962)

Louise Bogan
(1897-1970)

Langston Hughes
(1902-1967)

Theodore Roethke
(1908-1963)

W. H. Auden
(1907-1973)

Richard Wright
(1908-1960)

Elizabeth Bishop
(1911-1979)

A Gallery of Poets   551

John Berryman
(1914-1972)

Robert Lowell
(1917-1977)

Dylan Thomas
(1914-1953)

Gwendolyn Brooks
(b. 1917)

Lawrence Ferlinghetti
(b. 1919)

© 1980 Thomas Victor

552   A Gallery of Poets

Denise Levertov
(b. 1923)

Allen Ginsberg
(b. 1926)

Robert Creeley
(b. 1926)

W. S. Merwin
(b. 1927)

A Gallery of Poets 553

James Wright
(1927-1980)

Anne Sexton
(1928-1975)

Adrienne Rich
(b. 1929)

© 1980 Thomas Victor

Ted Hughes
(b. 1930)

Gary Snyder
(b. 1930)

Sylvia Plath
(1932-1963)

Imamu Amiri Baraka
(b. 1934)

June Jordan
(b. 1936)

Margaret Atwood
(b. 1939)

Seamus Heaney
(b. 1939)

Alice Walker
(b. 1944)

Acknowledgments (continued from page iv)

GWENDOLYN BROOKS: "We Real Cool: The Pool Players. Seven at the Golden Shovel" from *The World of Gwendolyn Brooks* by Gwendolyn Brooks. Copyright © 1959 by Gwendolyn Brooks. Reprinted by permission of Harper & Row, Publishers, Inc. "An Aspect of Love, Alive in the Ice and Fire" from *Riot* by Gwendolyn Brooks, copyright, 1969. Reprinted with permission from Broadside/Crummel Press, Detroit, Michigan.

AUSTIN CLARK: "Penal Laws" from *Selected Poems* by Austin Clark, published by The Dolman Press. U.S.: Wake Forest University Press, Winston-Salem, N.C. 27109. By permission of The Dolman Press.

SARAH N. CLEGHORN: "The Golf Links" from *Portraits and Protests* by Sarah N. Cleghorn. All rights reserved. Reprinted by permission of Holt, Rinehart and Winston, Publishers.

LUCILLE CLIFTON: "Good Times" from *Good Times*, by Lucille Clifton. Copyright © 1969 by Lucille Clifton. "In Salem" from *An Ordinary Woman*, by Lucille Clifton. Copyright © 1974 by Lucille Clifton. Both reprinted by permission of Random House, Inc.

HART CRANE: "The Air Plant" is reprinted from *The Complete Poems and Selected Letters and Prose of Hart Crane*, edited by Brom Weber, with the permission of Liveright Publishing Corporation. Copyright 1933, © 1958, 1966 by Liveright Publishing Corporation.

ADELAIDE CRAPSEY: "Niagara" and "November Night." From *Verse*, by Adelaide Crapsey. Copyright 1922 by Algernon S. Crapsey and renewed 1950 by the Adelaide Crapsey Foundation. Reprinted by permission of Alfred A. Knopf, Inc.

ROBERT CREELEY: "The Flower." From *For Love, Poems 1950–1960* by Robert Creeley. Copyright © 1962 by Robert Creeley. Reprinted by permission of Charles Scribner's Sons.

COUNTEE CULLEN: "Saturday's Child" from *On These I Stand* by Countee Cullen. Copyright 1925 by Harper & Row, Publishers, Inc.; renewed 1953 by Ida M. Cullen. Reprinted by permission of Harper & Row, Publishers, Inc.

E. E. CUMMINGS: "next to of course god america i" and "my sweet old etcetera." Selections are reprinted from *Is 5* by E. E. Cummings with the permission of Liveright Publishing Corporation. Copyright 1926 by Horace Liveright. Copyright renewed by E. E. Cummings 1953. "O sweet spontaneous," "All in green went my love riding," "the Cambridge ladies who live in furnished souls," and "Buffalo Bill's." Selections are reprinted from *Tulips and Chimneys* by E. E. Cummings, with the permission of Liveright Publishing Corporation. Copyright 1923, 1925 and renewed 1951, 1953 by E. E. Cummings. Copyright © 1973, 1976 by Nancy T. Andrews. Copyright © 1973, 1976 by George James Firmage.

ANN DARR: "The Gift" from *St. Ann's Gut* by Ann Darr. Copyright © 1971 by Ann Darr. By permission of William Morrow & Company.

JAMES DICKEY: "The Poisoned Man." Copyright © 1962 by James Dickey. Reprinted from *Poems 1957–1967* by permission of Wesleyan University Press. "The Poisoned Man" first appeared in *The New Yorker*.

EMILY DICKINSON: "Baffled for Just a Day or Two," "I Died for Beauty—But Was Scarce," "Because I Could Not Stop for Death," "A Narrow Fellow in the Grass," "Some Keep the Sabbath Going to Church," "I Heard a Fly Buzz—When I Died," and "The Soul Selects Her Own Society." Reprinted by permission of the publishers and Trustees of Amherst College from *The Poems of Emily Dickinson*, edited by Thomas H. Johnson, Cambridge, Mass.: The Belknap Press of Harvard University Press, Copyright © 1951, 1955, 1979 by the President and Fellows of Harvard College. "After Great Pain, a Formal Feeling Comes" from *The Complete Poems of Emily Dickinson* edited by Thomas H. Johnson. Copyright 1929 by Martha Dickinson Bianchi; Copyright © 1957 by Mary L. Hampson. By permission of Little, Brown and Company.

H. D. (Hilda Doolittle): "Helen" from *Collected Poems* by H. D. Copyright 1925, 1943 by Norman Holmes Pearson. Reprinted by permission of New Directions Publishing Corporation, Agent.

ALAN DUGAN: "On Hurricane Jackson" from *Collected Poems* by Alan Dugan. © Alan Dugan 1961 and reprinted by permission of the author.

ROBERT DUNCAN: "My Mother Would Be a Falconress" from *Bending the Bow*. Copyright © 1966 by Robert Duncan. Reprinted by permission of New Directions.

RICHARD EBERHART: "The Fury of the Aerial Bombardment" and "The Groundhog." From *Collected Poems 1930–1976* by Richard Eberhart. Copyright © Richard Eberhart 1960, 1976. Reprinted by permission of Oxford University Press, Inc. Reprinted from *Collected Poems 1930–1976* by permission of Chatto and Windus, London.

T. S. ELIOT: "The Hippopotamus," "Journey of the Magi," "Gerontion," and "The Love Song of J. Alfred Prufrock." From *Collected Poems 1909–1962* by T. S. Eliot, copyright, 1936, by Harcourt Brace Jovanovich, Inc.; copyright © 1963, 1964 by T. S. Eliot. Reprinted by permission of Faber and Faber Ltd. from *Collected Poems 1909–1962* by T. S. Eliot.

MARI EVANS: "And the Hotel Room Held Only Him" and "I Am a Black Woman" from *I Am a Black Woman* by Mari Evans. Published by William Morrow and Company, 1970. Reprinted by permission of the author.

LAWRENCE FERLINGHETTI: "In a Surrealist Year" and "In Golden Gate Park That Day." From *A Coney Island of the Mind* by Lawrence Ferlinghetti. Copyright © 1957 by Lawrence Ferlinghetti. Reprinted by permission of New Directions.

DONALD FINKEL: "The Father." From *Simeon* by Donald Finkel. Copyright © 1963 by Donald Finkel. Reprinted by permission of Atheneum Publishers.

ROBERT FROST: "Design," "Dust of Snow," "Fire and Ice," "After Apple-Picking," "Out, Out—," "Nothing Gold Can Stay," "Stopping by Woods on a Snowy Evening," "The Draft Horse," "Mending Wall," and "Birches." From *The Poetry of Robert Frost* edited by Edward Connery Lathem. Copyright 1916, 1923, 1930, 1939, © 1969 by Holt, Rinehart and Winston. Copyright 1936, 1944, © 1958, 1962 by Robert Frost. Copyright © 1964, 1967 by Lesley Frost Ballantine. Reprinted by permission of Holt, Rinehart and Winston, Publishers.

ALLEN GINSBERG: "To Aunt Rose" from *Kaddish* by Allen Ginsberg. Copyright © 1961 by Allen Ginsberg. Reprinted by permission of City Lights Books.

NIKKI GIOVANNI: "Nikki-Rosa" from *Black Feeling, Black Talk, Black Judgement* by Nikki Giovanni. Copyright © 1968, 1970 by Nikki Giovanni. "Winter Poem (3 feb 72)" from *My House* by Nikki Giovanni. Copyright © 1972 by Nikki Giovanni. Both by permission of William Morrow & Company.

ROBERT GRAVES: "Galatea and Pygmalion" from *Poems 1914–1926* by Robert Graves, published by Doubleday & Co. Reprinted by permission of Curtis Brown, Ltd. Copyright © 1929 by Robert Graves.

THOM GUNN: "Lebensraum" reprinted from *Positives* by Thomas Gunn. By permission of The University of Chicago Press © 1966 by The University of Chicago. Reprinted by permission of Faber and Faber Ltd. from *Positives* by Thom and Ander Gunn.

ARTHUR GUITERMAN: "On the Vanity of Earthly Greatness" from *Gaily the Troubadour* by Arthur Guiterman, © 1936. Reprinted by permission of Louise H. Sclove.

DONALD HALL: "The Sleeping Giant" from *Exiles and Marriages*. Reprinted by permission of the author.

THOMAS HARDY: "Ah, Are You Digging on My Grave?," "The Man He Killed," "Channel Firing," "The Ruined Maid," "The Going," "The Voice," "I Found Her Out There," "Drummer Hodge," "The Subalterns," "The Darkling Thrush," "In a Wood," and "The Convergence of the Twain." From *Complete Poems of Thomas Hardy*, edited by James Gibson (Macmillan Publishing Co., Inc., 1978). Courtesy of Macmillan Publishing Co., Inc. and Macmillan Press Ltd.

ROBERT HAYDEN: "The Whipping" and "Witch Doctor." Reprinted from *Angle of Ascent*, New and Selected Poems by Robert Hayden, with the permission of Liveright Publishing Corporation. Copyright © 1975, 1972, 1970, 1966 by Robert Hayden.

A. D. HOPE: "The Brides" reprinted from *A. D. Hope: Collected Poems 1930–1970* by permission of Angus and Robertson, Publishers, Sydney, Australia.

SEAMUS HEANEY: "Mother of the Groom" from *Wintering Out* by Seamus Heaney. © 1972 by Seamus Heaney. "Bog Queen" from *North* by Seamus Heaney © Seamus Heaney 1975. Both reprinted by permission of Oxford University Press, Inc. Reprinted by permission of Faber and Faber Ltd. from *Wintering Out* and *North* by Seamus Heaney.

GERARD MANLEY HOPKINS: "Heaven-Haven," "Binsey Poplars," "Spring and Fall," "Pied Beauty," "I Wake and Feel the Fell of Dark, Not Day," "Thou Art Indeed Just, Lord," "God's Grandeur," and "The Windhover." From *Poems of Gerard Manley Hopkins*, Fourth Edition, edited by W. H. Gardner and N. H. MacKenzie. © 1967 by Oxford University Press and The Society of Jesus. Reprinted by permission.

ZILPHIA HORTON: "We Shall Overcome." New words and arrangement by Zilphia Horton, Frank Hamilton, Guy Caraway, and Peter Seeger. © Copyright 1960 and 1963 Ludlow Music, Inc., New York, N.Y. Used by Permission. Royalties derived from this composition are being contributed to The Freedom Movement under the trusteeship of the writers.

A. E. HOUSMAN: "Loveliest of Trees, the Cherry Now," "Is My Team Ploughing," "To an Athlete Dying Young," and "With Rue My Heart Is Laden." From "A Shropshire Lad"—Authorized Edition—from *The Collected Poems of A. E. Housman*. Copyright 1939, 1940, © 1965 by Holt, Rinehart and Winston. Copyright © 1967, 1968 by Robert E. Symons. "They Say My Verse Is Sad; No Wonder." From *The Collected Poems of A. E. Housman*. Copyright 1936 by Barclays Bank Ltd. Copyright © 1964 by Robert E. Symons. "Eight O'Clock." From *The Collected Poems of A. E. Housman*. Copyright 1922 by Holt, Rinehart and Winston. Copyright 1950 by Barclays Bank, Ltd. All reprinted by permission of Holt, Rinehart and Winston, Publishers, and The Society of Authors as literary representatives of the Estate of A. E. Housman and Jonathan Cape Ltd., publishers of A. E. Housman's *Collected Poems*.

LANGSTON HUGHES: "Merry Go Round." Copyright 1942 by Langston Hughes and renewed 1970 by Arna Bontemps and George Houston Bass. "The Negro Speaks of Rivers." Copyright 1926 by Alfred A. Knopf, Inc. and renewed 1954 by Langston Hughes. Both reprinted from *Selected Poems of Langston Hughes*, by Langston Hughes, by permission of Alfred A. Knopf, Inc.

TED HUGHES: "The Dove Breeder" from *The Hawk in the Rain* by Ted Hughes. Copyright © 1957 by Ted Hughes. Reprinted by permission of Harper & Row, Publishers, Inc. "Owl's Song" from *Crow* by Ted Hughes. Copyright © 1971 by Ted Hughes; "Theology" from *Selected Poems* by Ted Hughes. Copyright © 1961 by Ted Hughes. Both reprinted by permission of Harper & Row, Publishers, Inc. and reprinted by permission of Faber and Faber Ltd. from *Crow* and *Wodwo*.

DAVID IGNATOW: "The Dream." Copyright © 1961 by David Ignatow. Reprinted from *Say Pardon*. "Oedipus." Copyright © 1955 by David Ignatow. Reprinted from *Figures of the Human*. Both reprinted by permission of Wesleyan University Press.

RANDALL JARRELL: "Gunner" and "The Death of the Ball-Turret Gunner" from *The Complete Poems* by Randall Jarrell. *Partisan Review* copyright 1944, copyright renewed © 1973 by Mrs. Randall Jarrell. *Poetry* copyright 1945, copyright renewed © 1974 by Mrs. Randall Jarrell. Reprinted by permission of Farrar, Straus and Giroux, Inc. "Bats." Reprinted with permission of Macmillan Publishing Co., Inc. from *The Bat-Poet* by Randall Jarrell. Copyright © Macmillan Publishing Co., Inc. 1963, 1964.

ROBINSON JEFFERS: "Shine, Perishing Republic." Copyright 1925 and renewed 1953 by Robinson Jeffers. "Hurt-Hawks." Copyright 1928 and renewed 1956 by Robinson Jeffers. "To the Stone Cutters." Copyright 1924 and renewed 1952 by Robinson Jeffers. All reprinted from *Selected Poems of Robinson Jeffers*, by Robinson Jeffers, by permission of Random House, Inc.

ELIZABETH JENNINGS: "In Praise of Creation" from *Collected Poems*. Published by Macmillan Press Ltd. Reprinted by permission of David Higham Associates Limited.

JUNE JORDAN: "A Poem About Intelligence for My Brothers and Sisters" from *Passion* by June Jordan. Copyright © 1980 by June Jordan. Reprinted by permission of Beacon Press.

DONALD JUSTICE: "Counting the Mad." Copyright © 1957 by Donald Justice. Reprinted from *The Summer Anniversaries* by permission of Wesleyan University Press.

GALWAY KINNELL: "For the Lost Generation." From *What a Kingdom It Was* by Galway Kinnell, published by Houghton Mifflin Company. Copyright © 1960 by Galway Kinnell. "Last Songs." From *Body Rags* by Galway Kinnell, published by Houghton Mifflin Company. Copyright © 1967 by Galway Kinnell. Both reprinted by permission of the publisher.

MAXINE KUMIN: "The Absent Ones" from *House, Bridge, Fountain, Gate* by Maxine Kumin. Copyright © 1975 by Maxine Kumin. Reprinted by permission of Viking Penguin Inc.

STANLEY KUNITZ: "The War Against the Trees" from *The Poems of Stanley Kunitz 1928–1978* by Stanley Kunitz. Copyright © 1957 by Stanley Kunitz. By permission of Little, Brown and Company in association with the Atlantic Monthly Press.

THOMAS KINSELLA: "An Old Atheist Pauses by the Sea" from *Nightwalker and Other Poems* by Thomas Kinsella. Copyright Thomas Kinsella. By permission of the author.

PHILIP LARKIN: "Church Going" and "Toads" are reprinted from *The Less Deceived* by Philip Larkin by permission of the Marvell Press, England.

D. H. LAWRENCE: "Mystic," "Snake," "How Beastly the Bourgeois Is," "Piano," "Bavarian Gentians," and "Gloire de Dijon." From *The Complete Poems of D. H. Lawrence*, edited by Vivian de Sola Pinto and F. Warren Roberts. Copyright © 1964 by Angelo Ravagli and C. M. Weekly, Executors of the Estate of Frieda Lawrence Ravagli. Reprinted by permission of Viking Penguin, Inc.

DON L. LEE: "Man Thinking About Woman." From *Directionscore: Selected and New Poems* by Don Lee, copyright 1971. Reprinted with permission from Broadside/Crummel Press, Detroit, Michigan.

DENISE LEVERTOV: "Sunday Afternoon" from *Jacob's Ladder* by Denise Levertov. Copyright © 1958 by Denise Levertov Goodman. "To the Snake" from *Collected Early Poems 1940–1960* by Denise Levertov. Copyright © 1966 by Denise Levertov. "What Were They Like?" from *The Sorrow Dance* by Denise Levertov. Copyright © 1966 by Denise Levertov Goodman. "What Were They Like?" was first published in *Poetry*. All selections reprinted by permission of New Directions.

PHILIP LEVINE: "To a Child Trapped in a Barber Shop." Copyright © 1966 by Philip Levine. Reprinted from *Not This Pig* by permission of Wesleyan University Press.

Acknowledgments 557

VACHEL LINDSAY: "Abraham Lincoln Walks at Midnight." Reprinted with permission of Macmillan Publishing Co., Inc. from *Collected Poems* by Vachel Lindsay. Copyright 1914 by Macmillan Publishing Co., Inc., renewed 1942 by Elizabeth C. Lindsay.

AMY LOWELL: "Wind and Silver." From *The Complete Poetical Works of Amy Lowell*, published by Houghton Mifflin Company. Copyright 1955 by Houghton Mifflin Company. Reprinted by permission of the publishers.

ROBERT LOWELL: "Robert Frost" from *History* by Robert Lowell. Copyright © 1967, 1968, 1969, 1970, 1973 by Robert Lowell. "The Old Flame" and "Middle Age" from *For the Union Dead* by Robert Lowell. Copyright © 1962, 1964 by Robert Lowell. "Skunk Hour" from *Life Studies* by Robert Lowell. Copyright © 1956, 1959 by Robert Lowell. All reprinted by permission of Farrar, Straus and Giroux, Inc. "After the Surprising Conversions" From *Lord Weary's Castles*, copyright 1946, 1974 by Robert Lowell. Reprinted by permission of Harcourt Brace Jovanovich, Inc.

HUGH MACDIARMID: "In the Children's Hospital." Reprinted with permission of Macmillan Publishing Co., Inc. from *Collected Poems* by Hugh MacDiarmid. © Christopher Grieve 1948, 1962.

ARCHIBALD MACLEISH: "The End of the World" and "Ars Poetica." From *New and Collected Poems 1917–1976* by Archibald MacLeish, published by Houghton Mifflin Company. Copyright © 1976 by Archibald MacLeish. Reprinted by permission of the publisher.

JAY MACPHERSON: "Ordinary People in the Last Days" from *The Boatman and Other Poems* by Jay MacPherson. © Oxford University Press (Don Mills, Ontario) by permission of the publishers.

JOHN MASEFIELD: "Cargoes." Reprinted with permission of Macmillan Publishing Co., Inc. from *Poems* by John Masefield. Copyright 1912 by Macmillan Publishing Co., Inc., renewed 1940 by John Masefield.

EDGAR LEE MASTERS: "Carl Hamblin," "Elsa Wertman," "Hamilton Green," and "Anne Rutledge." From *Spoon River Anthology* by Edgar Lee Masters, published by Macmillan Publishing Company. Reprinted with permission of Mrs. Ellen C. Masters.

J. PETER MEINKE: "Advice to My Son." Copyright © by the Antioch Review, Inc. First published in the *Antioch Review*, Vol. XXV, No. 3. Reprinted by permission of the editor.

W. S. MERWIN: "On the Subject of Poetry" from *The Dancing Bears* by W. S. Merwin. (Copyright 1954 by Yale University Press) in *The First Four Books of Poems* by W. S. Merwin. Copyright © 1975 by W. S. Merwin. "Another Year to Come" from *The Moving Target* by W. S. Merwin. Copyright © 1960 by W. S. Merwin. Appeared originally in *The New Yorker*. "For the Anniversary of My Death" from *The Lice* by W. S. Merwin. Copyright © 1967 by W. S. Merwin. All reprinted by permission of Atheneum Publishers.

EDNA ST. VINCENT MILLAY: "Grown-Up." From *Collected Poems*. Harper & Row, Publishers, Inc. Copyright 1922, 1950 by Edna St. Vincent Millay. Reprinted with permission of Norma Millay (Ellis), Literary Executor.

MARIANNE MOORE: "Silence" and "Poetry." Reprinted with permission of Macmillan Publishing Co., Inc. from *Collected Poems* by Marianne Moore. Copyright 1935 by Marianne Moore, renewed 1963 by Marianne Moore and T. S. Eliot.

EDWIN MUIR: "The Annunciation." From *Collected Poems* by Edwin Muir. Copyright © 1960 by Willa Muir. Reprinted by permission of Oxford University Press, Inc. Reprinted by permission of Faber and Faber Ltd. from *The Collected Poems of Edwin Muir*.

FRANK O'HARA: "The Day Lady Died" from *Lunch Poems* by Frank O'Hara. Copyright © 1964 by Frank O'Hara. Reprinted by permission of City Lights Books.

CHARLES OLSON: "La Chute" from *Archaeologist of Morning* by Charles Olson. Published in 1971 by Grossman Publishers. All rights reserved. Reprinted by permission of Viking Penguin Inc. From "The Songs of Maximus" (Songs 3, 4, 5, 6) in *The Maximus Poems* by Charles Olson. © 1960 by Charles Olson. Published by Corinth Books in association with Jargon Books. Reprinted by permission of Corinth Books.

GREGORY ORR: "In an Empty Field at Night" from *Burning the Empty Nests* by Gregory Orr. Copyright © 1973 by Gregory Orr. Reprinted by permission of Harper & Row, Publishers, Inc.

VINCENT O'SULLIVAN: "Medusa" from *Our Burning Times*. Copyright © by Vincent O'Sullivan. Reprinted by permission of Hawthorn Properties (Elsevier-Dutton Publishing Co., Inc.).

WILFRED OWEN: "The Parable of the Old Man and the Young," "À Terre," and "Futility." From the *Collected Poems of Wilfred Owen*. Copyright © Chatto & Windus Ltd., 1946, 1963. Reprinted by permission of New Directions. From *The Collected Poems of Wilfred Owen*, edited by C. Day Lewis. With permission of The Owen Estate and Chatto & Windus Ltd.

DOROTHY PARKER: "Résumé" from *The Portable Dorothy Parker*. Copyright 1926, 1954 by Dorothy Parker. Reprinted by permission of Viking Penguin Inc.

RAYMOND PATTERSON: "When I Awoke" from *The New Black Poetry*, edited by Clarence Major. Copyright © by Raymond Patterson. Reprinted by permission of the author.

SYLVIA PLATH: "Tulips." Copyright © 1962 by Ted Hughes. Originally appeared in *The New Yorker*. "The Rival." Copyright © 1962 by Ted Hughes. "Daddy." Copyright © 1963 by Ted Hughes. All from *Ariel* by Sylvia Plath. "Mirror" from *Crossing the Water* by Sylvia Plath. Copyright © 1963 by Ted Hughes. Originally appeared in *The New Yorker*. All selections reprinted by permission of Harper & Row, Publishers, Inc. *Ariel* published by Faber and Faber, London © Ted Hughes, 1965. "Mirror" in *Colossus* published by Faber and Faber, London. © Ted Hughes, 1967. Reprinted by permission of Olwyn Hughes.

EZRA POUND: "The Encounter," "Hugh Selwyn Mauberly" (V), "The Temperaments," "In a Station of the Metro," "A Pact," and "Portrait d'une Femme." From *Personae* by Ezra Pound. Copyright 1926 by Ezra Pound. Reprinted by permission of New Directions.

JOHN CROWE RANSOM: "Piazza Piece." Copyright 1927 by Alfred A. Knopf, Inc. and renewed 1955 by John Crowe Ransom. "Bells for John Whiteside's Daughter." Copyright 1924 by Alfred A. Knopf and renewed 1952 by John Crowe Ransom. Reprinted from *Selected Poems*, Third Edition, Revised and Enlarged, by John Crowe Ransom, by permission of Alfred A. Knopf, Inc.

HENRY REED: "Naming of Parts" from *A Map of Verona* by Henry Reed. Published by Jonathan Cape Ltd. Reprinted by permission of the publisher.

ISHMAEL REED: "beware : do not read this poem" From *Conjure Selected Poems, 1963–1970*. Copyright 1972, © 1972 Ishmael Reed. Reprinted by permission.

KENNETH REXROTH: "The Bad Old Days." From *The Collected Shorter Poems* of Kenneth Rexroth. Copyright © 1956 by New Directions. Reprinted by permission of New Directions.

ADRIENNE RICH: "From a Survivor" is reprinted from *Diving into the Wreck*, Poems 1971–1972, by Adrienne Rich, with the permission of W. W. Norton & Company, Inc. Copyright © 1973 by W. W. Norton & Company, Inc. "Bears." Copyright © 1955 by Adrienne Rich. Reprinted from *The Diamond Cutters* (1955) by permission of the author.

EDWIN ARLINGTON ROBINSON: "Richard Cory." From *The Children of the Night* by Edwin Arlington Robinson. Copyright 1897 by Charles Scribner's Sons. Reprinted by permission of the publisher. "The Mill." Reprinted with permission of Macmillan Publishing Co., Inc. from *Collected Poems* by Edwin Arlington Robinson. Copyright 1920 by

Edwin Arlington Robinson, renewed 1948 by Ruth Nivison. "Miniver Cheevy" from *The Town Down the River* by Edwin Arlington Robinson. Copyright 1907 by Charles Scribner's Sons; renewal copyright 1935 by Ruth Nivison. Reprinted by permission of Charles Scribner's Sons.

THEODORE ROETHKE: "Root Cellar" copyright 1943 by Modern Poetry Association, Inc. "The Bat" copyright 1938 by Theodore Roethke. "Elegy for Jane" copyright 1950 by Theodore Roethke. "The Meadow Mouse" copyright © 1963 by Beatrice Roethke, the Administratix of the Estate of Theodore Roethke. "My Papa's Waltz" copyright 1942 by Hearst Magazines, Inc. All from the book *The Collected Poems of Theodore Roethke*. Reprinted by permission of Doubleday & Company, Inc.

J. R. ROWLAND: "Seven Days" from *A Feast of Ancestors* reprinted by permission of Angus and Robertson, Publishers, Sydney, Australia.

MURIEL RUKEYSER: "Effort at Speech Between Two People" from *29 Poems* by Muriel Rukeyser. Reprinted by permission of International Creative Management. Copyright © by Muriel Rukeyser 1962.

GUADELUPE DE SAAVEDRA: "IF You Hear that a Thousand People Love You." By permission of the author.

SAINT JOHN OF THE CROSS: "Song of the Soul in Rapture" from *Poems of Saint John of the Cross* translated by Roy Campbell. Reprinted with permission of Hughes Massie Limited. "O Living Flame of Love" from *The Poems of St. John of the Cross*, translated by Willis Barnstone. Copyright © 1968 by Indiana University Press. Reprinted by permission of New Directions.

CARL SANDBURG: "Fog." From *Chicago Poems* by Carl Sandburg, copyright 1916 by Holt, Rinehart and Winston, Inc., copyright 1944 by Carl Sandburg. Reprinted by permission of Harcourt Brace Jovanovich, Inc.

SIEGFRIED SASSOON: "Does It Matter" from *Collected Poems* by Siegfried Sassoon. Copyright 1918 by E. P. Dutton & Co., renewed 1946 by Siegfried Sassoon. Reprinted by permission of Viking Penguin Inc. and G. T. Sassoon.

ANNE SEXTON: "The Moss of His Skin." From *To Bedlam and Part Way Back* by Anne Sexton, published by Houghton Mifflin Company. Copyright © 1960 by Anne Sexton. "Welcome Morning." From *The Awful Rowing Toward God* by Anne Sexton, published by Houghton Mifflin. Copyright © 1975 by Loring Conant, Jr., Executor. Both reprinted by permission of the publisher.

LOUIS SIMPSON: "My Father in the Night Commanding No." Copyright © 1963 by Louis Simpson. Reprinted from *At the End of the Open Road* by permission of Wesleyan University Press. "My Father in the Night Commanding No" first appeared in *The New Yorker*.

WILLIAM JAY SMITH: "American Primitive," excerpted from the book *New and Selected Poems* by William Jay Smith. Copyright © 1953 by William Jay Smith. Reprinted by permission of Delacorte Press/Seymour Lawrence.

W. D. SNODGRASS: "April Inventory." Copyright © 1957 by W. D. Snodgrass. Reprinted from *Heart's Needle*, by W. D. Snodgrass, by permission of Alfred A. Knopf, Inc.

GARY SNYDER: "Some Good Things to Be Said for the Iron Age." From *Regarding Wave* by Gary Snyder. Copyright © 1970 by Gary Snyder. "For the Children" and "The Uses of Light." From *Turtle Island* by Gary Snyder. Copyright © 1974 by Gary Snyder. "The Snow on Saddle Mountain" translated from Miyazawa Kenji. From *The Back Country* by Gary Snyder. Copyright © 1968 by Gary Snyder. All reprinted by permission of New Directions.

HELEN SORRELLS: "From a Correct Address in a Suburb of a Major City" from *Seeds as They Fall* by Helen Sorrells. Vanderbilt University Press, 1971. Reprinted by permission of the publisher.

STEPHEN SPENDER: "Words." Copyright 1948 by Stephen Spender. Originally published in *The New Yorker*. "I Think Continually of Those Who Were Truly Great." Copyright 1934 and renewed 1962 by Stephen Spender. Both reprinted from *Selected Poems*, by Stephen Spender, by permission of Random House, Inc. Reprinted by permission of Faber and Faber Ltd. from *Collected Poems* by Stephen Spender.

WILLIAM STAFFORD: "Traveling Through the Dark." Copyright © 1960 by William Stafford. "For the Grave of Daniel Boone." Copyright © 1957 by William Stafford. From *Stories That Could Be True* by William Stafford. Reprinted by permission of Harper & Row, Publishers, Inc.

JAMES STEPHENS: "The Wind." Reprinted with permission of Macmillan Publishing Co., Inc. from *Collected Poems* by James Stephens. Copyright 1915 by Macmillan Publishing Co., Inc., renewed 1943 by James Stephens. "The Wind" and "What Tomas Said in a Pub" from *Collected Poems* by James Stephens. By permission of Mrs. Iris Wise and Macmillan, London and Basingstoke.

WALLACE STEVENS: "Anecdote of the Jar," "Disillusionment of Ten O'Clock," "The Snow Man," "The Emperor of Ice Cream," "Peter Quince at the Clavier," "Thirteen Ways of Looking at a Blackbird." Copyright 1923 and renewed 1951 by Wallace Stevens. "The Plain Sense of Things." Copyright 1925 by Wallace Stevens. All reprinted from *The Collected Poems of Wallace Stevens*, by Wallace Stevens, by permission of Alfred A. Knopf, Inc. "Bowl" from *Opus Posthumous*, by Wallace Stevens. Copyright © 1957 by Elsie Stevens and Holly Stevens. Reprinted by permission of Alfred A. Knopf, Inc.

YURI SUHL: "The Permanent Delegate." By permission of the author.

MAY SWENSON: "The Secret in the Cat." From *New and Selected Things Taking Place* by May Swenson. Copyright © 1964 by May Swenson. First appeared in *Harper's* Magazine. By permission of Little, Brown and Company in association with Atlantic Monthly Press.

EDWARD TAYLOR: "The Souls Groan to Christ for Succour" and "Christ's Reply" in *The Poetical Works of Edward Taylor*, ed. Thomas H. Johnson (Princeton Paperback, 1966). Copyright Rockland, 1939; Princeton University Press, 1943, pp. 60 and 61–64. Reprinted by permission of Princeton University Press.

DYLAN THOMAS: "Do Not Go Gentle into That Good Night," "Fern Hill," "In My Craft or Sullen Art," and "A Refusal to Mourn the Death, by Fire, of a Child in London." From *The Poems of Dylan Thomas*. Copyright 1946 by New Directions Publishing Corporation. Copyright 1952 by Dylan Thomas. Reprinted from *Collected Poems* by permission of J. M. Dent, Publisher, and the Trustees for the Copyrights of the Late Dylan Thomas by David Higham Associates Limited.

EDWARD THOMAS: "The Gallows." Acknowledgment to Faber and Faber Ltd., publishers of *Collected Poems* by Edward Thomas, and to Myfanwy Thomas. Reprinted by permission of Myfanwy Thomas.

JOHN UPDIKE: "Winter Ocean." Copyright © 1960 by John Updike. Reprinted from *Telephone Poles and Other Poems*, by John Updike, by permission of Random House, Inc.

VIRGIL: Excerpt from The *Aeneid* Translated by C. Day Lewis. Copyright © 1952 by C. Day Lewis. Reprinted by permission of Literistic, Ltd.

ALICE WALKER: "Medicine." From *Once*, copyright © 1968 by Alice Walker. Reprinted by permission of Harcourt Brace Jovanovich, Inc.

ROBERT PENN WARREN: "Apology for Domitian." Copyright © 1958 by Robert Penn Warren. "Bearded Oaks." Copyright 1942 and renewed 1970 by Robert Penn Warren. Reprinted from *Selected Poems 1923–1975*, by Robert Penn Warren, by permission of Random House, Inc.

RICHARD WILBUR: "Two Voices in a Meadow" © 1957 by Richard Wilbur. Reprinted from his volume *Advice to a Prophet and Other Poems* by permission of Harcourt Brace Jovanovich, Inc. First published in *The New Yorker* Magazine.

Acknowledgments 559

"The Pardon." From *Ceremony and Other Poems*, copyright 1950, 1978 by Richard Wilbur. Reprinted by permission of Harcourt Brace Jovanovich. "A Late Aubade." Copyright © 1968 by Richard Wilbur. Reprinted from his volume *Walking to Sleep* by permission of Harcourt Brace Jovanovich, Inc.

SHIRLEY WILLIAMS: "You Know It's Really Cold" (The Peacock Poems: 3). Copyright © 1975 by Shirley Williams. Reprinted from *The Peacock Poems* by permission of Wesleyan University Press.

WILLIAM CARLOS WILLIAMS: "Poem," "Tract," "The Red Wheelbarrow," "This Is Just to Say" and "To Waken an Old Lady." From *Collected Early Poems* of William Carlos Williams. Copyright 1938 by New Directions Publishing Corporation. "The Artist" and "The Dance" from *Pictures from Brueghel and Other Poems*, by William Carlos Williams. Copyright 1954, © 1962 by William Carlos Williams. All reprinted by permission of New Directions.

JAMES WRIGHT: "Saint Judas." Copyright © 1971 by James Wright. "Revelation." Copyright © 1957 by James Wright. Both reprinted from *Saint Judas* by permission of Wesleyan University Press.

JUDITH WRIGHT: "Woman's Song." From *The Double Tree: Selected Poems 1942–1976* by Judith Wright, published by Houghton Mifflin Company. Copyright © 1978 by Judith Wright. Reprinted by permission of the publisher. Reprinted with the permission of Angus & Robertson (UK) Ltd. from *Collected Poems* by Judith Wright. © Judith Wright 1971.

RICHARD WRIGHT: "Between the World and Me" from the book *White Man, Listen!* by Richard Wright. Copyright © 1957 by Richard Wright. Reprinted by permission of Doubleday & Co., Inc.

ELINOR WYLIE: "Velvet Shoes." Copyright 1921 by Alfred A. Knopf, Inc. and renewed 1949 by William Rose Benet. Reprinted from *Collected Poems of Elinor Wylie*, by Elinor Wylie, by permission of Random House, Inc.

WILLIAM BUTLER YEATS: "Long-Legged Fly" and "The Circus Animals' Desertion." Copyright 1940 by Georgie Yeats, renewed 1968 by Bertha Georgie Yeats, Michael Butler Yeats and Anne Yeats. "The Second Coming." Copyright 1924 by Macmillan Publishing Co., Inc., renewed 1952 by Bertha Georgie Yeats. "The Coming of Wisdom with Time." Copyright 1912 by Macmillan Publishing Co., Inc., renewed 1940 by Bertha Georgie Yeats. "The Four Ages of Man." Copyright 1934 by Macmillan Publishing Co., Inc., renewed 1962 by Bertha Georgie Yeats. "The Lake Isle of Innisfree." Copyright 1906 by Macmillan Publishing Co., Inc., renewed 1934 by William Butler Yeats. "Crazy Jane Talks with the Bishop." Copyright 1933 by Macmillan Publishing Co., Inc., renewed 1961 by Bertha Georgie Yeats. "Leda and the Swan" and "Sailing to Byzantium." Copyright 1928 by Macmillan Publishing Co., renewed 1956 by Georgie Yeats. All reprinted with permission of Macmillan Publishing Co., Inc. from *Collected Poems* by William Butler Yeats, and M. B. Yeats, Anne Yeats and Macmillan London Limited.

ONAKATOMI NO YOSHINOBU: "The Deer on Pine Mountain." Kenneth Rexroth, *One Hundred Poems from the Japanese*. All rights reserved. Reprinted with permission of New Directions.

ART AND PHOTOGRAPHY

BEN SHAHN: *Hunger*, © Estate of Ben Shahn, 1980. By permission of Visual Artists and Galleries Associations, Inc.

THE GRANGER COLLECTION, New York: Imamu Amiri Baraka, Gwendolyn Brooks, Ralph Waldo Emerson, Thomas Hardy, George Herbert, Gerard Manley Hopkins, John Keats, Wilfred Owen, Percy Bysshe Shelley, William Carlos Williams, Elinor Wylie, E. E. Cummings, Ezra Pound.

THE BETTMAN ARCHIVE, INC.: W. H. Auden, William Blake, George Gordon, Lord Byron, Robert Browning, Samuel Taylor Coleridge, Stephen Crane, Emily Dickinson, John Donne, T. S. Eliot, Robert Frost, A. E. Housman, Langston Hughes, Ben Jonson, D. H. Lawrence, Robert Lowell, John Milton, Marianne Moore, Edgar Allan Poe, Alexander Pope, Edwin Arlington Robinson, William Shakespeare, Christopher Smart, Wallace Stevens, Jonathan Swift, Alfred, Lord Tennyson, Dylan Thomas, Walt Whitman, William Wordsworth, Richard Wright, William Butler Yeats.

© 1980 THOMAS VICTOR: Margaret Atwood, Elizabeth Bishop, Allen Ginsberg, Seamus Heaney, Ted Hughes, Denise Levertov, Adrienne Rich, Anne Sexton, Louise Bogan, Robert Creeley, Lawrence Ferlinghetti, Alice Walker, W. S. Merwin, Gary Snyder, James Wright.

© 1961 ROLLIE McKENNA: Sylvia Plath.

© MARY RANDLETT, 1981: Theodore Roethke.

Courtesy MINNEAPOLIS TRIBUNE: John Berryman.

Courtesy of JUNE JORDAN: June Jordan.

Index of Terms

terza rima, 128
tetrameter, 122
theme, 33
tone, 203
trimeter, 122

trochaic meter, 122
trochee, 121

verbal irony, 213
villanelle, 126, 219

Index of First Lines

Index of Authors and Titles